M2M

New Literary Fiction

M2M

New Literary Fiction

Edited by Karl Woelz

AttaGirl Press
San Francisco, CA

Published in the United States of America by AttaGirl Press, a division of
Damron Company, P.O. Box 422458, San Francisco, CA 94142-2458.
Printed in China
Cover Photograph: Paul A. Borja
Cover Design: Kathleen Pratt
Book Design: Kathleen Pratt
First Edition

ISBN 0-929435-72-9

Library of Congress Cataloging-in-Publication Data

M2M : new literary fiction / edited by Karl Woelz—1st ed.
    p. cm.
 ISBN 0-929435-72-9 (pbk.)
 1. Gay men—Fiction. 2. Short stories, American. 3. Gay men's
writings, American. I. Woelz, Karl.

PS648.H57 M26 2003
813'.01089206642—dc21

2002151463

Acknowledgments/Permissions

"Rabbit Chase" by Michael Carroll. Copyright © 2002 by Michael Carroll. Published by permission of the author.

"Dust Storm" by Mitch Cullin. Copyright © 2002 by Mitch Cullin. Published by permission of the author.

"Baked Alaska" by John Donahue. Copyright © 2002 by John Donahue. Published by permission of the author.

"The Wrong Kind of Queen" by W.C. Harris. Copyright © 2002 by W.C. Harris. Published by permission of the author.

"Jolly-Olly Petey" by Joe G. Hayes. Copyright © 2002 by Joe G. Hayes. Published by permission of the author.

"Sacajawea" by Trebor Healey. Copyright © 2002 by Trebor Healey. Published by permission of the author.

"Stigmata" by Greg Herren. Copyright © 2002 by Greg Herren. Published by permission of the author.

"The Incontinents" by Andrew Holleran. Copyright © 2002 by Andrew Holleran. Originally appeared on-line in *Blithe House Quarterly* at www.Blithe.com, Spring 2002. Published by permission of the author.

"To My Former Mother, Mrs. Callahan" by Tom House. Copyright © 2002 by Tom House. First published in *Antioch Review*, vol. 60, no. 2, Spring 2002, and reprinted in *Grain*, vol. 30, no. 9, Summer 2002. Published by permission of the author.

"That Boy This Day" by Daniel M. Jaffe. Copyright © 2002 by Daniel M. Jaffe. Published by permission of the author.

"The Real, True Angel" by Robin Lippincott. Copyright © 1996 Robin Lippincott. First published in *The Real, True Angel*, Fleur-de-Lis Press, Louisville, 1996. Published by permission of the author.

"Same Situation" by Paul Lisicky. Copyright © 2002 by Paul Lisicky. First published in *Famous Builder*, Graywolf Press, St. Paul, 2002. Published by permission of the author. "Same Situation" copyright © 1973 (Renewed) Crazy Crow Music. All rights to the four aforementioned songs by Joni Mitchell are administered by Sony/ATV Music Publishing, 8 Music Square West, Nashville, TN 37023.

"Disability" by Vestal McIntyre. Copyright © 2002 by Vestal McIntyre. Published by permission of the author.

"All There Is" by Craig T. McWhorter. Copyright © 2002 by Craig McWhorter. Published by permission of the author.

"An Encounter with the Sibyl" by Felice Picano. Copyright © 2002 by Felice Picano. Published by permission of the author.

"Gorgon" by J.E. Robinson. Copyright © 2002 by J.E. Robinson. Published by permission of the author.

"Skins" by Rakesh Satyal. Copyright © 2002 by Rakesh Satyal. Published by permission of the author.

"Give It Up for Billy" by Edmund White. Copyright © 2002 by Edmund White. First published in *Granta 78*, Summer 2002. Published by permission of the author.

"Japanese for Blurred Image" by Robert Williams. Copyright © 2002 by Robert Williams. Published by permission of the author.

Contents

For Krandall Kraus,
who continues to say yes

Introduction

I'm not a big fan of Introductions when it comes to short story collections because, really, what's there to say? *Here's an assortment of stories I think are well worth your time—read and enjoy in good health!* As a reader, I just want to get to the good stuff as quickly as possible. With that in mind, I'm going to keep these introductory remarks as succinct as I can so that you *can* get to the good stuff as quickly as possible.

Just a few years ago, readers such as yourself had a choice—unprecedented in contemporary publishing—between *several* collections of gay literary short fiction. You could pick up the most recent volume of Dutton/Plume's long-running *Men on Men* series, the latest copy of Little Brown's *Best American Gay Fiction*, or the newest edition of *His* from Faber & Faber. But you no longer have that choice. All three of those anthology series have been killed by their publishers. And books like them—produced by mainstream publishing houses—aren't coming back anytime soon. Nor are gay publishers rushing in to fill the void.

Many publishers, whether mainstream or gay, don't believe that there's a market for gay literary fiction. This belief is based upon the assumption that gay men aren't interested in "serious" gay fiction. That they're more engaged by style than substance. That they want only to "escape." That younger gay men would watch a DVD before ever picking up a book. That in a world of cyber-*everything*, reading has become little more than a quaint pastime, practiced by only an anachronistic few. These assumptions are untrue, of course, but they are shaping the way you read, telling you what you want, defining your "consumer trends," and forever narrowing your options.

And that's why *M2M: New Literary Fiction* is here. The editors of AttaGirl Press *do* believe that there's a market for "serious" gay fiction. We know how difficult it is for many gay writers to get their work into print (without being forced to either "de-gay" it on one hand or to hyper-sexualize it on the other). We're aware, too, of the increasing numbers of publishers (for whom even more-than-respectable profits are never sizable enough) who are abandoning their gay readers. We believe both in gay writers *and* in gay readers, and we are committed to creating a space in which the two can come together to support and sustain one another.

You've noticed, no doubt, that the word *gay* doesn't appear anywhere in the title of this book. I think the phrase *M2M*—shorthand for "man to man"—does a more than adequate job of establishing that this is a *gay* book. And if that doesn't do the trick, the photograph of the attractive man on the cover (*de rigeur* these days) should clinch it. Let there be no doubt: this is a collection of short stories written *by*, *for*, and *about* gay men.

I also decided not to include the word *best* in the title because I think it's a *given* that the stories in this book represent some of the best, most talented gay writers at work today. I did, however, decide to include the word *literary* in the title. And though this might sound like an egregious example of stating the obvious (after all, what else could short stories *be* but "literary"?), I'm using the word to differentiate between *literary* fiction and *genre* fiction—that is, erotica, science fiction, fantasy, horror, romance, and mystery. This is not a collection of gay vampire stories or gay ghost stories or gay stories to be read with one hand holding the book and the other holding something more ... fleshy. These are literate fictions, skillfully crafted, engaging and entertaining, that honestly render the complexity of our lives.

I'm never quite sure what to say when people ask me to define "literary" fiction. My initial impulse is to reply, "fiction for grownups," but I always worry that this response might be misunderstood as either imperious or dismissive—when it's intended to be neither. There's nothing wrong with wanting to be "entertained" or wanting to "escape" from the grind of your day-to-day existence for 200 pages—or for two hours at the local cineplex. There are many books, and a great many movies, that will do exactly that for you, and when you're done you can leave the book on the plane or you can throw your empty popcorn tub in the trash and stroll through the rest of the mall.

I bring up film because I think literary fiction is much like independent cinema. Independent films are, more often than not, less "commercial" than their Hollywood counterparts. Less manipulative. "Quieter" and less "obvious." Less driven by the need to create huge spectacle and even bigger box office. More thoughtful in subject. Less constrained by plot and freer to explore depth of character. Willing to take chances. Committed to making us think and reflect upon what we've seen. And not treating each and every one of us as if we're a fifteen-year-old straight boy. These are the kinds of things, I think, that also characterize literary fiction.

Literary fiction challenges us as it entertains us. Forces us to reexamine the world around us. Makes us think about who we are, how we are, and where we're going. Sometimes, as we read, we see ourselves reflected in the story's characters and situations, and sometimes we're asked to step into the shoes, or slip under the skin, of someone so completely unlike us that the world opens up for us anew. Literary fiction is a mirror, a window, a way to see the people and the world around us with heightened vision. It compels, completes, and sustains us.

You're about to meet some familiar faces—writers like Andrew Holleran, Felice Picano, and Edmund White—authors whose skillfully crafted and beautifully written prose has engaged and compelled us for a quarter of a century. You'll also be reunited with more than a few writers whose names might ring a bell—authors like Mitch Cullin, Daniel Jaffe, Paul Lisicky, and Robin Lippincott—but who have *yet* to become household names. And then, of course, you'll be meeting a couple of writers—John Donahue, W.C. Harris, Rakesh Satyal, Robert Williams—with whom you're probably not at all acquainted. But whether or not their names are familiar, the nineteen writers whose work you now hold in your hands are *all* incredibly talented craftsmen. I wish them (dear writers) and you (dear readers) only the very best. Read and enjoy in good health!

If you're interested in what I have to say about the state of contemporary gay fiction, meet me at the Afterword when you're done with the following stories, and I'll tell you what I think about the state of the gay literary nation, circa 2003.

Karl Woelz
Shippensburg, Pennsylvania
October 1, 2002

Baked Alaska

John Donahue

T he heat arrived unannounced, its full humidity and oppression delivered with the dawn. A summer day, misfiled in the spring.

Ray didn't feel the brunt of the mercury until he left the apartment and headed to the car rental place. At first he welcomed the weather until the smell of the street rose buttery and unclean, sapping his energy before he'd driven a mile. Then the wait in the airless office while the girl tapped his info with curved and painted fingernails, a miniature palm tree decorating each one. Released to pick up his subcompact, he headed north for what he hoped was cooler air.

The card with the directions was tucked under the sun visor. Two and a half hours, it read, if you're coming from the city. He brought the invite too; he wasn't certain if he'd be required to surrender it for admittance. He wasn't sure the way these things were done.

The service wasn't planned for this kind of heat. The hall of the old inn lacked air-conditioning and the windows were thrown open to the limp air. Traffic sounds and kids' shrieks floated over the guests, who waited till the last moment before finding their seats. The gathered friends and family, fanning themselves with their invitations, presented a restless picture, their thoughts more on escape than the enduring happiness of the bride.

Ray sat on the side of the stage. Carol had told him, since you can't be a bridesmaid, you'll have to be an usher. He was her friend, not Ted's. Ray and Ted had two topics, mutual funds and real estate, they could discuss without much awkwardness. Yet in their disinterest, they maintained a friendly rivalry for Carol's affection. From his fellow usher, Frederick, he received only looks of puzzlement concerning his role. Best friend of the bride.

Carol, ever practical, spoke to the minister, who agreed to shorten the service. Unaccustomed to wearing a suit, Ray felt the heat burden his collar and armpits; under his jacket his shirt turned leaden. The exchange of vows was muffled by the heavy air and the electric whirl of useless fans, yet his impatience eased for a moment at the exchange of rings and when the veil was lifted for the kiss. During the exit procession he linked his arm with Carol's sister and they began the slow shuffle down the aisle through the folded chairs. Everyone looking, roused from their stupor, putting on a face.

A string quartet played in the back of the room. The sound of the cello cut through the humidity while at the same time seemed warped by it. Its ribbon of sound drew Ray's gaze to the hands of the man playing. Long-fingered and earnest in the melody. He among the musicians seemed lost in the music, immune to the heat. His glance at the passing bridal party remained inward, his eyes blank. Like he was having a stroke, Ray thought, or a visitation.

Ray felt an inappropriate arousal. Built on the musicians elbowing their strings and the processional music they produced. From the sweat that defined his body inside his clothes. The thought of it all to come. The wedding night. The excitement a wedding night contained. This heat from nowhere. The inappropriate heat.

After the receiving line, the toasts and dinner, the musicians reappeared, amplified this time, augmented by a drum kit. Despite the temperature, there was to be dancing. Carol was adamant about that.

Dresses became marked with sweat. Neck ties abandoned. Everyone grew a mustache of wet beads. After a round, the parents were deposited to the side with tumblers of ice water. The cliques that had dissolved during the ceremony and the toasts reemerged, splitting up families and age groups. Ray felt an awkwardness among the alliances. He was the only gay on the guest list. He could hardly spend all his time with Carol. She said to him after a giddy embrace, has my makeup slid off my face? Then she spun off to visit with her aunties.

He had his camera, which kept him occupied. Allowed him to skirt the edges of the party yet be a part of it. Everyone on their best behavior for the lens.

He reconsidered his singular status during the band's break, when he watched the cello player shift his instrument to the side and survey the party with a slight panic in his eye. Moving to the bar, the musician grabbed a beer and left the hall for the porch, pushing a pack of cigarettes out of his shirt pocket. Ray followed him outside.

Young kids fought and tumbled on the square of grass and a few adults smoked cigars supplied by the best man. This was now done, Ray realized, now done at weddings. Cigars and girls in strappy dresses choking on them. Ray leaned against the wooden rail.

Ray introduced himself and they shook hands. The cello player's name was James. His face, when seen up close, was scratched by some acne, had a small history of it written on his jaw.

Are you playing much longer? Ray asked.

James looked at his watch. There's a short set. Some of the same songs though. Let's hope no one notices.

James had a nervous way of talking and didn't look at Ray until each sentence was complete. Each thought followed by a quick nod of the head. He seemed on the brink of bolting, but went nowhere.

I don't think they will, Ray said, surveying the drenched crowd.

I probably should get back, he said, looking out to the lawn before cocking his head in Ray's direction.

Those not staying over at the inn began their good-byes and filed into the parking lot as the last song of the evening was played. Some rooms had been reserved for guests staying the night. With their honeymoon postponed until August, Carol and Ted were down the hall from Ray.

Ray paced the veranda, dividing his time between watching the cars drive off and looking through the watery and bubbled hundred-year-old glass to where the musicians packed up and talked among themselves. James taking the longest, dawdling with the padded case, as big as a man. Or maybe he was a bit scrawny. James waved good-bye as the pony-tailed guitar player departed, leaving him alone.

Ray brought over two beers from the bar and handed one to James. The large instrument case made for an awkward transfer. The little wheel went off when James reached for the bottle.

Let me dump this in the car, James said.

Ray followed him out with the beers. Neither said anything as the wheel crunched over the gravel drive. Ray put the bottles on the ground and helped fit the case into the trunk. A few drinks under his belt made Ray feel both cool and pleasantly off-balance. He was glad to be away from the party and the closeness of the inn. He leaned against the car, offered his bottle for a toast.

James said, You know I haven't done this in ages.

Ray tipped back another sip and smiled. Done what?

You know … this, he said.

Ray thought to himself, what, drink? Maybe he doesn't drink much.

James said, Had a guy buy me a drink after cruising me all night.

Okay, Ray said as he straightened up a bit. He saw James smiling his first real smile of the night and he said, I guess the wedding has me all worked up. Which was true enough.

I see them all the time, James said. This one wasn't too bad.

Oh, I guess you do.

We were here last weekend. We're booked here next weekend, too.

Ray found James' mixture of forthrightness and reserve both endearing and abrupt, was thrown off balance by his life. A career it seemed of playing music at weddings. They talked as the inn quieted down, the last of the guests gone. It seemed a decision must be made.

Ray said, Have you ever seen the inside of a guest room?

Once in the room Ray undressed without ceremony while James sat on the bed half-looking around. Smiling in half. Everything in half. Ray started pulling it all off, maybe to prove something. I'm from the city. I'm active. I have a gym membership. I can remove my clothes. I can be nude.

James glanced around the room and twiddled with a button on his shirt. It's been a while, he said. I don't remember how to do it.

Ray melted at this joke, which he knew contained some truth, more than he himself was willing to venture. At the same time doubts began to creep into his head.

Turning off the light, Ray said, Sometimes it's easier remembering things in the dark.

The walls of the room were patterned with flowers, as were the chairs, bedspread and curtains. It was decorated for girls. Just the fact that there were two men in it, one of them nude, seemed to defile it, to overwhelm the potpourri. James undid his shirt and stood to meet Ray. 'Cause until that little bit of initiative, Ray had worried James was lost. Instead, James met Ray's mouth with a little yelp of lust. His long-fingered hand pressed against the small of Ray's back, and despite the heat, James shivered.

The next morning Ray awoke and watched James asleep in bed.

Curled onto his right shoulder, his skin rising and falling on their bed of flowers. He blamed this thought on the quaintness of the inn, but for a moment he thought James looked like a foal, or some long-legged bird in its nest.

Ray pulled on his underwear and went next door to Carol's room. He tried the knob.

Carol and Ted were still in bed and Ray crawled in beside them, on Carol's side.

I hope I'm not too early, he said.

She propped her head on her elbow and smiled at him.

During the night the weather had broken and cool air ruffled the curtain.

That was a great wedding. I have to say. Which made Carol laugh.

Ted said, I'm a little hungover. Take over for me, Ray. I don't feel so good.

Ted left the bed and entered the bathroom. He was wearing his blue pajamas. Carol once claimed their shared fondness of pajamas as a basis for their marriage.

Carol and Ray began their wedding postmortem. My dress, she said pointing to it hanging off the closet door, soaked through. I thought my mother was going to have a heart attack.

Their talk was interrupted by the sound of Ted farting in the bathroom. They paused a moment, waiting for it to end, smiles suspended on their lips. Ray felt this was a more intimate moment than crawling into bed with them. When the string of gas continued unabated, they began laughing and couldn't stop. They stuffed sheets and pillows into their mouths. Their laughter shook the bed frame.

Is this what married life is like? Ray asked.

Carol buried her head into his T-shirt. I'm gonna wet the bed, she said. Still the gas wouldn't end. Ten minutes.

They sputtered out on the wedding. He never mentioned who slept in his bed next door, but he realized he had been waiting for an opening the entire visit. Carol fell back asleep.

He laid back in the bed. The shower started running and soon Ted began to sing. Ray tried to listen to the words, the melody half-familiar from last night. He listened to the words and for a moment dozed.

Ray returned to his room and found that James had gone. His last glimpse of him, calm, creamy-skinned, and he thought, fast asleep. The conflicting thoughts of relief and regret chased across his brain. He went to the nightstand thinking there might be a note, and when finding none there, he shook out the bedding. He went to the window and found his view of the parking lot blocked by a wing of the building. He dressed and descended to the lobby and out onto the porch. Behind the moistness of the new day he felt the sun's growing acreage. The car was gone. He left the porch and went down the front walk to the street. No one else was out except a woman walking her golden retriever along the road's sandy shoulder. Every time the leash became tangled with the dog, she twirled herself around instead of freeing it from the dog. This happened several times, and Ray watched her spin herself down the street. This made him crazy.

He returned to his room. Regret at finding it empty emerged stronger this time round, polishing over his original thought, the one of relief.

During breakfast, after he had eaten the eggs, folded the last of the toast into his mouth, he asked Carol, Where did you find the band?

From a list the inn provided. They were good, huh?

He begged off the nature walk scheduled for the afternoon and returned to the city.

He collected the photographs at the lab around the corner. He didn't want to return to work and look through them at his desk, or on the street. The cold weather had returned. He sat on a box built over the radiator that served as a bench underneath the front window. The shop was empty and reeked of developer's liquid, which, he supposed, discouraged lingering.

He paused before opening the envelope to look through the shop window, at the double row of traffic and the people crowding the sidewalk. There was always that moment before opening the pictures when what you remember becomes diminished by the record.

Some shots were old. From as far back as Christmas at Carol's, when he passed the camera around and asked each person to shoot whomever sat across from them at the dinner table.

There were one and a half rolls of the wedding, and on several the lighting was dim, the focus blurred. Many of the murky photos featured the slightly older bride and groom dipping and hugging, a little wrinkly, prone to bad angles and red eyes. He came across many people he couldn't identify, which came as a surprise, and when viewed through the stink of developing fluid lent a melancholy air to his task.

There was a picture of James. He hoped there might be one. He too looked less than remembered. He was behind the subject of the picture, Carol, our bride for tonight. Ray's memory had tricked him up, thickened James' torso, smoothed his brow. The lab gave him a duplicate set and Ray placed the two shots of James, each with a different tint, side by side. He wasn't sure how to think about him, blurred into the background, but he thought about him. He would be thirty years old. That would be my age, Ray thought. Two years ago.

Was it reluctance to return to work, he didn't know, but he remained seated and pulled through the pictures again. His third time round. Someone must have gotten hold of the camera for there was a three-suite of images that weren't taken by him. One of Ray drinking. The scarred underside of his chin. Completely unflattering, he tore it in two.

He walked back to his office, the pictures wrapped in the photo shop's plastic bag. He stuffed them in his backpack under his desk, then suffered the remaining hour of the day. Made more difficult as he sank back into the wedding and their wedding night together. The hot weather had come and gone so quickly it was like a brief, false summer.

On Wednesday the idea first surfaced. It was tamped back down in the morning only to rebound in the afternoon. He called the inn, inquiring about room availability, and would the dining room be open? There was a wedding Saturday? At what time? Five o'clock? It's all booked? Okay, thanks, I'll look someplace else.

These are all things I could do, he thought, even though I have no intention of doing them. He called and reserved a larger car than his previous model, thinking that it would be more comfortable to sleep in should it come to that. In his head he went through his closet searching for a clean shirt. That night he found the directions to the inn on the table where he dropped his mail and keys.

Ray, whose rule was to decline all wedding invitations, found himself on Friday night preparing to attend another.

He didn't realize how different this ceremony would be from the last. When Ray slipped in the back the quartet was playing alongside the stage. Again Ray watched James' engagement with the music, his withdrawal, his unseeing eyes circling the room. Ray watched his delicate way of stowing the bow as silence descended for the vows. And at a nod from the woman whom Ray had dubbed the head mistress, the resumption of song.

When the ceremony dissolved, Ray hung around, smiling at the other guests, the whole time watching the musicians. Besides James, the band consisted of two women and another man, the women wearing long skirts and the men in white cotton shirts. Their gender balance must have added to their wedding appeal. He had prepared nothing to say. When the guests wandered off, Ray moved himself forward, closer and closer until James did a double take.

There was some confusion, alarm even as Ray explained he wasn't really a guest. Then a furrowed brow on Ray's part when he learned there wasn't to be a dance.

They have a dj, James said.

Oh, a dj. So you're finished already? Or do you dj as well?

No, he said, the words spoken to the wall. I don't dj.

So your day is over?

Pretty much.

That's good.

There was a moment of silence.

You got any plans? Ray asked.

We're invited to drink something but I think I'll head home.

There was another pause.

I feel bad about last week, Ray said. I had gone over to see Carol, and I only thought I would be gone a minute. We got to laughing about married life.

Yeah. I didn't know.

His fellow musicians returned and Ray wished they would go away. The violin player pecked James on the cheek and said, Call me later. She seemed to be the one in charge, chatting with the wedding party and checking her watch. Protective of James as well it seemed, she looked Ray over and returned his hello with a silent nod.

James brought his attention back to Ray. What are you doing?

Not much.

Do you want to come over?

Okay.

My mom would love to meet you.

He wasn't sure this was a joke. I'm not good with mothers. Only their sons.

James laughed at this. You can follow me in your car.

Ray trailed the beat-up Volvo out from the inn, his hands gripping the steering wheel. He turned off the radio and concentrated on the car's tail, rimmed with rust, and hoped James didn't live in a trailer. A twenty-five-minute ride down small roads, past farms and dumps and some modern places too. They turned in at a smallish house hidden behind tall hedges, whose base leaves, he learned later, had been chomped over the winter by hungry deer. A large yard contained a fenced-in garden, with three ancient, lichen-covered apple trees bearing mutant fruit. Some tough old apples holding on from last season.

James rolled the instrument case up to the house. There were two doors to slap through, which Ray always thought of as a country thing, for no one had time for that in the city. Ray kept thinking, Is mom going to appear? A thought that made him shy. He'd thought he'd be at the wedding dance at this point, he'd thought maybe he'd talk to James during his break or something. Drink a beer. Look at him play from a safe distance. He'd thought of the floral room of the inn and how with the lights off the flowers turned black. The naked body of James in his arms, spinning through the black flowers. The cheap sheets that burned against his knees.

The two rooms on the ground floor were divided by a staircase, with a kitchen and screened porch set off the back. The space was neatly arranged and dense with books and pictures. A row of white pottery on one shelf, a collection of old cameras on another. For a moment Ray regretted coming. It had been easier in the inn with only James' underpants lying on the floor. The plainness and whiteness of briefs tossed on the ground and all that could be possible. As a vessel for your dreams, he thought, nothing could beat a pair of shorts.

James found a dusty bottle of Campari which they drank on the porch. There was the sound of ice cubes in a glass, wind caught in the trees, crickets and night birds. Some candles burned. Ray didn't want to question James too much, but remained curious about his life. How he spent his days. He wondered about his nights. All alone was it, in the woods? Making his bachelor meals. The band mistress calling to remind him of rehearsals.

There was a diner near Ray's apartment; he didn't like revealing that he often ate his meals there, and at other times had them delivered. Even some mornings, a single coffee, milk, no sugar. A dollar for the coffee and a dollar for the tip.

James said, I moved here with Peter, who found this place. Before that, I lived over in Ashton in an apartment. A lot of this stuff is his. He left it here when he left. You know. But we had a couple of happy years, and then one that wasn't so great.

James paused and fussed with his glass, adjusting its distance between the bottle. He said, Winters can be long. Summers are beautiful.

He looked up and Ray understood this was his time to share, but he suddenly felt inexperienced and naive. Randy or Steve, didn't they hang around for six weeks or so? He thought of all his names and said, But you stayed?

Here I am.

Ray looked at his soft brown eyes, then toward the open door of the kitchen, warm with light.

What's upstairs?

James led the way up one flight where two bedrooms shared the floor. One room, reserved for guests, contained two single beds. For a second he thought he was being directed in there, until James led the way to his room.

He followed James into his bedroom and stood a moment while James turned on then dimmed the light. James pointed out the room, its closets and view, using two fingers like a flight attendant showing the emergency exits.

I'm not really interested in that, Ray said, meaning it as a joke but it came out harsher.

No, James agreed.

What he had thought of all week, through every sales call, and the miles driven in the rented car, were James' hands plucking the catgut. James' hands working his fly, freeing his buttons, holding him.

I'm glad you came back, James said, as he hooked a finger round Ray's belt loop.

When he finally sank against the pillow, Ray's head filled with the drive back to the city. Leaving about ten in the morning would be best, he thought. There was a movie to see with Carol and the laundry basket was spilling over. In this half-sleep state the traffic appeared heavy, cars closed around him in what the radio reporters call a pocket of volume. His legs jerked involuntarily in a pre-dream flash and James circled him with his arm and pulled him in.

He remembered this plan Sunday morning when ten o'clock arrived and all he had accomplished was a cup of coffee. Eleven o'clock found them back in the sack, and at twelve they ventured down for a nibble. Two o'clock outside in the yard for an underpants sunbath and skin-reddening snooze. At six James threatened to rattle some pots on the burner.

With a disbelieving snort Ray found himself in the car at ten o'clock at night, a hand-scrawled map in his hand. His body raw from everything, skinned from sun and beard, in equal measure sore and tender.

His Monday began, at once familiar and distant. A salesman for a fabric company, Ray visited his clients, complimented the new watch or haircut before displaying his samples. This piece will be such and such amount. And such and such for the collection. All this provided a good salary as well as social connections.

Kenny, the dewy-eyed representative of DKNY asked, after slowly turning through the portfolio, if he was going to the new restaurant opening this weekend. What's it called, Napkin, I think? Suddenly Ray felt the weight of a return visit to James' weigh heavy.

Did I say for sure I was coming? Ray thought. I'm sure I didn't. He had the habit, as did many busy people, of loading his acceptances with ambiguity and escape clauses.

You'll be around Friday? Kenny said.

Yeah, I think so.

If you want to come I can put you on the list. You know, you can be my guest.

Ray felt the invitation was a life preserver thrown to a drowning man. He said, I'd love that. He looked Kenny over. His sweater tight against his throat; it was next year's color. Prune.

Kenny closed the book of samples and pushed it toward Ray. It's nice work. I'll tell Karen.

Ray wasn't one who had boyfriends. In a bar he could locate what he wanted, whether a blow job or a Sea Breeze, without much delay. That was more than enough excitement. He liked the city and enjoyed watching the caravans of Friday afternoon traffic leaving him behind.

Nevertheless, when Thursday arrived Ray found himself losing interest in the party and searched online for the train schedule, printed it out and pinned it to his cubicle wall. The departure times highlighted in yellow.

As she handed over a licorice-flavored tea, Carol said, You have to find your boyfriends out of town so as not to ruin your reputation.

I don't have a reputation.

You do. We all know it. You never call back.

Nobody calls back anymore. It's gone out of fashion.

So when can I meet him?

He works most weekends or has rehearsals.

Why doesn't he visit during the week?

That's when I'm working and I put in a lot of hours.

Yeah right, she said and threw a cookie at him.

He couldn't hide the fact that he had never, as yet, invited James into the city. The map he had bought for the first drive had an amber circle imposed around the city highlighting its 75-mile radius. Seeing James' town just outside this marking was a relief. Comfortably out of reach of the city and its brown haze.

Ray looked up at the skylight in Carol's kitchen. The sun lit the semi-transparent glass and glittered off the safety wire. The glass was splashed with the shadows of swaying leaves, and beyond that blotches of green. The sight transported him, at least for a moment, back into the country. Into his hazy and blurred weekend escapes.

One of these days, he said, but she was at the sink rinsing her cup and didn't hear him.

A new life began: city living during the week and cabin fever on the weekends.

Wednesday night generated the most distraction. He stopped at the window and peered at the rain strafing the avenue. The view from his studio apartment, three stories above tree line, contained a mix of air shaft, pigeon, and water tower. His alone for six years. It was always a happy day, signing the renewal of his lease.

During the train ride he felt another person stir, another voice begin to speak inside him. He sat back to watch. As the train left the tunnel and picked up speed, Ray tried his best to relax. He picked up the abandoned newspaper on the seat beside him and read and reread the leads. This eruption of some other Ray, claiming to be true.

This is what James looked like. A drained-of-blood paleness that shone cleanest down his back. Eyes that wore green well under the heavy brow. A longish swag down the left side of his head. The thin wrist didn't prepare you for the hand. Long-fingered and nimble in the joint. If he straightened his spine he could beat Ray by an inch, which always was a surprise. His teeth set in a slight wobble. A streak of hair marked his haunch. Some mornings during the week, he woke early, he said, and went running down the path by the stream. For his legs, he said. But when Ray examined them, you knew they weren't, they just weren't.

His tongue set in a wet mouth. The lip-curl half-snarl of a smile.

Could hop out of bed in a flash when a sudden downpour required all windows be shut. A swan neck that held the secret of his voice. His breathing abdomen with its highway to hell. His shoulder held up by prominent blades. Some gray hairs sprung behind his ears. His underarms were practically clean. His whiskers came in blue.

Ray had a slowness assembling all the parts. They were all separate and dear to him, enshrined in a museum of body parts. His coloring bitter around the edges.

A slow assembly constructed during the train ride, with each stop more complete.

The reverse upon return, when Sunday nights became a dead zone. All he could do was lie on his bed and stare at the ceiling, concentrate on his breath. After an hour or so he was happy once again, alone in his home. He picked up the phone and ordered in Chinese.

This was new: he'd never felt this hungry before. The mild gurgling of his stomach replaced by a sharp pain that demanded immediate attention. An ache appeased by filling and suffocation. At work, he rode down the seventeen flights to the lobby newsstand and rustled through the packages. He hid pretzels in his desk. He began thinking about his next meal, which he thought both rudimentary and unwelcome. He didn't have time for that. When the pretzels ran out, he went desk to desk begging snacks from co-workers. Eating seeds and sour balls, whatever anyone could spare.

A midsummer Friday found Ray outside James' house. He liked arriving early, knowing he had an hour or two before James was due. He parted the leaves of the tomato plant; hefted a giant zucchini and examined its pale underside. He looked into the woods, which always appeared green despite the parched lawn. He waited around, and even though he was waiting around, he was happy doing it.

He headed into the woods and followed the narrow river, walking against the current, along the companion path. As he walked he imagined James running through the woods, which he claimed to jog even when there was snow. He ran as far as the lake, he said, which Ray had never seen. The air was warm and dry. Orange mushrooms sprouted on the side of the path. He had the time and decided to find the lake.

He walked and wondered when James would arrive home. With each step away from the house, he felt closer to James. Why is that, he thought, treading over the soft piles of pine needles lining the path, what's with that? He linked his incomprehension to the reams of sheet music he found scattered around the house. Ray couldn't read a note of music, it was just so much bird feed spilled over paper. Nevertheless, his incomprehension gave him a thrill. Left with the words, the brief instructions to the musicians, his only clue to what he would hear.

After about twenty minutes' hike, the river widened, swallowed a few small islands, then widened farther to make a lake. It was larger than he'd imagined, maybe half a mile across. The path crossed over the bent trunk of a tree that had bright green leaves with long pods hanging off its branches. He sat on the trunk and looked out over the water. The skin of the lake was smooth, yet teeming above it were all kinds of winged bugs that lit and sped and jerked.

He thought of James living out here in the country, away from everything. And he thought of himself in the city, sleeping alone in his bed on the seventh floor. He wished he could harness the flying sewing needles, flashing cerulean in the sunlight; he wished he could harness a squadron of them to sew his life together. Watching them dive and chase each other, he realized that they were not team players. They would be no use at all.

From where he sat facing the lake, a small breeze stirred and cooled his face. Small waves, they couldn't accurately be called waves, ripples maybe, formed by the wind, were sent his way. He watched their progress toward him and their disappearance on the shore. It seemed to him after a few minutes' hypnosis that the wind carved the shape of a smile in the water. A small, soft smile, the kind James specialized in. It seemed a drug-induced image, a fleet of smiles coming after him in the water, then breaking at his feet. An endless supply of them, sailing toward him as he sat under the bean tree.

With this thought his heart slipped, its beat felt wide and unhealthy, transplanted from another animal.

Maybe I need to buy a car, he thought with a start. That may help me out, free me from the train schedule. There's probably good deals out here in the country. James would know.

For this distance, he realized, the mileage between him and James, was what it required for him to love. He knew James would be home by now, that he had gotten out of the car, looked around, wanting him too.

He thrust his hands in the lake and found it warm, his skin magnified under the clear water to a map of cracks, his pores big and open. This word *love* was one he used during sex, when he loved your ass, when he loved your big cock, when he loved your nipple. He hadn't used it before for the whole person.

The form his love took, of hunger and hallucinations, came as a surprise. This love—it took him a while to figure out what was happening—made him feel cool and contracted in his muscle but warm on his skin, like a Baked Alaska.

He ran his wet hands through his hair. He felt stupid about the future and happy. Pond water dripped down his face. God only knows what was in it.

John Donahue
John Donahue is a writer and graphic designer who lives in New York.

Skins

Rakesh Satyal

"I didn't know it would be so warm up here, or I'd have picked a lighter suit," he said, embarrassed by the activity of his skin.
– *Willa Cather,* The Professor's House

After running across the field, his cleats digging up mud chunks and flinging them in fans, Bryon stops behind the other boys and feels his face flush with blood. He is eleven years old, his lungs stretchy, and the crisp October air enters him unhindered.

Bryon has stopped outside the semicircle around Coach Baker, like an electron distanced from a nucleus.

"When ya pass, ya gotta use yer instep. Yer *in*step."

The Coach holds up one foot and rubs what should be his *in*step. Instead, it is convex, his fat foot pushing against its well-worn sneaker, mouthwash-green grass stains settling into the creases of the shoe like sweat into the Coach's wrinkles.

"Ya gotta place that ball in the sweet spotta yer foot."

He swings his leg back and then brings it forward diagonally, lifting it higher than any of the boys would have ever imagined. Carl Buschman, a boy with one curl of hair at the base of his neck and the stomach of a kangaroo, has to move to avoid getting hit in the face.

"Who wants to deminstret? Toby, why dontchyou?"

Bryon is paying no attention to the Coach, such talk just another mosquito whirring in his ear. Instead, he is studying the silver, fingerprint-laced sheen of the Coach's whistle, which nestles between the unbuttoned collar of his white polo shirt, brown and gray chest hairs wrapping around it. Bryon also gives sideways glances at the boys in front of him. Sweat wets the tips of their hair, blond turning brown, brown turning black. Whereas Bryon stands with his arms at his sides, hands limp, legs perfectly parallel, knees locked, his only movement the rise and fall of his chest, the boys around him assume a different stance: one leg bent, knee popping out, the finely woven threads of the wool socks they wear stopping just under their kneecaps; chins tilted downward, eyes looking through brows as furrowed as they can be in their youth; hands on hips or tucked under their T-shirts, fingers scratching the soft skin of their stomachs, as they have seen their own fathers do in front of the TV during *Monday Night Football.*

October is the perfect month for soccer. It is no longer the scorching summer, especially August and September, which, in Indiana, are beastly, unforgiving, certain to leave casualties in their wake: the fifty-year-old grandpa who swam laps at the Y every morning for thirty years, but who had no defense while mowing the lawn on a hot Sunday afternoon; the frantic single mother, sweating in a living room with nothing but three small children and a pile of unpaid bills – General Electric, Indianapolis Bell, Fun & Learning Daycare Center – a mother whose face baked and baked to a golden brown until there was no way out but under the smoking wheels of a fast car, off the scalding tar of her apartment building's roof, or surrounding with fiery insides the emerald gelcaps of a Tylenol bottle. These are the deaths of local news lineups, lives eulogized in small rectangles at the top right of a TV screen, a computer-generated image of a burning sun and the word "HEAT" beneath it like a commandment.

October sweeps away this landscape of hot death. It gives Indianapolis a chance to rest before winter starts to whisk souls away again with snowstorms, frostbite, hypothermia. In October, heat and cold co-exist, shake hands, and make a deal, just like the Coach makes his center forward do with the other center forward before the start of *real* games, on Saturdays, not here at this practice field in the park, but on the other side of town. With each passing sunset pushing September into October, the flame in the air curls into itself and becomes wet pollen, carried on ever-cooling winds. Milkweed that sprouted thickly along paths now droops and succumbs to hikers' feet, which thresh until the whiteness unravels in the grass. Trees suck the heat into their leaves, and the fire that once turned so many necks tan – then red – now burns only in these branches, green lit into red, orange, and yellow fire.

Bryon Thomas stands surveying the burns that summer has left on the back of the boys' necks. Jimmy Deermore, shock-blond with a smattering of freckles bursting from under his collar, burnt the worst during those last weeks of August, before school began, and the dark redness under his hairline has started to peel. Other boys whose mothers were more generous with the sunscreen do not bear these badges of courage; they left pool parties with their oil still oozing, protecting them from UV rays until their mothers took them home, scrubbed their skin, and left it as clean as newly washed peaches. Free of peelings, these boys either have a downy fur trickling across the small bumps of their vertebrae, or just smoothness. Bryon runs his hand along the back of his neck and knows himself to be in the latter category. No covering. Just skin.

"Bryon! What did I just say?"

Bryon looks back to the front of the semicircle. Toby Martin, a lanky boy with sunken cheeks and ostrich legs, is just finishing his exemplary pass. He is always chosen for tasks like this, half because he is the best player on the team, half because he is Coach Baker's nephew. He brings his leg down with a plop, in rigor mortis, and looks at Bryon with a hint of spite. But only a hint. After all, he has, like everyone else, come to expect Bryon to act strange.

Being put on the spot by the Coach is certainly not new for Bryon, but his embarrassment always is, as inevitably and implacably bitter as the first bite of a crab apple. Bryon sees fewer neck-backs now, half of the heads having turned to see what his answer is going to be. The heads that haven't turned belong to boys who gave up on Bryon long ago, who will forever see him as the boy who lost Portfield.

"What did I just say?" the Coach repeats, putting his arms akimbo. The V of his collar widens with the movement and reveals several more hairs, more than Bryon would have ever expected. The whistle seems doomed in its entanglement.

Despite his embarrassment, Bryon is experienced enough to make quick work of it. He looks down and says, with a grace he has learned from his Memphis-born mother, "I don' know, sir. I'm sorry." For some reason he cannot explain, Bryon suddenly feels as if his blond curls are turning browner, as if summer has been sucked out of him once and for all. It is no longer September, and the heat is moving somewhere else. The Coach has gotten used to Bryon, so he nods and has Toby demonstrate once more, making him freeze at the end of his trajectory, pointing at, not touching, the frozen leg, which flushes and quivers with tension.

"Right here's what I mean," and the Coach sweeps his hand in a sickle over the instep of Toby's foot. "That's where yer gonna smack it during scrimmage, right, boys?" He doesn't wait for an answer. "That's what I thought. Okay, bathroom break and then scrimmage time. Shirts versus Skins."

And Bryon's head pops up again.

They play soccer in a very large, open field, a perfect rectangle bordered on all sides by an alternation of evergreens and maples, all of them taller than Bryon's apartment building. The field is so large that, from one end of it, if Bryon holds his hand up, the trees on the far end fit snugly onto his palm. Along one of the shorter ends of the field runs the road that cuts through the park; it continues past this rectangle, farther uphill, until it wraps around a gigantic flagpole flourishing the Stars and Stripes. This flagpole marks the highest point in Carrollsville; the only flag bigger than this one is at the local Perkins restaurant.

Far away, in the western corner of the field, are tucked two squat, tan-brick cubes that serve as restrooms. The insides stink of urinal cakes and mildew. Flies feast on the trashcans and on the yellowed rings of the toilets; they creep up the blue-tile walls and then fly out of the windows, narrow slits that run just under the ceiling.

On the east side of the field are four tennis courts, their nets sagging and swaying in the breeze. The Parks and Recreation Department does not want to spend money on lights, so the courts are useful only half of the time, destined to be cast in shadow too soon.

Strangely enough, however, this near-dusk seems to enhance soccer practice. There is something subtly energizing about the rawness of the hour, when the scent of hot earth still hangs in the air. This is when the Coach seems most passionate about practice, this time when the fireflies have just begun to bruise the darkness with pokes of yellow light. This is the time of the scrimmage.

"Bryon, ken I see you fer a minute?"

Coach Baker beckons Bryon forward with one squat index finger. He blows air from his nostrils, his nose hairs pushed out then sucked in. Bryon stumbles forward, his desire to run away, his instinct to suppress this desire.

"Bryon, I jus' don' know what to do with ya," the Coach says, wiping sweat from his forehead with the back of one hairy forearm. "Ya practice to do good in the scrimmages, and ya do good in the scrimmages to do good in the games. And *you* shore know how importint games are." The Coach leans in and knowingly raises one eyebrow. "Like Portfield?" His eyes open wide, questioning. Bryon answers by lowering his head, guilty as charged.

"I'm gonna have ya play 'gainst Toby," the Coach says. "So's you ken see how he passes."

Bryon looks blankly at the Coach.

There's nothin' in this kid, the Coach thinks. Bryon's eyes are round and empty, their bleak gray somehow the perfect color for them.

The Coach leans into Bryon and grips him by the shoulders. Bryon freezes up. His spine and his collarbone burn.

"When are ya gonna join the team, son? Why dontcha just *play*, son? C'mon. I'm beggin' ya."

Bryon reddens. He reddens as the boys line up next to him, Jimmy Deermore on his right, Carl Buschman on his left. He reddens as the Coach walks down the line, drawling, "One, two, one, two," assigning them scrimmage teams. He reddens as the Coach goes out of his way to make Toby a One and him a Two. And Bryon prays, as he always prays, "Not the Skins. Not the Skins."

"Okay, Ones are Shirts. Twos are Skins. Piss and then play, boys."

Bryon's face pales, composure sucked into the pit of his stomach. Under his shirt, his skin is blood red, hot, fighting instinct, fighting desire.

"Why do ya want to be like all those other boys? So many boys spell it that way. Yer Bryon. Yer special."

"But it sounds the same!" Bryon pleads over his waffles, which have gone cold, syrup-soggy. With his fork, he mixes his tears into the congealed butter. He tries every week to get his mother to change the spelling of his name. He would fight to change it entirely, but he knows his mom. She would just ignore him if he suggested this. Still, he comes so close to asking it. One of the girls in his class used to be named Erica Jenson, but when her parents got a divorce, her mother changed not just Erica's last name but her first name, too. Said Erica's father picked the name and she hated it. Now Erica Jenson is Crystal Hicks. And Crystal

Hicks is Bryon's biggest source of hope.

"Bryon, honey, it's early. Please. Mom's gotta get to work." For a second, she looks at her son and, instead of seeing his big, gray eyes and blond curls, she sees herself as a girl, hair only an inch longer than Bryon's, although her mouth and cheeks were less pink than his. He whines more she ever did as a child. What she doesn't know is that he never whines at school. He just stiffens and turns away.

As his mother fixes her short, sandy bob, then puts on her apron and nametag – a black "Donna" wedged into a teal rectangle – Bryon sniffles and exaggerates a sigh. If she knew what school was like, she would let him change it. Bryon shakes his head and then suddenly sees the man from yesterday. And for some reason – perhaps skin – there is a glimmer of hope.

Yesterday, it was Wednesday, and on Wednesday mornings, Bryon has computer class. His teacher, Miss Smith, takes the class in one large group to the computer room, a windowless box with Macintoshes that hum and exhale hot breath. For one solid hour, the kids are supposed to research on the Internet. No guidelines, "Just somethin' that will make ya smarter," as Miss Smith puts it.

Most often than not, however, Miss Smith is too tired to supervise, tucking herself into the corner and gossiping with Mrs. Frazier, who used to be Miss Kramer but who got married in July. Every Wednesday since school started, the two teachers have spent the entire period talking about the honeymoon in Hawaii. They both have perms that stop just short of their shoulders. The fake curls hardly move as the teachers bounce with banter.

"So, did you go hula dancing?"

"Oh, no, they … Well, they just did that when we went out to dinner and stuff. There was a class at the hotel, but I … didn't really get to it."

Miss Smith giggled and leaned in, clutching her lesson plan to her small chest. "Didn't really get to it, huh?"

Bryon watched their slim bodies writhe with laughter. As always, he watched the ring sparkle, then rubbed his own ring finger. He didn't know exactly what the ladies found so funny right then, but he was close. He knew it had to do with John, Mrs. Frazier née Kramer's new husband. They talked about him all the time. Bryon had seen him talking to Mrs. Frazier in the hall a week ago. He was thick and hairy, and his T-shirt looked too tight for his body, the muscles beneath it like Batman's.

Suddenly, Miss Smith was talking directly to Bryon.

"Bryon, what are ya supposed to be doin'? Do ya wanna detention?" She instantly looked older, like Bryon's mom.

Bryon turned around and faced his screen. Closed his eyes and shivered once. Then opened them and looked down at the keyboard. B-R. Then, I-A-N. He smiled briefly before Stacy Anderson started in on him.

"Let's type Bry-*on*'s name in!" Stacy said, and Bryon turned to her. Stacy's parents run a construction company that has built three subdivisions in the past year. Stacy has shock-blond hair that she always wears in a ponytail. In computer class yesterday, she was wearing a pink blouse and white capri pants. A bracelet shone on her tan wrist, a ring on her pinky. Gloss was on her lips, the kind that Bryon's mom puts on when she goes out on a date.

Stacy and her friend Heather, an equally pretty girl with brown hair and a ring on her finger, too, had pulled up Google.com on Stacy's computer, and now they typed in Bryon's name. Bryon watched helplessly. He could never challenge girls like Stacy. As she pecked Bryon's name into the keyboard, her thin, tan forearms seemed stronger, much stronger, much fiercer, than the kicking, stabbing legs of the boys on the field could ever be.

"There he is!"

The boy on the right....

And there he was, this strange, exotic man, white-faced, round-chinned, a treble clef of a mustache sprawled over his top lip, and then a golden, patterned cloth wrapped over and over around his head, no hairs popping out, just this shimmering wrap, like one of those things men in India wore on TV. So white-faced, this man, his whole face so clean, but at the same time, so strong because of its mustache, grown-up and handsome, like a king's. And for some reason that he just couldn't understand, Bryon felt as if he were looking in a mirror, as if this were his destiny, to have this face and, above all, that grown-up pallor, invincible and perfect. And as Stacy and Heather's muffled cackles increased, Bryon both wished he could be the man in that picture and worried he could never be, his heart snapping again and again. He touched his hand to his cheek and imagined his face changing color, his chin growing fuller, a sprig of black hair curling off his top lip. Even as he heard Stacy and Heather, and now Jessica and Crystal, snicker more, he touched his face and grew more beautiful.

After computer class ended and the room was empty, Mrs. Frazier went around restarting the computers. She came across Stacy's computer. On it was a picture she hadn't seen since the British Lit class she had to take her senior year at Berea. As she closed the browser and made the man disappear, she sighed.

"Lord Byron? These kids are gittin' way too smart for me."

Half of the boys are pulling their shirts over their heads and flinging them away.

Their skin is tight over their ribs, except for Carl Buschman, whose fat jiggles like wind-blown water. Tight or fat, the skin is all bare. At first, it is smooth, and then October brushes past and awakens goose pimples.

These are fifth grade boys. There is not yet any hair trickling from their belly buttons to the waistbands of their shorts. But there is the thin stripe of whitest skin running just above the waistband, the border of the private area that has been protected from the summer sun but that peeks out, as if to catch a breath of autumn. The stripe wavers gently at the hips. It is straightest at the small of the back, just between the beginnings of buttocks.

Bryon would never show his stripe, let alone the whole bare plane of his torso, to the other boys, his body open to the crisp autumn air, nipples hardening. Only in the privacy of his small room in the apartment can Bryon take off his shirt, can he look at himself in the dresser mirror. He feels guilty every time he does this, a wave of tension moving up his back and turning his neck to cement. He feels eyes all over him: those of his stuffed animals, held in a hammock-like net above his bed, the tiger that his mother won for him at the Carrollsville Community Carnival goofy but unflinching; those of his action figures, pinpoint black dots in peach wax sockets, rife with concentration. Even the round, wooden, knotted posts of his bed seem to sprout irises, moving their stare from his shoulder blades to the puckered skin at his elbows.

Bryon must use his time wisely. There are only a few minutes in the day when he is free from his mother's constant worry the minute she steps in from her day shift at the diner and starts to bother him about getting ready for soccer practice, about setting the table for supper, about doing the dishes, about doing his homework. And then there is Anna, who, in her fourteen-year-old whirlwind, cannot take long periods in the apartment gracefully, who, if not jumping into an older friend's Bronco, jumps into Bryon's room.

"Hey, Brat!" she says as she plops down on his bed, the springs creaking. She has just washed her hair, and as it falls upon Bryon's blanket, it sends a wind of wet jasmine wafting into Bryon's face. "Whatcha doin'?" This question makes Bryon overly cautious.

"Nuthin'," Bryon replies, placing his Road Rage truck on the dresser and hunching over it. Out of the corner of his eye, he looks into the mirror and sees Anna running her fingers through her hair, drenching the bed.

"Hey!" Bryon whines, turning around. Without a thought, he hits his sister's arm.

"Fuckin' brat!" Anna yells, and she twists his wrist. Bryon uses his open hand to hit her again. He swings without aim, simply in the general vicinity of her person. The more she twists his wrist, the more he bends toward it, to leverage out the pain. Now his nose is buried in her hair, his face wet with processed sweetness. And now, even though Anna is pelting him again and again – with the heels of her hands, like a girl does, unaware of just how much it hurts – Bryon feels nothing, because there is something totally disarming about the smell of her hair, its fragrant dampness. Soon, he is sniffing it. Then he wants to taste it.

"What are ya *do*ing?" Anna squeals. As she pulls away, she sees a strand slip out of Bryon's mouth.

Anna cannot speak. She stares at Bryon, the glaze over his eyes slowly fading as he pulls out of his reverie and realizes how ridiculous – how unwise – he is being, entrusting his secret, closed-door, mirror-time self to someone else. Anna looks at him and sees the only man left in the house, not even a man, certainly not the tall, beer-smelling father who tousled her hair ten years ago and then walked out the front door. He didn't even close it, the wind blowing and making it knock against the wall. Anna pulls away from her brother and walks out of the room, gathering her wet hair behind her in one long bunch, as if to wring out the memory of that phantom father. She gives one more look at her brother before leaving.

"Please don't tell Mom," Bryon falters, but the last two words come out in a whisper. Bryon knows what Anna is thinking. He knows, just as she passes through the doorway, that he, Bryon, has flashed through her mind: she sees that afternoon two winters ago, just three days after Christmas, when she walked into her room and found him on the floor with her new Ken doll in his hand, the doll's clothes – a yellow Hawaiian shirt and tiny, sky-blue shorts – in a tidy pile at his knees, and Bryon's eyes transfixed on the plastic perfection of Ken's chest, orange as a sunlit eyelid. Bryon knows, as Anna passes through his doorway, that the next time he stands before his mirror, pulls his shirt off, and sees what he has hidden from the other kids on the field, there will be a million more eyes that make him turn away in shame.

Shame is what restrains Bryon this October almost-evening, as he hears cotton shirt after cotton shirt land on the grass with a *swish*. It is fall, and just as the trees are dropping their leaves in crisp skirts, baring their wooden skeletons to the dusk, so are these robust precursors of men, running to the bathroom, these little trees turned inside out, smooth, sun-darkened milkiness exposed to the breeze, rugged competitiveness locked deep within.

"Be aggressive, honey," Bryon's mom said, so many times, so many nights before leaning over his bed and kissing him on the forehead. So Bryon sucked it up and was aggressive for a morning.

Last November, on the real fields, on a real game day. Uniforms washed the night before, as the boys tried to sleep, bellies expanding with butterflies. Fervent Lord's Prayers newly offered, perhaps for the first time with true sincerity and humble penitence, all to beat Portfield, the one true rival. Now the boys line up on the field, parallel to the daunting, confident row of Portfield competitors, all faces flushed with spite. That is, except for Bryon's, which pales with fright, not just of the sport but also of the stirring of his body. He digs one foot into the grass.

Bryon is always fascinated by the intricate system in which he has to put on his footgear. First comes the firm shell of the shin guard, the padding of its inside almost the same texture as the Styrofoam from

26 **Rakesh Satyal**

which Bryon carefully pulls out his toys. Then comes the thick, wool sheet of his socks, usually just white cotton with two blue stripes at the top, but, during games, royal blue, the same color as the team T-shirts they all wear, the collars and shirt cuffs ringed in white, Carrollsville Kroger Store, their sponsor's name, sprawled across the front in a cloud of cursive.

Then the shoes. For some reason he can't understand, Bryon loves the way they constrict around his feet, both the toughness of their black leather and the fatness of his socks making the contour fit fiercely around his insole, the fan of his toes, his heel. He loves cinching the leather even tighter as he pulls on the long, thin laces and ties them into a double-knot. He also loves evening out the rings of the bow his knot has formed. Always, before standing up, Bryon leans forward and grips each foot with its respective hand, feeling the thick cylinders of the cleats press into his fingers.

He thinks of his sister. Anna has taken ballet for nine years. Just two years ago, she began to dance *en pointe*; for her birthday that September, her teacher gave her a brand-new pair of toe shoes, their pink satin crisp and shiny, the matching ribbons that curled off them long and much thicker than the laces of Bryon's soccer shoes. It took Anna several tries to get the ribbons to crisscross her thin calves in that fluid manner, as gentle as strokes on a candy cane; in the end, it was their mother, who had taken lessons herself eons ago, to create the satin lattice. Before Anna's first *pointe* piece in a recital, Bryon marveled over the dexterity with which his sister recreated the X's, then the painful-looking but irresistible manner in which she pushed her toes into the floor and made the shoes stand on their noses.

"Soccer is *your* recital, hon. But be aggressive, hon. Be aggressive."

But even at this moment, as Bryon stands across from boys more determined than he is, his performance will falter, because he will spy the tallest boy on the Portfield team, a boy whose face looks older than everybody else's, a boy whose upper lip bears the messy, black fuzz of a budding mustache. Pimples, small pricks of red, lie under the fuzz. This boy's legs are dark, obscured by a layer of curling leg hair, which fades gently at his kneecaps before disappearing under his soccer socks.

Instantly, Bryon thinks of the pink satin of Anna's shoes, then a bow the same pink color. Anna's thirteenth birthday. That day, Anna received a book from Karla, her mother's best girl friend from the diner. It came wrapped in black paper, that pink bow tied around it. The title of the book was *You're a Teenager!* On the cover was a pretty girl with long, blonde hair, a red purse in one hand. Her head was thrown back, her chin up, her body frozen in a giggle.

"That's a private book just fer you, hon," Karla whispered to Anna, smoothing Anna's hair back with red-painted nails and kissing her on the forehead with red-painted lips. "You read it and you lemme know if you have any questions." She exchanged a knowing look with Bryon's mom.

Of course, Bryon could not wait to get his hands on it, and later that afternoon, he grabbed the book from the kitchen table and leafed through it. The tips of his fingers left crescents of sweat on the pages. Bryon hardly paid attention to the spine cracking under his excited grip. Because in those pages were pencil drawings of things he had always imagined but had never gotten to see. A long-haired girl placing her hands on her nude hips, looking at her nude body: round, awkward breasts, the triangle of her sex, which made Bryon turn away, hot-faced and tingling. On another page was a close-up of the triangle, but Bryon did not understand what it was; he tried for two whole minutes before turning the page and gasping:

A pencil drawing of two boys standing next to each other, naked, unashamed. Under the picture was written, "Two thirteen-year-old boys." The boy on the left had a hairless form, the plane of his torso a white nothing contained by thin black lines. His penis dangled as innocently between his smooth legs as his arms dangled at his sides. The boy's face was happy and bright, like a Disney character's, his smile saying that he did not even know – or did not even care – that he was naked.

But the boy on the right was different. He had his arms raised over his head. His face was a squiggle of lines, features scrunched together in either pain or laughter. This boy *did* have hair on his body: a trail of tiny, straight lines moving from his belly button to his penis, which, unlike the other boy's, bore a soft mane; a puff in each underarm, like a pair of mini-pompoms; and a dotted line of a mustache, matched by the faint curls off his legs.

Bryon decided in that moment, the book wet in his hands, his face flushed with knowledge, "I will be the boy on the right. I wanna be that boy."

And here, on this field, facing Portfield, Bryon faces the boy he has always wanted to be. He sees, in this tallest member of the Portfield team, his face darkened with hair and puberty, the meeting of dream and reality. Except now, instead of empty whiteness contained by spare black pencil, the boy he has always wanted to be is alive and pink with life and possibility.

"Be aggressive, hon. Kick that ball. I know ya can do it, hon."

In retrospect, it is so simple, the mistake that costs them the game, the mistake that belongs to one person and one person alone, this dreamer of a boy who simply chose the wrong time and wrong place to dream. This boy who was aggressive, who saw the boy he wanted to be and followed him. A minute left in the game, 0-0, but this is the regional championship and Coach Baker watches how that little shit Cody Johnson, two years older than everyone – "They shouldn' even let 'im play" – pushes Bryon Thomas, who has been lingering around Cody the whole game, kicking extra hard around him, until the two boys' legs share hugs around the ball, Bryon's hands traveling to Cody's shoulder to, it would seem, steady himself. Coach Baker sees the word push spiteful from Cody's lips, "Feggit," as Bryon hits the ground, his legs totally giving out, his back striking the grass hard and flat. And then, with only thirty seconds left, it is Bryon Thomas, of all boys it is Bryon Thomas, who has the chance to win with a penalty kick.

It is so simple to all involved. It is simple to Bryon's mom, who watches her son from the sidelines, calling his name again and again, this name that she spelled differently because she always knew her son was special, and now he stands at the height of the game, resurrected from a fall dealt by a jealous older boy, and she will hug and kiss him at the end of the game, when he has won it for everyone, a feast of Capri-Sun and Little Debbie oatmeal cookies awaiting him and his teammates. But this is before she knows the failure of forcing aggression.

It is simple to Coach Baker, who says a prayer in his head again and again as Bryon runs to the ball, then feels his guts wrench as the kick strikes the ball.

It is simple to Toby Martin and Jimmy Deermore and Carl Buschman and all the other boys, who pray, as well, who see the kick coming, and who know It before It even happens.

And it is simple even to Bryon, who rushes to the ball with tears still in the sill of his eyes, the remnants of the devastating push and curse that the boy he has always wanted to be has just spat at him. It is simple to him, as he runs to the ball chanting, "Be aggressive, Be aggressive," as if running to this ball and kicking it with everything in him will bring him one step closer to the boy on the right, the right boy. And just when his foot hits the ball, the world goes satin-pink, bow-pink, boy-pink, and as the ball flops up and skews to the left, traveling no farther than five feet, Bryon knows he will never be aggressive again.

He lets the group charge ahead of him to the bathroom. Meanwhile, he digs his cleats into the grass, dawdling, the way he usually does, although he usually isn't aware he is dawdling. Now, he pays attention to every effort he makes to linger; he feels the wind of the other boys' bodies sweep past him, and he quickens his pace, determined to stay just close enough to seem a part of the bathroom line, just far enough to make his escape. He has planned to follow them to the tan brick of the bathroom and then hide behind it. But when he is twenty feet away, he sees a tiny dirt path, just one foot's width, cutting through the trees on his right, a miniature forest of poison ivy and vines acting as its border.

Bryon sees in the path, in its light dirt, the stripe he saw sprawled along the boys' waists. He will never show his stripe, his skin, to these boys, these too-confident boys. He will never be aggressive like that. Better to take a path resembling the stripe than to show it.

He begins to swerve to the path, keeping an eye ahead of him to see that the other boys have reached the bathroom. Already, most of them have disappeared into the building, their voices echoing off the insides. Even from here, Bryon can smell the mixture of cooling rot and warm urine. He can imagine the tinkle of the boys' piss, their laughter tinkling in turn around it. He ducks his head and moves quickly to the path, not looking behind him, determined to disappear.

"Where the hell do ya think yer *going*, kid?"

Bryon doesn't even turn around. He knows what the Coach looks like, knows that the Coach has put his arms akimbo again, knows that the whistle-tangling chest hair has opened back up to the air. But most of all, Bryon knows the look he would see spackled across the Coach's eyes, the same look he saw on Anna's face that day with the Ken doll, the same look he saw on Miss Smith's face during computer class, the same look he saw on his teammates' faces at Portfield. So he doesn't turn around but stays looking at the vines sprouting at his feet.

"Well? Whatcha doin'?"

The voice has come much closer now. The Coach can't be more than five feet away. Bryon can hear the nose hairs sucked in and blown out again.

"I asked ya a question, kid."

The voice is too close, and suddenly the Coach twists Bryon's arm and makes him turn around. Bryon stumbles back, pulling his hands up to avoid touching the poison ivy behind him, whose sharp, lotiony scent fills his nostrils.

"I'm tired of all yer mischief, kid!" The Coach's voice is a whole octave lower than usual, the Coach's lips chomping the words forcefully. "I can't let Portfield happen again. Either ya join the team, kid, and play good, or that's it!" His voice reaches a frightening crescendo here, and his face, especially his temples and cheeks, turn purple with anger. The Coach turns away, takes off his baseball cap, and scratches his head, a round circle of baldness surrounded by peppered hair. Then he says under his breath:

"Fuckin' feggit."

The moment Bryon hears the first F, he turns on his heel and dashes down the path, scalding remembrances of the word the boy he always wanted to be shouted to him that fateful day. Bryon threshes through the plants, not caring now if the ivy spreads its poisonous salve across his arms and legs. The fading light leaves him in nothing but a constant *whack* of thin, leafy branches and fireflies. At one point, a single fly lights just before his face, and he sees in his right eye a rife flicker of yellow. The world goes dazzling-dim. Tonight has become a series of both dying heat and darting energies. And so Bryon darts farther away, tripping over ragweed and Queen Anne's lace, undoing dandelions' embraces with the ground, digging up more mud with his cleats and sending it far away from his feet.

He stops after five minutes, having charged deep into the woods. Vines are so thick here that they turn the trees into trellises. Moths and mosquitoes brush past Bryon's body and make him tremble. Everything is so close together and thick that it is instantly night in this forest, the evening light far up past the canopy of trees, eye-shaped slivers of red above his head the only sign for Bryon that the sun is still casting its last glow across the sky.

He touches his face and realizes it is damp with tears. Only now does he realize that he is not panting simply from running; the firm push of his exhalations has been the trembling of crying, and now that Bryon understands this, he commits himself fully to the act, kneels among the weeds, and bawls. He hunches over, holding himself as if injured in the groin. He spits. He watches his tears wet the ridged blades of grass. Right now, the other boys have probably lined up for the game, not even caring that he has left. Or no, they probably do care; they are probably celebrating, giving Coach Baker the best-played scrimmage he has ever seen. Coach Baker, who probably stands on the side of the field, his cap back on his head, his hands clapping, "Yeah yeah yeah!" as Toby Martin drills his way through the Skins, his shirt flapping around him.

Bryon thinks of the Coach, how he hates him, those chest hairs, but suddenly he sees, as if for the first time, for it is so vivid, the picture of the man from computer class, the exotic wrap around his head, the regal pallor of his cheek, and just when Bryon doesn't think the picture can throb with life any more, he looks up and sees it framed by the darkening dusk in the forest.

"Hi," it says.

Bryon rolls back on his haunches and stares, enraptured. Here is the man, except he has shed his wrap and stands with his thumbs tucked into the pockets of faded jeans. He wears no golden, shiny jacket but a musty blue shirt, which he has unbuttoned all the way, his chest and stomach revealed between buttons and buttonholes. His skin seems to glow, like moonlit marble; Bryon thinks of fairy tale movies he has seen on TV.

"What are you doin' all the way out here, boy?"

It seems so strange for this man to have such a normal, real-sounding voice, despite the celestial way his body shines. And yet Bryon loves it. He loves the joining of this voice with this body, which seems so familiar—the bulge of its chest reminds him of Mrs. Frazier's husband, John. But something else, too.

"What—dontcha talk, boy?"

"Yessir," Bryon replies, getting up from his kneel and feeling awkward. He is again aware of the rigidity of his body, so unlike the posture of his fellow soccer players. His arms dangle limply at his sides, as if he is in shock.

"Ah, that's a good boy." The man takes a step closer, a web of light and dimness covering his skin. "What's yer name, boy?"

"Bryon."

"Brian?"

Because it is Brian this man says – really Brien the way it sounds. Bryon reddens in the dark, except this time it is not embarrassment but joy.

"Yessir, Brian. B-R-I-A-N."

"Ah, big boy! Spellin' pro, huh?" the man jokes.

Bryon laughs timidly.

"So, Brian, ya playin' soccer?" The man nudges Bryon's cleated foot with his boot.

At this lightest touch, Bryon realizes who this man is. Not just the beautiful man from computer class.

The boy on the right....

"Ya don' say much, do ya, boy?"

The man kneels down, and now Bryon sees the treble clef of a mustache more than before. Its hairs prickle over the man's lip, almost reaching into the black sliver of his mouth. The man's breath is warm and damp, like the woods. Now, as he kneels so close, Bryon can see the sparse hair on the man's head, his encroaching baldness tapering along the crown of his skull. Bryon dares a peek to the man's torso again and sees the shirt has widened, not the ugly V of Coach Baker's sweaty polo shirt but a large gap, revealing two hair-pricked nipples and a belly button lost in fuzz. Lost in the boy he has always wanted to be. Slowly, the gap widens even more, and now there is no gap at all, only bare skin, the shirt another weed in the grass, faded and lost.

"Y'ever seen a man naked, boy?"

The air has gently sweetened, and Bryon thinks of Anna's wet hair. He feels as if it is back on his tongue again, leaving him cotton-mouthed and dumbstruck. And suddenly—supremely—he realizes, "No, I have never seen a man naked." He has only seen them in books, or as Ken, or in his imagination, but never upclose. He has pictured the boy on the right time and again, or the exotic man from computer class, but he has never seen them straight-on. Soccer flashes through Bryon Thomas' mind, and he realizes that in everything, everywhere—not just on the field—he has been dawdling and dribbling, never really kicking *at*, only *around*. Bryon shakes his head, answering, "No," and then a wave of hot fire rises through him, and he realizes, No, summer has not left him. The heat has simply moved somewhere else.

"Well, we'll hafta change that, boy."

As the man bares himself, as Bryon finally sees the boy and the man join, sees them upclose, he knows what he is ready to do.

Be aggressive....

Bryon pulls off his shirt.

Rakesh Satyal

Rakesh Satyal is a recent graduate of Princeton University, where he studied comparative literature and creative writing. His work has also appeared in *Vanity Fair*, *Out*, and in the anthology *The Man I Might Become: Gay Men Write About Their Fathers*. He works for the Doubleday Broadway Publishing Group, a division of Random House.

All There Is

Craig T. McWhorter

If I thought in terms of enemies, you would be one. I have been avoiding you because I'm here, in Provincetown, on vacation, and you represent far too great of a reality to allow me to vacate. Turning from you in the streets and on the beach, I do not want to speak to you. I do not know what I would say, how anyone could possibly say the right thing in such a situation.

And yet, there you are, walking toward me on the beach, three days after I first saw you, and as utterly unavoidable as the greenhead flies whose sole intention in life seems to be to bite my skin. Of course you are here, because nearly every scene of this particular drama sits among the men on this beach.

The sweat gathers at the rim of my cap, and I slip it off to let the breeze cross the bald skin on my head. And, in the distance, you still approach, much smaller than my raised cap so that if I lowered it you would disappear. Magic. The cap returns to my head. You are still there. And when you are so large that a hat would no longer make you disappear, when my staring might be noticeable, I turn and stare out to the ocean instead, waiting for you to pass. But it is so long before you cross my line of vision that I wonder, *where did he go?*, and turn back to my right only to find that you have stopped, that you are standing, that you are smiling and shielding your eyes with your hand in a mock salute, mere feet from my blanket, all because you know the friend, TJ, at my side.

You squat near his feet, just to my right, and the two of you acknowledge that you've seen each other at the guest house where apparently you're both staying. As I've avoided you this past week, your eyes avoid me. They travel from the sand encasing the tops of your toes to TJ's crotch and perhaps his eyes.

Despite being naked, I feel invulnerable. I'm surrounded by an invisible force field of martyrdom. I have been wronged.

Eventually, our proximity requires that we acknowledge the situation, but I refuse to go first.

And so you ask, almost state, "You're Tim, aren't you?"

It is brave, I think, to look at me sideways and acknowledge with one question, who I am and what you did to me.

The answer is yes. I'm Tim. You know, the man whose lover you fucked, here, on this same beach last summer while I was safely returned to Boston, summer over, back at work. It was my house where you must have shared coffee with him, my bed in which you must have slept with him. I was the one on the other end of the phone hearing explanations from Scott that he'd "made a new friend," that the two of you had gone to the movie, that you'd had dinner at Lorraine's. Were you there for any of those phone conversations? Waiting in the room while he spoke, perhaps admiring walls I painted, idly fingering door pulls I attached, perhaps impatient that he hang up with me so that he would come to bed with you? I have seen you there so many times in my mind that you are now a part of the furnishings, seated in the corner chair shredded by the cats until it looks like angora, standing next to the abstract painting we bought at the flea market in Wellfleet. I've never even seen you in that house, and yet, I can no longer picture it without you.

Sometimes I think that house was why I fell in love with Scott. We'd been on the beach—a first date if "Maybe I'll see you later at the beach" counts as making a date. Then, with my bike stuck in the back of his car, we went back to that house. I watched the bubbles in my water navigate the ice cubes in my glass while he played the messages on his machine, not minding if I heard his life speaking at him from the black plastic box next to the phone—a *Who's Who* of "Hey, Scott"s. I thought, *This man has nothing to hide.* No one could hide anything in this perfect little house. And when we had sex, most of the water still in my glass on the bedside table, his eyes confirmed my suspicions. He did not look away. He had nothing to hide. And so I stayed that night and the next and the next until my own apartment was just an overpriced closet and his friends starting making jokes about lesbians and U-Hauls.

I loved the sounds of Commercial Street that drifted in through the front windows: the soft whir of bike tires and the occasional ting, ting of a bell mounted on the handlebars like we did when we were kids, "girrrl" groups of men and women headed into town for tea dance or older couples who stopped at the picket fence and pointed out the lupine and peonies, the trolley and its drivers who slowed around the bend and then announced to the tourists, "Provincetown as we know it today began off to the left at Long Point Lighthouse." They always said the exact same thing at the exact same place. I loved that the house was so filled with sun that no matter what time of day, I could lie on the couch with a book and pretend to read, bathed head-to-toe in light, enough light for him, me, and the cats. I loved coming home from the beach, sticky with salt and sweat and not being able to decide whether I wanted a cold beer or a hot shower first. Each seemed to be reduced to an absolute sensual purity by context and contrast, the ultimate clean, the ultimate refreshment. And at night, the ultimate sleep, curled around Scott, hugging his back into my chest, one knee pillow spanning between our legs.

He was always there that first summer, intrinsic to my contentment as if he were a wizard casting spells and mixing up the sounds that thrilled my ears or seducing the sunlight into his house to keep me warm. He got up every day at seven even though he was on vacation. I followed shortly thereafter, and we sat on the front stoop and drank coffee with the crossword between us. Nearly every day, we played tennis, went to the beach, cooked, and then walked from one end of town to the other, seeing the same paintings in the same galleries, the same people on the streets. And I never got bored. I waited for the restlessness, for the desire to prowl bars and beach for new men, to stay out late drinking and sleep late into the hot part of the day while he did the crossword alone. But then, late into the summer, waking from a nap, cat purring on my chest, I realized, *This is all there is, all I want.*

TJ invites you to join us for lunch—the sexual potential between the two of you is obvious. Annoying. The three of us, TJ in the middle, all naked and munching on deli sandwiches brought from town along with the towels, bottles of water and suntan lotion in our backpacks.

I'm halfway through humus with roasted red peppers on a baguette and these are the things I've thought since you slept with Scott. I thought about burning the book you wrote, a gift you signed to him, that I had read before I knew. Somehow, I thought, you would feel the heat, like pins stuck into the padded body of a voodoo doll. Onto the pyre I would add every picture of me and him and the contents of a drawer filled with relationship memorabilia—cards and letters all signed with his initials in a heart, and thus I would voodoo him too. I thought, *Maybe this will make it not hurt anymore.*

I thought about finding your email address and then spamming you with an infinite chain of vitriol. I hate you. I hate you. I hate you.

I thought about catching you in a crosswalk, cluelessly ambling across an intersection in front of my car, and how maybe the indentation of your face in my windshield, your body on my car's hood, would remove the equally graphic image of you with him having sex on this beach from my mind.

I'm done with my Cape Cod chips, and when you mention how hot it is, I nod in agreement. These are the places I've been since you slept with him.

For a while, I still lived with him in Boston, even after Scott had told me about you, and I walked the streets of the South End at night so I didn't have to be near him. The wizard had lost his powers. All the eccentricities I'd once thought so charming, seemed suddenly obvious for what they were, deep insecurities.

Each step against the brick sidewalk compacted the anger and hurt within me. I imagined every narrow side street to be a canyon, the rows of town houses its steep stone walls. The curves of bowfronts and bays, the layers of red brick became the strata of a geological record. I wanted to record my own petroglyphs on those walls—stick figures of you and Scott on the beach, being swallowed by an enormous tidal wave, eaten by sharks, hunted by bands of warriors riding stick figure ponies with smooth oval bellies and horizontal tails trailing behind like hyphens.

My mind reached out to passing strangers and said, *He cheated on me. He's not the person you think he is. He's not spiritual and gentle and honest. He cheats and he lies and he uses people.* I wanted them to hate him too.

I have sat in my new home, and watched TV—endless reruns of *Roseanne*, fund-raising specials for PBS like *1000 Years of* Les Mis and *Songs You Never Knew Andrew Lloyd Webber Wrote*. I did that for a long time. Sometimes I even cried during the Andrew Lloyd Webber specials.

I've been in a bar in Cambridge dancing shirtless with a man who exploded with muscle and power. The first man to touch desire within me since Scott, and we were on our second date. He was drunk when he arrived.

The only two dancing, we were also the only two shirtless and he pulled me close, angling his head toward my chest, tongue extended to my nipple. I backed up, I said no again and again, and each rejection of his tongue pushed him to lap up beer instead. He became more insistent, the mouth ever nearer my nipple until I pushed him away.

With the other, with Scott, I did not say no to any excess, even when I knew it was killing us. He always got what he wanted. The third summer, I sat on this same beach, drowning in the cum of men we had picked up together, our new routine, but threeways with him were like having sex with *two* strangers. I sat and watched my life become ephemeral. Who was this man who seemed to know no other goal than the next dick? When had he left me behind? Was he any different, any more sober, than the man who now wanted to lick my chest, who could no longer dance or speak he was so drunk?

So I kept saying no despite the temptation of clarity and of his mouth hard, suckling and needy on my nipple. I thought of my voice leaning to the arc of his ear and saying "Bite it" above the drone of music and how the sting of his teeth edging into my flesh and cutting through the soft focus of my recent life could mean only one thing—he wants me, here, now, in front of all these people. But only here and now, and I kept saying no 'cause he seemed too much like Scott, too high on temporary. Another bottle, another dick, another nipple. It's all the same, they're all the same. I left when he started stumbling around me in circles, calling me a bitch.

Out the cab window I could still see the flashing lights of the dance floor through the transom windows above the doors, and they reminded me of car wrecks or crime scenes in TV movies.

I have been in a closet of a bedroom in the Fenway where five of us struggled to undress in the small spaces around the mattress. Five strangers lit vaguely by the light of a desk lamp shining into a corner while digital fish wandered across a computer screen dodging bubbles. A collection of unfamiliar shadows, white flashes of teeth and rolled eyeballs, four men who had followed one from a nearby bar like rats following the Pied Piper. I only learned some of their names on the walk over, and then we were all naked, and I watched as the bodies coupled and tripled and invaded each other. It was all slick with lube, frantic and intoxicating. Slick like condoms and AIDS didn't exist. For a moment, it was like my life with Scott had never existed, and I plunged again and again into the bodies as they were offered. Four strangers. Four unknown sexual histories. Four different opportunities for infection. I came last and left first.

Crossing the bridge on the way to my car, I looked into the reeds of the Fenway beyond and knew that they were full of men and that many of those men were doing the same things I'd just done. We were all taking the same risks. We were all the same.

I'd thought I was safe with Scott, safe from disease and pied pipers. Safe from myself. Safe from loneliness.

I have been on this beach with TJ, talking about all the sex going on in the dunes behind us, all the sex that goes on in the reeds and the bathrooms and the bars. "We're all the same," he said. "We all want the same thing. We want to not feel lonely." And I thought, *I just want to forget.*

It is very hot, and after lunch, the three of us walk to the water that the Florida boys all insist is too cold for swimming. When the waves rise above my knees, I dive out toward Plymouth and the relief is immediate. The contact of water on skin is more tangible for the temperature difference, like a crisp apple, sour and sweet at once, and I stay under, stretching out my arms then forcing them back through the water, pulling me deeper, farther from the shore, an anemone undulating beneath the surface. When I come up for a breath you are next to me, you have followed me, and we turn and look together at TJ who is still wading along the shore. Quietly, we tread water and watch the traffic along the beach, somehow removed from it, so that all I hear is the gentle splash of our hands at the surface of the water and the loudspeaker from a whale-watch boat passing half a mile off the coast. Then you dive back under, the white skin on your ass flashing and disappearing into the almost black ripples.

The three of us stand where the water reaches our waists, lifts and pulls at our flaccid penises, inches below the surface. We talk about books that TJ hasn't read, both of us recommending them to him. We talk about faculty we both know, conferences we've both attended or will attend. It scares me that we have things in common other than Scott. But I like it too, like talking to you.

When the water finally becomes cold rather than relief, we all three head back to the beach.

All day, below the surface of our conversation, my mind rebels again the situation. *When do I get up and kick sand in his face? When do I scream? When do I demand retribution? Why the fuck am I being nice to someone I've dreamed about hitting with my car?*

But I'm also taking inventory, not cruising, just assessing. *I remember his dick being bigger, his body tighter. He's definitely put on some weight.*

The thing is, you were supposed to be mine. I was the one who said how cute you were all summer as you walked past and smiled. I liked your barely goatee, a cluster of dark whiskers circling your mouth. I liked your smooth, flat chest, the way your surfer shorts rode low on your hips so that from the front I could imagine glimpses of the dark hair spreading immediately below the waistline. And we had you together, the first time. You were part of that third summer of three-ways. I assumed while we three were together that you *were* mine. That you were there because of me, and that for Scott, it was just another way of being with me.

But even then, I must have known. The following week, after watching Scott stare all day at a man two blankets over, I finally said, "Could we just go home and have sex. Just you and me." We did and for two days it was like it had been that first summer—ultimate. For a while, we stopped making each other feel alone. Then, I went back to Boston, and he went after you, and there was nothing for a very long time.

Later, he would tell me that you were a way of hurting me, that he saw how I desired you and wanted to take that, my desire even, and make it his own. He wanted to prove to me or to himself that he was good enough. Now, I look at you making plans to meet TJ, who is packing up to leave, later in the afternoon for a "drink," and I think, *good enough for what?*

We both watch TJ go, and I realize that it is not being wronged that has protected me all afternoon, but TJ's presence, like a padded glove couching the emotional blow of your fist in my gut. Suddenly, mouth dry, heart pounding, I look across the blanket gap where he used to be, and say, "I'm glad you came here. I'm glad you talked to me." I don't know why, but it's true. The emotional blow is more than just pain or anger.

You say, "You know that I didn't mean for it to happen."

I know that's true as well. You let it happen. Scott's the one who meant for it to happen. When he wants something, he gets it. I used to admire that about him. Then you tell me that he wanted a relationship with you. He flew out to see you in Chicago, and I think of him on that plane, doing the crossword in the in-flight magazine, sitting alone but imagining that he wouldn't have to be that way anymore, the way I made him feel. At least you told him no.

You pause and, staring down at the pattern of your towel, say, "I'm sorry."

I sit with that for a while, like ice cream that you don't want to eat, but you don't want to melt. Finally, I say, "He isn't." And then when you don't respond, "I really hate him." You only nod.

Shortly after, you leave, chasing men back into dunes, and I cross over those dunes to the lake of a tidal pool that separates the beach from the roads and houses of Provincetown several hundred yards beyond. Part of me wishes you were still here, walking beside me, probably because our afternoon together seemed so pregnant with dramatic potential and I had the lead role as chief martyr. Partly because I liked you, liked talking to you.

The tide has started on its way out, and the water tugs at my legs below the knees, threatening to pull my feet from beneath me. Horseshoe crabs lose their tenuous hold to the sand and float with the tide, riding it like hang gliders. I am headed for the love canal, a break in the head-high reeds, just where the tidal pool is deepest, that winds and cleaves its way through the grasses back toward town. When I reach the entrance, the current, forced to travel in a narrower channel, is much stronger and it beats against my chest and then against my thighs as I ascend an invisible sand hill below.

The course of the canal is serpiginous, hairpin curves and an ever narrowing path, and as I round each corner I expect to see men coupled together, hands and mouths working overtime. I half expect to see you and wonder what would happen if I did. Would I join you like Scott must have, like I wanted to for so long? Would I feel better if I did?

Instead, I see more rushing water and floating crabs and after one corner, a long black eel that swims across my path and mimics the shape of its larger geography. Along its back a ribbon of a fin flutters rhythmically before the eel disappears into the reeds in front of my feet.

When those same reeds begin to touch my shoulders on either side and the canal has become more of a crack, I stop and turn around, facing the unseen dunes and beach beyond. A yellow bi-wing plane, laden with tourists, flies overhead and its shadow momentarily darkens the green of the reeds before disappearing on the other side of the dune.

The water now pushes at my back, urging me forward. I let it take me, and I do not fight or dive, but float along with the current headfirst, the rocks and algae zipping along beneath me, the path becoming wider again before me. At each curve, I bend my body to follow the water, imagining that I too have fins that guide me like sails. And it's so easy, this tumbling, this giving in to kinetic energy, this gentle, twisting float out to sea. It consumes me and I think, *This is all there is.*

The love canal ends, its mouth opens to the larger, less defined tidal pool. In that pool, I stand sideways to the current, forcing a hole in its flow where the water must divide and curl around my front and back before rejoining itself. My back is to town and before me, the one, single dune which defines Herring Cove Beach stretches left and right toward distant lighthouses. Men walk along the top, carrying backpacks, some with their towels wrapped around their waists like sarongs. Sand kicks up behind their feet and filters the late afternoon sunlight. The boys are heading back to town, to tea dance and cocktail parties. They will line up along the curb of Commercial Street, waiting for tables at Gallerani's, or cluster in front of Spiritus, eating pizza, cruising one another. They will walk the length of town seeing all the same paintings in all the same galleries and smiling at all the same people.

You are somewhere in that crowd, will be somewhere in town tonight, and I replay the day, hearing again and again your apology. I say now what I should have said then.

Thank you.

Craig T. McWhorter
Craig T. McWhorter has published stories in a number of anthologies and journals including *Men on Men 2000*. He holds an MFA from the University of New Orleans and currently lives in Denver. Comments are welcome at cmcwho@estreet.com.

Sacajawea

Trebor Healey

Alex woke up with a hangover. Jesus, he thought, all that Tanqueray bullshit he was pushing at me. Like he thought he was that guy, Mr. Talbot?—whoever—on the fucking billboards. Same goddamn haircut and snobby attitude. Then he smiled remembering the substantial take, before recalling as well the tourist-prick and the HIV incident up in the park last night. Things had a way of coming back to that. Cruel, stupid people and cruel, stupid diseases. That just kept comin', like rats and roaches and the white man.

The damn Damron guidebook had gone on and on about the statues—The Coming of White Man among them—and how there was some kind of consequential mysticism to the fact that the gay cruising area—cutely dubbed the Daisy Patch—ran figure eights around them, somehow legitimizing gay sex as historically significant or fated or some bullshit. We are making history! It had shrilly exclaimed.

Well, I only need forty bucks, thanks.

Alex didn't see any gay people around however. Just a whole lot of statues and some homeless people, and Portland's requisite gaggle of dirtbabies—the drifting, patchouli-scented, punk-garbed runaways and anarchists who migrated each year up and down the West Coast between Tucson and Seattle. So he sat at the base of a statue and waited. Waited and breathed deep the rich summer grass of Washington Park, watched the pine boughs roll on the wind like big waves.

Thirty-six hours on a Greyhound had left him punchy and irritable, and he wondered if he looked as frazzled as he felt. But he dismissed the notion. Alex was the kind of boy who didn't have any trouble attracting guys. Though 30, he looked 22, which made him cute and handsome at the same time, and if he looked frazzled, he knew frazzled would suddenly look good to whoever was watching. It was a kind of vulnerability after all, and he knew the asset of that.

And then he spotted the strolling queens, back near the "Coming of the White Man." The Coming and the Going of the Whiteman, he thought, the Trolling of the Whiteman. Walking alone, in loafers or clean white sneakers, pretending to be appreciating the flowers and trees—Alex could spot a cruising homosexual from a mile away. They eventually led him to the aforementioned Daisy Patch, with its wilted greens and the two bronze Indian men who looked noble and alarmed all at once—the romantic versus the stoic stance. The latter was for books. He looked up at the glorious larger-than-life figures. They looked frightened, like they'd seen Jesus rise from the dead or some-thing, but in their line of sight 50 yards east were only empty tennis courts. Perhaps their countenances were simply an admonition about public obscenity—a service to the queens or the Portland PD.

Alex turned away from the first two men he encountered. They were young and unkempt. He'd do them for free; tonight he needed money. He just needed a hundred bucks, a place to stay, some food. It wasn't asking too much. Not for Alex—and he knew it. He sat down again, this time under the Indians. Then he saw one coming. A little bit heavy, loafers, locking the driver's side door on a late-model sedan. A tourist or a married man for sure, Alex figured. He smiled once as the man approached the statue. A huge grin suddenly covered the man's face, enough to make those bronze Indians wince. Bagged him, Alex congratulated himself. I'll ask for $150. He don't get out much I'll bet and takes what he can get. I'm the best he's had in years, if ever, I'm sure of it. And I know he has paid. Oh, I'll bet he's paid.

"How's it going?" the man said, sort of like a coach would say it.

"Fine," Alex said.

"Pretty nice evening out here." Oh Jesus, get to the point. Alex wanted to say Let's go, or, Wanna get out of here? Or, That'll be a hundred and fifty bucks, bozo. But he held his tongue. Any eagerness could knock his price down by twenty or thirty bucks.

Instead he blurted: "It's a real nice town in summer, Portland is."

"You from around here?" the man asked with just a twinge of nerv-ousness. Alex was playing him now.

"Sometimes," he answered vaguely. Married johns liked drifters, someone they wouldn't run into again.

"Well you either are or you aren't," the man added gruffly. Alex thought that was a bit brazen, a bit prying. He didn't like it.

"Actually I'm not but I come here sometimes. Course I'm leaving tomorrow morning." Make the pathetic thing feel secure he thought.

"Where are you staying?" the man continued. But Alex just looked at him then coyly. "Uh, you wanna go somewhere?" the man continued.

"Yeah," Alex said boyishly. The man smiled, and they headed to his car.

But the interrogation apparently wasn't over: "Let me ask you something," the man said as he pulled out his keys, but before he reached to unlock the passenger door to let Alex in, "… are you HIV-positive?" Alex felt insulted. He was surprised and humbled all at once. Suckerpunched. Who the hell was this john asking him in a fucking park if he was positive? It crossed his mind to clock the guy. It crossed his mind to lie. It crossed his mind to just jump the guy and take his wallet. It crossed his mind that nobody had asked him that question in a long, long time.

"Fuck you, bozo!" he blurted. "You goddamn right I am, you clos-et queen!" Then he raised his voice and yelled: "Hey, is there anybody here who's HIV-negative? This fuckin' queer don't suck positive cock!" By this time the man was in a panic and scurrying around the front of the car, fumbling with his keys. An awkward man, unable to move gracefully at a fast clip in loafers. Alex went on at top volume: "HIV-negative married man, father of 3, license plate NKY459, Oldsmobile '98!" The engine revved. Alex turned and slammed both fists down hard on the back trunk with his whole body screaming out: "You fuck-ing homosexual, cocksucking, motherfucking faggot!" And with a skid, the car was gone.

The cruising faggots had disappeared into the bushes. Always dis-creet, you could count on that. There were a few straight couples—women with bad hair, men with white socks pulled far too high—star-ing from over near the tennis courts. The glorious red men in bronze watching the white men come for the last century ignored him. He found himself looking back toward the statue he'd first sat down on, over among the homeless people and dirtbabies: a woman with her hand up as if she were hailing a cab. As if she cared about what had just happened and wanted to somehow deliver him. The only face out there that didn't stare or duck into the bushes, if not completely ignore him. And then, indeed, a cab appeared. He chuckled and thanked her, looking back over his shoulder at her as he hopped in. "Take me to a gay bar."

"Which one?" the cabbie replied.

"I don't care. Any one."

"Well, there are several," said the cabbie.

"Oh, Jesus, I'm in no mood to be making decisions. I'm sure this fuckin' town's got an Eagle if it's got any gay bars at all, so take me there."

"Yeah, sure thing."

And he banged his meter, as if to remind Alex of his empty wallet. But since a statue had hailed the cab, he thought this cab ride was on the universe. It wasn't. Charm was all he had to work with. It momentarily crossed his mind that the cabbie was gay and might have been on a break and might even be cruising himself. If so, Alex knew that cock beat charm every time. Charm was like the free clinic—it could help you out in a pinch. Maybe. But cock, cock was like PPO health insurance, a gold standard.

"What's your name?" Alex ventured, but the cabbie only glared in the rearview mirror.

Stuck with charm. "That statue back there, of the lady—who is it?"

"Sacajawea," the cabbie answered, without explanation.

"Sacaja-what?"

"Sac-a-ja-we-a," he repeated, slowly, syllable by syllable.

"Who is she?"

"She's that Indian girl who showed Lewis and Clark around; brought 'em all the way out here to the Pacific."

"Why'd she do that?"

The cabbie glared again in the rearview mirror. "Just a nice lady, I guess. They didn't know where the hell they were going. She showed 'em the way."

"Like a cab, eh?" Alex chanced a smile. It fell dead, face-to-face with the glare. He had a problem.

"I don't think she took a fare for it," the cabbie answered after a substantial pause.

Alex wanted to add that Herr Glare wasn't going to be getting one either, nice lady or no.

Momentarily, they pulled up in front of the Eagle, and the cabbie craned his neck around to deliver the bad news: "That'll be four bucks."

Alex considered throttling the man for a second, or threatening him with his hand playing pretend-gun in his jacket pocket. But he looked out the window instead, stalling. A cute Deadhead-looking boy with baggy pants was ambling down the sidewalk. Alex instinctively rolled down the window and said: "Hey dude, I'm in trouble. I need four bucks. Sacajawea hailed this cab, and then she split on me. I'll make it up to you, I swear...."

The boy, who should have said, Who the fuck are you? and Why should I refinance the poor business decisions of a half-baked hustler, lit up with a smile when he heard Sacajawea's name and began laughing.

"She'll do that," he said with a big smile. "That woman is all over this town." And he pulled out his wallet and handed the driver a five.

Alex climbed out of the cab. "Thanks a lot man. I don't like doing that kind of thing. I'll get you the five bucks within a few hours. Give me your number or something."

"Don't worry about it," the cute boy said. "I'm a friend of Sacajawea's," and he vanished into the Eagle. Fuckable for sure, but Alex needed more than five bucks, and he was already running a deficit with the lad though his cock hadn't even left his pants.

Instead, Alex stood on the pavement, and though at first unawares, prepared for the coming of the white man, who was just now weaving down the sidewalk toward him. Staggering he came with his mane of white hair, his tanned, furrowed face. Alex smiled, and when the man's brows jumped up an inch and the corners of his mouth followed, he knew he had a gimme.

The man blurted out in a drunken, far-too-loud and eager invitation: "I'm headin' to the Silverado, cutie. Care to join me?"

"I'd love to," Alex answered, mustering another smile. Shit, he thought, I'm gonna run out of these one of these days. Six drinks later and some of the worst conversation he'd ever had to put up with, Alex was on his back in some fancy antique-strewn gingerbread bungalow overlooking 23rd Avenue, getting the most drunken, slurpy blowjob of his life. All he wanted to do was get out of there, so he lifted himself up on his elbows, yanked a white clump of that Newport, Rhode Island-yachtsman hair to free his penis, and grabbed his big cock and jacked it off, much to the aristocratic drunk's delight, shooting his load across the man's red wrinkled neck with a great grunt that made the soused fool cry: "Yes, yes!"

"That'll be a hundred and fifty bucks, sir," followed right on the heels of Alex's orgasm. He was already up and climbing into his jeans, his still-hard cock a bit of a chore to shove into the crotch of his Levi's.

The startled man, climbing up off his knees with some effort and tottering, started making excuses. "But I bought you all those drinks .... You listened to me .... I thought you liked me .... You don't look like a hustler .... I'm not that kind of man."

Alex had to look at him then. "And just what kind of man are you?" he asked bluntly, looking him squarely in the eye.

"I'm ... ah ... a highly respected investment analyst. I ... ah ... I ...."

"Same difference," Alex snapped as he pushed the man back onto the bed with a shove. He dropped easily, pickled as he was. Then Alex grabbed the man's trousers and pulled out the wallet.

"Hey, don't rob me!" the panicked man feebly implored.

"I don't like to have to do this, but you've heard of collection agencies, right? People who don't pay their bills?" He pulled out four one-hundreds, a fifty, two twenties, and three ones. "That oughtta do it," he said with satisfaction, raising his brows from the pleasant surprise of so much cash. He threw the pants onto the floor and walked out.

"Hey, you come back here, young man!" the patrician gentleman cried.

"Nice knowin' ya," Alex called back over his shoulder, and he was out the door and down the steps, on his way to the Ben Stark for a room and a shower.

From which he now emerged into the too-bright light, four hundred and ninety-three dollars richer, minus the twenty-five for the room, of course.

He ended up in a coffee shop on 23rd Avenue called Coffee People. What the hell was that supposed to mean anyway? Coffee People? People made of coffee? People identified with coffee? Did it need a comma?

"You know this place has a real stupid name," he said to the blonde cashier at the counter.

"Hi, I'm Sandy!" was her answer.

"Forget it," he muttered. "Give me a triple latte." When it came back with a bean balanced on its lid, he considered pursuing it, but thought better of it and dropped the bean in Sandy's tip jar. She beamed. Like I thought, a bunch of zombies, Alex mused.

What if they had gay cafes called HIV People or Buttfucking People or Cock People or Bottom People or Cocksucking Faggots or not people at all but Sodomizing Beasts! He told himself to drink the coffee and calm down. Jesus, they could drop a load of cum on the top of every coffee instead of a fucking bean. Or float a condom in it. Everybody's goddamn gimmick coming at you gets oppressive, he concluded. Mine's FUCK YOU, and he said it aloud to no one in particular.

The coffee kicked in and it started to rain too. And Alex started to feel better. Everything started to look beautiful to him. There were two birds that started messing with something on the sidewalk. There were the leaves that fell from the tree and those that didn't. The children who'd gambol by or even the older folks, their faces worn and sagging. Sagging in a somehow beautiful, unsymmetrical way. Alive. Everything alive looked utterly beautiful to him, and he liked being alive right then and wanted to stay alive. And it wasn't just the living things he realized. It was everything else too—a peeling billboard across the street; the way the brick was getting wet on the outside of the shop; a dent in a car parked on the curb; the way metal bent and stone crumbled. Whatever crossed his plane of vision, he added to the list. Everything perfect.

Like how it must have looked to Sacajawea when she showed it all to Lewis and Clark, before there was a Daisy Patch, and another sad statue about the coming of the white man, and cabs to be hailed. He thought of what she must have looked like. He tried to reconstruct her dark, shadowy, bronze image from the statue he'd seen. She looked depressed and kind of broken, he thought. Who wouldn't be, giving it all away. She must have sensed what she was setting into motion.

Just then, Alex spotted a woman across the street, struggling with an umbrella. It was obviously and hopelessly broken, its thin metal skeleton protruding in several places. She finally jammed it into a trash can and stepped to the curb, pulling her coat tight around her body like a blanket. Her hand went up to hail a cab, and it struck him. It's fuckin' her! Fuckin' Sacajawea! She owes me five bucks! He stood up, but she was already climbing into the cab.

I must be losing my mind, he figured, and gulped down his coffee. She had looked beautiful, this woman, a natural progression of his thought after all the perfection he'd seen in the street: the children, the faces, the billboard, the wet bricks. Even this damn white-man world has its beauty. He suddenly felt where this was going and became angry. Well, I suppose HIV is just perfect too. He felt he'd tricked himself into a reverie, like the one out cruising in the Daisy Patch where no one would ever ask. Then he remembered that Tibetan Buddhist fag from the hospital in LA who'd talked about something called *Dzogchen*, some sort of realization that everything's perfect as it is. Well, it ain't, he retorted to himself. I'm fucking dying and so was that fag and how the hell could he talk himself into that bullshit? He remembered the guy telling him that only his own ego was getting in the way of his realizing this. He'd snapped at him: "Yeah, that and my lack of T cells and the pneumocystis virus and this fuckin' thrush and the fact I have no money, no family, no fuckin' clue and no patience for your bullshit!" He saw it all as a traffic jam, and here's this guy with no car hitchhiking for answers, trying to tell him that we're already at the place we can't get to. That's when he got up out of his hospital bed, resolving to get the fuck out of California and its bullshit explanation for everything, once and for all.

He scrunched up his coffee cup and turned to leave, noticing Sandy smiling at him from the counter. He never knew what to do with these clueless straight girls. He thought of saying something like You can suck my cock for a hundred bucks, but laughed at the impossibility of such a notion and at how different it was with men and women.

She said good-bye flirtatiously. He couldn't give her the satisfaction or the dishonesty of flirting back, so he just let his thoughts run out his mouth—"Sandy, right, like the Boulevard?"—referring to a major thoroughfare that ran east of town.

I don't take shit from no one, he told himself as he pushed open the door onto the sidewalk—Tibetan Buddhists, married closeted tourist homos, white-haired businessmen and straight girls who want to flirt to feel pretty. I ain't gonna put up with it. I'm not gonna just accept it. Take it. It seemed like everyone was saying just take it, put up with it, find a way to feel satisfied. But he saw it all a different way. Yeah, just take it. I'll take whatever I want. If I need something, I take it. That's how I accept what life throws at me. You need justice, food, money, shelter, sex? Take it. Don't sit around consoling your sorry ass for having none of it. That's just what the fuckhole politician Christian corporate motherfuckers want you to feel. Jesus, I'm sick of religion. He laughed, having addressed Jesus, who could only reply, "Why the fuck you telling me this?" He laughed out loud as he did more and more these days. He found it empowering to have everyone around him stare and think he was nuts. Young, cute, and crazy. Can't get much more powerful than that. Nobody will fuck with me. But they'll all want to fuck me. Same difference.

That's when he heard the sirens and saw the fire trucks leaving the fire station. He didn't think about the fantasy right off. He just got alert because that's what sirens are for, right?

He'd done it with cops, security guards, a soldier once when he was traveling in Eastern Europe.

Mostly he remembered the gun. Cradled in the soldier's arms when he first approached him to ask for directions. He was surprised when the soldier slung his rifle back onto his shoulder, said something to the other guard, and motioned him to come up the stairs and into the building. Alex followed him right into the bathroom where the soldier turned and looked right at his dick. Alex grabbed his crotch hard, and then the soldier leaned his rifle up against the tile wall as he undid his zipper and pulled out his meaty, uncut cock. Alex was watching the rifle as he dropped his own pants, allowing his half-hard cock to flop out, when he suddenly realized that it was the soldier's gun he wanted even more than his dick. He got on his knees and sucked the soldier's thick, uncut, veiny penis and tried to ask about the gun in broken Polish but didn't make his point. Sex was hard to communicate and yet so easy. The details, the fetishes are what were complicated. The rest was easily understood without language. But he wanted that gun, and all he knew were phrases like, Where is the train station?; How much?; and Which bus? Hardly helpful, but as the guidebooks didn't tell you how to say, Will you put that gun up my ass? or Fuck me now with your firearm!, he had to improvise.

Alex just pointed at it. He licked his lips, smiling. Then he stuck his finger up his ass and moved it back and forth. He pointed to the rifle again. The soldier seemed to understand suddenly, and while his own hard cock bobbed straight out in front of him like a loaded pistol, he hoisted Alex's legs up onto his shoulders, resting them on his rough green wool uniform that felt suddenly somehow comforting to Alex, like a blanket he remembered from his childhood, or like something an Indian maiden might wear over her shoulders.

Then the soldier began to feed the rifle into his ass. It hurt. Alex had never felt anything so unforgiving. Alex was groaning and jacking off and so was the soldier, both of them losing any sense of tenderness as the rifle forced its way further up Alex's ass. That's when Alex dropped his left leg and kicked the safety catch open near the far end of the rifle. The soldier hesitated, slightly alarmed, but he was lost in his own antic- ipated orgasmic fuck-everything, who-cares, I-wanna-cum agenda. Alex thought and hoped the soldier might have half-considered kicking the trigger and giving this fucking American punk what he wanted, fill- ing his body with communist-archenemy-evil-empire lead and the toi- let stall with his splattered guts. And fuck the consequences. Alex want- ed nothing more than to cum looking at this boy's face as the bullets filled him. He wanted to feel himself choking and coughing up mucousy clumps of blood as the thick white gobs of soldier jism and his own white magic plopped onto his chest, which would now be torn apart from the inside out. He wanted to feel his and the boy's cum run down his torn-up skin and drip onto his exposed heart as he expired.

Instead, he ended up with an anal fissure that required emergency surgery.

That was in Poland almost ten years ago. Now here he was in Portland. There were no soldiers here. Though it struck him how close the two words were. Poland and Portland. It gave him a strange kind of synchronistic courage as he walked determinedly into the fire station. Suddenly it all seemed predetermined. This fantasy would happen and he could take it from life. It was like fate; like being queer; like HIV; stupid, cruel people; and, death. Like roaches, rats, and the coming of the white man.

I know there's someone still here, he thought, left behind as the trucks roared away. That's the lot of faggots among groups of men, he laughed. He proceeded through the garage, right into the locker room, where he encountered a man in his late thirties sitting on one of the wooden benches while he wrapped up one of his calves with an Ace bandage. Alex asked him what had happened, and without flinching or showing any surprise that this dude had just walked uninvited into the station, the man answered that he'd been hurt in a fire last week trying to save some Indian woman from a burning apartment house out on Sandy Boulevard. Alex looked directly into the man's eyes and grabbed his own crotch firmly. The man let go of his Ace bandage and let it unravel and fall toward the floor, leaning back with a smile.

"Let me suck you off," Alex said, knowing he needed to get the guy hot before he asked for what he really wanted. The guy looked around momentarily, and assessing that the coast was clear, quickly pushed his pants down to his knees without even standing up, while Alex quickly got on the floor and began blowing him. The fireman started to groan, massaging Alex's head with greater and greater force as it bobbed off his swollen cock. Alex knew then it was time to ask for what he wanted.

"I want you to fuck me, fireman. Fuck me." The guy looked at him and said, "Yeah, yeah," in a deep voice, not really like a question, but more like an assurance of sure I can do that. But would he really? And where?

"I want you to fuck me, right here, right now," Alex insisted.

"Whatever you want kid," the fireman muttered, seductively. He got up and pulled off his shirt and kicked off his pants. Then Alex seasoned his wish:

"I want you to fuck me with a fire hose."

"You want me to—"

The fireman's lower lip dropped, but only briefly, before a big smile spread across his face. He turned around, his hard, veiny cock bobbing in front of him like an insect's antenna, as he looked behind him toward the remaining fire truck where the big raveled-up hose displayed its weighty nozzle like an uncut Puerto Rican homeboy with attitude. He looked around again before proceeding to the fire truck, where he quickly unraveled the hose. Just his hands unwinding the thing—the heft and weight of it—caused Alex's full, vein-marbled shaft to shutter and jump up like a dog. If it could have yelped, it would have.

Now he was coming back through the door with the hose trailing behind him. The head of the thing was shiny and brass. It must have been two inches in diameter, and behind it, snaking seemingly to eternity was the long burlap-cloth fire hose. Alex was already on his back fingering his hole, a mean furrow on his brow, begging for it.

The fireman got on his knees, and looking Alex directly in the eye, asked, "You ready? I'll go easy." Alex ignored the last part, as the fireman, now firmly stroking his own cock, began to push the hose into Alex with his free hand. Alex's asshole was expanding like it never had before. This too was cruel, like the gun, this fire hose, but it was polished smooth and it got wider and wider the more he took of it. He was aiming to get to the burlap when it happened. They both heard the maintenance man pull the lever.

He'd arrived just a few minutes ago and was cleaning things up in the garage, trying to get a jump on his chores before the firemen returned from their last call. He'd been surprised to see the hose unwound and leading through the door to the locker room, but he remembered seeing a fireman do that before when they were emptying out the hoses after a fire. They'd run them through the locker room and empty them in the showers. He also noticed the lever wasn't open, which was odd. Why would someone go to all the hassle of unwinding the hose to get the water out of it and not even turn it on? He flipped the lever, not knowing that it carried a full load under pressure.

A stare of terror filled the fireman's face, reminding Alex of the scared Indians, running last night from Jesus. The coming of the white man indeed.

Alex's body lifted off the ground, as he shot a fat load of cum straight into the air almost immediately. The fireman had since turned, and fumbling to pull on his pants, was tripping toward the door, the once-slack hose now full as a snake and writhing like a python on the floor. He looked back at Alex for a split second, who just then wanted to ask him if in fact he did save that Indian woman in the fire. But Alex felt his throat swell so he couldn't speak, and he only saw the fireman scream, "Jesus Christ!"—but he didn't even hear it, his ears were ringing so. Alex had never felt anything so incredible as this divine pressure on his prostate. It was like every pioneer who'd ever come west had joined together into one giant human tide of a cock and had rammed him as if he were history itself. Coming again and again, he flung every orgasm he felt he ever had in him, or ever would, up and out into space.

Lost in an ecstatic mania of orgasm, his eyes had rolled back, gushing with tears of every emotion imaginable, and when they did, he saw above him a calendar—and printed across the bottom was "Courtesy of the Portland Historical Society." By the time he looked to see the picture of her he was already full of her—the rivers ran in him like the ones she'd guided Lewis and Clark down in search of the farthest shore. Like a thousand-armed Shiva, the rivers branched out in him blue and full as Sacajawea's hands and arms massaged and tickled the inside of him, hailing a final cab as his body exploded like a star, giving the firehouse a fresh coat of red paint and Alex the orgasm of spirit, shooting out the top of his head like cum out of a cosmic cock.

Showed him the way, she did.

Trebor Healey
Trebor Healey's fiction can be found online at the *Blithe House Quarterly* and *Lodestar Quarterly*. Anthologies include *Best Gay Erotica 2003*; *Queer Dharma: Voices of Gay Buddhists*; *Wilma Loves Bette and Other Hilarious Gay and Lesbian Parodies*; *Mama's Boy: Gay Men Write About Their Mothers*; and *Beyond Definition: New Writing from Gay and Lesbian San Francisco*, of which he was co-editor. Trebor has also written a hit single, "Denny," for Pansy Division. His first novel, *Through It Came Bright Colors*, will be published in Spring, 2003.

Fall

Mitch Cullin

1.

Before moving into the dormitory for the fall semester, Willy Keeler had visited Moss University several times during the summer, had even attended spring training while still a high school senior, but it wasn't until last night, four days prior to the start of classes, that he actually paid any serious attention to the ivy-covered buildings encircling the quadrangle. Then for a while he stood beneath the statue of Herbert R. Moss, the institution's benefactor and namesake, whose towering marble likeness existed at the university's epicenter (around which, no doubt, had sprung the administrative offices, the library, the architecture building, and then, following the Great Depression, the Moss Center of Economic Studies).

Yet Willy sensed from Moss' chiseled expression—those serious gray eyes, the long gray sideburns, the thick gray hair forever swept to one side—that little pleasure was ever felt for what his final testament would eventually bequeath: the finest private university in Texas, built near Houston (only to be swallowed by the city many years later), with the school's credo written by Moss himself—*Souls not yet born, let them be free to consider everything when they come here, where no possibility or dream shall be denied*—and now carved ornately into the pedestal of his monument.

"It's ol' Herbert's tomb," his suite-mate Tadpole once said, mentioning that Moss' remains were encased somewhere within the pedestal, a revelation that, at the time, had given Willy the creeps.

But when finally pausing below the statue on such a quiet and unseasonably cold night, gazing upward at the elaborately rendered head and body, he didn't conjure troubling visions of the benefactor's corpse, or consider the fact that the edifice of Herbert R. Moss was nothing more than a rich man's fanciful gravestone. Instead he found himself memorizing and pondering the credo, hoping to gather some meaning from the words as he walked away.

Let them be free to consider everything, Willy thought again and again.

"No dream shall be denied," he whispered, singsong-like. "No dream shall be denied—"

Not even the dream that startled him awake in his dorm room, the same nightmare that had surfaced twice since his arrival at Moss. How stupid it was, how minor, hardly worth the fear it produced or the need to return to sleep with the bedside lamp on. Still, it bothered Willy profoundly, and he wasn't sure why. Perhaps because it was based on a true thing. Perhaps because the nightmare originated from Lionel Meredith, a recruiter who had signed him to play football for the university.

"Glad you signed on with us," Lionel had said during the summer, bringing an arm around Willy's shoulders as he showed him the campus, "otherwise I'd have been pissed—you know, you made me a killer, son. The very day I first drove out to Claude to watch you play, I killed something. So if you hadn't come to Moss then I'd have gone and massacred one of God's creatures for no good reason in the world, some poor dumbass coyote."

Lionel didn't spare Willy any of the details, explaining with slight amusement how he and Sal Dignetti, another recruiter, hadn't seen the coyote. They only felt the impact as the car dipped over a rise. But while U-turning and then parking on the shoulder, they saw the coyote laboring near the center of the road, trying for a moment to stand.

"Then she just quit making an effort but we could see her still breathing."

Both men lit cigarettes and leaned against the car, waiting for the coyote to die. But she wouldn't; she continued panting and shuddering. So they waited a bit longer, taking a moment to inspect the grille and the hood, and, aside from the spray of blood across the license plate, there was no sign of damage to the vehicle. Then they wandered into the two-lane for a closer look.

"We thought it was a small dog, then Sal noticed the large pointed ears, I spotted the tail tipped with brown. Two of her legs were stumped, deformed. You know, it's amazing she could survive like that—I mean, I suppose she was born that way, right? Then I spotted this cottontail on the other side of the asphalt, all rolled up like a ball of fur—the rabbit had blood and stuff coming from its throat and so I figure it was probably between that coyote's teeth when I hit her and got knocked loose."

But the coyote kept panting and panting—shuddering, twitching a paw—even as gore spilled from her mouth, even as Sal poked at her with a stick. Yet something essential was lacking, Lionel told Willy. He understood that shock was usually succeeded by mild elation.

"Seen it happen to ballplayers all the time," he said. "Wasn't much different, except the hit she took was about a million times harder than what any of you kids get dealt on the field. Anyway, we decided not to wait any longer or we'd end up missing your game. And I guess I felt kinda bad about her, and if you hadn't signed on, Willy, I'd have hated you for causing me to kill that pitiful thing."

"Well, I'm glad I'm here, glad you don't hate me either."

Lionel burst out laughing. He laughed so abruptly, releasing a deep and somewhat forced cackle, that Willy cringed: Ain't funny, he wanted to tell the man. There ain't nothin' funny about it.

"I'm jokin' you, kid. It's not like I haven't clobbered living things in my car before, you know?"

"Sure, I know."

Willy understood all along he wasn't responsible for the coyote or the cottontail or for anything Lionel Meredith did. In fact, where the recruiters were concerned, he had no say or control over anything. The day the coyote was hit, he didn't know they were coming to watch him play. Furthermore, he'd had no knowledge about the late-night meeting with Bud Warfield, the football coach for Claude C.S.D.: a meeting in which Lionel and Sal praised the young running back's performance on the field (on the first play the boy effortlessly took the hand-off, dodged a cornerback, and sprinted into the end zone; the rest of the game featured the same deft ability), and, without reservation, they were certain Willy would be a welcome addition to Coach Hawk Haskins' team at Moss.

"It's a good program we got going."

"As you know, Hawk is a top-notch coach—"

So Bud heard them out, sitting thoughtfully behind his desk with a wad of Red Man in his cheek, spitting every now and then into a

Styrofoam cup as the recruiters made their case in his dim office.

When the pair had finished, when they had concluded singing Willy's glories to the heavens and telling Bud exactly why Moss University was the best place for such a naturally talented kid, Bud spit once into his cup before speaking.

"But the thing is—this boy's wanting me to guide him—he ain't got much of anybody else to—so he'll sign where I tell him to."

Lionel began to speak, but the words came from Sal instead: "I can tell you now that Hawk is very interested. We all think there's plenty of potential there."

Bud nodded as if concurring, yet his voice turned strident.

"Now that there POH-tential is something I want to make clear to you boys early on. I want Willy at the top—and Hawk is damn sure that—nobody here denying that—but college is just a stop to where we're headed—"

And Lionel had to smile.

So did Sal.

"Where *we're* headed?"

But Bud wasn't smiling; the only thing appearing from his lips was brown saliva, squirting into the cup with a hiss that somehow conveyed loathing. Then he looked Lionel in the eyes—then Sal—then Lionel—until both men shifted awkwardly in their chairs.

"Let me tell you boys a little something—I watch things close from out here—I have for years now. You know, I've waited a long time for a blue chipper, and I finally got me one now—I know it, and you boys know it. And here's the thing—Mister Hawk Haskins is up there on his throne with his pick of the crop—and he's always getting this twig up his ass about taking some speed-burner kid and putting a lot of lard on him and making him a backer—or a blocking tight end, or some shit like that—and I'll tell you two this, I don't like that kind of POH-ten-tial."

Then no one was smiling.

"You know Hawk can't make any guarantees, Coach. He can't do it—"

"Nosir, I know he can't. So let's put her this way—my boy's a running back, pure and simple. If we go on and sign, that's how he's going. And if Hawk wants to dick him around after he's got him, I'll pull that boy in a wink. We'll blow a year and go out shopping somewhere else—now, that's a guarantee I can make."

Lionel sighed.

Sal shrugged.

Both men stared at Bud as if expecting more from him, but Bud simply spit into the cup and then wiped his mouth on his forearm.

"We'll give Coach Haskins the message," said Lionel.

"You do that."

Except all Willy ever knew about that night was this: two recruiters watched him play, Coach Bud met them briefly after the game, and by the spring, he had been committed to attend Moss University in the fall.

So the coyote really meant nothing, and the way Willy figured it, he and Lionel were square—Lionel killed a coyote but got a hot running back, Willy was set to play college ball but suffered the occasional nightmare.

"No dream shall be denied—"

He was sick of saying it, had grown bored with pondering the credo.

Bunch of bull, he thought. Meaningless words sounding important.

"Let me be free not to consider a goddamn thing—"

While wandering the desolate campus, peeking in the library windows, urinating in bushes beside the astronomy building, he attempted clearing his mind of everything—no thoughts, no dreams, no problems, no voices annoying his ears. But while strolling within the pitch of the stadium parking lot, he heard people chanting in the distance, a faint racket that started on the opposite side of the lot and gradually grew louder and louder. Presently he spotted bodies jogging toward him, emerging from the darkness, appearing ghostly and pale. As the group drew closer he realized they were fellow students, twenty or thirty of them dancing in a row, mostly male, completely naked in the midnight hour—and covered in shaving cream.

How ridiculous they looked, laughing and carrying on, doing the Bunny Hop, seemingly oblivious to the cold front that had chilled the city, chanting, "Join us! Join us! Join us! Join us!"

The four bodies leading the dance held cans of shaving cream and, when spotting Willy, they took aim, shooting streams of foam in his direction.

"Join us! Join us! Join us!"

And if Willy had been in a better frame of mind, if he hadn't felt so miserable and lost, the spectacle of the dancers would have cracked him up. But instead they unnerved him. So he turned and ran.

"Join us! Join us! Join us!"

He ran as fast as he could, tearing across the lot—arms swinging, sneakers pounding the asphalt—until the voices disappeared altogether, until the only noise he could hear was his heartbeat pulsing at his eardrums.

His pace slowed when he entered the quad again, inhaling as he reached the wide-open concourse. Just then he wanted to go to his dorm room, except he didn't want to encounter Tadpole or anyone else (everyone would probably still be awake, they might also be waiting for him). Anyway, he believed the night air was best for him; it was good breathing the coldness into his lungs as he walked, good taking in crisp healthy air so his body could refresh and his brain could get less muddled.

For a while he stretched out in the grass in front of the library, relaxing long enough for his heartbeat to slow, for his nerves to settle.

Then he crossed the sidewalks and walkways leading to the architecture building, finding the clever slots that adorned the bricks around the main door, a flourish that brought endless amusement to first year students—quickly sliding a fingertip over the holes produced a series of quasi-musical toots.

"Frog farts," Tadpole had called the sounds.

So Willy attempted frog farting "Yankee Doodle Dandy" and "Mary Had A Little Lamb," but was unable to create anything other than the expected pops.

"—had-a-lit-tle-lamb—no—yan-kee-doo-dle—dammit!"

But soon growing bored, he returned to the statue and sat, pressing his back against the pedestal, gazing forward with the same hard and humorless expression, he imagined, as Herbert R. Moss' likeness.

He pulled his knees to his chest, scanning the vacant quad (all that grass and sidewalks and red brick and dark windows—and not another soul in sight). A dull throbbing flared in his right knee, an infrequent reminder of the high school injury that almost ruined him as a player. His skull ached.

And huddling beneath the credo, Willy wished he had somewhere to go, somewhere far from Moss University. He wished he could throw his belongings in a box, slam his dorm room door shut, and head home without explaining his reasons to anyone.

2.

Last December, after viewing a video tape of Willy's knee injury, Hawk Haskins had no questions in his mind—he needed the running back from Claude, and he would get the running back from Claude.

And Sy Morley, the head trainer for Haskins' team, could tell from Hawk's face—the manner in which the man shook his head as if awestruck, the way he grinned slyly at the corner of his mouth while watching and re-watching the footage—that Willy Keeler had just gained an important admirer.

"Roll it, Lionel. Let's see that shit again."

Lionel pointed the VCR remote at the big-screen TV in Hawk's office, punching the play button with his thumb.

Then Hawk, Sy, Lionel, and Sal watched the video for the sixth time, staring intently at the screen as the Claude Tigers battled the Lefors Leopards—as Willy gained yards with the football, got nailed by an opposing cornerback, stumbled briefly, broke free from the tackle and shook the cornerback to the grass—then he cut left, then he cut right—then another tackle was attempted by a second Leopard, but Willy continued onward, dragging the opponent with him—then a third Leopard appeared, driving helmet-first into Willy's lower back. Down the boy went, cradling the ball, and disappeared under the chests and elbows and cleats of additional tacklers.

"There it is," said Sal. "Right before the dog pile."

Lionel paused the video, rewinding it several seconds, then advanced the action frame by frame so they could study the moment of injury (Willy collapsing from the tackle, his right leg twisting unnaturally at the knee as he fell).

Pause, rewind, repeat.

"Damn," said Hawk.

Pause, rewind, repeat.

Lionel stopped the VCR.

"Well—?" Hawk asked Sy.

"No way to know for sure, Hawk, but damn few kids I've seen wouldn't have been stretchered off from it."

Hawk glanced at Sal.

"Must've hurt like a bitch. Played it out, did he?"

"Sure did, Hawk. All of the fourth quarter."

"Goddamn, he's a tougher hoss than most, that's for certain. All right, I say go and wrap him up."

"That's the last ticket for that position, you know. What about Cody Graham?"

Hawk threw his hands up.

"Nah, hell no. Came in to see me the other day with his ol' man for chrissakes—and his ol' man starts telling me what formations his boy fits best and silly shit like that. Anyway, I got me a feeling we want this kid from Claude—iron balls and poorer than a shithouse mouse—now there's where the real ballplayers come from."

"Got a slight problem though, Hawk," said Lionel. "The ol' guy's fishing around. How do we handle him?"

Hawk squinted and stared at Lionel.

"Who you talking about?"

"Bud Warfield—the kid's coach—he knows what he's got—might be shopping him—"

"He's shopping it all right," offered Sal.

"Will he call it?"

"No question. The kid's got no father. Warfield will call it."

Hawk closed his eyes, rubbing at his eyelids while thinking. "Hell, that's fine," he finally said, opening one eye while still rubbing at the other. "I've seen them—poor bastards stuck there in the sticks all their lives—why in God's name would a man go and coach out in Claude?" Then he nodded and sighed. "Sure, work with him, fellas. Give Toad Farley in Tulsa a call for what you need. I'll square it."

"No problem, chief," said Sal.

"We'll get him here," said Lionel. "Don't worry about that."

And when Lionel brought Willy to the university for spring training, Hawk welcomed him with a bear hug, saying, "Hell if you didn't make the right choice, son. Now if you need a thing, any damn thing, you stop by my office, understand? If you need to shoot the shit or get something off your chest my door is always open. You're part of the family, okay?"

"Okay."

But during all those summer visits, even after moving into the dorm nine days before fall classes began, Willy had yet to share a private conversation with the great Hawk Haskins; he hadn't had a chance to recline alone on that leather couch in the man's office and discuss life and football, hadn't found the right opportunity to tell Hawk how much he respected him—because someone was always around (Lionel or Sal or Sy or other players from the team, dominating the conversation and unintentionally ignoring the nervous, quiet kid from Claude—a clueless newcomer who looked confused when Hawk called the football season *wartime*, who didn't laugh when Hawk jokingly suggested he be addressed as General Haskins instead of Coach Haskins).

Except today will be different, Willy thought. Today I need to talk.

He'd decided last night while sitting beneath the statue: he would go to Hawk and say, "Can I speak with you, just the two of us?"

Then Hawk would reply, "You got it—what's troubling you, son?"

Simple as that.

It helped that he was already expected at Haskins' office ("Whatever you do, don't be late tomorrow," Lionel had informed him yesterday afternoon. "Coach has serious business regarding you."), so today the fat would get chewed and the shit shot, today Willy would get something important off his chest.

But now on this chilly August morning, while heading across campus to Hawk's office, he suddenly found it difficult going forward. Or perhaps he didn't want to.

Pausing on a pathway lined with oaks, where birds chirped and warbled among the branches, Willy leaned into a tree. For a while he listened to the birds, watching as leaves fluttered toward the ground and floated past his head and landed near his sneakers. Then how lifeless the university seemed to him, how dead.

Everybody's hungover, he thought, or sleeping—or they haven't got here yet.

His hands were trembling, his guts grumbled and churned. But he wasn't hungry, couldn't remember when he last ate, and worried that he might be falling ill.

Or, he wondered, was it fatigue slowing him down, making him feel strange? And had he slept at all following his long night of wandering?

"No," he said as a sharp pain coursed through his belly.

"Good," he whispered when the pain subsided.

He'd had diarrhea earlier, then there was light-headedness before showering. Still, the shower seemed to help. With the water running hot, burning his chest and back, he soaped himself thoroughly at dawn, washing away the pathetic evening of beer and rowdiness he'd experienced with several teammates, rinsing clean the aftermath that had sent him to every dark corner of the university.

Except he didn't want to think about it now, not until he spoke with Hawk. And he didn't want to think about it then either, not while relaxing with the water pouring over his body: Forget the drinking and driving and the stupid craziness and fighting that erupted, he told himself. You'll explain most everything to Coach soon enough.

Though he wouldn't mention the shower—or how he dried himself and then wiped steam from the bathroom mirror with his towel. He wouldn't tell Hawk how surprised he was to find his face lacking bruises or scratches—or that when he pulled a comb through his hair he nearly passed out from the pain (he knew the lump was hiding there, like a golf ball with tender nerve endings, he imagined, embedded in his skull). No, he wouldn't whine about getting kicked in the head, or point a finger at who kicked him. He'd only say things got out of hand yesterday evening, and he didn't feel so happy about it, and maybe his teammates didn't like him.

"Coach," he'd tell Hawk, "maybe I shouldn't be at Moss, maybe the team is better off without me here."

He'd composed his speech at the statue, had uttered the lines to himself while massaging his bum knee, then rehearsed it after showering; he stretched naked on the floor of his dorm room and spoke.

"Coach, I don't want you to think I'm a tattler or anything 'cause I ain't. It's just where I come from team spirit is very important and everything—and if a bunch of guys on the same team don't see eye-to-eye on things—or if some of those guys gang up on one guy 'cause he doesn't like how they're behaving off the field or whatever—and then they go and knock him silly—then maybe it ain't good for the team spirit is all I'm sayin'—"

And while speaking almost silently, Willy's upside-down gaze went to the poster hanging above his roommate's bed, the framed lithograph that he vaguely associated with the coyote nightmare—four dog skeletons standing upright (a dog playing a flute, a dog beating a drum, all four waving bony paws) and dancing in a circle around an open grave. Dead Can Dance, proclaimed the poster at the top, publicizing his roommate's favorite band.

Dead can dance, thought Willy. Doesn't make a lick of sense.

He wasn't talking anymore, wasn't mumbling under his breath. For a few minutes he tried resting, but the bad dream quickly surfaced, emerging with disturbing clarity, as if it had been lurking in his brain all along; and when he stirred—blinking awake on the floor, glancing again at the poster—the vision remained: a coyote limped upon a two-lane blacktop. Her left front and right hind paws were missing, a malformation which gave her a peg-legged, rocking beam motion as she trotted. In the middle of the road she encountered another coyote, a dead one. The carcass—split at the gut, the head and throat and belly more damaged than the rear quarters—was stretched sideways over the broken white stripe; the eyes were open, the irises yellow. Telling skid marks led to and from the remains.

And there was blood.

So much blood, in fact, that it stained the asphalt and mixed with the curvy, uneven departing tire tracks. The crippled coyote sniffed at the dead coyote, then she hunched across the carcass and urinated. Soon she would shake and push and worm her snout into the cleaved belly—presently she would begin eating.

The dream was always the same.

Pointless, Willy thought. Not that interesting, not worth the fretting.

"Ain't worth getting down or spooked about when you're alone," he said aloud, taking comfort in his own voice.

He wished his roommate wasn't always sleeping at his girlfriend's apartment. If they were better acquainted, had spent a day or two hanging out—if his roommate stayed at the dorm, if they'd talked somewhere besides on the practice field or in the locker room—he wouldn't think twice about giving the guy a call and saying, "Top 40, I really need to talk—I'm kinda confused on everything and lonely."

Or he could ask him about the poster, maybe mention the dream and the rotten night he'd had.

Then they could meet for breakfast like best friends.

They could share each other's highs and lows—because they both played football for Moss, they both came from West Texas, and, of course, they were supposed to live together.

But five days had passed since his arrival and, aside from the occasional visits of his suite-mates, no one else had entered the room.

"Don't worry, you ain't missing much," said Tadpole, replying to Willy's first day inquiry regarding his roommate's whereabouts.

That was also the day he got nicknamed Dust Storm by the older players, joining the ranks of Eagle Eye, Kabob, Communion Sunday, Tereus, Otter, Full Tilt, and Wastewater.

That was the same day he learned that Tadpole, a lean and fast free safety, was actually named Steve. Then there was Duke (Eric), a captain and a wide receiver. And Top 40 (Mike), a captain and the quarterback and Willy's roommate, who, fellow teammates were eager to point out, was cocky on the field and difficult to like when he wasn't playing ball.

"Dust Storm, your roommate's an asshole," Duke had said on Willy's second evening at Moss. "Top 40 wants a fuck buddy so awful it hurts. So all I'm sayin' is you best padlock your butt before sleeping."

They were cruising in Duke's Jeep Cherokee (along with Tadpole and Otter and Eagle Eye), splitting a six pack after practice and taking Willy on a drive-by tour of what Duke called "the big city stankies"— past the porn shops and strip clubs dotting Richmond Avenue, the gay bars and piercing palaces on Westheimer, the projects and shotgun shacks of the Third Ward.

So Willy took it all in, amazed at the sprawl and urban weirdness of Houston. He enjoyed the company of his new friends, felt comfortable sitting in the backseat beside Tadpole, sipping on a Coors while the others joked. Duke, who was a little buzzed and driving a little too fast, seemed like someone he might have known in Claude, an old buddy from high school with a crass sense of humor and infectious laughter. Except Duke grew up in the Dallas suburbs, had never worked on a ranch or hiked the Caprock canyons, and preferred rap music to country music.

"This track is fuckin' dope," Duke kept saying, rewinding the same hip-hop song over and over, smiling as the bass thump thump thumped from the speakers. And every so often the others would join him in singing—

> *Ain't no nigger gonna get me down*
> *Ain't no nigger gonna push me 'round*
> *Ain't no nigger gonna get me down*

You ain't showin' like no punk, bitch
I gotta .357 says different
I gotta mind that bleeds
I ain't no nigger, nigger

Even Tadpole liked the song—and it bothered Willy that he did. Maybe because Tadpole was black. Maybe because, in Willy's mind, the word *nigger* was cruel; it didn't matter if the rapper was black or not. But eventually he stopped paying attention to the lyrics, allowing instead for the pounding bass to dictate his mood: how good the beats felt, how wild and tough, vibrating his body in the backseat, throbbing in his head while the others sang and joked and showed him the sights of Houston.

Then Duke turned the volume low and glanced in the rearview, saying, "Someday they're going to write a book about me being so fucking brilliant. Ain't that right, Dust Storm?"

"About you being so fucking dumb is more like it," said Otter.

"I ain't joking," said Duke. "Know how it's going to end? I'm eighty-six and in bed with a teenager. No shit. I'm doing the bitch sideways. That's how it ends."

"Nobody's going to make some book about you."

"Hell, I'll write it myself."

Tadpole said, "Man, in my book, the way it ends, you know, I'm living in Hollywood. I've got the pool, the car, titty girls all over the place. That's how it ends. I'm floating in my pool with a beer. I'm the shit. The end."

They seemed like good guys, Willy thought last night. But they're not my friends anymore, probably never were.

And today, when proceeding on the pathway and moving now between the oak trees on this crisp morning, he hoped Hawk would listen patiently to what had to be said. Then possibly everything could get sorted out. Then, perhaps, he might not feel so awful.

3.

So yesterday—before Willy sat at Herbert R. Moss' tomb, before encountering the naked Bunny Hoppers—there was another evening drive in Duke's Cherokee, evidently a post-practice ritual. Once again, to Willy's chagrin, that one hip-hop song came thudding from the speakers—*ain't no nigger gonna get me down, ain't no nigger gonna push me 'round*—inciting Duke, Tadpole, Otter, and Eagle Eye to bob their heads rhythmically while chanting the lyrics. Then more alcohol was consumed (Duke having purchased a half case of Miller's Genuine Draft with a fake ID card).

But it wasn't to be a leisurely cruise on the highways or through the side streets; they were on a mission, heading into the Montrose area of Houston, where, as Duke had said, "We can find us some cash, some funny money."

That made the others laugh, made them start giggling like kids.

"Welcome to Queersville," Otter told Willy.

Duke said, "Ever rolled someone, Dust Storm?"

Willy didn't understand the question, so he glanced at Tadpole, who was grinning, and replied, "Can't really say."

Then Duke asked, "Ever been rolled?"

The others cracked up again. And Willy joined them, though he couldn't figure out what was so funny.

Just drunk talk, he imagined. Just acting goofy in front of the new guy.

"You're a hoot," Duke told Willy as he pulled into a parking space behind an old warehouse. "Dust Storm, you're priceless. A real keeper."

"Thanks," said Willy, popping the top on a beer. "You are too."

Except Duke didn't hear him; he was busy removing the key from the ignition, was gazing into the side mirror that reflected the rear entrance of the warehouse—an open and dimly lit portal, beyond which blue and red strobe lights flickered.

"What's going on?" Willy asked.

No one answered; they had suddenly fallen silent and anxious (each twisting around to follow Duke's stare, chugging their beers as if absorbed in a drinking match, eventually crushing the cans).

Without the tape player going, without the conversation and jokes, Willy could hear techno music throbbing within the building. He offered Tadpole a sip of his beer, but Tadpole shook his head and said nothing. So Willy shrugged. Then he drank quietly, barely paying attention to what the others were doing—or to the men occasionally crossing the parking lot by themselves, wandering to and from the warehouse.

"What about him?" said Eagle Eye, pointing at a man who moved past the Cherokee in tight jeans and a white T-shirt.

"Nope," said Duke.

Then came a couple, an older man pressing a hand gently against a younger man's neck. As the pair walked toward a Jaguar, Willy suspected they were more than close friends.

Takes different kinds, he thought.

After all it was Houston ("Bigger than Austin and almost as strange," his mother had informed him.), a no-zoning city where adult video shops existed between churches and schools, and drag queens and male hustlers roamed the sidewalks of Westheimer along with hip married couples and college students.

"Nope," said Duke, "two faggots is one faggot too many."

Willy finished his beer and reached for a second, pulling it from a plastic bag on the floorboard.

"Nope."

"Come on, Duke, we don't got all night—!"

"Nope."

Ten men, Willy finally counted.

Ten men by the time he killed his second beer, and ten *nope*s from Duke.

"Okay, how about him?" asked Eagle Eye, nodding emphatically, indicating a guy with a shaved head and black leather pants: He had strolled casually from the warehouse, then paused a few feet behind the Cherokee to flick a cigarette butt down, snuffing it under a boot heel.

When the guy didn't proceed, when he remained standing there and looked upward at the starless sky, Duke went, "Yep, Black Pants is in trouble—let's go!"

But afterwards, while sitting beneath the statue, Willy tried convincing himself that what happened earlier in the parking lot was completely unexpected. Forget that he left the Cherokee with the others, forget that he ran alongside his teammates, charging at that poor guy.

"I didn't know," he planned on telling Hawk. "I didn't know."

Black Pants never flinched or attempted to flee. He just seemed bewildered, perhaps slightly amused as they surrounded him. And right before Duke threw an elbow into his chin, he actually smiled.

"Faggot!"

Willy wasn't surprised by the use of strength, wasn't shocked when

Black Pants spun and fell (those things occurred on the practice field every afternoon, that was how Duke played ball).

"Think it's funny," said Duke. "Don't think it's funny now!"

Black Pants covered his face, moaning through his hands while squirming on the ground—so Duke kicked him in the chest.

"Shut the fuck up!"

"Fucker," yelled Eagle Eye.

"Silly faggot," said Otter, "dicks are for chicks!"

But Tadpole didn't say anything.

And neither did Willy.

The two simply watched as Duke began searching Black Pants' pockets, yanking the contents out (folded bits of paper, some loose change that sprinkled to the pavement, car keys that were promptly flung across the parking lot and came crashing down on the windshield of someone's Buick).

"Here we go—"

Duke held the wallet, waving it so everyone could see.

Good, Willy thought. All done.

Except it wasn't done: Black Pants only had three dollars—no large bills, no credit cards—and that made Duke angry.

"Motherfucker," Duke said, throwing the wallet. "Goddamn shit!"

Later that night, when rehearsing what he planned to tell Hawk about the incident, Willy said, "See, this is what gets me. I mean, it was bad enough what Duke did. It was bad enough because this guy hadn't done no harm at all. We should've just got our asses on back into that truck and left. But Duke was pissed crazy. He wouldn't have it no other way. To be honest, Coach, I hadn't given that fellow a proper look until everybody started laying into him."

"Stupid fuckin' faggot cocksuckin' stupid shit fucker," Duke kept saying, a sneaker whacking Black Pants in the ribs and stomach and neck.

Soon the others, including Tadpole, joined in—encircling their victim, kicking and nudging at his body.

But Willy couldn't move or look away.

"Fuckin' faggot cocksucker—"

"You like that? Huh? You like that?"

Two eyes caught Willy—wide and scared, peeking between fingers and fixing on the one person who wasn't attacking.

"Coach, that about drove me crazy then. Jesus, any other day I might be having a beer with this guy, might be saying to him, 'How about them Oilers?' But goddammit what was I supposed to do?"

Otter pressed a sole to Black Pants' crotch—"Know what your ass-hole's for?"—and began stomping.

"Careful, Otter—man, you'll get AIDS!"

But it wasn't the blood dripping past Black Pants' shielding hands that made Willy yell—not the dull-sounding kicks delivered by his teammates, or their taunts—rather it was those frightened eyes, locking on Willy and imploring him, begging him to shout, "Quit it! That's enough already! Cut it out!"

Otter heard him first.

Then Eagle Eye.

Then Tadpole.

All three stopped, glancing at Willy with expressions that looked perturbed and almost shameful.

But Duke: "Didn't make a hell of a difference to him, Coach. And it's funny, because I don't remember getting in there. Can't recall how I got on top of that guy. But I was there all right. I was all over him and trying my best to keep him protected. I mean, it wasn't easy doing two things at once, you know, covering his body with my body and fighting Duke's feet with my hands."

"Goddamn you, Dust Storm, dumbass freshman fuck—!"

Duke's left leg swung like a frenzied pendulum, back and forth, back and forth.

Then it was Willy's turn to gaze imploringly at those who stood by (Otter and Tadpole and Eagle Eye returning his stare with frowns and wrinkled brows). Duke's shoe struck Willy's forehead, then jabbed his chin, then pounded his right ear—as if his head were a lead football that desperately needed punting.

The chin again.

The forehead.

And then Willy lost consciousness; he went limp on Black Pants and faded away.

So maybe it was in that moment he blamed the coyote. Or perhaps when stirring inside the Cherokee. Or was it later, while wandering the quad, that he thought: Stupid coyote, putting yourself in the wrong place and getting smashed.

Because if the coyote had hesitated for only a minute, if she had stepped on a thorn or rested beside a mesquite tree, then Lionel wouldn't have hit her. Everything would be different. It was like the poem he read in high school, a villanelle about butterflies landing on a flower in Japan and, as a result, a mine shaft collapsed in Alaska.

"Cause and effect," his teacher Mrs. Christian called it. "A seemingly minor and unrelated event can possibly have dire consequences."

Like a miscalculated play in a game, thought Willy, or a well-intended signature on a piece of paper.

Like Lionel and Sal eating dinner with his mother at the Dairy Mart in Claude.

And if the coyote had lived, what would be so different?
Probably nothing, concluded Willy, not a single thing—except one coyote living and breathing, that's all.

Either way, the recruiters would have still shared a basket of French fries with his mother, and Lionel still would have told her, "The letter of intent means that Willy is committing himself to attend the university, and it allows us to designate and hold a specific scholarship for him. It does require the signature of a parent or guardian."

Dead or otherwise, no coyote had any influence on his mother shrugging and sighing and saying, "Willy going to college—we've talked about it, but I guess I always figured it was like everything else—you think on it, and then it's something else you just can't afford."

Sal dipped a fry in ketchup. He said, "You need to understand, Miss Keeler, that we have a total supervisory and counseling program—academic excellence is a high priority. Our real and first concern is for Willy's education. We have counselors for that, and we have student work programs in the off-season. There are all kinds of avenues open through his scholarship to prevent his education from being a burden on you."

"He'll be in good hands, Miss Keeler, believe me," said Lionel. "It's one of the finest universities in the country."

"Pug, call me Pug. Miss Keeler was my mother."

"Okay, Pug it is."

Sal leaned in at the table, his chin hovering above the fries basket. "So listen, Pug," he said, lowering his voice, "we understand your concern—we know there'll be incidental expenses involved in Willy's graduation and getting him ready for school—maybe this will help out a bit."

As if on cue, Lionel dug into a coat pocket, removing a letter-sized envelope, which he then slid across the tabletop toward Pug.

"Go ahead. It's yours. Has nothing to do with us or the university—it's from friends of the university who simply want to give deserving young people a little help when it's really needed."

With three fries pinched between a thumb and index finger, Pug cocked an eyebrow and glanced uncertainly from the envelope to Lionel, to Sal, then—after letting the fries fall to her plate, after wiping her fingers on the thighs of her jeans—she lifted the envelope, felt its bulk in her palm, and looked inside.

"Good Lord," she said softly, gazing up at the recruiters. "Good Lord," she repeated, pressing the envelope to her chest and covering it with both hands.

"You sign this." Sal had already unfolded the letter of intent on the table, had already smoothed the paper and flipped the top page. "We'll meet later with your son and Coach Warfield."

"Until then," said Lionel, setting a ballpoint pen in front of her, "let's keep this between the three of us, okay?"

"Of course," said Pug, "I won't utter a thing."

And almost before the ink had dried, both recruiters were in Bud Warfield's office, standing below a high window (moonlight fell upon the tile floor, spreading cross-shaped shadows over their loafers).

"The Hawk will take care of him," Lionel was telling Bud, "college to grave—"

"You know I got eighteen other good offers, don't you?"

Bud propped his legs on a corner of his desk.

"We don't doubt it."

"Offers," said Bud, popping the knuckles of his right hand and leaning back in his chair, "not inquiries—"

"I'm sure you do."

Bud grinned. "So let's get her down." He tilted his head to one side, spitting tobacco juice at the trash can, then said, "You're telling me no red shirting?"

"That's right."

"A pure running back—nothing else—"

"You got Hawk's word."

Bud's mouth opened wide as if he were yawning—the wad of chew rolled off his tongue and sailed into the trash can. Then he pulled his legs from the desk, pushed forward in his seat, and brought his elbows to the desktop: "There may be one thing more."

"We thought there might be."

Bud pursed his lips for a moment, weighing the implications of what was about to be spoken. Finally he said, "I got a brother in Clayton, New Mexico—sells insurance—folks around here don't even know him. Now, he could take something and hold it for me as long as need be."

Lionel nodded as Sal dryly said, "We got a sponsor in Tulsa—give us your brother's name and his address—this is something the sponsor wants to do. It's got nothing whatsoever to do with the university."

"I understand that," said Bud, taking a pen from a desk drawer.

"You won't be disappointed."

On a yellow Post-It note, Bud quickly wrote his brother's address and a dollar amount. Then he handed the note to Lionel—"This is what I need and where it should go."—and was surprised when the recruiter stuck the note in a pocket without as much as a glance at it.

"It'll get taken care of."

"When do I tell my brother it's coming?"

"The day after the kid signs."

For several seconds all three men went quiet in that dim office—Bud staring at the recruiters, the recruiters staring at Bud—each hearing the faint raps of winter moths hitting the high window.

"Guess that's it," said Sal.

"Yep," said Bud.

Then handshakes were exchanged.

As the recruiters began to leave, Lionel told Bud, "We'll sign him here—get him to the campus to announce—you'll get calls from the press—we'll mail you what to say about his selection of the university."

"That's fine."

"We're heading to Amarillo—we'll be back here on Friday night for the game—we'll sign him the next morning after the deadline."

"No problem," said Bud. "I promised Ben Denton at the Daily News that I'd let him know—"

"You're not doing that," said Sal, shaking his head. "You don't let anybody know anything, understand? We'll take care of it."

"Whatever works for you," Bud replied lightly, though he wanted to say more. He wanted to point at the door and say, "Get the fuck out of my world, we're done," but the note in Lionel's pocket made him think otherwise. So instead he watched silently as Lionel and Sal walked from his office, exhaling relief when they vanished within the dark locker room. Then he eased back in the chair, inhaled a long breath, and proceeded to study the tobacco stains on his fingertips.

So if that coyote had lived, figured Willy, I'd end up at Moss no matter what. I'd still have climbed on into Duke's backseat and drank that beer and got the shit knocked from me. It was meant to happen—the whole business was out of my hands anyway.

Street light traveled across Willy's lap and thighs.

Duke was speeding along Montrose, and Otter was saying, "Should we take him to a hospital?"

"Are you kidding?"

Tadpole went, "Dust Storm? Hey, you hear me?"

"He's full of shit," said Duke. "I didn't nail him that hard."

"You did, man, you really did."

"Got him hard, Duke."

In the backseat, Tadpole jostled Willy's shoulder. "Dust Storm—?"

"Maybe he's dead," said Eagle Eye, reaching over Tadpole, slipping an arm between Willy's knees so he could fish a beer from the plastic bag.

Willy moved his lips, mumbling with eyes shut—"Yes, sir, that's the truth of it."—then he faded again.

"Hon'," his mom was suddenly telling him, "I'm a phone call away."

And Coach Bud: "Son, stay tall in the saddle."

Streetlights came and went.

Then, having passed the iron gates of Moss University, the Cherokee loitered at a stop sign. The following morning, Willy wouldn't remember throwing open the door and fleeing, but he'd still recall Tadpole shouting his nickname as Duke yelled, "Christ, Tadpole, who gives a fuck!"

Suddenly it was as if he awoke from a nightmare, startled, and found himself running for his life.

Sleep running, he thought later.

And he didn't slow until entering the empty quad, until coming to stand beneath the statue—and he didn't run again until encountering the shaving cream dancers in the stadium parking lot.

"Join us! Join us! Join us!"

Then he might have run all night, he might have run well past sunrise and continued onward—if only he had somewhere to go.

4.

Perched at a corner of Hawk Haskins' desk was a taxidermied chicken hawk (frozen in a position of descending attack, its claws affixed to a lacquered base). Hanging on the wall behind his desk were photographs: Hawk with George Bush, Hawk with Ann Richards, Hawk with John Madden. Below those photographs—reclining in a swivel chair, legs outstretched and snakeskin boots crossed—sat Hawk himself, absently picking his teeth with a toothpick, grinning as Willy stood facing him.

But today, like every day, they were not alone. From the moment Willy entered the office—hands trembling, eyes darting nervously—he was put next to Susan, a dark-haired coed who greeted him with a firm handshake and red fingernails, who made smacking noises as she worked and chomped a piece of chewing gum.

"Willy, this is Susan—Susan, meet Willy—"

She didn't notice those shuddering hands (twitching so badly now that he hid them behind his back after they shook). Then how pleased she acted, standing beside such a handsome and reserved young athlete, holding him at the elbow.

"Smile, Willy—"

A picture was taken.

Then another.

Another.

Like the prom, thought Willy, like the sports banquet.

Except he didn't know his date, even though she behaved like she had known him since childhood, saying his name with a pestering familiarity: "Willy, don't be shy—smile, Willy—come on, you've got a nice smile—"

Good thing he wore pressed Wranglers and a clean Polo shirt.

Good thing he had showered, otherwise the fatigue would've been more apparent.

So he tried smiling, tried keeping the corners of his mouth curved upward—but the photographer was distracting (overweight bald guy ducking here and there—"look this way, that's great"—clicking and clicking, breathing raggedly through his nostrils). The headache pounding inside his skull, intensified by the camera flashes (all fireworks and glare, white bursts stunning his sight), forced his smile into a grimace.

Flash

Susan playfully tugged at his elbow, as if attempting to jar Willy's reticence.

A real pro, he thought. Miss Charm, Grace, and Style—a big bunch of roses should fall into her arms, a crown should drop on her head.

Flash

Hawk wasn't the only one enjoying the spectacle: Lionel and Sal were there too, along with Sidney Charlton, the Sports Information Director; all three men standing near Hawk's desk like vigilant sentinels.

Flash

Then the photographer was finished. "Nice-looking kids," he said, giving Willy and Susan a nod and a wink before heaving his equipment bag from the floor—and Sidney came forward, patting him on the shoulder, saying, "We appreciate it, Steve, especially considering the short notice."

"No problem, Sid. I'll get a contact sheet by tomorrow."

"Excellent."

Then it became Susan's turn to receive a pat.

"Thanks, Susan," said Sidney, "you'll be seeing more of our boy here."

Susan's grin blossomed, baring shiny teeth and red-pink gums.

"I hope so," she said, touching the bangs of her hair and glancing briefly at Willy (such pensive eyes met her look, such discomfort).

"Done good, sweetheart," said Hawk, the toothpick dangling from his bottom lip. "Listen, when you see your ol' man tell him hi."

"I will, Coach," she said, following the photographer toward the door, walking very slowly and deliberately, as if studied in the art of sauntering from a crowded room—fingers fluttering, totally aware that all eyes would watch her ass wiggle past the doorway: "Bye, Coach—"

"Bye, hon'."

"Bye, everyone—"

When the door closed behind her, Sidney exhaled an exaggerated breath while pretending to wipe sweat from his brow. He nudged Willy, saying, "What you think, son?"

"She's nice," Willy replied halfheartedly.

"True enough," said Sidney, smirking at the others. "And dammit if you don't get to go out with her a time or two a week, how's that sound?"

Willy assented vaguely by shrugging, so Hawk scooted up in his chair, asking, "Say, you ain't got a girl there in Claude, do you?"

"Don't feel that hot today," Willy wanted to say, "and I'm not really sure what's going on here." But instead he shrugged again, saying nothing.

"Christ," said Sidney.

Hawk sighed: "Well—do you or don't you, son?"

Willy gazed down at his boots, shaking his head.

"That's good," said Hawk.

Then Sidney went, "You'll go out with Susan—her old man owns most of Galveston—and what'll happen is—she'll slip you a hundred or so on dates, so it won't cost you anything, understand?"

But Willy could only shrug, could only stare at his boots and lift his shoulders—and, sticking his shaky hands into his pockets, grinned like an idiot.

"Is this boy a beauty or what?"

Hawk started chuckling, so did Lionel and Sal.

"Willy, if she slips you some cash," said Sidney, "that's her business, right? I mean, it's got nothing to do with any of us here—or the university. So—what the hell, if you don't spend it all on the date, you got yourself a little something now and then to ride by on, right?"

Hawk uncrossed his boots. "Let me tell you something, son." He rose from the chair, carefully placing the toothpick on his desk. "I put a lot of stock in gut hunches," he said, striding over to Willy, throwing an arm across the boy's shoulders. "Sid and Lionel and Sal and me— we been talking a lot about you—"

Hawk guided Willy to the opposite end of the office, bringing him to stand in front of a large, sheetglass window—beyond which stretched a hard blue sky and low-lying clouds (on the rooftop of Texas, Willy imagined, miles above his teammates and Moss and Houston).

"We've been figuring maybe—just maybe—if you don't have to go waste your time on student jobs and such as that—if you got yourself plenty of time for weights and the right sort of training—give you, say, another thirty to forty pounds—then maybe we might have us the right recipe for a run at the Heisman—"

As they stared out from the window into the yawning and empty football stadium below, Willy smelled garlic on Hawk's breath. He could see their reflections in the window, could glimpse his own confused and forlorn expression.

"It'll take work on Sid's and my part—and the rest of the boys—it's going to take all you can give it if it's going to work. It's going to take all you got for four years. Maybe five if it takes red-shirting—you think you got what it takes to get there, son? Because if you do—I think we just might do it—we might just pull it off—"

When Hawk affectionately squeezed his shoulder, Willy felt the twisting pain in his gut, and for a second he worried that he might shit himself (not now, he thought, not until after I can talk to you, Hawk, not now).

"I don't have to tell you—the Heisman—that's the mountain top—the real mountain top—yessir—you reach up and get that one, and it's the power and the glory, son—the power and the glory—"

Willy tried concentrating on Hawk's words, but how weary he felt, hungry now and unfocused; so it was easier to shut his eyes and conceive the stadium below as being packed, the spectators and players as small as ants.

"Son—?" Hawk was saying.

And Willy knew there was something that needed to be said, something important that brought him into Hawk's office—but the speech he'd rehearsed had drifted from memory and he didn't feel like talking much anyway.

"I want to go home—"

"Sorry, didn't quite catch that. What is it you're saying?"

Then with eyes closed, Willy saw himself as a small boy, agilely climbing to the top of Claude's water tower on game nights. Sometimes the wind was so soothing and warm up there he would fall asleep. But not before spotting the bleachers on both sides of the football field, the bright lights shining on the grass—not before applauding the cheering voices that always carried to where he sat. Sometimes he cheered too, regardless of who was winning. Or, for the hell of it, he would drool over the railing and pretend his dribble was a football sailing toward goalposts a hundred miles away. On those nights, he knew everybody was down below, the people from his life, and Willy was so far above them that he was certain his spit evaporated while approaching the earth.

"I think I'm going home, Coach."

So there he was again—reaching the water tower catwalk, inhaling the dry air. Even as Hawk shook his shoulders and spoke his name, Willy was sitting beneath that mural of peeling letters—*Claude, Home Of The Fighting Tigers*—and hanging his legs into space, taking it all in from above: the mesquite branches ruffled by a flat breeze, the thick oil rig fires that burned amongst a maze of chinaberry sprigs.

In the distance, a coyote cried from the blackness of wide pasture: a mournful, high-pitched howl that faded into a series of yips and yaps. Then other coyotes joined in the chorus, yip-yaps mixed with drawn out howls. The wails ricocheted between canyons and hills, sounding as if every coyote in the world had come together to lament.

To the west, the lights of Amarillo spread across the horizon, and headlights floated in the darkness between Claude and its larger neighbor.

To the east, the soil remained impermeable at the bottom of dried watering holes—in the arid dirt of abandoned homesteads, along overgrown cattle trails—where a deep stillness existed, present only to the flatland scrub and the first norther that washed clean the simmering heat of unbearable summers.

Mitch Cullin

Born in Santa Fe, New Mexico during the "crossfire hurricane" year of 1968, Mitch Cullin is the author of five highly acclaimed books: *Whompyjawed, Branches, Tideland, The Cosmology of Bing*, and the story collection *From the Place in the Valley Deep in the Forest*. His short fiction has been widely anthologized, most recently in *Best American Gay Fiction 2* and *Gay Fiction at the Millennium*, and his novels will soon be published internationally in forthcoming editions from England, the Netherlands, and Japan. With his writing described by *The New York Times* as "brilliant and beautiful … rhythmic and telling," he has also been the recipient of many awards and honors, including a Dodge Jones Foundation grant; writing sponsorship from Recursos De Santa Fe; the Stony Brook Short Fiction Prize; a poetry fellowship from the Arizona Commission on the Arts; and a nomination for inclusion in the American Library Association's "Notable Book List, 1999." He currently resides in Tucson, Arizona, where he lives with the artist Peter I. Chang—the pair having previously collaborated on *Safe Places to Die* (2000) and the graphic novel *Undersurface* (2002).

Give It Up for Billy

Edmund White

Harold's lover Tom didn't come with him to Key West that winter. Tom thought the heterosexual snowbirds (those who winter in the south) were too old in Key West and the younger gays who worked there year round were too stupid. Since South Beach had become the destination for A-list gays (celebrated decorators, real estate speculators, media moguls and their satellites, muscle builders and models), Key West had turned into a backwater for balding gay couples from Toledo, the sort who owned and operated their own neighborhood dry cleaners and whose foreheads burned easily in the semi-tropical sun. These guys, the Toledo drycleaners, immediately took up with a similar couple from Lubbock they'd just met. The foursome were happy to go on a glass-bottomed boat out to the reef or to play bridge at night back at their all-male compound where the only men under thirty worked behind the desk.

Harold didn't mind how dowdy Key West had become with its main street lined with Israeli-owned T-shirt shops, its commercialization of Papa Hemingway's bearded face on the coasters at Sloppy Joe's bar on Duval, or its Conch Train that puttered down shaded streets and informed the tourists in shorts and sun hats about the Hemingway House and his cats with six toes or about Truman's Little White House or the Audubon House. Harold accepted that the world was becoming a product to be consumed by the world's leading industry, mass tourism. He looked at Japanese tourists as models for us all. They didn't seek out private, authentic experiences while traveling, or so at least he imagined. They didn't claim to be the exception, to be solitary and romantic. They weren't a headache for their group leader. No, they were content to buy the best-known, most easily recognized, luxury brand names at airport shops and to take their photos of the Whaling Museum or the Eiffel Tower or the Oldest House from the exact spot the guide indicated. Harold had been coming here for a few weeks every winter over the last twenty years and he'd seen Key West go from a rough town of drifters and trailer trash to an elegant stronghold with artistic pretensions, including an annual literary conference on themes such as "Nature Writing" or "Journaling" or "Fact or Fiction?" Property prices had gone up tenfold.

And he was no longer young and wouldn't figure on anybody's A or B list. He was sixty-three, in a few days to be sixty-four, and about to retire from the New World History department of Princeton with a handsome teacher's union portfolio. He had an arthritic neck and cataracts he wanted to have removed as soon as they were a bit riper. Tom, his forty-five-year-old lover, worked for Johnson & Johnson in public relations. Tom ran several miles a day and had no wrinkles, possibly because he used Retin-A.

They had an extremely open, easygoing relationship. Their heterosexual friends—and almost all of their friends were heterosexual in Princeton—said they envied them their relaxed attitude toward each other's extramarital adventures. Actually the adventures were embarrassingly rare and the friends found their non-possessiveness confusing since it seemed to mark yet another spot where there wasn't a perfect fit between homosexual and heterosexual couples. People liked homosexuals if they were a sort of fun house reflection of their own image. They didn't want them to be completely different.

What no one knew was that Harold and Tom had long since given up having sex with each other. It was as if their original friendship had flared up into sexuality and jealousy for a few years before subsiding back into mutual esteem. Harold wanted Tom to have fun, even sexual fun, so long as he didn't fall in love with someone else and leave him. He couldn't bear to live alone in Princeton. Or anywhere, for that matter. Though Princeton, with its acres of mansions and lawns and its lonely winter nights and its absence of all gay presence, seemed particularly daunting for a single gay man. Recently Tom had begun to date a woman from his office, someone who did community relations, and she represented a more serious threat to their life together. Women played for keeps, Harold believed. He thought female seriousness was biological and had something to do with sperm being cheap and eggs dear, or was it to do with spreading a favorable mutation quickly through the species, but such theories always struck him as kitsch. He knew that straights took their lives more seriously than gays did, and straight women most of all. He also knew that Tom had begun to despise the Chelsea-style gay men they saw when they went into New York City for dinner or a concert. Tom couldn't resist making a nasty comment every time they passed a muscle boy. Anyone who looks like that must be putting in four hours a day at the gym, he'd snarl. For Harold it was not an issue. Neither Chelsea Boys nor skinny East Village bohemians looked at him. Nobody did.

Tom would say, I'm glad we don't live in the gay world. It embarrasses me; it's so mindless and narcissistic. Give me the eternal verities any day—children, the future, self-discipline, altruism.

Harold relaxed back into his old Key West routines. He rented a bike and went everywhere on it, even on cold nights and rainy days. Literary friends his age thought it absurd that he didn't rent a car and drive around in dignity as they did. They thought it ridiculous that he insisted on teetering around with his big po-po hanging out over the saddle, but Harold loved the boyhood associations of riding a bike, especially at night down the cat-busy lanes and under giant palms churning in the wind. Most of the time he was tired and a bit dazed, as if coming out from under a sedative, but when he was alert, as he was at midnight on his bike, he felt as he always had.

He'd looked forward to going back to Scooter's, the go-go bar, which in the past had been on the edge of town where Truman Avenue shaded into Highway 1. It had been a rowdy but innocent place where skinny, Florida blonds and small compact brunets from Montreal came out on the tacky runway, one by one, in jeans and layered shirts. Each did two numbers, the first one clothed and the second stripped down to a G-string. The unseen announcer at the end would say, "Okay, fellas. Give it up for Ronnie," a locution Harold had never heard before; apparently it meant "Applaud Ronnie."

He found that there were more and more things he didn't know about. Almost all the guests on late-night talk shows he'd never heard of—pop singers or actors in TV series, which he didn't watch. He didn't follow sports and never knew the names of tennis players and football stars. He could identify most of the current and past names in New World studies, of course, as well as many of the principle figures in

American history. He was convinced he knew more about his period, Woodrow Wilson's America, than about George W. Bush's.

Scooter's had moved into town. The bar was now smaller and cleaner and better lit. Instead of putting on stage any kid blowing through town, it now had a small permanent cast of dancers, mostly non-English speakers: a big blond Estonian, an intensely black Senegalese with biceps as round as cannonballs, a wispy Czech, a sulky Spaniard, a smiling Macedonian. They would dance for twenty minutes on the two podiums at the far end of the room, then jump up onto the bar and coax tips out of customers before working the room.

They'd dance standing up on the bar and customers would stick dollar bills in their gym socks, but after a while they'd crouch down, their legs spread wide, and let the older men touch their thighs and crotches. The tips were rarely more than a dollar or two, whereas at Teacher's, the heterosexual strip bar, the men handed out tens and twenties. Were gay men poorer or less competitive or did they think it a waste to pay out a lot of money to a member of their own sex? The seedy festive air of the old Scooter's was gone. With its tables and chairs gathered around the stage and the lights red or white, strong or soft, which the boys had kicked on with their toes, like Marilyn Monroe in *Bus Stop*. They no longer had an overhead pipe to do pull-ups on. And gone was the cubbyhole separated from the room by glass beads where customers could have extra feels in the dark for twenty bucks: lap dancing, it was called.

Now the proximity of the heavy foot traffic up and down Duval, those herds of tourists grazing along, released from the big cruise ships, acted as an inhibiting presence on the men in the new Scooter's. The whole place was just too visible and few locals dared to drop in.

But it was better than nothing. In Princeton there were no go-go boys, and in New York there were too many drag queens for Harold's taste and not much lap dancing. He admired transvestites—their courage, their art, their antic sense of fun—but they didn't turn him on. In Princeton, of course, for so many years the boys had been his students: superb, untouchable. Now that at last he was about to retire, he was the age of their grandfathers and unlikely to attract anyone. He sometimes fancied an older man, but they seldom looked his way. Almost no one looked his way.

Night after night Harold, after a dinner with elderly literary or

scholarly friends, would bicycle down the nearly empty streets to
Duval, which was always busy, and to Scooter's. Gay bars, straight
bars, closing restaurants, a big disco, the Ripley's Believe-It-or-Not, the
handsome spotlit façade of the Cuban Cultural Center, the slow passage
of cruising cars and pickup trucks up and down the main drag, the
clang-clang of bells rung by professional bicyclists conveying one or
two passengers in open rickshaws—it was all exciting, an animated little world. Harold chained his bike to a lamppost, visited the outdoor
ATM and ambled into Scooter's. He liked the glow of naked young
flesh under the spotlights, the smell of freshly poured beer, the pools of
attention as men gathered around a dancer drifting like a big, showy
chameleon through the crowd. He liked to sit at the bar and look up at
these kids with their powerful legs, sweat-drenched torsos, broad shoulders and unfocused smiles. Sometimes one of them would drip on him.
They were nude and extravagant as hothouse flowers blooming above
all these old men. In Italy he'd once seen rosebushes threaded through
gnarled olive trees: that was the effect. The boys were more often than
not bewitched by their own reflections, which they studied in the mirror with alternating smiles and frowns. As one would turn sideways and
suck in his gut, you could just hear him asking himself if he was really
getting a beer belly as his pal Tommy claimed.

The men, of course, had once been boys, too, but not boys like
these, not usually. These men were chemical engineers or hotel man-
agers or accountants: nerds. Two of them whom Harold had met were
English and ran a bed-and-breakfast in Brighton. A few, no doubt, had
been good-looking, but not in the way these dancers were. Back then,
very few men worked out, and almost no gays. These dancers had gym-
built bodies, legs bowed with muscle, tiny waists giving it up to flaring
torsos and wide shoulders, thick necks, cropped heads. "Give it up for
Bobby"—that was the phrase that kept ringing in his head for no good
reason. These dancers were shaved, tattooed, bronzed, tinted; even their
pubic hair, when they revealed a glimpse of it, was just a shaped,
trimmed patch, cut to the quick to make their genitals look still bigger.
Everything—sneakers or combat boots, thong or towel, nipple ring or
diamond ear-bob—had been thought out, but even so they had a reck-
less, raucous assertiveness that came through their primping like a
trumpet through a thicket of quivering strings. Most of them were
straight and spent the dollars they earned on local girls. He'd seen them

stumbling out of the Hog's Breath Saloon with girls. Harold liked them all, all of the boys, and when one of them strolled around the room in a gold G-string and gathered a group of old men (hands liver-spotted, backs twisted, mouths radiant with new teeth), Harold couldn't help but picture *Susannah and the Elders* by, was it Titian? That beautiful naked girl emerging from her bath, her flesh coveted by all the old men peeking through the bushes.

It took two or three days for Harold to decide he liked Billy the most. Billy was about five-foot-ten and he had a splash of peroxided hair, though in recent years peroxide no longer signified "cheap" or effeminate Now it read "punk" or just "young"—nothing clear, in any case. Billy had a knowing smile and a faint scar that traversed his nose. Just a seam, really. A ghost of asymmetry. He had a solemn, level gaze, something serious and noncommittal but friendly about his manner. He had what personal ads on gay websites called a "six-pack stomach."

He also had an immense uncut penis, which once or twice a night he worked up and gave quick glimpses of. Sometimes, when he danced on a dais, he pulled his shorts open and looked down at his penis, which he could see but the audience couldn't. He'd mime the sound, "Wow," and bug his eyes, as if he'd never seen it before. But he went lightly on the comedy. He wasn't a camp. He was a serious, virile man but not forbidding, certainly not unapproachable. A man's man, who treated customers as if they were almost pals, though he definitely maintained a professional distance.

Harold gave him five-dollar tips and never groped him. Sometimes Harold said friendly, noncommittal things, like, "The air conditioner's on the blink tonight?" or, "Where'd they get this music?" After four or five days, Billy would come over to Harold on his break. If Harold was seated at the bar, Billy would lean against him, throw a hot, heavy arm around his shoulders. "That guy over there," Harold would say, "was sure pawing you."

Billy said, "These guys must think we're really naive. Man ... That guy said he'd just bought a mansion quote-unquote in Key West and had decided he wanted to spend the rest of his life with me. He said he was a multimillionaire quote-unquote and would leave me well provided for. He'd take me away from all this." Billy opened a hand, then let it fall to his side.

"Jesus ...," Harold muttered with feigned disgust at the guy's chutzpah. But why not? If the guy were alone, not long for this world, rich enough to feather his last nest with a nice gigolo, why not buy a young man who looked thirty and seemed unusually solid.

"I said to him, 'Why not tip me a few dollars right now if you're so rich,' but the cheap bastard never parted with a penny."

"Hey, Billy," Harold said, wrapping a hand around his tight little waist, "where are you from anyway, Australia?"

"Zimbabwe."

"Oh."

"Do you see?"

"Yes, I see. Former Rhodesia."

"You'd be amazed how many Americans think it's next to Tibet."

"Hopeless …," Harold groaned.

Billy had a polite, deferential manner, an impenetrable but friendly regard, a deep reserve. He might throw his arm over Harold's shoulder but it all felt like a professional engagement; Harold could almost hear the meter ticking. A very tall blond man in his late thirties wearing a raspberry-colored polo shirt, pleated khakis, and gold-bitted loafers signaled Billy, who excused himself. Harold didn't want to stare but he saw the seated man draw Billy down onto one leg and idly stroke his hairless, oiled thigh. There was no lust in it, just intimacy, and the man spoke rapidly, even in a businesslike way, while Billy nodded agreement. They could have been two spies exchanging information while pretending to be dancer and client. In five minutes the conference was over and the man had elbowed his way out of the bar, uninterested in the other dancers, though he did shake hands with the bouncer at the door and even spared him a smile.

The next day Harold watched a porno film his landlord leant him; the eventless subplot was about twins from Hungary, identical down to the tiniest mole on the right forearm or the small, cantilevered buttocks or the overlapping incisors. They seemed happiest when stepping off each other's joined hands and doing a back flip into the pool and the most embarrassed when they had to kiss, and fondle each other's small-ish identical erection with an identical hand. They had identical pony-tails. The main story was unrelated, all about a superb, dark-haired boy with flawless skin who so enjoyed being penetrated by a blond Dracula that he begged the monster to bite his neck, a declaration so miracu-lously romantic that Dracula was turned back into an ordinary human being. And saved. From what? Harold wondered. Eternal life? Eternal youth? Harold worried about dying. He had de-dramatized every moment in his life, giggled at the over-the-top romantic scenes in movies, accepted his mother's death with equanimity, even indifference, though when he'd won a scholarly prize for his book on Wilson at Versailles, he'd wept, since his mother wasn't alive to enjoy his moment of glory. Egotism, he'd told himself. Egotistical foolishness. Life at Princeton, the university and the town, was so unchanging that he couldn't remember many key dates in his life there other than his five sabbatical years and the beginnings and ends of his three previous affairs.

He couldn't quite figure it out, but it was as if he'd worked out a strategy that if he didn't bear down too hard on his life, it would leave such a faint impression it wouldn't what? Count? Be noticed? Go through the carbon onto a master copy? He'd almost never been alone. He'd always had a live-in companion, although in the sixties he had still had to pretend that Jack, the man of the moment, was just rooming in his spare bedroom. By the mid-seventies the mores had so changed that he and Jack had been invited everywhere as a couple.

There had been so few ripples in his life. He'd produced only three books, but two were significant and still in print. He'd inched his way up the ladder to tenure and a full professorship. He'd had three or four star students who were now distinguished Americanists. One was even contemplating early retirement.

He felt he'd somehow slipped through. He'd not had to serve in Vietnam, at first because he'd been in graduate school and then because his asthma had been so crippling. Later, the disease had just gone away, even though central New Jersey was both polluted and saturated with pollen, the industrial Garden State. He'd been just a few years too old to become a hippie, and he was never tempted to drop out. He'd supported the student rebels in 1968, but no more so than most of the other junior faculty. He'd come out when he was in his fifties, back in the 1980s, when gender studies had become trendy and he was able to renew his scholarly image by arguing in an oft-cited essay that World War I had been a forcing shed for modern gay identity. He'd exercised moderately, had never drunk to excess, he'd been afraid to try intravenous drugs, and he'd smoked marijuana just twice, both times with a Puerto Rican trick, and had felt nothing. Just when AIDS had become a real danger he'd met Tom, who was then in his early twenties and virtually a virgin. They'd been faithful for nearly a decade and by then had mastered safe sex techniques, which they used with all their other new tricks.

But he knew he wasn't going to slip past old age, sickness, and death. No one did. He wasn't Dracula. He was considered practical and realistic and he'd take all the most rational steps toward the grave, or rather the crematorium. The other day Tom had read out loud from a new novel, "He was accumulating as many experiences as possible so he'd feel less alone when he died," but Harold suspected the author of irony. It didn't work that way. Harold thought most novelists were irresponsible, and those he'd known weren't very perceptive or worldly. That's why he seldom read fiction.

Harold knew that at best he had just twenty or twenty-five more years to live, which didn't sound very long. The previous twenty years had gone by so fast. Time was speeding up just as it was running out, like the last of the water draining from a sink. Back in the early eighties, Key West had been a good time-thickener because he'd known so few people and had done nothing but lie around and read. But now the island was so busy with elderly activity—luncheons, readings, cocktail parties, art openings—that the days sped by. Key West made Princeton seem tranquil by contrast.

Harold didn't tell Tom every detail about Billy during their daily phone calls but Tom certainly got the highlights. Tom had enough on his plate. Roger, their old wirehaired fox terrier, had become so ill with leukemia and was in such pain from arthritis that Dr. Wilkins had put him to sleep.

Harold knew he was being irrational, but he thought they should have waited until he, Harold, could have said good-bye to the dog. "Closure? Is that it?" Tom asked. "Everybody in America suddenly wants closure. Well, I wasn't worrying about your peace of mind, Harold."

A long silence set in. To change the subject Harold asked Tom about Liz.

"Her name is Beth. She's fine. We're seeing a lot of each other. How's Billy? When are you going to go to bed with him?"

"I'm not sure what my next move should be." Harold was grateful for this fake conversation to replace the real, painful one.

"Ask him over in the afternoon. If that man in the Gucci shoes is keeping him, the late afternoon may be the only time he's free."

"Don't you think it's odd he's from Zimbabwe?"

Tom laughed. "You don't keep up with the news but Zimbabwe is going through hell. The black president, Mugabe, has encouraged roving bands of black ex-soldiers to kill the white settlers and expropriate their farms, and the soldiers know nothing about farming and the crop yields are diminishing and the World Bank or whatever won't extend them any more loans; it's a nightmare. As for gay life, the gay guide forbids readers to go there at all. People suspected of homosexuality are pushed off a cliff—or is that Yemen? Anyway, it's dire, darling. Your little Billy has come to Key West to come out."

Harold said admiringly, "You always can orient yourself to a new person or situation within seconds. Whereas I feel like some sort of moral Mr. Magoo."

"That's right: I'm perfect," Tom said. He didn't take compliments well and was specially immune to Harold's, which were too flowery and heartfelt for someone like Tom, brought up on jokey, shrugging sitcom dialogue.

That night Harold invited Billy to drop by his place the following afternoon for a drink.

"I don't drink."

"For a fruit juice."

"But not orange or grapefruit," Billy said. "They're too acidic. Maybe a herbal tea would be best, or mineral water flat."

"What?"

"Non-sparkling. It's better for the digestion."

Although Harold found alimentary pedantry to be tiresome, he welcomed it as a diversion from the real question: Why should they get together at all?

"I can come by after my workout around four-forty-five or four-fifty," Billy said.

Despite the precision, he didn't show up until five-fifteen. He came speeding up in a red convertible with the top down and the stereo blaring a Mariah Carey tape (something Tom would have sniffed at). For Harold, who liked no music after early Stravinsky, it was all the same to him. The barbarians had broken through the gate, they were the rulers, there was nothing more to worry about.

They sat outside on a little veranda surrounded by shoulder-height bamboo walls. Harold had brought back from the expensive supermarket cooked shrimp, smoked mackerel bits, blue corn chips, and several kinds of water, as much as he could carry in his bicycle basket without losing control. Billy drank the water but didn't touch the food.

When Harold asked Billy what were his plans in life, the young man said, "You know the tall guy who comes into the club to see me?"

"Yes. Who is he?"

"His name is Ed. He's an agent for models. He arranged for me to be in *Frisk*. I brought you the February issue. It's in the car."

Harold had always imagined most of the readers of the "women's magazine" *Frisk* were gay men, closet cases who needed a heterosexual alibi in order to study other men's bodies. Maybe there were women readers, too. Certainly in this issue, he thought as he thumbed through it, there was a lean man in his fifties, a guy with a small penis and a beautiful face, and there was a photo essay titled "A Romantic Evening by the Fire," which showed a woman being undressed by an entirely depilated man. A hard-core gay magazine wouldn't have had any of these variations—the older man or the woman, but the guys would have had shaved bodies.

Billy's pictures made up the lead story. He was shown in various stages of undress, though the last spread revealed just how immense his "manhood" was, to use the language of the magazine. The text called him by a different name, Kevin, and said he was a corporate lawyer in Boston.

"So you want to be a model?"

"I'm already thirty and if I watch my diet and work out every day maybe I can stretch it out till I'm forty, but I'm saving every cent. Some day maybe I'll go into public relations. Right now I'm just making a quick buck. I can't work in America anyway, not at a legitimate job; I don't have a green card. Most of my money I'm sending back to my mum to install an electric fence around her house."

"Shouldn't you get her out of Zimbabwe altogether?"

"The cities aren't dangerous, not yet. She has a very nice house and servants. You can't believe how far the U.S. dollars I send her go. Anyway, she's running the family business."

"What is your family business?"

Billy looked at Harold in a penetrating way—frank, level, unsmiling. "Funeral parlor. My mum and dad emigrated from England to Rhodesia in the late sixties. They had a thriving business. When I was eighteen, my Dad sent me back to London for a two-year course in embalming techniques, grief counseling, and funeral accountancy. Then he died and I took over the business. My mum is the business manager. She's the one who has all the contacts in the community."

"Black as well?"

"About a third of our clients are black."

From the very beginning Harold had picked on something ... formal about Billy. When they were just standing around, Billy lowered his head, let a noncommittal smile play over his lips. He hooked his hands behind his back and widened his stance like a soldier at ease. Now Harold could easily picture Billy in a white shirt, dark tie and dark suit, producing a white handkerchief for the sobbing widow.

Harold asked Billy whether he'd been gay in Zimbabwe. "No, it's too dangerous. I had a girlfriend, though I spent a lot of time looking at her brother. She knew. We didn't talk about it, but she knew. I desired her, too. In fact, she's the most beautiful girl I've ever seen. She's going to move to London any day now."

"Are you bisexual?"

Billy looked vaguely cornered and said, "Let's just say I'm sexual."

Harold could tell it was a line he'd said many times before.

Billy took Harold for a ride in his car out to another island. His cell rang and he laughed and murmured into it, but he wasn't speaking English. When he hung up, Harold asked, "Was that Afrikaans?"

"Zulu. Well, our kind of Zulu."

"Were you speaking to someone in Zimbabwe?"

"Yes, it was my mate Bob. Great guy. We always have a bit of a chinwag once a week."

"Is he black?"

"What? Oh. No. He's white."

"You speak Zulu to another white guy?"

"We go back and forth."

Harold thought no one could argue that a Zulu-speaking, African-born Zimbabwean was an outsider.

Whenever Harold asked something about politics in Zimbabwe, Billy maintained a low-key tone. *Sixty Minutes* had just done a frightening segment on the deterioration of the country. In one scene a group of armed black men in rags crossed a lush, well-tended field and approached a young white farmer. Their discussion seemed more a dispute over something like a parking ticket, heated but containable, yet in another scene the charred, bloated dead bodies of other white settlers were shown.

Someone taped the program for Billy, who seemed shocked, silenced when he saw it. "I knew that young farmer. I knew him."

"The president was such an obvious hypocrite," Harold said. But Billy appeared to be way beyond outrage or anger.

They had sex every afternoon. Harold paid him two hundred dollars a session. After a few days he suggested they lower the fee to a hundred and fifty dollars, but Billy was firm. "I need all I can get, Harold," he said.

Billy would appear around five in his red convertible outside Harold's gate. They'd sip some herbal tea and then move into the bedroom for a "massage." Harold would apply a thick cocoa butter with an oppressively sweet smell to Billy's back and shoulders, then to his muscular buttocks, finally to his calves and thighs. It smelled like a Mars Bar.

Harold didn't really like massaging Billy's body, which felt too hard and unyielding. There was no mystery to it. It was like armor, not responsive flesh. Billy would talk in fits and starts, giving the news of the day, and Harold felt like his trainer. The problem was that Harold didn't really dote on other men, never had. He wasn't an idolater, though Billy was cut out to be an idol.

Decades and decades ago, back in the 1950s, Harold had been famous for his smooth skin; even the three women who had touched and held him had envied him his skin. He'd been lithe, small-sexed, boyish, though he'd dressed in chunky tweeds and worn wire-rims and seldom smiled with his thin lips. But for the handful of men who'd bothered to lift his fragile glasses off and liberate him from his heavy, thickening clothes, he'd been a bijou. Once when he'd been in Paris as a tourist, he'd been picked up by a couturier who lived in Sartre's old apartment. The man, all sprouting whiskers and smoker's cough, had stood back, slightly amazed at the boyish genie he'd summoned up out of the drab clothes: *"Mais tu es un bijou, un petit bijou,"* he'd said as he opened his hands, as if to bear witness. Harold still felt a bit like that, a jewel, and he half expected to amaze other men. On the phone his voice, apparently, sounded like a piping, eager, overeducated kid's, holding a laugh in, and young people who met him first on the phone warmed up to him, called him "Hal," and said funny, sly things to him. Later, when they saw he was old, they were taken aback.

After Harold had massaged Billy's back, he tapped his ass, as a trainer might, with an unsuggestive touch, and Billy turned over. There, suddenly, was the enormous uncircumcised penis, white and marbled and somehow assembled like sausage meat. And Harold applied himself to it, performed fellatio as if this were just a customized kind of massage, given the shape of the body part. Billy kept his eyes closed and made not a sound until the actual moment of explosion, and even then Harold suspected it was less a sensual moan than a warning to back off in the interests of safe sex.

Harold invited Billy to his sixty-fourth birthday party on another island not far away. They all sprayed themselves against the clouds of mosquitoes and Harold's friends, a dozen of them, artists and writers and teachers in their fifties and sixties, were charmed by Billy, who stood about with his hands hooked behind him, his eyes lowered: the perfect mortician.

He was unassertive but friendly and open. He talked about Zimbabwe and his fears for his mother and sister. "I'm trying to raise a bit of money so that my sister can emigrate to Australia."

"We saw the *Sixty Minutes* show," someone murmured sympathetically.

"I knew that farmer. My sister has a beautiful farm, but she can never sell it now. I've got to get her out of there as soon as I can afford it. Every day counts."

Billy played with someone's four-year-old daughter and even laced an arm around the waist of a big-eyed, short-haired woman who'd divorced her husband recently, though the husband was present if subdued. A man who wrote a column on labor problems for *The Nation* kept asking Billy questions about his job as a dancer. Billy smiled mildly; he had no hesitation in responding. Surely, Harold thought, he must be enjoying this freedom. He was never free in Africa.

One of the guests, a sculptor, invited them to his studio to pose for him. "I'm doing terra cotta figurines of lap dancers at Teacher's, women dancers and male customers, so I might as well do some gay pairs, if you're up to it. I don't know what will come of it, if anything."

They went to Sid's studio two days later, in the afternoon, at their usual hour. Sid paid Billy ten dollars for posing. By this time Harold's straight friends had all seen the issue of *Frisk* and they were all astonished by the size of Billy's penis. "But is that trick photography?"

"No," Harold said, lowering his eyes modestly.

Sid's wife said, "And he's a hell of a nice guy, too. He played with Annabelle's daughter for hours. I asked him to dance next month for our guests on Captain Bob's boat; we're giving a big party. Too bad you won't be here." It struck Harold as odd that straight people would want a go-go boy to dance for them, but Key West prided itself on being off-beat.

Harold enjoyed holding Billy's calves and staring up at him. Billy was wearing just a G-string, whereas Harold was in a shirt and slacks. Sid had rigged up a platform that simulated a bar. He kept pushing them closer together, not because he wanted intimacy. No, he just wanted to simplify their forms into a pyramid. Once again Harold thought of roses emerging out of a gnarled, twisted olive tree. Harold dreaded their sex sessions. The rancid, sweet smell of the cocoa butter which Billy had brought with him that first time and had left behind sickened him. The butter had almost been used up. He disliked the lengthy massage of this nearly inert and unfeeling body and the sausage-making which ended with a single groan. He resented the ruinous expense, which Harold thought he couldn't reduce or eliminate, since it was going to save Billy's mother and sister. Harold couldn't even convince himself he was bringing any special pleasure to Billy, since Billy complained that Harold's teeth were too sharp and hurt him. Of course Harold had never faced such a big challenge before.

Suddenly it was over. The vacation had come to an end. Harold had given his straight friends in Key West something to deplore or admire, in any event to discuss. Did they suspect Harold was paying Billy and so handsomely? Or did they think all the usual rules didn't apply to gay life and that young Susannahs gave freely, copiously, of their charms to their Elders? He suspected his friends thought he was exploiting Billy, but in fact Billy was exploiting him, with his full complicity. Harold sympathized with Billy's family's plight and respected Billy's serious-ness.

Billy drove him in the red convertible to the airport. He helped him with his luggage. They shook hands. For a moment Billy stood at ease, with his hands hooked behind him. Then he waved and drove off.

Harold thought that his decision to go on having sex at all was either a stubborn sign of the life force or a mere habit, depending on one's interpretation. He smeared Androgel on his body every morning, a clear salve containing androgens, the sex-drive hormone. Without it he'd never feel a twitch of desire. His doctor had prescribed it: "It'll give you some zest for life, improve your energy level. Appetite. Zest," he repeated. He rather liked it when he forgot to use the hormone salve and felt no sex desire (though that included other desires as well). Without a sex drive people became depressed, it seemed. Were monks depressed?

Was he lacking in zest? For sex, yes. But for life?

Yes, he thought. Whereas Billy had a survivor's instincts. He was determined that he and his family would survive.

Harold was so happy to be back with Tom, though he missed the dog, Roger. Tom was dating his girlfriend three nights a week now. Beth. Her name was Beth. A month after Harold came home, Tom said he was moving out. "I'm going to try to make things work with Beth."

"Really?"

"You know how much I've always wanted children. A child. I only realized that after Roger died."

"What?"

"Roger was our child. But when he died I thought how pathetic it was to heap so much tenderness on a poor, short-lived, dumb animal. I'd like a human child. Beth wants one, too."

Harold didn't like Roger to be called "poor." He was so shaken that he didn't think much about Billy. Once or twice he showed Billy's spread in *Frisk* to his friends in Princeton. They said, "Wow," but they were humoring him. They obviously felt sorry for him. Did they think he was to blame for Tom's change of heart, of life?

One day, while researching an article on Woodrow Wilson at Princeton, Harold came across a remark Wilson had made twenty years after graduation, "Plenty of people offer me their friendship; but partly because I am reserved and shy, and partly because I am fastidious and have a narrow, uncatholic taste in friends, I reject the offer in almost every case and then am dismayed to look about and see how few persons in the world stand near me and know me as I am."

Six months later he called Sid in Key West just to chat.

"Say, did you know Billy is getting married?" Sid asked.

"No," Harold said. "For immigration reasons?"

"Apparently it's a real romance. She's not even American. She's from South Africa." Sid downshifted. "I don't really get that, do you? Switch-hitting?" He didn't know about Tom and Beth. "You know Billy danced at our annual party. We took everybody on Captain Bob's boat and Billy was the entertainment. If I hadn't talked with him I wouldn't have known how serious and intelligent he is. I mean, he's such a thoughtful guy and then boom! There he was, bumping and grinding."

"Maybe Billy was never gay," Harold said. "Despite all appearances. I assumed he'd come to the States to enjoy sexual freedom, but now I think it was just to earn some quick money to relocate his family."

After he hung up, he threw some pumpkin-stuffed ravioli into boiling water. He was unaccountably hungry, in spite of the clammy summer day. A small, peevish voice somewhere inside of him said, "See? He was just using you and everyone else." But then Harold smiled, pleased at the simplifying form things had taken. He wondered if his understanding of the people around him was becoming as occluded as his vision. Were there moral cataracts that one could remove?

Edmund White
Edmund White has written fifteen books, including *A Boy's Own Story* and *The Married Man*. He has written two biographies (of Genet and Proust), two books about Paris (*The Flâneur* and *Our Paris*), and a collection of stories (*Skinned Alive*). He teaches creative writing at Princeton and lives in New York.

That Boy This Day

Daniel M. Jaffe

I've been continuing custom the past six months, sitting every day between 3 o'clock and 4 o'clock in Starman's Café on the outer edge of the French Quarter away from most tourists, although the occasional Yankee still manages to snake in, as Yankees have been known, for more than a century, to do. Like that baggy-shorted tourist this afternoon, wearing his "I Love French" T-shirt, its lascivious red tongue flicking at all onlookers. As if a lady such as myself would not understand or be offended by such vulgar display. It is Southern custom for a hostess to make her guest feel at home; it is also Southern custom for a guest to recognize that he is not at home.

This afternoon, sitting down in a cozy chair by the window, I did as always, set my black patent-leather purse on the table, removed my white gloves with pearl wrist buttons, gloves too large for me because they had belonged to Mister Thompson, but I wear them every day because she used to do so. I tugged off my gloves this day, one finger at a time, as always, laying one glove atop the other, thumb to thumb, pinky to pinky, and I smoothed them romantically together.

I then raised the steamy mocha latte I drink no matter what the heat and humidity out-of-doors, so cool and conditioned inside Starman's that Mister Thompson always wanted just to sit and "sip a steamy." "Let the sidewalks blister and the tourists melt like so many lumps of earwax," she'd say and we'd giggle. In memory of her this day, as I did every day, I dipped my wrinkled little pinky (with, I'm embarrassed to admit, chips in the red nail polish) into the foam, dabbing pinky against nose tip the way Mister Thompson would do after her fashion. How relaxed I felt, above all the world's tumult, and so princess-like that those credit card people could telephone all they wanted, it wouldn't bother me one weensy since I wasn't home to hear the ring.

"Missus Thompson," those people say, you owe you owe you owe you owe. "We waited a respectable six months." But now you owe you owe you owe.

I say, Where's the compassion in this world? And then I laugh, Hah hah hah hah. Go ahead, Mister Moses, I say, or Miss Moses, should it be one of those girls calling, go ahead. You just keep striking this poor widow rock in the hopes of finding water. No Promised Land for you at the end of your days. Where's the compassion in this world?

Five thousand dollars. As if they had buried Mister Thompson in gold. She was always perfectly content with cheap costume jewelry. Five thousand dollars for a burial! Where's the compassion in this world? But you looked grand, Mister Thompson, lying there surrounded by shiny pink satin, your pale blue cocktail dress with the frills suggesting a cleavage one was forever straining to see. The minister refused to look at you while saying his usuals, but I looked. I gazed. No other guests, as per your preference: "When my time comes, Missus Thompson, whenever my time comes—private in life, so … private in death."

"Yes, ma'am, Mister Thompson. Yes, ma'am."

I swiped a napkin across my nose to rid that stupid steamy drop. Five thousand dollars. And me alone at the funeral with the rigid frigid minister. I could have used some comfort, Mister Thompson. No one to show compassion to *me*. So private. The privacy you wanted and needed and had to have in order to be you. I made sure you had it, Mister Thompson, your privacy.

Alec came in this day like the good teenage boy he was, with a "Hello, Missus Thompson, How are you, Missus Thompson?" As always. Alec, in his short-sleeved white shirt and maroon tie, black slacks and shoes polished to a pretty-boy sheen, wavy brown hair neatly banged. I half-smiled at him, that handsome boy of 19 or 20 or maybe even 21, so difficult to tell—the farther one is from a point, the greater the distance, the more difficult to see it clearly even with thick bifocals in luscious pink frames that provide an alluring air even in these my sparkling twilight years.

"A real delish dish," Mister Thompson would say before patting my fanny as recently as six months ago. Mister Thompson would try to do so in public, but of course I'd never let her, only in private when a pat would lead to a caress to an around-the-waist embrace. And be I fifty or sixty or seventy, I still felt twenty with Mister Thompson's arms around my waist and her lips against mine, even when I could feel her dentures loosening behind those pruney pinks; still she was my Mister Thompson and I her delish dish. No one to hear me say this at the funeral except that minister who paled when I mumbled all this as eulogy, such truths, all my lovinglies.

I nodded at Alec, a slight nod, dignified. We would chat on occasion, not much more than "How's college, Alec?" "How are you feeling, Missus Thompson?" The young live actively in the world, the old live squeakily in our arthritic joints. I would sometimes compliment the wavy cut of his hair, the manly ruddy flush of his cheeks, and had even been known, when intoxicated by too much caffeine, to offer compliments such as, "My word, Alec, but swim practice is doing wonders for your shoulders and chest." He would start to smile then stop himself, look away from me, scan a respectable circumference, presumably to determine whether anyone had overheard.

Alec did not stop to converse today; not the end of the world, as long as he showed me the courtesy of hello, which he did, but a compliment on my beige blouse with the collar's green embroidered stitching would not have knocked the globe off Atlas' manly shoulders. Whereas my thought-voice places emphasis on *woman* in the phrase "old woman," one has been known to hear young men emphasize the *old*.

Alec did not order the same drink day after day, he liked va-ri-e-ty—one day hot coffee, the next day iced, one day Earl Grey, the next day English Breakfast. Fickle as a pickle from brine to wine. He probably didn't realize that I noticed such details, but I notice most everything. Most. Having missed all the signals before my wedding, I swore I'd never miss another signal in my life. But here you go—I did, nonetheless: Alec's inclination toward beverage variety should have been a foreshadowing clue. Apparently, no matter how I try, sometimes I'm dense and don't see what's right in front of my eyes. Poor Jacob in the Bible was fooled when marrying Leah-should-have-been-Rachel, but who could see behind that thick veil? So many veils in this world, not all of them dainty lace and gauze. The Bible teaches compassion.

I finally figured it all out earlier this day, when watching Alec's sapphire blue eyes. It's all in the eyes; I should have known that before. Just watch a man's eyes, a handsome man's eyes, a young man like

Alec with straight nose and creamy skin and lips a little too big for his mouth so they've nowhere to go except into a pucker, looking like he's offering a kiss even when he's not. I used to think menopause aptly named—a pause from men—but shame if I don't still notice pucker-lips all moistened by ice tea and that thick tongue flicking the end of a white straw. Even when he stopped to chat, Alec never sat with me, but he lingered sometimes, making me think maybe he'd sit down and lean across the table and kiss me so I'd know the touch of a real man once before I died.

A vow's a vow, I always say, have always said. I made those vows like Jacob and I meant them like Jacob and I kept them like Jacob, although I never took a second husband or concubine. But with Mister Thompson gone now … I fulfilled "'til death do us part," and am released from my vow, and I admit I'm weak flesh and would like to know the touch of a man needing to be unzipped from the front rather than the back.

Shame, Missus Thompson, shame. I know I know I know. What's the measure of a real man, I'd like to know? Is it in inches? Shame on me. Shame shame shame. Where, Missus Thompson, is your compassion for memory?

God bless Mister Thompson wherever she is, meaning well, trying so hard, not her fault she got in the wrong line when God was giving out plumbing, a hose instead of … what … a … a … drain? … a sewer? … is that all I am? … a pool of earthly delights, as Mister Thompson would say? Or was I just a backyard sump pump?

"Me on the outside isn't me on the inside," she told me that day in the Five and Dime, right there in the jockey short aisle. "A Mardi Gras mask, my life's one big Mardi Gras mask," and she wept against my bosom, this Mister Thompson who was supposed to have been my rock, my shoulder, my man. So mortified, I had to scream at the cashier, "My husband banged his appendix scar on one of your pointy shelves! You've reduced him to tears! We'll sue if there's infection, you just see if we won't!" The bells on the glass door chimed their fury behind as I hustled Mister Thompson out of the Five and Dime and across the sidewalk into our blue Buick sedan and home, Mister Thompson sobbing all the way, begging me to refer to him as "her" out loud and even in my thoughts. I had never before seen Mister Thompson sob.

Couldn't have told me before the wedding, could she-he? Waited two weeks, an entire two weeks. Three years of dating, but only two weeks after the wedding.

I'm not queer, I said handing him-her a hanky, looking out our new living room window for the brimstone or at least the fire. My new yellow chintz curtains would be burnt to cinders, the orange shag carpet from my cousins and the gray davenport with the knobby feet would all singe as crisp as Mister Thompson's skin surely would one day in Hell.

But no fire shot down from Heaven, so I listened to him-her. The Bible teaches compassion.

Always felt that way, she-he said, always an outsider, always different, wanting dolls, not sports, yet knowing not to show the perversion.

Children know these things. Children always know.

"You telling me you're a homo?" I asked, longing for a cigarette even though I did not smoke.

"No, don't you hear me, woman?"

"I'm not queer," I repeated. Would have tapped an ash pillar onto his thick blond hair right then, had I a cigarette. I remember thinking, ashes, ashes, we all fall down!

"It all works," she-he said.

"I know," I said, "Remember that pretty young thing sweating under you on our wedding night? For all of two seconds? I know it works. So what are you talking about?"

"Inside," she-he said, "not outside. Inside. My soul."

Finally, a word I understood. *Soul.*

I paced around the living room ... the body's just a vessel, I always knew that.... cheap endtable with an Aphrodite lamp and tasseled lamp shade—what had I been thinking when I bought that one ...? *Soul.* I'd never thought much about the difference between a man's soul and a woman's. Never thought would they be different or same ... hanging picture of a man on horseback over one side of the couch, woman on horseback over the other side ... a woman's soul. My husband had a woman's soul ... yellow chintz, Mister Thompson hated yellow chintz, but I'd insisted on yellow chintz ... the body may be Satan's territory, but the soul was God's. That much I understood, I read the Bible. "I'll take down the yellow chintz," I said.

"What?" he said.

"Never mind." I slumped onto the gray davenport with the knobby feet, between my husband and the davenport's sturdy arm.

I loved Mister Thompson. My high school sweetheart. Tall and gentle and smart with soft lips. He waited until our second date to kiss me, our fourth to touch my clothed breasts. He sighed on the porch swing beside me, that sweet boy feeling a girl's breasts for the first time. "So beautiful," he said, and I foolishly assumed him to be complimenting my body rather than fantasizing transfer of my parts onto him. Many many kisses and feels of my breasts and my hips. I once reached to touch him down there, but he shoved my hand aside. "You're a lady, you mustn't," he said, and I flushed with the shame of having forgotten the restraint expected of a good woman. Men are animals beyond control, which is why the Good Lord created woman—to rein in His initial flawed effort at humanity.

The day of his-her disclosure two weeks after our wedding, he-she hunched beside me on the davenport, hid his-her face, the whimpers as screechy-high as mine, then grumbly low the way one would expect a man's. It was all I could do to stop my arm from reaching round him, pressing his head to my shoulder. The ugly stench of a man's anxiety sweat. I loved Mister Thompson. So why not press his head to my shoulder?

God's will, I thought to myself. All is God's will.

A test from the Bible.

A vow.

I left our new living room.

Young Alec showed up at Starman's Café every day at 3:15, after some summer school class or other. Not remedial summer school, but extra courses, biology laboratories dissecting frogs and such. Bright boy, used to deliver our paper.

This day was a typical French Quarter July when the humidity lumbers through town like a gator too sluggish to open its maw, but no less ugly for sparing you a nip on the behind. The *barista* boy, as I've learned they're called nowadays instead of "soda jerks," the *barista* boy, Michael (according to his clip-on name tag), was new in the shop, short and wiry, dark unkempt curly hair à la that famous lewd David statue, bushy beard, rough farm boy hands. He stood behind the counter ready to take the baggy-shorted tourist's second order, that Yankee with the lascivious red-tongued T-shirt.

I'll never find five thousand dollars. So what will they do, unseal

Mister Thompson's mausoleum and toss her in the garbage? No, just me. Mister Thompson's costume jewelry wouldn't fetch more than a few pennies, and the house was already mortgaged beyond its worth. And our insurance—

"We must get insurance; death is a surety," I said.

"Not the death of my soul," said Mister Thompson. "Never the death of my soul." One of her romantic qualities I loved.
She agreed to purchase insurance.

Tall Alec stood in line behind the baggy-shorted tourist and stared at new Michael who had not yet seen him, stared, sucked in his already tight belly, stood tall at military attention, and that's when I understood something about Alec that I hadn't before. Alec's eyes, deep-set and sapphire blue.

After the baggy-shorted tourist left the counter and returned to his small table on the café's far side—at least he had the decency to sit on the far side with that flicking red tongue—Alec stepped up to the counter and stared again.

"How may I help you?" asked this Michael, his words forming a question, a solicitation even, but his intonation as flat as the page of a training manual.

Alec, apparently hearing the words but not the intonation, grinned broadly, said nothing.

"How may I help you?" More emphatic this time.

"Uh, what do *you* like?" Alec was looking directly into Michael's eyes, brazenly, à la Miss Lauren Bacall.

Michael's eyes shifted to the cash register. "I don't drink coffee."

"Wow," said Alec. "That's really funny. Working here and all."

"Yeah," said Michael, his eyes now meeting Alec's. A hint of impatience? "What can I get you?"

Again Alec grinned. Michael did not.

"Uh, coffee-of-the-day," Alec said, adding with a shade of supplication, "Please." Blind blind youth.

"What size you take?"

"Large for sure," said Alec, his eyes twinkling like the Devil's. Could he have meant what I knew he meant? Michael seemed oblivious. As Michael turned to fill the cup, Alec's eyes scanned below Michael's waist. Then the exchange of cup and money, and when Alec should have nodded a simple thank you, instead he said, "I like your beard."

Had Alec been older than Michael, one might have regarded such a comment as mere older-to-younger friendly, or a moment of wistful recollection … one's own whiskers of youthful masculine assertion. Had Alec been younger, the statement could have been mere admiration and some perverted Freudian envy of penis yet to mature. But these young men were peers, and Alec stared into Michael's eyes as he said what he said about that manly body part.

Not fair of Alec. This was Michael's workplace. Everyone could hear. How could Michael—anyone—possibly misunderstand? How could Michael possibly respond? He pursued the only gentlemanly option—to feign momentary deafness, fiddle with his green apron, wipe hands on thighs, the muscles of his chest constricting as blood rushed to his face in anger or shame or both.

After Mister Thompson's declaration of gender identity (I've learned the right phrases since that time), I left our new living room with those vengeance-inspiring yellow chintz curtains, strode into our new bedroom (four-poster bed, white down comforter trimmed in blue ribbons), returned with my largest skirt, pink and midi-length with a black poodle embroidered where the left knee would be. "Here," I said to Mister Thompson, "there's enough material inside for me to let this out at the waist."

Mister Thompson looked up and for the first time in my life I understood the liturgical word *beatific*.

He-she took me right then and there, on our new gray davenport with the knobby feet. A passion I had not seen in him-her those two weeks prior, one I learned to bring out in him-her any time by dressing him in a skirt or panties or brassiere (D-cup—Mister Thompson's soul was big-busted).

Not so bad, that passion, that loving, the adoration kisses after she smoothed the wrinkles in her skirt, the murmurs of gratitude. A friend with whom to share makeup tips and do my hair. With whom to notice other men—we both liked looking at stocky men with thick dark hair. "Look, don't touch" was a rule we shared. Harder for Mister Thompson than for me, I thought whenever we'd pass a football player or wrestler or strapping policeman on the street, when I'd notice that hunger in her eyes, a hunger my woman-soul understood, a hunger that belied his previous declarations of straight-as-an-arrow. I even once thought to give Mister Thompson permission to experience what she never had, but I just couldn't bring myself to say those mother-may-I words. Mean of me, I know, but I just could not. My compassion had its limits. Mister Thompson never strayed.

Six months now without Mister Thompson, polishing my nails alone, choosing nightgowns alone, hand-washing my delicates alone.

Five thousand dollars, Mister Thompson! Where on God's earth shall I find five thousand dollars? How unfeeling and selfish and unfair of you to impose such a burden upon me. A burden that will hang over my head like a sword of Damocles the rest of my days, its hilt encrusted with fake pearls and rubies, dangling over my head, maybe slicing me open one day. You told me you'd kept up the insurance payments. Whatever did you do with those premiums?

How much do callboys cost?

Through my thick bifocals in luscious pink frames I watched those boys, each of them, from my cozy chair by the window, and I could tell that Alec, at his own round little table now, stirring his coffee, sipping, examining the marble tabletop flecks of black and gray on white, that Alec was intentionally not looking at Michael so as to give Michael time to ogle him. But that's not what Michael was doing. Michael was ignoring Alec entirely.

Of course he was. And rightly so. Why must I spend the rest of my days wondering what you did with those insurance premiums? Did you stray? Did you?

Thinking those uncompassionate thoughts, I spilled my steamy.

Leezy rushed over. I hadn't noticed her begin her shift, the frowsy redheaded young lady, Leezy, all nimble-fingered and smiley beneath her puffball frizz. Too cool, too calm, too collected, eyes always off somewhere; thinking, no doubt, about last night's kiss or tumble with her latest Jimmy Dean Johnny Reb. Pleasant though, Leezy, always working late afternoons. Always a "Good afternoon, Missus Thompson. What's your pleasure this afternoon?" As if she didn't know I always ordered a steamy. And "Wishing you a nice day, Missus Thompson." I overheard her wish the same to every other customer, even tourist strangers in disgusting T-shirts, perfunctory politeness being preferable to sincere rudeness. She brought over several napkins, the dear, wiped up the mess and even smiled before stepping behind the counter, where she busied herself arranging pecan rolls and blueberry scones and Italian biscotti all behind glass.

The latte spill had spared my white gloves with pearl wrist buttons, but I felt modest embarrassment just the same. I am a mature lady, not a child. Calm yourself, Missus Thompson, calm yourself. Just a few drops, really, nothing to cause a scene or attract attention. Neither Alec nor Michael nor the tourist seemed even to notice. It was then I reminded myself as I had so many times during the previous fifty years: you chose to stay, Missus Thompson, no one forced you. Accept your own responsibilities.

"Hey Leezy, we're out of fives." Raspy and high, Michael's voice, still manly, but a young man's. As she sidled to the register, Leezy brushed her behind against the front of Michael's apron. Oh, how his eyes sparkled; all he could do not to grab her right then and there.

Alec—in his short-sleeved white shirt and maroon tie, black slacks and shoes polished to a pretty-boy sheen, wavy brown hair neatly banged—ceased his stirring, his sipping, just stared. How E.M. Forsterish, how Oscar Wildean—an attraction to a macho working man. Mister Thompson loved those writers and all the ones I used to read aloud in bed every night as we lay side by side, Mister Thompson in pink nightie, me in gray flannel. Her feet so cold against mine. Would it have killed you, Mister Thompson, to read your own damn books? What if I hadn't given in so easily to your perversity? What if I'd stomped my foot that day two weeks after the wedding and said, "Mister Thompson, I married a man!" Would that have been a greater display of compassion, shoring up your manhood instead of conspiring in its erosion?

At that defining moment—we all have them, do we not, moments we forever replay, can never alter but in fantasy?—after Mister Thompson had made his-her disclosure, when I left our new living room with its vengeance-inspiring yellow chintz curtains and crossed into our new bedroom with the four-poster bed and white comforter trimmed in blue ribbons, my initial intention was to march straight to the mahogany highboy, to yank open the top drawer and grab the stinky jockstrap Mister Thompson had worn days earlier while playing neighborhood basketball yet had not had the decency to toss into the bathroom's white wicker laundry hamper. My initial intention was to return to our new living room and shove that stinky jockstrap into his-her face. His-her declaration struck me as somewhat akin to one about cancer: no one requested the ailment, it simply befell; one had to endure the condition and all it brought, learn to incorporate sadness into life. What sort of woman would I be to abandon a husband with cancer?

What kind of woman was I? What kind of woman is found attractive by a he-she? Could a real man, a young man, a virile man, feel true desire for me? I suppose I shall never know.

There in the bedroom, as I fingered the elastic waistband of that extra-large jockstrap, I thought how lucky I was to have him-her, a tender man, a caring man. I suddenly realized in a rare (for me) moment of insight that if I forced him to be the man I wanted rather than the man she was, I might lose her, my husband, the only man I'd ever loved. So I walked past the mahogany highboy, opened the closet instead, rifled through my side, brought out my poodle skirt.

To whom was I showing true compassion, to Mister Thompson or to my companion-needing self? Shall I ever know?

Leezy took charge of the register and Michael left the counter to fetch bags of coffee beans from the storeroom at the far end of the shop, just beyond the baggy-shorted tourist with the lascivious red-tongued T-shirt. Michael walked around the shop, positioning the bags on display shelves here and there. Alec watched Michael's every move now, cleared his throat each time Michael passed. But Michael seemed wise to Alec, if only on some primal, don't-mess-with-me male plane, and studiously avoided glancing down when passing Alec's table while carrying, first, a couple bags of Sumatra under his arm and against his muscled chest, then Sweet Lite Blend in his rough farm boy hands, now French Roast.

Alec noticed, I could tell, his face taking on a grapefruity cast, sourish with a touch of despair. He sipped his coffee, his eyes focusing on Michael's muscled chest, the apron, the globe-like behind. It's all in the eyes.

How little I knew about Alec, this boy I'd been seeing in the neighborhood for years. A thank-you note each Christmas for the five-dollar bonus I'd leave him—such a good paper-delivery boy, always on the porch, never in the azaleas. Then the "Hello"s years later on the street and now the "Hello"s in Starman's Café. But what did I really know about him? Can one ever know the shape of another's soul?

This day I saw its major outlines for the first time, those of Alec's soul, suddenly, a soul in convolution, maybe even in convulsion. I could almost see Alec jealous of those beans, wishing Michael would hold him as close as those beans lucky enough to be pressed against Michael's muscled chest.

The frown, the furrowed forehead, the loosening of his maroon tie and Othello-like sucking in of lower lip just at the pre-murder crisis moment. Had Alec ever known the touch of another young man? I've heard there are possibilities in this delta city of ours, all those Yankee tourists importing heaven-knows-what practices. But Alec was so young. Old enough to know what he desired, certainly; but old enough to know how to find it? Not if his clumsy efforts of this day were any indication.

Michael returned to the storeroom; came back out with a long-handled broom. Sweeping the black-speckled white linoleum floor beneath this table and that. The baggy-shorted tourist, still here, lifted his sneakered feet like a child, allowing Michael to sweep beneath. Legs up in the air, jockey shorts visible through the shorts' leg holes, yet innocent because of the lack of perverse intent. Michael chuckled with a "Thank you."

As Michael swept near Alec's table, with no apparent intent to stretch his broom so as to sweep beneath it, Alec lifted his feet in turn, his legs, legs covered down to the ankles in long black pants yet the position somehow obscene. How obvious the young can be, not knowing shame enough to keep unseemly desires private.

Michael scowled at Alec long enough for their eyes to meet, he pivoted, shook his head. He rested the long-handled broom against the counter, walked over to the storefront window, beside me, adjusted a "Come on in and cool a spell" sign. Why, Michael, I thought but didn't say, how nice of you to step so close. Come here, baby, let Mama comfort your day. He smelled of fruity cologne, and I inhaled deeply, straining to detect the underlying sweat, which I did. I smiled broadly. More delicious than sweetened coffee is the mix of a man's sweat and cologne meant for a man, not perfume meant for a woman.

Michael picked up a bag of Ethiopian something-or-other beans that had fallen from the window display, held it in one of his rough farm boy hands, and stalked back toward the storeroom.

At just that moment I saw what was about to happen but could not stop it. So fast, these young people.

Alec stuck out his foot. Just like that. When children demand attention, they will not be ignored. Alec darted his foot out, too late for

Michael to stop himself. Michael tripped, fumbled the bag of Ethiopian whatever beans, tried to catch the bag as if it were a football. The bag tore. Beans spilled all over the black-speckled white linoleum floor. Michael fell flat on his face.

"Oh no!" Alec sputtered, and he dropped to his knees, helped Michael sit up, rested Michael's back against the counter.

What had Alec been expecting? What had he thought would happen after he darted out that foot? Of course Michael would fall. Isn't that precisely what Alec had wanted? Perhaps he didn't know. Youth.

Michael shoved Alec away, stood, braced himself against the counter.

Leezy rushed to his side. "You all right, sugar?"

The baggy-shorted tourist, meanwhile, in a surprising gesture of Northern civility, grabbed the long-handled broom and moved to sweep the spilled beans.

"That's okay, Mister, I'll get it," said Leezy, dabbing a napkin against Michael's split lip.

Alec was still on his knees by the counter, and I thought … I thought … oh, please don't. Please don't approach Michael now, not on your knees while he's standing, don't rub your face against—

No, fortunately that's not what Alec did.

Instead, he began to sob, softly, almost in a whimper. And to crawl slowly, on hands and knees, wherever the coffee beans had spilled. Right onto them, onto each and every coffee bean. One knee, the other knee, onto bean after bean, Alec wincing through his whimper-sobs. How painful, hard coffee beans sharp against his knees, his palms. I suppose Alec was Catholic.

"Man," said the baggy-shorted tourist with the lascivious red tongue on his T-shirt, "You Southerners really are freaky."

"How dare you!" spouted out of me like a gush from an opened hydrant. "How dare you, sir!"

Everyone looked over at me, even Alec. He stopped crawling, just stared.

I grabbed my black patent leather purse and white gloves with pearl wrist buttons.

I rose.

I walked as quickly as my thick-soled black support shoes would allow, past fruity-smelling Michael and frowsy redheaded Leezy. I opened my purse, pulled out a ten-dollar bill, slapped it onto the counter. "That's for the spilled beans."

Then I snapped my purse shut, and through my thick bifocals with the luscious pink frames, I sneered at the baggy-shorted tourist, I snorted dismissal—of him, of the two sales clerks.

I leaned on the counter, worked my way down to the floor to a kneeling position not far from Alec. Oooh—arthritis. I knew about my arthritis, of course, but what was my pain compared to this boy's? He needed me. Was it not woman's helpmate role to support man? The Bible teaches compassion.

Flapping my white gloves with pearl wrist buttons, I brushed a path free of coffee beans, reached out to offer a comfort touch, an embrace of compassion, but Alec recoiled and I saw in his eyes, which reminded me so of your eyes, Mister Thompson, eyes which always looked at me with appreciation although I frequently wondered, couldn't help but wonder no matter how I tried to stop myself from wondering, whether you made love to me from church vow "I do" rather than from testosterone "I must have you." I even thought to ask, so many times, between kisses, but I'd learned my Bible and that ye must not seek what ye shall not survive finding.

If Mister Thompson had to choose between me and a boy like Alec, I don't mean for a lifetime, but for a good time, a one time, whom would she have chosen? And would Alec have looked at her with those eyes now looking at me and filled with, if not reptile-kissing revulsion, then mild repugnance at the nearness of aged flesh to young lips?

Suddenly I laughed. Suddenly. Oh, how I laughed. A laugh shrouded for decades within a fear-hope I had not realized lay within. All this time. How appropriate to discover a laugh-in-waiting within myself, me, forever a lady-in-waiting, waiting and hoping that one day Mister Thompson would surprise with an anything-but-expected declaration that I, his wife, now fulfilled his every co-human need, a declaration that his interest in female couture had burned off like hot summer mist, that he would no longer gaze at muscle-bulging T-shirted men along Bourbon Street because his Adam eyes were now filled to bursting with my Eve countenance. Yes, Mister Thompson had often touched me and elicited from my body those responses no other man ever had, but even so—even in those many moments while I was wrapped around and filled with him,—I wondered if I filled him in return, in that needy place within every man.

I doubt now that I did, although that's all I truly wanted. Ever. Ever. To fill the gap within him that I needed her to fill within me. Was it so terrible to have hoped, all those years, that she might one day change?

Terrible?—no; but so ridiculously foolish.

An old woman's laughter releasing to the winds her too-long-retained girlish fantasies.

I wiped dripping mascara, said, "Thank you, Alec. Thank you for the spark to awareness."

How much greater than five thousand fleeting dollars is the worth of permanent secure love, and how much more noticeable and scarring is its absence.

With a good deal of slow creaking, I raised myself to standing. Alec's eyes were filled with pain. At having momentarily forgotten his manners? At not having welcomed my comfort? At the thought that I might leave without pressing his head to my shoulder?

Oh, Good Lord, will I never shed my inclination to fantasy?

He blurted, "I'm sorry!" Perhaps the apology was meant for Michael, but I chose to regard it as directed to me.

Alec covered his face, his eyes—as though by refusing to look at our shames, we can ever prevent ourselves from seeing them. "How foolish," I mumbled. "How ridiculously foolish." I then opened my mouth to say, but shut it tight so as to stop myself from saying for the second time in my life, "I'm always here for you, baby. Mama's always here."

Daniel M. Jaffe

Daniel M. Jaffe's novel, *The Limits of Pleasure,* was a finalist for *ForeWord Magazine*'s Book of the Year Award, and was excerpted in *Best Gay Erotica 2003*. Dan's short stories and personal essays have been published in dozens of anthologies and literary journals such as *Found Tribe*, *Kosher Meat*, *Bearotica*, *Rebel Yell*, *The James White Review*, *The Florida Review*, and *Green Mountains Review*. Dan edited *With Signs and Wonders: An International Anthology of Jewish Fabulist Fiction* and translated the Russian-Israeli novel *Here Comes the Messiah!* by Dina Rubina. Dan's website is: http://danieljaffe.tripod.com.

Jolly-Olly Petey

Joe G. Hayes

We stare out at the sky-water and the sky-water stares back. At times past this exact spot my feet, my eyes have been shown the sea as mirror, the sky another one above and back and forth with themselves; but now the sheet is a seethe, a bubbling of seethes. Danny don't go in till you feel it staring b-back at you, Petey would say whenever we'd go swimming. Swumming, Petey always called it after his accident. No special reason. I'll tell you why, his fascination with the sea—I was a little late catching up to him in this; no surprise in that—but it's come to me at last: half o'er, half o'er, to Labrador. Like Petey said. The expansiveness of it. Outward, outish. Away to the shimmer. In search of a land beautiful, big enough, to contain the all of our love.

A saffron wash blossoms up around the cloud-louvered moon and the night becomes electric. Storm's coming, almost here. An explosive slip-sliding of systems in the North Atlantic waters, in the North Atlantic skies over us. An interior something spurts up in sympathy, writhes. Clouds scuttle. They cross the moon and you can see their innards like an X-ray. Terminal beauty. Traveling terns rake the sky over us, like its their Nature Company Zen bed and they're trying to de-stress as they race their invisible highways southward. The water tries on a silverish-green varnish, throws it off like a late-for-a-date dresser, glows brighter as the moon seeps out again and its color not a color at all but a blur on a thousand white-topped towers.

The wind puffs up and strokes our leg hair, mine as orange as carrots on the boil, Petey's a black stubble. It's growing back now, Petey's leg hair, and him having shaved it a week or two ago I suppose. The navy clouds, gathering like anger over the sea, turn red as your blood. Inky at the edges. Inky-dinky-parlez-vous. Dad sang that song when the family with the French mother moved next door, never again, Mom went on the warpath, denounced his upbringing, hid the remote and the *Sporting News* on him.

The tang of oceanscent so strong now you don't even smell it, you'd only notice its calamitous absence. I'd take a deep breath but I don't even have to, I open my mouth and the sea-wind purges in. I Michelangelo-reach for Petey and life begins. I touch him, finger his soft hair to the side of his forehead. Gently. I look at him, right in the eyes. Acute compassion. I don't look away when his eyes meet mine. My life has been a labyrinth, now finally I've found the sodden throbbing heart at its middle.

I look at Petey. For once finally I don't hide behind my lust, my fear, my drunkenness, my Marine-ness. My Dawgness. Whatever I am, whomever, it's showing in my eyes. For once. I'm showing Petey. Showing him, I start to see who I am. Self-realization? Go in for sure but don't forget to go out. In, out, like the ocean, like the breath of any living thing. Like how we're made. Like Petey always said. The people who love us are often clearer mirrors than the confounding ones we consult daily, alone and wondering. Who do you say that I am?

I shift his weight again—he's heavier than I thought or maybe it's this ghastly sleep-lack. I run one finger along the wet indent in his head—just there, just there. A shiver jags through me, like I was the one whose skull got crushed. And maybe I was.

I pull him into me until it feels like we're the same body. Siamese twins connected at the—at the everything. The moon slurs in, slurs out, stippling our flesh. Impossible to say where his flesh ends and mine begins. Squeeze.

I speak finally, tell him things. I don't mince my words or hold back.

I want to wander in the Southland Of Your Heart, Petey, I tell him. Not a word out of him.

He doesn't want to stop this, or maybe he's that shocked he can't speak.

His eyes look right through me—that old way, as if they're peepholes to the sea. As unknowable, twice as deep. I take a pulling breath—

Petey lookit—ahh—if I wasn't the first, Petey—just say I'll be the last. Happy Land. Lets go to Happy Land.

My words are jangly. Not used to telling the truth. See it was never safe.

It's time now. I remember reading when there's a Big Wave, there'll be two more right behind it, Big Waves come in threes. Who said that? Beston, in *The Outermost House*. In one chapter he admired a solitary male bather, a Caravaggian local yokel smashing nudely joyous into the waves, unaware he was being watched why is it that we are more what we want to do, rather than what we do.

Well, whether he will or nil, his wave theory's true, I count, and here comes Mr. Second One, Mr. Third right behind like a comedy troupe. Now for it—uhhhh! we launch ourselves into the sea. The wave explodes, grabs. Seeking out the cracks and holes and fissures of us, squirming wet into those places. Must be cold but funny I don't notice, nothing now but me and Petey. The green-white-black water assumes us. Assumption Wednesday or whatever fuckin' day this is. Breathless, gasping. Laughing if you can believe it. These waves, that once watered Babylon, swirl in, sweep us away, and what paw prints do any of us leave really if not on the hearts and faces of others. Sans surgery, we all get the faces we make in this life.

I shove my wet hand Down There and see if Petey will take the cure again.

See, I come to love Petey not to bury him. And to atone.

Mmmmmmmmmph, Petey says. D-Danny.

His eyes shift, focus, find mine. Must be the only person in the world who wouldn't jump, ask where he is.

Instead, he smiles.

Danny, he says, Danny. Is this h-heaven then?

Yes, I say, yes, it is.

I hold him tighter, bring my mouth to his.

The moon comes out and there is nothing but light.

The end of one world. The beginning of another.

We used to half-watch after-school cartoons, the off-white noise of American children, in Petey's musty basement while we played

Monopoly when we were kids. This commercial would blare on a lot for these drinks, you made them from a powder. Probably just sugar and food coloring right, FDC # 1975975333, triclyethylenesorbital added as non-caking agent but kids don't give a fuck, they trust no one's out to poison them, we loved them, loved the names of the different flavors anyway, loved the commercial New, exciting flavors! Goofy Grape! Rootin' Tootin' Raspberry! Lemony-Lime! And Jolly-Olly Orange!

It was two months after Petey's accident. We were twelve almost thirteen, and this was the odd first thing that had thrummed the strings of delight inside the strange new Petey.

It-it-it it's o-on! Petey roared this one afternoon from the basement—'The Rumpus Room' his mother always called it with her brogue Rrrrrrruuuum-puss Ruuum. I was taking a pee break up in his family's pink-tiled bathroom, reading the T&A mags his dead father had kept hidden under a stained mattress pad in the bathroom closet. I came bombing down the stairs at his call—

We were twelve and our mothers were upstairs in Mrs. Harding's kitchen, trying to find things to say to each other. The dust was that thick under the kitchen table, my mother reported later. As for Mrs. Harding, she thought my mother had airs.

The grandeur of that one, I overheard her say to Petey. She's so high she's haute.

Jolly-Olly Orange! Jolly-Olly Orange! Petey was shrieking, not stuttering at all like he did most times. He was holding his stomach and rolling on the floor, laughing, wiggling his thrown-out arms and legs like a spider I watched once after inundating it with Raid.

"Jolly-Olly Orange! Jolly-Olly Orange!"

When the commercial was over, Petey calmed down a little and we went back to our Monopoly game, set up on the drunk-legged card table Mrs. Harding used for ironing, she was kinda short. There were whole years when we played Monopoly, both post- and pre-accident, we'd get so into it we'd have one game set up at my house and one at Petey's.

This particular afternoon I was murdering him, kicking ass and taking names as the local phrase went. I'd just about taken over the whole world of Atlantic City with my lucky boot and Petey—Petey was always the little doggie—was holed up down in scumbag Baltic Avenue, maybe one railroad, awaiting a final fatal pass on my hotel-charmed chain of greed. Like teeth those hotels, red bloody teeth ringing the board and all mine. My bills tucked away by the neat pastel denomination partway under the edges of the board, lifting up the board in their swelling largesse.

Petey's love of Monops as he called it was one of the few things that hadn't changed after his accident. I fustily rearranged my red hotels back in their precise lines—Petey's only delight when I was winning was to muss them up, accidentally on purpose. They went awry and I can't s-say why, he'd explain, when I'd turn back/come back and find them askew. An act of God, I s-suppose.

I handed him the dice, trying to look like I was trying not to gloat.

Don't get a one, three, four, seven, eight, nine, eleven, or twelve, whatever you do, I said. He hated when I did that.

Up y-y-your, up y-your a-a-ass.

I catch your general drift Petey, I said, his stuttering always worse when the blood rose in him. No need to wear yourself out.

He flung the dice his black hair flung too and they bounced within the box's cover, little tiny rattling pieces of fate. Like bones they sounded. They came up seven, considered most times a lucky number but not right now for Petey, but before I could proclaim, Oh what a shame, Pacific Avenue! You owe me $1700, Petey turned and grabbed this floor-mopping bucket he must've filled up with water when I was upstairs peeing and snooping.

OH GOD, A TIDAL W-WAVE OUTTA NOWHERE HITS ATLANTIC CITY! he roared, dumping the water onto the board, sweeping all the pieces and money and cards and hotels onto the floor. I lost my breath, the table imploded in sympathy, amusement overcame outrage and I dove on top of him laughing. We rolled around on the floor, wrestling and shrieking on the soggy money and the soddening board.

Act of G-God, game c-cancelled due to Act of G-God! Petey cried as I knuckle-sandwiched him on the head. On the opposite side of course from where his indent was.

I like to remember Petey that way. I should say, it's one of my favorite cards in the infinite Rolodex in my head marked Petey.

Petey wasn't the sharpest tool in the shed in school stuff, though he could've been if he wanted. But a pulling something in his eyes made you believe he knew everything important. You know that look, some dogs and cats have it, certain strangers on the bus you wish you could ask them. Ahhh, life, right? Like what's the story? Petey didn't have that look before The Accident, even though everyone called him The Golden Boy. No one called him that after The Accident.

The Accident. Might as well tell you about that now. You tell me was it my fault.

It was deep in the green tangle of June. Not that there were any more trees in Southie then than there are now—it's the least vegetated part of the city, I read that just recently. So what there was of green stood out all the more. Shimmery. The neon tufts of grass beside the buckled continental plates of sidewalks, and you'd always have to look, like pubic hair on the very young and the very old, that much of a surprise. The explosion of sumacs and ailanthus from ends of alleys, from mere fissures in industrial parking lots. Squirming unstoppable some of them up from miasmic subway vents and where are their roots, you wonder. Springtimes, you'd almost swear the smokestacks and asphalt roofs, the soot-draped fill trucks that rattley-roared through the West Side at night, took on a softer color in sympathy with the reputed rebirth of the world, elsewhere.

One of them summer days in late June you dream about all winter, weird that It should happen then. Forever after referred to as The Accident, from the Expressway to Pleasure Bay.

We were still locked up in school, tight as tiny drums the last week before vacation. Must Be Hard On The Kids, Weather Like This, everyone says, but I never minded, dreaming out the lifted windows. Buildings had windows that opened then, so the mind could wander when the body couldn't. Windows should be a compound word, no? Lifted-. Liftable-, but instead nowadays it's a case of No You Don't, and toxic-breath industrial carpet to boot.

But it was Then, and Summer smells sifted right on into class: dropped window-wash blue Popsicles, melting sticky in the streets and the dogs would lick them found treasure. French fries and dogs from Sullivan's when the wind was from the east. The yellow smell of ancient dandelions shoveling up puffs from the sidewalks and alleys. Always, the sea-aroma, vital and variable as breath. At night hanging out on the top slick stoop you could almost lick the air so sticky with city summer smell, bricks and backs of necks sweating. Ma wouldn't

call you in till eleven and the neighborhood crones concurred, Too Hot
To Sleep Anyway Kids. Unless your window faced the ocean: You kids
behave yourselves, I'm putting yez all in Christopher's room tonight,
there's not a breath anywhere else, and when Petey slept over with all
windows agape we could hear the neighbors in their living. We devised
blackmail schemes to get-rich-quick at what we heard in the lights-out-
ness; but these were all forgotten by the morning, left behind as we traversed the flashing Timbuktu of 11-year-old boy dreams.

Me and Petey both played Little League then. Senior Division that
year, we were eleven almost twelve and on the edge of Something.
Changes but not the Bowie kind, we'd no idea what we were going
through. Petey played for the GasCo Cardinals. I should say he was the
GasCo Cardinals. They'd picked him, Old Colony Glass picked me,
there wasn't a thing you could do about it. They had tryouts the last
blue-blowy Saturday of March and then they'd call you that finger-bit-
ing week. A man's gruff voice, calling for you. A stranger to tell you
your new team and that was that. You pictured a basement somewhere,
men and smoke gathered. Rosters and charts and a lightbulb a-swing-
ing like a Detective Movie and your name written down. Your abilities
being bandied about, extolled or repudiated.

Me and Petey got called for different teams. Petey got picked
Saturday night right away, me they didn't call until Thursday.

Until Thursday.

Don't worry Danny, Petey said all that week. That smile. Don't
worry, Danny. They're fightin' over you!

We were playing against each other that June night, me and Petey's
teams. I was okay. Petey was the best in the League. Both teams 11-0
undefeated, one week before the play-offs started, believe me it was the
talk of the town. Ouf, that game of yours is a nine-day wonder, Mrs.
Harding said when she puffed in from the butchers that afternoon. She
went on to report that Mr. Green and the Kenealley Girls had asked her
all about it. She always called it sporting, Are you sporting tonight
then? when she'd see Petey in his uniform.

Who's gonna win tonight? I remember Mr. McGillicuddy asking
when we traipsed into his store after school that afternoon for lucky
green ice-pops. I felt integral, a necessary part of things. A part of the
sun slanting sideways through the thick-as-mud ketchup bottles on the
third shelf, the winning scratch cards Scotch-taped to the cash register

fluttering temptation, jiggling and bobbing in the open-door seabreeze.

Here we go then, Danny, Petey said later, right before that night's game.

He'd showed me before but I could never see it enough. His pre-game ritual. We were in his bedroom, the tiny one that looked out onto the alley. It glowed from above, that room, the light fell down between the buildings and then wobbled into his room. Gobs of light but once removed. So hot, his mother had wedged the old rattley fan into the window. An old white sock with a green stripe stuffed between the fan and the paint-peeling sill lessened the vibro-hum a little, not too much but that was fine, a summer sound and welcome back to you. The fan was an old GE model, gray. It looked like it belonged on a battleship, or in an office where battleships were planned. Funny how you remember. The fan's breath lazy, half lift-stirring the pictures of knights and Red Sox players Scotch-taped to the Old Roses wallpaper in Petey's bedroom. Any one of Petey's six wild older brothers would've received a fanny-warming remembrancer from Mrs. Harding for doing such a thing, not Petey though, never Petey, he was her favorite. Even then, before The Accident. All of them redheaded but for Petey, Petey's hair like wet coal, the fair-haired boy nonetheless. He could've Scotch-taped the world. Okay, probably oldest brother Donnie would get away with it too, just little things you notice, tone of voice, the lift and shift of eyes, smiles and sighs given or held in pursed-lip reserve. If I have to come over those stairs, Mrs. H's refrain those days, she'd shout it from the first floor hall, everybody's bedroom upstairs, If I have to come over those stairs, and I pictured her like a wave rising up the stairs, coming like God in wrath with a rolling pin, but she never did except once when Sean set Matty's bed on fire.

He was the world's favorite then, Petey. Like I say referred to as The Golden Boy. A straight-A student and so polite you'd think it was parody, the nuns smiled when they saw him coming. The girls had always loved him, but more now, our backs shoved up against the abyss of puberty. An altar boy, and a light around him after Communion. So clean and pressed and slicked, even after screaming recess. Smiles and yes please thank yous and a clean smell oozing out of him at all times. That good in baseball, the other boys worshipped him. And the only parents who didn't like him had to be jealous like my mother. That went back ages, one of the big department stores downtown used to have a portrait studio on the basement floor, and every year they ran their Beautiful Baby of Boston contest. Petey won it three years in a row and my mother never forgot it.

That family belongs in the Projects, she'd mutter over the sink. Beautiful Baby, my ass.

She referred to Mrs. Harding as The Babymaker, though seven kids was hardly a freak in town those days. There was just the one of me, my older brother Brian having died before I was born. The last shake of the stick, eh? ancient Mr. Crosby next door used to call me, before they took him away.

In addition Ma couldn't figure out how Mrs. Harding did her vacuuming without leaving any lines on the carpets, and was too proud to make inquiries. And then, the whole Donnie and Brian thing, which I didn't know about then. Ma would do anything for me, her only child, but there's a toughness about her you'd never guess, or, well, I don't know maybe you would. The tenderest parts of you are your fake fingernails, Dad said to Ma once when he came home with a drop-in. And that puss on your face would scare Jesus. They were blurt-arguing, splotches of words hurled like paintballs, Ma irrevocably committed to the final word.

Not without a sense of humor though, Ma. When we were eleven, and Sap was the saying at school when something bad happened to you, as in you are one, it was constantly falling from my lips. When the can of cocktail sauce Ma was trying to open exploded thirty seconds before company came and she'd just had her hair done; when her lucky numbers never came out of a night; one time helping her with the shopping during a wild March deluge and her umbrella buckled, became airborne in the parking lot, Sap, I'd intone at her, but drawn out in a pre-pubescent shrill, mocking, pointing at her, Saaaaap. She'd give chase but could never catch, my legs like sticks but endless in their energy, a few months later, tired, not feeling good, Dr. McCarthy told me, You've got mono young man, you'll be in bed for a month, summer was just starting and on the crowded elevator ride down from the doctor's office Ma turned to me, waited till I looked at her, Saaaaaap, she whispered as the doors opened to the lobby and the little bell went ding.

But Petey now, there was a shine about him, some kids just have it, you wouldn't be surprised if they turn out to be President or at least very rich, postcards from Bermuda every Christmas like the Barrys who owned that fuel oil company.

But I used to wonder what people would say if they saw Petey's pre-game ritual. Petey's uniform laid out on his bed. The whole thing, like a flattened Fab-ed version of himself. The shirt by the head, the pants along the spread, the little puckery jockstrap with the frayed leg straps on top of the pants, even the sanitary socks and cleats. The shirt arms outstretched like an appeal. His glove threaded into one cuff sleeve, right at the edge of the bed. The smell of fresh bargain laundry detergent staining the hot room.

It was still about 90 degrees even though it was like seven o'clock. The game started at eight, Night Game! and the nuns wouldn't mind much if you were late the next morning, they'd ask you in front of the whole class and you'd try not to smile when everyone-turn-around and tell 'em how you won. Well ahhh, see I was on third, right? Last inning two outs, right? Booger McPhee on deck? And then?

I was already in uniform, slouched in the tipply green chair, watching Petey. I was a sloucher, a watcher, not smart at all. Nothing special. Intensely normal, forgettable Danny? Oh yeah, Danny. Yeah. Petey lived closer to the field than I did so I'd called for him. I was sitting in the green chair in the corner, watching Petey, my left hand sweating inside my Henry Aaron glove on my lap, the smell of it I still remember. Petey's room immaculate. Always. Petey had no clothes on at all. Our bodies were exactly the same, we'd measured them.

Come to life now and we bless you and give you the honor, Petey said, waving his hands over his uniform. He was always getting these weird prayers and blessings from the knight books he read all the time, old history books from the library's tag sale every Memorial Day for a grubby quarter and they smelled like old people's breath when you flipped the pages, brittle and tired yes, but whispering of mystery and ways of living long gone by now. I couldn't be bothered, the writing too small, way too much to say, and you pictured a withered hand up on the brow covering the eyes as they murmured endlessly and you couldn't be bothered when you're young. Except for Petey, Petey wanted to know things.

Petey walked over to his bureau and took the tiny beveled-glass bottle of miraculous Lourdes Water that The Mission Monks sent Mrs.

Harding once a month, along with their Heartfelt Blessings, for her little something. He unscrewed the black cap carefully with nimble antennae fingers, then sprinkled a bit of the Holy Water onto his white and red uniform. Number 7 he was, that was always a precondition.

He closed his eyes.

We ask to win without bragging, and to lose without excuse, Petey continued. He had such a way of speaking then. All you could do was stare.

We seek to bring honor to the game, to ourselves, and to our God, he finished. Petey opened his eyes.

Then he began dressing, solemnly. Not a word out of him, the way we'd put on our cassocks and surplices when we did altar-boy duty. Always in the same order. Petey sat down on the end of the bed, the cups of his hipbones pulling at muscle and flesh so white it was blue, and me watching from the corner in fluttery fan shadow. He pulled on the right sanitary sock, then the left. Then his stirrups, Cardinal Red that year of course. The stirrups would have to be exactly as high as the sanitary socks, Petey was most particular about that. Then he'd stand up and wiggle into the little cotton jockstrap, putting those tiny white and pink things safely away where they belonged. Much was expected of them later, we didn't know that then. Our families, the Church, advertisers, all the world really, had plans for them. These expectations and boundaries. What were these expectations.

Then the shirt next, a baseball jersey underneath if it was chilly, but not tonight it was roasting, my ears red with the heat, nothing redder than a redhead's ears when he's flushed with June. Next the pants, and the matte black belt always too long and wrapped halfway again around his tubular white waist. Now, Petey's cleats. Always the right one first. Finally the hat, like a coronation. Petey would turn to the mirror to do this, lower it slowly with both hands onto his black hair. Sometimes he'd ask me to put it on for him, not tonight though. He'd stare at himself for a bit, then turn to me—

Who do you say that I am Danny? he'd ask. He didn't stutter then.

Petey Harding, I'd answer, though I felt funny. My … ahhh … best friend.

Bestest, he'd say.

That smile. Something inside rising up to meet it.

———　　———　　———

We march down to The Game on the clacky river of the sidewalk, which sighs out the day's heat. The air swings like a carnival. Our cleats clickity, we walk in unison. People shout out encouragement, luck as we stride you stride we all stride for baseball by their door-stoops, everyone sitting out. Mrs. Lally now, relishing the view from her top stair, smoking a Tareyton, but she's a lover not a fighter, housecoat and scuff slippers and Good luck to you, Brian, she sings out to me. My name is Danny. Brian was my older brother I never met, my only sib like I say, he died the year before I was born, he was 16, drunk driver, and that was that. This name fuckup happens sometimes, I guess we look alike. Can't tell Ma, can't talk about Brian wit' Ma.

Take it easy on the hills, boys, some cackling old man calls out from across the street. He's standing in the open maw of a barroom, Pat's Place. You can see the smoke twirling lazy out into the honey twilight. There's no wind, it just sort of sifts out, that smoke. Wanting out.

I still don't know what he meant by that. Bored? Launch yourself into the streets, walk by people, say hi. You walk out that door, never knowing what will happen. What they'll say to you. What you'll imagine they're thinking.

Look, Petey says as we click round the corner of East Broadway and Farragut Road. Beyond the tops of the triple-deckers there's a sharp glow to the south that is not the sunset, edging things in surreality.

We both come up short, stop.

The lights are on at Columbia Park, Petey announces. I gulp. This means we're playing on the Big Field. The Big Field's only for play offs and the 16-18 Senior League that lies in wait for me like all other good things. Panting like tigers in the midnight jungle of my upcoming teen years, these good things, then I realize I am the tiger, and the good things waiting for me to pounce upon. Soon. Soon.

For a second breathless, and a jiggle bounces between us, but then Why Not The Big Field, we're young and it's Summer and we're playing ball, Night Game! and the world belongs to us. Miracles come every day, like the paper, like the first pubic hair and me waiting by the hour.

Depending on their sympathies, cars honk out derision or calls to Kick Ass as they pass other shuffling knots of green-bubblegum players on their way to The Game. When they come to me and Petey, one from each side, the red and the blue, they get confused and a general

tumult of noise ensues, it's Southie and that kind of night. I totally forget that other people driving by have other lives this night, totally
unconnected to The Game. Then I remember that they do and pity poor
them. The ocean fifty yards across Day Boulevard shines pink and silver and flat, but way out at the horizon the shrouded light is green and
yellow, with an ugly black oval like a bashed eye in the middle.

Queer-looking sky, Petey points.

Huh? Oh. Oh yeah.

The ancients always said such signs portended doom! Petey waves
his fingers in my face at these last words, blows a bubble and snap it
goes. He laughs. Ironic now, looking backward.

Can you say it in English.

Here, Petey says, thinking of something else. I want you to have
these.

He pulls a box of Good 'n Fruity from his back pants pocket with
a flourish and a dimpling. Some kids are already warehousing cigarettes or airplane-model glue for sniffing in those pockets, not Petey.

Win or lose, I want you to have these Danny.

Good & Plenty is like horseshit, it's everywhere, as my grandfather
would say. Which isn't exactly true, there are in fact no horse poopsters
in Southie anymore, but that doesn't matter. Good 'n Fruity on the other
hand is hard to find. Some of us at school that spring have chin-rub
speculated about its disappearance from local stores' shelves. They're
not making it no more 'cuz one of the factory workers put LSD in it and
some kid from Maine died, Blubber Hogan, the school's rumormonger,
announced solemnly one lunchtime. My cousin Eddie O'Brien told me
so.

I've ordered it, Mr. McGillicuddy would say when we'd make
inquiries. He'd scratch behind his cauliflower ear. I did order it.

AWE-SOME! Where did you find them Petey?

At this spa over in Dorchester. Cambodians run it. You should hear
their music.

Petey was always off on his bike wandering. My mother keeps a
much tighter rein.

If Petey Harding painted his ass purple, you'd do the same thing!
she's said more than twice. The Halloween before, we'd done just that.
I told Petey what Ma always said, so we got finger paints and painted
each other's bums purple. When we went trick-or-treating an hour later,

ski masks to protect our identity, everyone asked us what we were, dear.

The Purple-Butted East Side Boys! we screamed once we had the goods in our pillow-sacks, running down the tenement steps, then we'd moon them at the bottom. I chucked my white Fruit of the Looms into a trashy can in an alley before I went home that night, that would be something I'd never be able to explain to Ma, who did me and Dad's laundry with the eye of an archeologist. I used to wonder what some-one would think, if they found that underwear. Like I'd eaten a lot of purple plums and shit myself maybe. I mentioned this to Petey.

Purple Plum Poopsterinis, he said. That's called alliteration, when the words start with the same letter. They roll off the tongue like wigg-ley red Jell-O, no, Danny? Wa-wa-wa-wa-wa!

Half the town is clutched at the edges of the neon-green ball field when we get there, and they've summoned legions of lawn-chair-toting relations from Quincy and Milton, Dorchester, Hyde Park. Big Game. Day has shattered into night and you don't even notice. Where goes the day when comes the night? Petey asks but I ignore him, I'm nervous and not in the mood for Petey nonsense. Smaller children overflow the stands and spill airplane-arm screaming onto the adjacent playground, the excitement is Croupy-contagious. Three competing ice cream trucks perfectly work the four sides of the Park, turning the square back into a circle and the geometry of it puzzles. Each one playing jingles that smear into a cacophonous symphony and a contented sigh from the ocean just across the rusty street. A jagged line of ruffling seagulls set-tles in on the telephone wires, peering, taut with Tonight like everybody else around here. Mothers muddled together, hobnobbing while check-books get balanced and diets get exchanged, This is that one Marie Boyle lost ten pounds on and you know the appetite on her. Young fathers are here, with three-year-old sons dressed in hats and baseball shirts too big for them, and as the squatted fathers point, trying to explain the holy intricacies of bats and balls and bases, their sons look skyward, their heads full up with baby blue thoughts.

May the best team win, Petey says, extending his sweat-free hand to me as we part to our own sides of the field. He has to shout almost, it's that loud with the crowd and all. Petey's always saying stuff like that. We have this bearded long-hair of a janitor at Gate of Heaven

School, one of the nuns' nephews I think, must be the last hippie in the world or at least in Southie. Yes thanks, he's been to Vietnam and writes dirty-worded poetry on a filthy yellow pad he keeps in the back pocket of his greasy green chinos. He calls Petey 'Peter Platitude.' Petey's mother refers to him as That poor miserable cray-chure. His name is Larry but everyone calls him Scratch and Sniff, self-explanatory I trust. Went off to Vietnam shy and crew-cutted, big-eared, so tall yet baby-faced for eighteen. Came back wild-eyed long-haired, apt to declaim on the Broadway Bus, missing something, God Help Him everybody said, but perhaps instead having been given something not entirely propi-tious. My mother says he resembles a vacant lot on the West Side gone to seed, and what's he doing anyway working in a school where he might do anything. Everyone except Petey and the nuns laughs at him. Petey, though, calls him Lawrence, and every day at school gives him an encouraging saying, Good Things Come to Those Who Wait, Lawrence; next day, It's Darkest Right Before Dawn, Lawrence, or whatever. That's Petey. Larry always just grumbles back. But he cried when he heard about Petey's accident, Cried like four babies, Mrs. Harding reported glumly. Even came to see him at the hospital after-wards but Someone Called Security and they made him leave looking like that, the cut of him, the old Irish matron at the Registration Desk kept saying to anyone who would listen. So many people visited Petey in the hospital. Even the Mayor and the Cardinal and the pictures of it in the papers clipped out and sent back to the cousins in Ireland, along with fervid scribblings to Storm Heaven for Petey, prayers and novenas would you please to this saint and that.

Petey was the most popular kid in school, maybe in town. The Golden Boy. All that was about to change tonight.

Listen what happened.

It was in the third inning when that wind came.

One minute even oceanside here people fanning themselves with flattened empty popcorn boxes, the sports section from the *Herald*, any-thing, not a breath and the women's perfume spurting into the sweat-and tobacco-ridden air like flowery unseen ejaculations. Then quick this invisible something whooshes in from the sea right across the Boulevard. If someone had gotten up from their lawn chair to pee in the sumacs behind left field or go talk to somebody about the upcoming Primary, Say Billy, could you and Trudy give Danno your vote next

month? For my sake? the chair flips over. A few caps swirl off the players on the field like twirly maple seeds except up not down. An angry
loop of sand raises itself like a fist between third and second and drives
in towards the plate. About a hundred people go, Ooooooooooooo, and
the ump raises both hands time-out. A lady's hat becomes airborne and
goes campaigning off into right field, tumbling over and over with
urgent intention. Haystack Hogan's grandfather goes hobbling after in
chivalrous but comedic pantomime pursuit.

Everyone looks up and around like they've forgotten we live in a
Natural world. These big inky clouds puffing in from the ocean, lowering as they advance the very weight of them, black-purple water bal-
loons swollen to the limit, and they've chewed away the stars and moon
and us not even hearing. The temperature dives about twenty degrees
instantly, like in a cartoon when they show the thermometer plummet-
ing, turning ice-crusted blue to Goofy's a-DUH chagrin. At first it feels
good after the day's heat but then seconds later no, too cold. All of a
sudden you can't see the Hennessey twins, can't see Little Pinky Quinn
out in the center field so good, it's like misty or whatever.

Then the wind gone. Poof. Like the snuffing of a candle. It's so
quiet, what is up with that. But a heaviness stays in the air like a
stranger in your dark bedroom. That hanging quiet before the thwack.
Everyone stops for a minute. Sniffing around. A lady of a certain age
breaks the ice, she's having none of it she's buried two husbands, cackles, Oh Cripes! and reaches with salamander-spotted fingers and fuch-
sia-pink fingernails for her More 120 cigarettes in the maroon
leatherette case with the lighter tucked in its built-in pocket.

Play Ball! one of the umps roars, and everyone back to normal,
though if they've left a sweater in the car they dash for it. The hip-
saunter of Mothers after their children, but they don't have to go far, the
chilly kids are seeking out Ma, the girls holding their skinny bare shoulders, the little boys with finger and thumb abstractedly grabbing their
peepees through their shorts, looking around. The men remain motion-
less, pretending still to sweat.

Petey's oldest brother Donnie is sitting on the guardrail up there by
the Boulevard, alone, married with two tots but mostly alone. He used
to mind us a lot when we were younger, before he got married himself.
Quiet. Alone even in a crowd that one, some people just are you know.
He's hung up his happiness for sure, Mrs. Harding says with a shake of

her head, can't say Donnie's name without eliciting that response.

Tinker Kelley strikes out and whips his bat, the ump snarls a warning, then Petey steps up to the plate and applause all round. Our best pitcher Billy Donovan's going for us tonight. Jimmy Whelan's our other pitcher and his turn was tonight but he got benched for this Big Game, see, Jimmy's okay for six innings but completely falls apart in the seventh (the last), gives up homer after homer which is why he's Way-Back Whelan. So it's Billy tonight instead of Jimmy. Petey in the first inning is the only one so far to get a hit off of Billy, a long screeching double it was, then Petey stole third and came home on a suicide squeeze bunt. There's something about watching a boy do something to fluidy perfection, you wonder what ever will stop him when he's a man. It's one to nothing now, Third Inning. Two outs. Not a soul on base. The grass twice as green under the funky night light. Three seagulls pecking and preening out in right field, oblivious but still a part of it all.

I'm playing first like always. Leaning in. Bum shoved out in a disdaining crouch, left right left right left, I'm lightly grazing my glove against the dirt three times before each batter just for green luck, luck's always green to me, it just is.

Billy and Petey stare at each other, then Billy vaults his whip frame into a windmill windup. He has dick bush but not me yet, he laughing showed us after a game when he was taking his cup off, Wouldn't you little pukes like to have this now? He throws a fast ball. Petey's ready but swings a hair too soon. He cracks a screamer down the right field line, just one foot foul. It almost takes my head off, I feel the wind of it whiz by me. No one can hit Billy Donovan's fastball except for Petey, he creams it most every time. If there's a thing Petey can't do no one knows it yet.

Sorry Danny, Petey calls out to me. It's the very lastest thing the old Petey Harding says. He whacks the dirt of his cleats with his bat, one at a time, spits, peers.

The next ball is a curve, low, in the dirt, a worm-killer, and the next one same thing but too high, a rainmaker. Coach calls Time Out and hustles out to talk to Billy on the mound the way they do. I think Coach wants Billy to walk Petey intentionally, because Billy keeps shaking his head, no no no. I go over to see what's up. Coach falls asleep in Mass, never during a game, but nevertheless Mrs. Harding vouches for his deep devotion to Our Lady, he's a member of the local chapter of The

League of Mary and she should know, isn't she the recording sec-a-terry. Big hairy paws I always notice, but something heartbreaking in how they fumble with a Rosary when he jump-awakens right at the Final Blessing, never married as his fiancée married someone else while he was in the service, and his life now is all about Mary and Baseball. He was made to kill people in Vietnam. Signed up for a stu-por-second tour when the loved one repudiated him via Par Avion. One time after a team meeting at his house he showed me and Petey his collection of cards, greeting cards birthday cards get-well cards Mass cards, not the usual like you'd find around here there and everywhere in overly-lit fluorescent shops A Niece Is A Special Person, A Prayer For You Father in Law On Your Birthday, but crinkly missives of wonder: rice paper ones from Southeast Asia, some hand-lettered in gold by Capuchin Monks in Italy, another, layered tissues of paper thinner than butterfly wings, all unique but each a hallmark of wonder. I'm just telling you because TV would have us believe Coaches are just coaches, half-dimensional recipients of indigestion right before the Big Game, shillers of Athlete's Foot and Jock Itch remedies, and I want to set the record straight before Coaches themselves start taking their cues from same like everyone else.

What are you doing? Coach is saying to Billy, not rhetorically, when I join them at the mound, I'm not sure I'm supposed to be here, but this is what the Big Leaguers do when there's a Conference on the Mound, the first baseman will trot over sometimes, in an Assistant-Secretary-of-State-ish advisory capacity.

I can get him out, I know I can! Billy whines. He's six-foot tall and has dick bush already but his voice hasn't changed yet which is strange, but I guess This Thing Coming to us all is like that telescope I got in the mail that year from Aunt Jean Marie for Christmas, the shafty-thing part came in December, the lensy thing not until March. But it was cracked and Ma wouldn't let me send it back because that would be rude Danny, but I ask you, isn't it just like that side of the family.

Billy splays a cleated foot into the dusty pitcher's mound. The dust rises up, does not settle down and I watch it, wondering where does it go as it vanishes.

One more pitch, Coach says, shoving his hands into his back pockets and rocking back and forth. No strikes, hear me? If you don't, then you walk him. Hear me?

Play Ball! the home plate ump bellows. Coach slaps skinny Billy on his non-bum and trots back in. He's put on his Veterans of Foreign Wars Post # 1964 blue nylon jacket.

Billy is a sore sport and hates to lose. He's mad now and going to throw the fastball, I know it. People who can't control their emotions you can predict what they're going to do ten out of ten times, no? I want to yell that out to Petey but I know he knows this too, fastball coming. I want my team to win but I always root for Petey too. Once Paul O'Rourke said to me—whispered it really on the way home from Altar Boy Guild, Petey was still back at church getting his picture taken for *The Pilot* for his Altar Boy of the Year Award, he whispered, Paul did,

Okay Danny listen—Petey, right? Sometimes, I want to see him—not fail, I don't mean like fail. Just maybe not be so perfect.

Why? I asked. Then, Shut the fuck up, Paulie, before waiting for him to answer. The shove I gave him, you should've seen it.

Petey digs his cleats into the dusty home plate soil. From where I am, crouched beside first base, I can see Petey tighten up his grip on the bat. Fingerlings. He becomes absolutely still, a Hall-of-Fame statue in the making and me knowing the inevitability of this twenty years before the rest of the world and why me as his best friend when he could have anybody. An accident of kindergarten seating and not a day's gone by since that we haven't been the sight and light of each other. Billy Donovan's eyes are wimply and leaking nervousness, fierceness, but Petey's are hearing music. And Petey's uniform still gleaming in the gloaming, how he manages to keep it white the way he plays. There's some people and it just comes natural, all you can do is stare. For a second I picture Petey in his batting stance without any clothes at all. Just his cleats and helmet. I wonder what everyone would think if they saw Petey doing his ritual dressing. But I know it's something you don't talk about with anyone else. How do we know we shouldn't. I look down, spit nervously, try to reach the edge of the grass with the dollop but it plops far short.

Petey! C'mon, Petey! Petey, give it a ride now Petey! All the way, Petey! But there's just as many calls out to Billy to blow it by him whip it by him, strike him out for Cris'sake and a boozy laugh. Billy's mother in particular with the brassy red hair: a wicked whiny voice and her incessant call a rising crescendo like a stain above everyone and everything: Ca'mooooOONNNNNNN, BILLY! over and over again till you want someone to slap her please. For the sake of your own concentration. Billy's father, a cop and works nights watching from the edge of the road above the field in his uniform not too far from Donnie, spitting with a snake-jerk of his head. Staring down in a way that makes me glad he's not my father.

Billy winds up The Wind comes back as if Billy's Merlin movements have summoned it. It cuts in like a rumbly driverless miscarriage of something from left field and roars right for the pitcher's mound. It knocks over somebody's camera-tripod thing. Patsy Flynn over on third does a little dance, he gets twirled around by the wind and looks like a dust devil with all the sand. Billy Donovan closes his eyes as he hurls the ball. His gloved hand shoots up to his face to cover his eyes from the sand. I remember that. He half-stumbles as he lets the ball go, dick bush and squeaky voice and inherited nasty spleen and everything else he's got thrown into that pitch, half the universe thrown into that pitch. I know the fastball will be wild. I know the fastball will be wild. Everything slow motions. The ball rotates as it approaches and its coming is comet-like, calamitous and heraldic.

Petey! I roar, to warn him, can't help it my best friend, everything oh Jesus—

Petey squints and his head shoots a look at me. We stare at each other for a second. The ball hits him then right over the eye, in between the helmet and his eyebrow. It came out of the sand while he was looking at me. The thwack of it. Crunch. It shatter-bounces his helmet off. The impossible has happened, Petey has erred, next the planets might go spinning out of their orbits—

Petey is still looking at me. His eyes rise big like moons.

I'm numb! I'm numb! he wails, dropping his bat and reaching for his head with both hands. Everyone hears this.

Then a silence as everyone watches. Silence is wonderful in a monastery, awful when there's so many around—

Petey's eyes shutter-shut, slow. How they louvered—how it reminded me of blinds quick-yanked down inside a house where something horrible has just happened. His arms pause halfway to his head, then flop.

He heaps to the dust. Buckling and the slow pulling in of knees and elbows. Crumple. There is a second when nothing happens, then blood curdles from his ear onto the dusty dirt. The dust is too dry, it won't accept it. The blood makes a crooked spiral as it leaks from his ear. Something monstrous seems to travel underground out from home plate, out to me where it splits the ground between my legs.

It rained for three straight days after that.

Joe G. Hayes
Joe G. Hayes is a writer and landscaper living in the Boston area. He is the author of *This Thing Called Courage: South Boston Stories* and is finishing a novel entitled *A Map of the Harbor Islands*, of which Jolly-Olly Petey is an excerpt.

Gorgon

J.E. Robinson

The class was bedlam. As the recording on the loudspeaker began its second verse, Roger Archer hopped onto his table and began to air guitar. He stopped long enough to hurl his Blues baseball cap across the room, freeing his platinum forelock. The other kids giggled. Some clapped their hands in time. A few sang "Mrs. Robinson" with him.

The middle school principal, Miss Stirrat, opened the room door. "Roger," she said.

Roger hopped off the table. "Ah, Miss Stirrat."

"I mean it this time, Roger," she said.

As the music subsided, Miss Stirrat returned to me, standing in the hall. I still had the letter. I was unable to look at it any longer. I felt as though I had been struck with a commode. Miss Stirrat, a large, maternal woman, had been in education almost thirty-six years. Nothing could have taught her the words to say to me.

"I know it's a shock," she mustered. "Keith said you can bring anyone you'd like. A minister, a doctor, witnesses. Your parents."

"May I bring a lawyer?"

"I don't think you have to go that far, Skip."

"Really."

Miss Stirrat held my wrist, a friendly gesture. I didn't reciprocate. "You can bring your parents. That will keep this in the family."

This talk of family, I could have said, made me feel like a bastard. Even at that moment, I had more tact. "They're both lawyers."

I couldn't say much more. In the months since I'd come to the Muir School, Miss Stirrat was one of the few people to have been on my side. When teaching seventh graders the intricacies of grammar and the nuances of *The Red Badge of Courage* and *The Catcher in the Rye* got too much for me, I rejuvenated in her office, after a talk. Now that my predilection had betrayed her trust, I could scarcely look at her.

For a moment, I looked through the glass at Roger. He seemed such a happy boy. Who would have believed I had done something to him, as the headmaster thought?

His lean jock's body, dressed in blue jeans and a blue and red rugby shirt, stretched into the aisle. I almost tripped over him.

"Sorry, Mister Macalester."

"That's OK, Roger," I said. "That's OK."

I almost patted his shoulder. I would have, but I knew I was being watched.

Thankfully, that was the last hour of the day. Hell, it was the end of my week. I bundled a week's worth of chewed and discarded pencils in a rubber band and dropped them into my desk. I stuffed the day's spelling tests—eighty in all—into my lawyerlike briefcase. I made a note to get Monday's tissues. I was winding down, when DeWolfe Penny opened the door.

"Mister Macalester?"

I looked up from what I was doing. I was standing at my desk, a pile of books and papers so deep Schliemann could have excavated. I was digging from the pile my grade book.

"School's out, Dee," I said. "Time to go home."

"I know," DeWolfe said. "But, my car pool … the guys left without me. I need a ride home."

Stunned, I didn't know what to say. "I'm not going directly home. I have a few stops."

"Please?"

What do you say to a thirteen-year-old kid, brown hair thick and full of cowlicks, who needs to travel almost thirty miles in the middle of January? All I could say was yes. After all, we practically lived in the same town, as DeWolfe well knew.

Getting my overcoat, I took my briefcase and turned off the lights. It was Friday, just past three-thirty, and the place had been cleared out, leaving just discarded notebook paper. DeWolfe almost looked as disheveled: he had icing smeared on his chin. In the hall, I pointed it out.

DeWolfe gushed, "*That.*"

"Mrs. Robinson's birthday party?"

"Yeah."

He reached to wipe it off, but I cleared it with a finger and licked the icing. It was chocolate, my favorite. Mrs. Robinson, a Social Studies teacher, was a good woman. I'm glad she had cake I would have enjoyed. And, since the school played Simon and Garfunkel on the loudspeaker to help celebrate, it must have been an excellent day.

Perhaps it would make little sense to you now that I agreed to drive DeWolfe back to Illinois. I doubt it would make sense to anyone rational that a man barely twenty-six, who was being watched for touching, would add to his reputation by escorting a lone boy out the front door. In a way, I thought the headmaster, Keith, a big man who rarely left his office chair for anything short of a bequest, would stride out and snatch DeWolfe from my side like the Erlking. Perhaps I was tempting. Perhaps I was tempting fate. Perhaps I was tempting the fate of a fool. Perhaps so.

"When the snow melts and it gets nicer," DeWolfe said, approaching my car, "maybe you should take your car to the car wash."

"Are you saying my car needs a bath?" I laughed.

"Sorry, but, yeah."

Opening the passenger door for him, I had to admit my car, a silver automatic Fox with soot and salt stains, needed a cleaning. Even though I had served as DeWolfe's backup ride since soccer season ended in November and he was somewhat used to my unkempt ways, he still gave me a look of complete astonishment when I asked him to shift scattered magazines and cups to the backseat. He still wanted me to throw them away.

I had to move quickly to put the book I was reading for recreation, *The Coming Storm*, with its cover of a disheveled prep schooler, with my briefcase before DeWolfe saw it and asked questions. The book was on my dashboard; I put it behind the seat, on the floor. There, the book's suggestive cover would not spark his curiosity.

As was my practice when getting behind the wheel, I lit my pipe. A plume of vanilla-scented smoke lifted from me. DeWolfe, as always, coughed.

"Sorry, Dee."

"That's okay, Mister Macalester. I forgive you."

DeWolfe was a banker's son. His father, a robber baron who made a killing in commodities, owned the largest bank in Whitman Township, as well as another bank near Springfield, Illinois. The Judge knew Mr. Penny. He said Mr. Penny was in one of the first Government classes he visited as a judge, my lifetime ago. When I talked to him at open house, Mr. Penny said he sent DeWolfe to the Muir School because of its athletics, and because he didn't trust all the "niggers" in the public schools.

Little did he know the Muir School had its "niggers." Mrs. Robinson and I were the Black teachers, but, as Keith so often said, he didn't think of us as Black, but as part of "the family," like Lilly in the TV show *I'll Fly Away*. Between us, Mrs. Robinson and I rolled our eyes. "Would Keith let us eat dinner at the kitchen table?" Mrs. Robinson asked. I wondered.

DeWolfe, a good kid, removed his hood as the Fox started to heat up.

"Might as well unzip, Dee."

"Unzip my coat?"

I nodded. "You don't want to get too hot, do you?"

DeWolfe unzipped his coat. He revealed his bright red ski sweater. Red was one of my favorite colors. It looked good on him.

"We'll be in here for at least a half hour," I said. "Slip it off, so you can be comfortable."

DeWolfe slipped the coat off his shoulders. He looked at me. He had brown eyes. Doe-like brown eyes.

"There," I said. "That's better, isn't it?"

DeWolfe nodded.

I puffed my pipe and pulled out of the school parking lot.

We were in the suburbs west of St. Louis, where, we teachers reminded ourselves every morning, the rich bastards lived. The Muir School was one of the best schools—public or private—in the St. Louis area. When I arrived there from the University of Chicago in July, Keith, the headmaster, greeted me with his set speech, replete with talk about the Muir family, the number of Merit Scholars the school sent to the Ivy League each year, and how well it competed on the athletic field. "The one thing we're not good at is theater," Keith said, rocking in his chair. He had a habit of fiddling with his Harvard tie. "You can do theater, can't you?"

Dressing the theater queens? "Sure."

"Can I ask you something, please, Mister Macalester?"

"Sure, Dee. What?"

"Can we … you know."

"Sure."

I changed the station from classical music (they were playing the English Bach) to a hip-hop station. DeWolfe smiled and started to bop.

"Poser," I said.

"Nuh-huh. I'm a homeboy!"

He started to rap with the lyric. The sound reminded me of being almost sixteen and having Reverend Shuddlesworth on my back. When I was almost sixteen, when he did that thing to me, I was barely strong enough to bear him. Dee, could you be as strong as me?

I couldn't see my father, for he stood in shadow. "Does it surprise you?" I had asked him.

"Not really," the Judge sighed. "I thought something would happen sooner or later. I should have done something about it when you tried attacking Alan."

He was referring to my attempted assault on my cousin Alan Morgan, when I was almost sixteen. How did he know about that? "When I tried *what*?"

For a moment, he looked at me. The muted stove hood light silhouetted his head. Then, he looked away. "Really, Skip. Don't play stupid. It is very unbecoming."

The letter from Keith informing me of my hearing crinkled in my inside breast pocket. It was too soft a sound for DeWolfe to notice.

"You think we got time to get something to eat?" DeWolfe asked.

"Why?"

"I'm hungry."

I turned the Fox onto Lindbergh Boulevard. "Dinner's just around the corner. You mean you can't wait until dinner?"

"Indulge me. Please?"

Putting his hands together in prayer, he pleaded with me and batted those doe-like eyes. "Oh, all right," I said.

You have to know Lindbergh in West County. It is a divided highway. Heading north, there were plenty of fast-food establishments, but they had access to the southbound lane. To reach them, we would have to stretch over a three-foot-tall concrete divider.

Roger Archer, I remember, put a hand on my leg and sent a shock wave. He pointed at a McDonald's. "Mickey Dee's!" he exclaimed. "Turn here!"

I did as I was told. It was still soccer season. The fall had just begun. I watched Roger lead three other boys into the restaurant. He looked every inch the jock in his black satin shorts and electric blue goalkeeper's jersey. In spite of myself, I let my mind float to things I had tried repressing since returning to St. Louis.

"Did you handle it?"

Marshall wouldn't answer me. Just out of law school that year, he had a way of not answering me, like a brother. I stopped trying to keep up.

"Marshall," I whined. My voice resonated over the snowy, dark parking lot. He turned to face me.

"*What?*"

"Did you—you know?"

Having grown up with me, my cousin Marshall Langston was just like a brother. He was just like my twin, the spat-upon image of the Judge. We were tall enough to look each other in the eye. In Marshall, I saw ambition. What did he see in me?

He huffed. "Yes, I did." He started walking.

"And?"

"And," he said, "it's not your problem anymore!"

The price for dropping a morals charge against me at twenty-five, when I was still in Chicago and when a law professor's teenaged son took my heart, was the postponement of Marshall's run for the Illinois state legislature. Someone else got the seat, and promised to keep it for a generation.

I stared at DeWolfe as he whipped back his winter coat and pulled out his wallet. I remembered the worn impression his wallet left in his back pocket. It was nice watching it. DeWolfe turned back to me as the McDonald's staff got his order.

"Pretty soon, you'll need new jeans," I said.

DeWolfe's eyes sparkled. "You're gonna buy me some?"

"Tell your old man to get you some," I laughed.

"*Please*—another bunch of corduroys and khakis. I need a cool dude like you to buy me some."

It was October, around my birthday. My soccer team had just won a home game. Everyone else was gone. Roger stood beneath the showerhead in the stall facing me. Soaping up, he let the spray cleanse the grass stains on his thigh.

I had walked in. When my shower was done, I flew out on cicada wings.

"You have no control over yourself," the Judge said once when I was home from graduate school. He looked up from his hands. He leaned back in his chair. "You're like a kid in a candy store, my son. All you do is stuff peppermint and chocolate in your mouth."

"*Well?*"

"You were asking me, Dee?"

DeWolfe nodded. "Ain't you gonna get something?"

"No," I said, "and, it's 'aren't you?'"

He picked his tray up from the counter and sprinkled salt on his fries. "Ain't, aren't. I'm rich. Who cares if I don't know my verbs?"

I thought about patting his shoulder, but the McDonald's counter lady, a grandmother in bifocals, stared at us. I looked at my feet, and mustered a smile. "You gotta know when the secretary screws up."

"I'll just get my other secretary to check her work."

"What if it's a him?" I asked.

"Whatever," he shrugged.

DeWolfe took the tray of a Big Mac, fries, and a root beer to a table and sat where he could see Lindbergh buzz by. I couldn't believe it. It was already approaching four.

"Dee—we gotta go. They're going to think I kidnapped you."

Mostly, I was joking. DeWolfe looked at me. He had Big Mac special sauce on his fingers.

"*You* kidnap *me*? That'll be the day." He sucked special sauce from his fingers, a tip at a time. "Gimme a few minutes. I'll have this gone in no time."

Pointing at a chair, he made me sit. I crossed my legs and folded my hands. "Am I supposed to wait?" I asked.

"Yes," he said. He started eating his Big Mac.

Just before Christmas, I waited for Roger to join his classmates to watch *The Nutcracker*.

"I'll only be a second," Roger said from the other side of the men's room door.

"Come on, Roger," I said," the rest of the students are waiting."

"I'm almost—" There was an audible sigh, then, after a few minutes, a flush. Roger came out to the hall immediately afterward. In the auditorium nearby, an orchestra tuned up.

"Did you wash your hands?"

"Mister Macalester." Roger smiled. He tried to blush. His eyes were the flavor of crisp graphite.

"Go and wash your hands."

"But, Mister Macalester, the guys are waiting!"

"For this, they can wait longer." I held the door open and led him to the men's room basin.

A strange thing about those Muir School rich kids: they are proud of their calluses. Roger's hands were strong and rough from handling a baseball bat. In the spring, he was a slugging third baseman. His hand felt warm. His thumb scratched against my knuckles. "*You have no control over yourself.*" The Judge's voice, as stern as a thunderbolt, pierced me. Not wanting to indulge my predilection to spite myself, I dropped Roger's hand. He looked at me with those graphite-flavored eyes, big as Orphan Annie's, once abandoned by Daddy Warbucks himself. Aside from that, there was nothing to report.

DeWolfe wiped his mouth with a napkin, which, balled up, he placed in the center of the Big Mac box like a pearl.

"Now, can we go?"

DeWolfe smiled. "Sure thing, Mister M."

Dropping off his garbage, he led me outside. A typical January day, it was overcast, and the sky reflected the dinge in the snow. There was already eight inches on the ground, and it looked like it could snow some more.

DeWolfe took me to my car, which, once started, warmed up quickly. He unzipped his coat and let it slip from his shoulders. "Where's next?"

I was surprised he was asking me. I was more concerned with getting back to the right side of Lindbergh Boulevard. "Illinois," I said.

"You said you got some stops to make."

"I'll make them over the weekend," I said.

"What's wrong, Arthur? You don't wanna be seen with me?"

"I beg your pardon? Did you call me 'Arthur'?"

I remembered the kids knew my first name. DeWolfe smiled broadly. He let the moment settle for a bit. "You don't want to be seen with me, do you?" he asked.

"That's not the issue, Dee," I said, putting on my seat belt.

"Then, what gives? You say you gotta make some stops, then you don't. I was wondering what's what. Is it me, or what?"

"It's not you," I said, pulling out of the parking space.

"Then, what, huh? I didn't embarrass you in there, did I?"

"No."

"Then, what?"

I looked at him. He was every bit the kid. He was acting his part. I needed to play mine. "My schedule has its reasons."

He shrugged. "Fine time to spank me, Mister M."

I nodded and pulled onto the right side of Lindbergh Boulevard. For the first few minutes, I contended with the start of rush-hour traffic fairly successfully.

DeWolfe's class was a scared bunch of kids. Being seventh graders, they were new to the school. An eighth grader ushered them into my room a week before the school year started. I was typing a lesson. "Have a seat," I said, "I'll be with you in a minute." When I talked, they hung on every word. They sat quietly, with their hands folded before them. DeWolfe was the one with impassioned eyes.

"What can we call you?" he asked.

The standard was to call teachers by a title and a last name. I used the standard. "My name is Arthur Macalester," I said. "You may call me Mister Macalester."

I was comfortable with it because no one called my father, ever the Judge, "Mister Macalester." Like the problem Mrs. Robinson initially had when she began teaching there, some tried calling me by a familiar name. Like DeWolfe.

"It's 'Mister Macalester' to you," I said.

DeWolfe started singing "You Picked a Fine Time to Leave Me, Lucille." It was plaintive, like the baying of a basset hound. Then, he flashed those doe-like eyes. "Please," he said. "*Please!*"

"Do people really call you 'Arthur'?" Roger asked, dribbling a soccer ball like a basketball on the parking lot. Though school had not started yet, being still August, soccer practice was well under way. Having finished the day, Roger and I waited for his older brother to pick him up.

"Most people just call me 'Skip'."

"Can I call you 'Skip'?"

I looked at him. In the setting sun, a puff of shadow raised the fine hairs on his leg. It was after practice; almost everyone was gone. He had his shoes and socks off. I looked down at his feet. Does he know? Does he know? Nothing is a bigger aphrodisiac for me than bare feet.

"No," I said. "It's best not to."

My pipe started to spit back at me. I had to get it out of my mouth, and let the moist tobacco dry out to get rid of that cinder taste.

"You really don't like things in your mouth," DeWolfe said. "Do you?"

"Just cinders and a bite in the bowl. That's all, Dee."

"No. You don't like things in your mouth. I can tell."

"The kids here are so—so—" The words were caught in the mouth as my colleague, my friend Ian, toweled sweat from his glasses after playing a tennis match in September. His freckles and red pompadour made him favor Danny Kaye. All he needed to do was a benefit for UNICEF. He returned the glasses to his face. "It's like they're from a bakery. They're all so very fresh."

"Really?" I asked.

"Haven't you noticed? The kids here can be so seductive." Ian smiled a little. He always smiled a little. I had heard he had an affair with one of our colleagues in the English Department when she was a Muir student eleven years before. As often as he smiled at me, I wondered if he wanted an affair with me.

DeWolfe became animated as we approached an intersection. Three lines of cars slowed and waited for the stoplight to change. Was that what got him going? He grabbed my thigh. "Right here," he said. "Right here!"

DeWolfe was like a spaniel that had just seen a fire hydrant. Wagging his tail, he rolled down the window as I took our place in the line, then he reached out for the car next to us, a St. Louis County police car.

"Hey!" DeWolfe shouted at the officer, a young, clean-shaven man wearing a wool hat. "Hey!"

"*Dee!*"

"I know what I'm doing," DeWolfe said. Leaning out of the car, he flailed at the officer. "Hey, man! Please!"

The officer rolled down his window. He gave me a skeptical look. "You in trouble, son?" he asked.

DeWolfe shook his head. "My name is Dee." He drummed on the car door in a beat. "Wanna push your broom in me?"

"*Dee!*"

DeWolfe started laughing. The officer was too young to know what to say. I grabbed DeWolfe by the belt and pulled him back into the car seat. Thankfully, the light changed, and we both lurched forward. DeWolfe was laughing uncontrollably.

"You get that look on his face?" DeWolfe asked.

I did. I wouldn't call that look, that disgusted look that could only be directed at a catamite, anything to laugh at.

I checked the Fox's rearview mirror. No sign of the officer. "Is he coming?"

"That prick?" DeWolfe laughed.

"Wait until he calls that in."

That cracked DeWolfe up even more. "Wait until he tells his wife!"

"I don't think that's funny, Dee."

He stopped laughing. "Why not?"

I looked at him. He flashed those large brown eyes and brushed a cowlick from his forehead. I couldn't think of much of an explanation. I continued driving, folding into traffic as harmlessly as a rabbit.

"The sad thing is, you must go through your life looking in the rearview mirror," the Judge said. It was dinner and he was eating medium-rare prime rib. "I know of no father who'd wish that upon his child."

For the next few miles, I was quiet, thinking about how to handle my hearing with Keith. Maybe, I thought, I should ask Mom to attend.

The Judge will agree. "Rose is an excellent lawyer, even if we are no longer married. Sic her on them and they'll sue for peace."

I imagined my mother, in her coldness, doing interrogatives with the Muir "family." "Are you *really* family?" she might ask. "Are you part of my son's family, Doctor?" she might ask Keith. Then, amid her hot strain, he would collapse and acquiesce. "You aren't so big, Doctor. Charging my son with molestation. The way you enticed him, teased him, and treated him, you are no more than a molester yourself. Tell me, good Doctor, have you ever touched thirteen year olds yourself?"

"Mom," I will say on the phone. "I have to tell you something."

She will seem still. "I already know, Skip."

Would Marshall brief her? Would the Judge? I could doubt it. "I don't think you know about this," I would finally say.

"I'm the mother. The mother always knows."

"Who's going to be home for you, Dee?" I asked.

"I dunno." He wiped car soot onto his jeans. "Maybe my mom. I guess I'll have to take a bath before I see her, huh?"

I nodded, a little enticed by the thought.

I had not met DeWolfe's mother. Until the boy showed me a picture of her, I thought his mother was a figment of his imagination, something designed to keep the rougher kids from wagging on about DeWolfe and his father, who walked around with his arm over the boy's shoulder, like a pal. Because Mrs. Penny didn't travel in our circle, I had a feeling neither the Judge nor Mom knew anything about her. I could tell them DeWolfe favored her. Once, in detention, he put on a girl's ruby red lipstick and used her pencil liner. He looked just like Mrs. Penny in that picture. When Miss Stirrat saw him, she personally washed his face. "Keith must *not* see this," she said. "We'd be in a life of trouble!"

"Can I take a bath at your place?" DeWolfe asked.

"In this weather?" I said. "You'll catch your death."

"No, I won't. I won't. Promise."

I dared not look at him. All he needed to do was flash those big, brown eyes at me, and I would have been his prisoner. I shook my head. "No, Dee. No, Dee, you can't."

"But, I won't tell, Mister M."

"You don't have to tell, because I'm not taking you. So, you can just forget it."

I could hear his hands clasp. "*Please*, Mister Macalester? *Please*?!"

I didn't even answer verbally. I shook my head. But, though I was in trouble, being investigated, some thoughts traced through me. I felt a small, experienced hand on my thigh. We were approaching the airport. Some jets landed. I tried to drive.

"Please, Mister Macalester," DeWolfe said. It was no longer a question, or a request. It was, how should I say?, a direction, like "turn here to fly."

"My answer's no," I still said.

"But, if you don't," DeWolfe said. "I'll tell."

"You'll *what*?"

"You heard me," he said clearly. "I'll tell. Everyone. The whole school. Everything."

I hadn't touched him, I was sure. Now, this kid threatened me? "I don't respond to threats."

"You'd do anything to keep people from knowing your thoughts," he said." Like any guy."

He kept his hand on my thigh. It was a queer sensation, his hand on my thigh. His eyes flashed and he drew a smile. He patted my thigh, then sat back.

"You know what it is," he said. "I want to see the inside of your bathroom."

I shook my head. "There's nothing for you to tell."

"That's what you think. How do you know I haven't told already?"

Would DeWolfe have told about a me and him or about the me and Roger? Someone already knew about the me and Roger. Would I be willing to damn myself further by agreeing to take DeWolfe to my place—to my father's house—for a bath, to watch him undress, to dry his back? At some stoplight on Lindbergh (a long road, as you can see), I glanced at DeWolfe. He had the look of a bow hunter. He had horns.

"My father might be home," I said.

"At this time of the day? *Please*."

He was right. DeWolfe knew my father well enough, by reputation, to know he was not home. His wife, Eugenia, my stepmother and a high-school English teacher, was most likely still tutoring at her volunteer job. I needed an out.

"I'm not taking you any place but home," I said. "To hell with the damn consequences."

DeWolfe shrugged. "Suit yourself. It was nice, you teaching me."

He was quiet for most of the rest of the drive, whistling the school song occasionally. It seemed to remind me of my "duty" to the Muir family. I could almost hear Keith, leaning forward, urging me to do right and keep such things about Muir at Muir. But I had to face fact: was I really a part of Muir to begin with?

When we reached Illinois, I headed for his house. "The evil men do," I heard myself say, paraphrasing Shakespeare, "live long after they are dead, while the good is oft interred with their bones. So let it be with Caesar."

We reached his house in Whitman Township, a baronial French colonial two-story overlooking a pond that had frozen over into a hockey rink.

DeWolfe looked at the house and sighed audibly. "Guess this is it.

The dice is cast."

"You mean, the *die* is cast."

"Whatever." DeWolfe rested his hand on my thigh again. When I turned to face him, he kissed me on the cheek. Not a heavy, sensual kiss, but a puppy-love peck, the kind you see girlfriends doing before going to the teacher and telling tales. He sat back and smiled. I picked up my pipe and puffed it.

"Good-bye, Dee," I said.

He twinkled fingers at me, as quick as tinkling a piano scale. It seemed so strange he would do that, as though we were brothers.

J.E. Robinson

J. E. Robinson's short stories have appeared in *Best Gay Erotica 2003*, *Harrington Gay Men's Fiction Quarterly*, *Men on Men 6*, and *Rebel Yell*. He is working on a novel, *Skip Macalester*, which is forthcoming. He lives in Southern Illinois, near St. Louis.

Stigmata

Greg Herren

"You know your trick last night was a priest, don't you?"

I had lost track of the conversation. Wool gathering as usual. It was just the standard Sunday-brunch collection of who picked up whom, who was wearing what, and who was developing a drug problem. A complete rehash of the events of the weekend, over toast, grits and Bloody Marys. I had been watching an older couple seated by one of the windows, who were having a rather heated discussion. The younger man looked on the verge of tears. I looked back at my own table to find three pairs of eyes staring at me. "What?"

My best friend Dennis rolled his large brown eyes. "Pay attention! I asked you if you were aware that your trick of last evening, he of the pitch-black hair and the impressive pectorals, is a priest?"

I looked at Dennis and then at the other two faces. Rodger was smiling, his reddish-blond eyebrows raised in anticipation of my reaction. Travers, who lived in the apartment below me and cut hair in the daylight hours before transforming himself into Uneeda Biscuit, drag queen extraordinaire, at night, managed to look pitying and compassionate at the same time. I looked back at Dennis and sipped my coffee. "No, I didn't know."

"Typical." Rodger's eyebrows came back down. He buttered a piece of whole-wheat toast. He could be a bitch, and had a mean streak in him, but now he was on my side. "I wonder if he goes to confession? I wonder how many Hail Marys you get for a blow job?"

"My first lover was a priest." Travers sipped his Bloody Mary with a sigh. "Father Sean. He was such a dreamboat." He scratched one of his plucked eyebrows absently. His head was shaved completely to make room for Uneeda's fabulous wigs. He was small and delicately built, with long tapering fingers and manicured nails. His voice was soft and soothing, like gentle rain on a spring morning.

"How old were you?" Dennis turned his attention away from me.

"Eleven. I was an altar boy."

"That was child abuse, Travers!" Dennis half-shouted, and other tables turned to stare. He lowered his voice, and the three of them got into a quiet-yet-furious discussion of priests and the sexual abuse of children.

I stared at my plate and felt sick to my stomach. Tony was a priest? It couldn't be true, yet it had to be. Dennis wouldn't have brought it up unless he knew for sure. Why hadn't he stopped me from leaving with Tony then? He was too busy having fun was the answer. I'd left the three of them dancing at Oz at two-thirty. They were doing coke or crystal or whatever it was that required them to make frequent trips to the stalls in the bathroom, and by two-thirty I was tired of that scene, tired of the sweaty boys dancing mindlessly with their shirts off, the loud music that required screaming to be heard over, and so I just walked out of the bar and up Bourbon Street to Lafitte's. I got a beer, went upstairs and out onto the balcony.

Which is where I ran into Tony.

I'd seen him around before, of course. He looked to be in his late thirties, maybe a well-preserved early forties. Pure-blood Italian, with the round brown eyes and the dark skin and the pitch-black hair. There was a slight touch of white at the start of his part, violently contrasting against the dark. His body was thick and solid, and he always wore tight shirts that emphasized the strength of his arms and the thickness of his chest. I'd made eye contact with him once or twice, and he's always returned my smile, encouragingly. But I was always too nervous to approach him, kept hoping he'd follow up on the smile, but he never did.

Until last night.

The balcony was deserted when I'd walked out there, which was fine with me; I didn't want to be around people. The night air was close, heavy, and uncomfortable. The thicker smell of grease hung like a film in the air from the Clover Grill across the street. I could see through their plate-glass windows that every table was full, and all the stools at the counter were taken. All I'd eaten for dinner was a salad I'd bought prepackaged at the A&P on Royal Street, with lettuce that was starting to wilt and turn brown and baby carrots that were starting to soften. My stomach growled, and I decided to answer the call of the grease. As soon as things died down at the Clover, I'd go over and have a mushroom bacon cheeseburger. It would mean an extra step-class next week, but I didn't care. It sounded good and I wanted one.

"Nice night," said a voice from behind me. I hadn't heard the door open. I turned and there he was, in the reflected light off of Bourbon Street, with his black hair with the touch of white, those beautiful soulful round brown eyes, the arms and pecs bulging out of a white ribbed tank top.

"I'm talking to you, Brian, hello?" Dennis' voice cut into my reverie. Startled yet again, I almost spilled my coffee. I could feel my face reddening.

"Relax, Dennis." Travers smiled at me and the shot a look at Dennis that had annihilated many a heckler during a Uneeda Biscuit performance. "Isn't it enough that you broke her heart already this morning? Do you have to be so beastly rude on top of that?" He patted my hand. "There, there, darling. Pay no attention to your evil stepmother."

"I asked you if you were going to see Tony again." Dennis' eyes were wide open, eyebrows up, forehead wrinkled, lips pouting. I looked at Rodger, who was avoiding my eyes. No help there. Travers was putting sugar into his coffee and determinedly looking into the cup. Maybe he was looking for grounds to read. I shrugged. "I guess I'll decide that if he calls me."

"HE didn't give you his number?" Rodger looked at me with disapproval. "Always get their number, Brian."

"What's he going to do, give the number for the Archdiocese?" Dennis exploded. Again, all eyes in the restaurant were on our table. I hated it when Dennis did things like that. His need to be the center of attention sometimes bordered on the pathological. He's only being overprotective because he cares, I told myself while I mentally calmed down. Being yelled at always made the bottom of my stomach drop out, my body temperature rise, and my voice along with it. Unlike Dennis, I don't enjoy public scenes.

"Fuck off, Dennis," Travers' voice lilted and drawled. But it wasn't Travers speaking, it was Uneeda. Travers switched between personas so gracefully and with such ease that I sometimes wondered if he had multiple personality disorder. "No one died and made you protector of Brian's virtue." His left eyelid slid down in a wink at me. "Such as it is."

"I'm sorry for shouting," Dennis said meekly to Rodger. Not to me. Never to me. He never apologized to me. It isn't as though he behaved so nicely to me that he never needed to, it was just always left unspoken. He would take me out to lunch; he would buy me a new shirt that would look "hot" on me or new workout clothes or something for the apartment; he would take me to a movie—but he would never say he was sorry. I don't know why he had such a block. But I do know he never spent money on Rodger or Travers. Ever. Not even on their birthdays. He would go down to the Marigny Bookstore and buy them a card with a scantily clad muscle stud on it, but never a gift. Never a celebratory cocktail. He looked at me. The waiter was refilling my coffee. "I don't understand why you won't have a Bloody Mary with us," he commented. He sounded curious rather than in attack mode. I just shrugged. "Are you going to go out with him again if he calls?"

"I don't know." I didn't know. What kind of future was there in a relationship with a priest? Weren't nuns supposed to be brides of Christ? Wouldn't that make priests husbands of the church? That was all I needed, to cheat on God. I wasn't Catholic, so I didn't believe in vows of celibacy. I was raised in a Protestant sect so militant in its beliefs that musical instruments weren't allowed in the church building. I had been brainwashed from birth to believe in the ethic of work, of tithing twenty percent of all income, and spending the rest of your time either studying the Bible or spreading the word of God to all non-believers. Catholics were sinful idolaters to be avoided unless they could be converted.

"I think it's kind of romantic, like Richard Chamberlain and Rachel What's-her-name in *The Thorn Birds*," said Travers. He was still talking like Uneeda. "A priest torn between his great earthly love and his love for God."

Dennis snorted and polished off his Bloody Mary. "Yeah, and look how that turned out!" He lit a cigarette. "And don't fool yourself— Father Ralph was torn between his ambition and his lust for Meggie. Love for either God or her didn't enter into it at all."

I wasn't in love with Tony. Father Tony. I tried picturing him in his clerical collar. It was easy enough to do. Was that where he was now, conducting mass in one of the many Catholic churches in the city? Passing out the Communion wafers while a boys' choir sang in their high voices, standing before an altar, Christ hanging, bloody and dying, on a cross behind him?

We had talked for a while on the balcony before we left the bar together. I couldn't really remember what about. But I could remember, through the fog induced by too much beer, that we had laughed and joked and cautiously, exploratorily touched before I asked him back to my apartment. Once we were there, inside, the door shut tightly behind us, we had kissed. His body was hard, unyielding to the touch. His torso was almost completely hairless except for a wiry patch in the direct center of his chest, which led to a thin trail that led to his navel and the thick patch at his pubis. His touch was gentle. His lips were soft, and he moved slowly, softly, in no hurry to bring either of us to a climax. He wasn't like the others I had brought home: hurried, desperate to come and then clean up, pulling their clothes on as though afraid of overstaying, perhaps to turn into pumpkins at the next stroke of the clock if they weren't gone, the mad dash to get out and away, to escape, before a conversation might turn serious or might even begin, other than saying "thank you," trying so desperately to get away through the door and into the night. I had lain in bed with Tony, our bodies entwined afterward in an intimacy that had felt nice, romantic, as though there had been more to it than just a frenzied animalistic coupling. It had been nice. I had lain there, his strong arms around me, thinking, "this is nice", thinking how nice it would be to wake up this way every day, how nice it would be to go to sleep like this every night, and then I had fallen asleep, to wake to an empty bed that still smelled vaguely of him, Tony, my trick, my lover—-

My priest.

"How was the sex?" Rodger asked as our waiter put the check down on the table.

"Nice." I said without thinking. "It was nice."

It had been nice. Yes, very nice. But it would remain that, a nice memory. I knew that. He wouldn't call. How could he? How could he come back to my bed again? We couldn't date. There was no possible future for the two of us. I looked across the table at Dennis. My best friend. Trying to save me from getting hurt. That was what was behind it all. That was why he told me, so I wouldn't have hope—hope that he would call, that we had a future together, turning it all into a romantic fantasy that would slowly begin to fade away into pain and hurt and rejection. I'd played that game too many times already. I looked at my friends. Rodger's freckled face as he counted out crumpled bills for his share of the check. Travers/Uneeda examining his long manicured nails.

"I've got yours, Brian." Dennis winked at me and smiled.

I smiled back. Apology accepted. "Thanks, babe."

We would all go back home from here, to take naps before heading out to Sunday Tea Dance. Uneeda was performing that night at the Parade, debuting a new number. We would be there, to cheer and applaud her as she performed to a remix of the latest Mariah Carey ballad, lip-syncing her heart out. Rodger would be avoiding his ex like always, trying to look like he was having the time of his life and his heart wasn't still aching. And Dennis?

Dennis wouldn't leave my side. He would buy my beers, dance with me, be overly solicitous to the point that people would think we were a couple, only he would be pointing out men to me, filling my head with all the gossip he knew about them, trying to decide if they were in fact good enough for me. Doing everything he could to mend my broken heart, to forget about Tony.

Father Tony.

We left the money on the table and walked outside. Dennis put his arm around my waist and I leaned into him. Uneeda was talking about her new number. Rodger asked the appropriate questions, little more than a word here or two there, just enough to keep her talking. Dennis and I dropped back a little.

"You okay?" he whispered.

"Yeah. Fine."

"Here's what we'll do today," and started laying out the rest of our day for me as we walked home.

Greg Herren

Greg Herren is the author of two novels, *Murder in the Rue Dauphine* and *Bourbon Street Blues*, as well as editor of the anthologies *Full Body Contact* and *Shadows of the Night*. He lives, writes, works, and plays in Sodom by the River, aka New Orleans. Formerly editor of *The Lambda Book Report,* he is now a contributing editor to that publication. His stories, literary criticism, and essays have been published in a wide variety of publications, from the anthology *Rebel Yell 2* to *Men* magazine. He can be reached at gregh121@aol.com.

An Encounter With The Sibyl

Felice Picano

I had become separated from the group of tourists in yet another of those interminable villages in the Tuscan hills when I turned a sudden vine-clustered wall and happened upon a tiny piazza. The past frantic twenty minutes I'd been threading my way through a high-walled labyrinth of narrow alleys, where every door seemed bolted shut and the lowest windows began some ten feet above my head, shielded from view by fractious-looking bushes. So the little open area I now happened upon was more than a mere opening out—it was a veritable expostulation!

Hardly larger than a tennis court, the little piazza, like the rest of the now nameless town—for in my panic, I'd forgotten its name—was surrounded by tall, tottering, umber brick walls. But as I stumbled out of deep shadow and into the glare of the late May mid-afternoon, I saw that one wall was lower than the others, indeed only thigh-high, capped with rough-hewn flower boxes, carnival with copious geraniums. And beyond the little wall and gala scarlet blossoms ... beyond was an astounding view from a great height: the depths, the widths of an unsuspected valley, traveling ahead so ruler straight, and for so distant a passage, I swore that if I squinted, I'd be able to make out the Tyrrhenian's triple-blue coast waters.

More surprising still, the piazzetta was inhabited and made use of. Since I'd left the others, I'd not seen a soul: not a grandmother lounging upon a towering windowsill, not a mongrel sunning amid the gnarled olives that eclipsed every tiny plot of garden. Along the view-end of the piazza, a miniature cafe had been erected: a mere three or four spindly white metal tables with elegant matching chairs, seemingly from some long-shuttered hotel—my only hint in the barbarous town

of a more elaborate way of life. A single octagonal fluttering tutti-frut-
ti umbrella had been raised between two tables. Grottoed within its
shade sat the oddest beautiful people I'd ever seen.

Either of them would attract notice on the busy modern thoroughfare of any metropolis. Because the young woman was in profile
to me, I suppose I noticed her first: her long neck; her honey skin; her
heavily lidded sloe-eyes; her nose, which while not quite aquiline, suggested Senecan tragedies; her full, unparted lips; the tiny brushes of
golden hair scalloped around her ear; the close fit of her oversized
bone-colored, raffia sun hat. She was sensual and chaste: all flesh yet
as though carved of alabaster; such a curious melange I'm afraid I
stared, rudely, astonished that she could also possess mobility. She
stretched a long, fine-fingered hand before herself as though in bene-
diction, or admiring her fingernails, and as she did, she caught not only
my eye, but that of her companion opposite and her lips moved.

She'd addressed a young man whose smashed gray fedora had
been tilted askew, framing in a nimbus of ash felt a richly colored, chiseled perfection. True, his nose was slightly snub for so refined a har-
mony, his lips fuller if possible than the woman's, his eyes more deeply
set, the shallow triangle of teeth open to view excessively white against
his tanned skin. Even within the shade of his hat brim, his eyes flickered darkly as he unconsciously lifted a hand in gesture to me, as
though encompassing the vista, reminding me of one of those burghers
of old Flanders, painted as an afterthought at the extremities of a vast
triptych, some merchant who sponsored the artist, and was thus allowed
to eternally present his city—minuscule in the background of some stu-
pendously dramatic, infinitesimally detailed Deposition From the
Cross.

The slightly over-elegant gestures of the two, as well as the evidence of napery, china and glassware, suggested a meal consummated,
and dawdling, as though neither wished to make a decision to move. At
first, I thought them siblings because of their strong resemblance in
beauty, then lovers from their languorous and wordless communication.
Until I noticed the third member of their party.

No wonder I had missed this figure, so ensconced was it in the
shell of a high, hooded, wickerwork chair. At first, all I could discern of
a personage was cloth, as though linens and pillows had been enthusi-
astically plumped and allowed to softly deflate.

In that moment of trying to make out the figure inside the hooded chair (for I'd convinced myself that it was a person), a very small peasant woman came into view on the piazza. She was quite round and wide-faced, with ebony hair pulled back into a doubly braided bun, mounted upon the back of her head like a spare tire upon the side fender of a Rolls Royce Phantom. Even more amazing was her costume, one almost parodistic in color and cut, it made her so much the tour guide's *contadina*. She'd stepped out of a double door from which she must have seen me stagger into the piazza and addressed me.

"*'Giorno, Signor. Voi rifrescarlei!*"

Her plump hand swept toward the tables, offering me a seat. Her words of welcome drew forth slow turns from the Etruscan couple.

When I didn't immediately answer her offer to refresh myself, she added brightly, "*Noi siamo molto gentile,*" attempting I guess to reassure me. Instead, she confused me further. Who of us, I wondered, were very civilized? She and I? Or the other three?

I took a seat at the only other already set table, sharing the umbrella a bit, and the taverna owner—for that was whom I supposed the plump woman to be—nodded in approval and after asking if I were hungry, and not waiting for a response, obliged me with an oral menu: pasta and risotto of the day, coffee, *gelati di noce*, and *delice*.

Thinking I would rest here a minute before venturing down into the aberrant little town again and attempting to locate the others, I ordered coffee—with milk, so I wouldn't receive the standard bitter, dark double sip of espresso.

"*Niente di mangiar?*" she asked appalled, as if I'd asked to drink blood.

I wasn't hungry. Couldn't eat a thing. Then, fatigue taking over, my little bit of Italian by now spent, I added in English, "Just something to drink."

The woman with the exquisite profile moved an inch to look at me better.

"She asks what food you will take," her companion said, turning in his chair just enough that I knew I was being addressed. He concluded by favoring me with the slightest hint of smile: it devastated me.

"Is it required?" I fumbled back at him.

The peasant woman waited, her apron edge twisting in her fingers.

"Not required," he allowed, and I couldn't for the life of me place his accent, which didn't match any I'd heard so far in this country. "Yet," he went on, and seemed at a loss.

"Yet preferred?" I tried.

He bowed almost imperceptibly in my direction, then smiled more fully. The pearly gates opened, irradiating the piazza, dazzling me.

"If I must eat … then … anything!" I said, casting my gustatory destiny to the winds that played with the stranger's lapels. To the woman waiting, I said, "Anything sweet. Anything but chocolate," I tacked on, as an afterthought.

A soft sputter of what I assumed to be a dialect of Italian between the man and the peasant woman conveyed the information. The *contadina* curtsied in our general direction and flounced off, like a dismissed *comprimario*.

"May I ask," his ravishing companion suddenly spoke up, "why not chocolate? Have we not heard it scientifically proven that chocolate is the food of love?"

Her accent was identical to his, and perfectly inscrutable, her voice as dusky in contralto as his had been burnished in baritone.

Under differing circumstances I might have disputed her statement, but I was weary and unwilling to extend myself. "I'm allergic to chocolate."

In truth, I liked chocolate as much as the next person, but the Italians' use of it so far in my trip had sated my limited palate for the stuff. I'd not eaten a chocolate I was comfortable with since I'd crossed the Grand Corniche into the country.

"Allergic? Exactly how allergic?" I heard twitter from the depth of the hooded wicker chair in a thin, high voice with a pure American accent, startling its directness.

"I get fevers," I fibbed.

"Hives too?" she asked primly.

"Not for years, no."

"Red streaks on your arms? Rashes on your abdomen? Blotches on your bottom?"

"Sometimes."

"High fevers?" she probed.

"Low but insistent."

"A dry mouth?"

"It's been so long since I …"

She ignored the attempt at qualification. "You see, Ercole. All the symptoms," and she seemed to subside back into the pillows of the wicker-work in what I was forced to assume was hypoallergenic musing. In the enfolding silence—striking by the absence of birdsong—I thought of the rising pitch of her interrogation, and the name by which she had called him. Something classical, no? Hercules? Yes. And the young woman then would be whom? Dejaneira? Diana? Aphrodite?

I must have muttered the last name aloud, in Italian.

"No, no!" the young woman laughed.

Ercole now motioned to me, clearly asking me to join them.

"American," the still nameless lovely young woman said, rather than asked when I took the fourth seat at their table. She swanned a long tanned wrist at me, and I took her hand, unsure whether to kiss it. The air around us smelled of almonds—almonds, spun sugar, something vaguely metallic. I took the soft hand, and she looked at me from within the striated illumination of her sun-hat.

This close, her eyes were rounder, hazel, green, golden: no, the same cream color of those long bars of *ciocolata* Jesu sold on the Via Urbana in Rome.

"The Grandmama believes it is a sign of old nobility to be allergic to chocolate," she now said, amused. "Having blue-blood. We—Ercole and myself—we eat liters of it. She laughed, sharing the secret with him, and I would have given her the keys to my house to hear that laugh again.

So charmed by her, and by the fact of the heap of white skin, white hair and bones I could now just make out among the purple material of the wicker chair, that I missed their names in the long liquidity of Ercole's "Pardon me to introduce ourselves, etc." I did regain presence of mind just long enough to register that he called the old woman "Principessa Someone or other."

Our waitress returned carrying a tray of milky looking drinks in tall mauve coolers, each glass set within a chased silver holder sculpted in relief, so that frolicking Nereids barely fended off the advance of amorous Tritons, all of them about to be swallowed by wide-mouthed, rather jovial looking, sea serpents. They looked old and valuable. Where was my coffee?

I turned to ask if one of these were it, and was interrupted by

Ercole, smooth as glass, saying, "Better than the coffee you ordered, signor. A dessert and drink in one."

I prodded it with a Bronzino-thin merman of a spoon, and sipped. "Amaretto?"

"Amaretto, yes," a touch of eagerness in his voice, "Something else too."

"Brandy? *Eau de vie de Poire*, perhaps?" I hadn't a clue.

"It is quite special," the young woman said, pointing to the old Principessa's nearly non-existent lap where I now made out a mauve glass flask, the same tint as the coolers, and like them encased in a chased silver carrier with nautical allegories.

"Absinthe?" I tried, half-joking.

They laughed and shook their head no, and I laughed, a bit bleakly, I admit, wondering if I were being slipped a Mickey, or if Ercole had mentioned, among that long list of surnames I'd scarcely listened to, the name Borgia.

"This is your first time here," the young woman asked, changing the subject. "You are here on vacation as a tourist? Or to study?"

"A little of both."

"You pardon my curiosity?"

She might have asked me the number of my bank account, and although it was so depleted now it would hardly matter, I still would have gladly given it.

"And you adore the country?" she enthused softly.

Well...." I began, and stopped.

Manners decreed that I ought to say yes, certainly, I adored their country. But the truth was a bit more complex. Not that it wasn't altogether lovely to look at, so many beautiful places and things to see. But I was more or less alone in Italy—and that seemed to make all the difference, didn't it? Unable to see Italy with Sarah, I was somewhat lost, even forlorn.

I ought to note here immediately that we'd had no falling out and that Sarah had abandoned me suddenly, without warning, two weeks before, outside of Monaco. She'd simply asked me to stop the Renault, and she'd stepped out, grabbed her two pieces of luggage out of the back seat where she'd placed them that morning at our pension in Nice, and she'd walked into the little train station and onto the steps of waiting train, taking her back to Paris. All without a word or a hint of explanation.

I'd still not gotten over her doing it, nor even worse, her utter calm in doing it. How she'd met the train precisely on time, how she'd known precisely where I had to stop for her to catch it. (Had she planned in the pension the night before, as I'd written out postcards, as I'd slept? She must have!) How she left me without a hint of complaint, or kiss or word of good-bye. I'd thought our trip together, our being together, heaven. How could she have thought differently? What could I have done to so alienate her? To not even deserve an explanation?

Once Sarah and the train were gone in the other direction, I sat in the rented car until the train barrier was lifted from the road in front of me. The cars behind me honked for me to move on and so I did. I drove to Florence, just as we'd planned, Sarah and I, in our carefully mapped-out itinerary, made months ago on the front lawn of her father's bayfront summer house.

I'd then continued to travel though Italy, following that itinerary. Not as though Sarah were still with me, naturally, but as though I couldn't admit that she was gone. I suppose, in some way, I expected to be stopped at another crossroads or train trestle and have Sarah, as suddenly, step out of a car with her two pieces of luggage and hop right into the Renault again, to continue our journey, without a hint of explanation. That would be unlike her, of course. But what she'd already done was so utterly unlike her, what difference would that make? And should that occur, I'd never ask for an explanation either.

I kept to our plan. I stayed at our decided-upon pensiones. I walked the foreplanned narrow alleys of Florence, purchased silver stuffs and tooled leather book jackets on the Ponte Vecchio exactly as we said we would, and I mailed them home in neat parcels from the American Express office near the Spanish Steps a week later, to announce my arrival in Rome. No letter, not a hint of a note to our parents about what had happened.

Once, only once in those weeks did the full realization of Sarah's deed impinge upon me fully—sickeningly. I was sipping Pernod and water and picking at some local variation of Nesselrode pie in an outdoor cafe on the Via Veneto. It was sunset, and all Rome appeared bathed in the final hot flush of twilight. Up the via, the Borghese Gardens had already flamed up and dimmed into moody shadows. But a small street perfectly perpendicular to where I sat was an eye-hurting red-orange, as though that half of the city was engulfed in fire.

The cafe was sparsely peopled as most Romans were returned to work or home after their mid-afternoon siestas. But a lovely young Scandinavian woman swerved off the via into the cafe and sat opposite me. She spoke in what I took to be Norwegian.

When I tried to tell her I didn't understand a word, she reached into a colorful woven carryall, and pulled out a dozen or so frothy-looking cookies, each wrapped in tissue paper. She unwrapped each sweet, popped it into her mouth, and offered me a few too, which I enjoyed. When we'd eaten them all, she lined up the parti-colored tissues on the edge of the table, crushed each in such a way it stood up, struck a match, and set fire to its upper tip. First one, then all the other papers lifted up off the table as they burned, flaming as they fluttered, rising a foot or more perfectly vertical in the air, and evaporating into lilac-colored smoke; not a jot of ash descended. Then she stood up and without a word walked off.

I was so delighted by the little performance, and the mystery of the papers rising as they burned, that I turned to my left and said, "Wasn't that strange and wonderful and exactly what you would have wanted to happen at dusk on the Via Veneto?" … And Sarah wasn't there.

Of course not. She hadn't been there in some time.

I remember seeing a documentary film about the Eichmann trial in Jerusalem, some years before. At one point, an accuser suddenly stops testifying. Holding onto the edge of the podium, the witness looks around the courtroom, then slides off, crumpling onto the floor, as men rush to his side. Explaining the incident to the camera later on in the film, the man—who'd suffered everything short of death in one of the Nazi camps—explained, "I realized all of a sudden that Eichmann was just a man. Only a man. But if one man could do that, well, then any man could. I could too. You too."

Something on the order of his sudden realization leading to an instant and overpowering emotion happened to me at that cafe table. William James called it a "vastation," a lovely turn-of-the-century word, don't you think? I stood up to leave the table and I realized not only that Sarah was not with me, hadn't been with me, and would probably never again be with me, but that I was alone: in Rome, in the world, in the universe, and I would probably always be alone. I reacted as that Polish Jew at the trial had, as William James said that he and his father before him had done: I fainted back into my chair.

Amazingly, I didn't hurt myself, and I came to soon after, thanks to the ministrations of the waiters.

That night, I didn't follow the itinerary Sarah and I had planned for our third night in the city—the Coliseum by moonlight (we'd even checked to be certain it would be a full moon), followed by dancing in one of the ancient Roman baths converted into a discotheque. Instead I remained in the room of my pensione and I pondered. I slept poorly. The morning following that, I checked out, obtained a road map, and left Rome for the hills, deliberately headed north and east, when our plan had meant for us to go south, to Naples and Capri.

From then on I would follow no itinerary. I would wander. I'd drive around at large, waste time, try to discover what I had done so wrong that Sarah had walked away from me without a word. Failing that, I would be miserable.

I'd left Rome two days before and I still remained haunted by questions. Earlier this morning, I'd awakened in a hotel in Lucca, walked out onto the terrace where a half-dozen other Americans happened to be breakfasting, and allowed myself to be talked into being part of their group on their visit to this particular town—Spiegato, was it? No, that meant mirror, didn't it?

Whatever its name, the town was completely off the beaten track for tourists and contained, they assured me, but a single attraction, an underground basilica dating from early Christian times. The Americans weren't a church group, so I never discovered why exactly they'd hit on this specific village and its single feature. But so they had. I'd followed their van for a few kilometers then lost them. Once arrived, I'd circumnavigated the lower part of the little place in fruitless search of the tour group, their ecru van, the ruins, or anything at all interesting. One time, I'd thought I'd seen two from the group strolling high up a road too narrow for the Renault to traverse, so I'd parked, and followed them on foot, and eventually arrived here.

"No?" the beautiful woman questioned me. "You don't at all adore our country. Not even a little?"

"Right now I do," I allowed. "Here. Now."

"Ah!" relief flooded her face, sending her from a momentary anxiety, leaning forward across the table toward me, back into her chair back smiling.

"He likes the place fine. He has a dilemma."

The accent of the sentences was American. Rather specifically, New England-sharp American. And the voice had issued from the depths of the hooded chair.

"Grandmama hears great sadness in your voice," the young woman said. I wondered if the old Principessa were blind, but didn't dare look closely at her to check.

"Hesitations," Ercole added. "A tragedy, perhaps!" He said it not to me, but to the air.

"No. No tragedy," the prim old voice declared with utter certainty.

If this was the family's idea of social chatter, I found it peculiar indeed. Even more peculiar when the old woman spoke again:

"She's gone back to Paris. To the man who seduced her."

I sputtered into my drink.

"You didn't know?" she went on. "It happened in an elevator. One of those large, over-elaborate pneumatic lifts. But he'll soon throw her over, of course. Her name begins with an S. Sandra. Susan...."

"Sarah!" I said, despite myself.

"Sarah, yes. Forget Sarah. You never belonged with Sarah. It was not a mistake, but mere propinquity. You'll do far better in life without her. Far better in all ways."

"That's hardly possible. Her family's terribly affluent. Whereas I ...."

"Please," Ercole softly tapped my fingers still. "Do not contradict." He put a finger to his lips. When I looked at his female companion, she too had a finger to her lips, and she even winked at me. Meaning what? That I was to humor the old woman?

"Your fortune, when it comes, " the old Principessa went on, "will be far more considerable than poor Sarah's. It is linked to a man. A man you haven't yet met. You'll encounter him in the corridor of railroad sleeper."

She paused, or fell silent.

As though she hadn't spoken at all, the others smiled, sipped their drinks. When the young woman spoke again, it was to say, "Tourists seldom find their way to our charming little piazza," which, following what the old woman had uttered, was a trifle banal.

She looked to me for response, as did Ercole. Unnerved by the sham conversation, I still managed to get out: "Too bad, as it's a spectacular lookout."

"Ercole said before that he thought he heard others also coming," she pointed to the steeply sloping road I'd clambered.

"A tour group. Searching for some ancient basilica," I explained. "You   know   it?"

They didn't seem to. "Few find their way here," Ercole said, I thought almost sadly. "Were you looking for the basilica yourself? Or for the others?"

"I'm not really sure what I was looking for," I admitted. "You live here?"

"Oh, no," the young woman answered with a laugh, as though a spectacular view, like too many sweets, simply wouldn't do. "Nearby."

"In a palazzo?" I wondered. I would look it up later in the guidebook.

"A very small palazzo," she admitted, playfully stroking my fingers. Meaning I'd be unlikely to find it listed, nor thereby discover the ancient Principessa's name.

I was about to ask where the little palazzo was located, not that I was trying to inveigle an invitation, when the old woman began speaking again.

"The man in the sleeping car will be immensely wealthy, extraordinarily powerful, and vastly influential. He will take an immediate and consuming interest in you. You will rebuff him, but he will persist. Finally, you will agree to dine with him."

What she said seemed so unlikely, so absurd even, that I let her words wash over me, uncontested. After all, I had this lovely company, this view, this marvelous drink—whatever it might be.

The old woman seemed to chuckle, "Just at the moment that you do decide to throw your lot in with his, the man will make certain demands of you." She laughed in a particularly smarmy manner, all the more lubricious coming from someone so proper. "Ah, how shame will blossom on your young cheeks as you perform what he requires of you. First shame. Then acquiescence. And finally, delight in your sordidness."

Well, really!

"I don't quite see the point in …," I tried.

Ercole and his companion hushed me.

"You'll think it sordid," the old woman said. "I, of course, make no such moral judgments. You, however, will think it very low. And you will then enjoy it all the more for how low you think it."

Her voice had grown weaker, her words softer.

"He will transform your life....," she added, by now in a whisper. "And eventually ... you'll come to ... thank him....To thank ... this ... Sandra ... Sarah ... even ... more.... " Her words trailed off.

I was suddenly aware of the sound of my breathing. I suppose I was waiting—dreading was more like it—for her to start up again.

When Ercole began to speak, I was almost rude in hushing him.

"No, my friend," he insisted gently. "No more will she speak. Now, Grandmamma sleeps."

Indeed, her light, irregular snoring could soon be heard, made the more resonant by her hooded chair. I was both relieved and, I admit now, disappointed. I'd wanted her to go on, to say more, balderdash though it seemed.

After several minutes more of silence, Ercole rose like a column of smoke, and appeared to float to the flower boxes atop the low wall that overlooked the valley.

As though she'd been watching from indoors, awaiting this very move, the peasant woman who served us appeared again and began to clear the table. As she worked, she sang a lilting, wordless, little tune.

Ercole's companion arose as liquidly as he had, and also, from awkwardness I guess, so did I. She strode over to where he stood and slid a tanned arm over his shoulder. Brother and sister—or were they cousins? lovers?—remained still and silent, out of reach of my many questions, looking over the magnificent valley. When they turned and separated, Ercole went directly to the wicker-work chair, which I only then noticed was mounted upon wheels. He tilted the chair gently, waiting. His companion came to where I stood.

I have to admit I was still so perplexed by the old woman, and even more by the suddenness of their departure, I thought I must ask at least one more question: any one would do, as long as it were answered.

"In the flask?" I asked. "What was it we drank?"

"Water. From a spring near our little palazzo," she laughed and moved away from me in a flutter of soft clothing across the piazza, toward a large, pre-war limousine I'd not registered as present until that very moment. It's huge back door was open, its darkly clad driver stood against the sweeping side fender, his hat-brim shadowing his face.

"*Ciao*"s were tossed at me, and answered by the peasant woman, busily folding up the big umbrella and wiping off the table. Any thoughts of payment seemed redundant.

The driver, Ercole, his companion, the wicker wheelchair and its occupant were all inside the car before I could move. The car doors were closed and the limo seemed to glide down the narrow hilltop street, vanishing in a silken putter.

"*Fortunato lei*," the peasant woman approached me. Lucky me.

When I asked her why, she pulled down the lid of one eye with a finger—a gesture I thought astonishingly odd—and replied, "*Parla La Cumaia.*"

"*La Cumadre?*" I asked back, not certain I'd heard her correctly, wondering if she meant that I was lucky to have spoken to the Principessa, who was her *cumadre*, some sort of honored relation.

"*No, no,*" she corrected, and repeated, "*La Cumaia,*" syllable by syllable. As I was still baffled, she shrugged, and still humming that careless tune, she went back inside.

I remained at the parapet, looking over the noble prospect another five minutes or so, embarrassment rising inside me. That Commedia dell' Arte gesture of the peasant woman, the absurd questions about chocolate, and finally the old woman's obvious delectation in spelling out in some detail an unsavory future for her own countryman—it all seemed some elaborate and tasteless joke, with myself the unwitting victim.

To hell with her! With all of them! Beautiful or not!

I traipsed angrily out of the pizza, and stumbled back down through the town. I didn't encounter the tour group again, and didn't see another human being. When I located my Renault, I drove out of the mountains and west toward the seacoast, headed for Genoa. I don't know why exactly. I guess I just felt like getting away from these damned hills and their bizarre denizens.

Later that night, I arrived at the pensione where I'd planned to be with Sarah. Although I was five days earlier than my reservation, they took me in. They also handed me a letter from Paris. Sarah had to leave me, she wrote, and she had to live her own life at last. She couldn't continue living a lie. She adored Eugen. She liked me as a friend. She hoped she hadn't ruined Italy for me. She would try to explain it all to me more fully someday.

After dinner, I went to an American movie playing nearby. It was subtitled in English, which I thought odd, but that dose of pure, unaccented English made me feel considerably better somehow. It also convinced me that I'd had enough of Europe for a while. It was time to go home.

On my way out of the cinema, I passed, then walked back to and into, a bookstore. To my surprise, I found some not too dated American newspapers and even a magazine. I scooped them up greedily, feeling a bit less homesick. I was now certain everything would be better when I left Italy. Sarah could do whatever she wanted, with Eugen or with whomever. I no longer cared.

About that, at least, the old woman had been right: Sarah and I didn't really belong together. We'd simply been thrown together early on in our lives and had hit it off and little by little we'd been persuaded by others that we were a couple, eventually persuading ourselves and each other that we belonged together and ought to be married. Why? We'd never been madly—not even tepidly—in love. Merely comfortable together. That might be fine if we were forty-five years old, or seventy-five. We were still young. There was nothing to stop either of us from having a perfectly marvelous life apart. And if I had been betrayed by her, well, better now than after we married. I would return home a "wronged man"—never a bad position to be in. And, after all, it was a new experience being dumped. One of many experiences I hoped to now acquire.

I'd paid for the magazine and papers and almost stepped out of the bookstore when I recalled the word the peasant woman had used to refer to the Principessa. My Italian had never been more than barely utile, but I was curious. I asked a clerk for and was shown to a large Italian-English dictionary.

"*La Cumaia*," it read. "The Cumaean. Said of a prophetess. Female seer. Specifically, the Cumaean Sibyl of ancient times mentioned by Virgil and Ovid." Still wondering, I asked the clerk in Italian how commonly used that word was in his language.

Not common at all, he replied. "Strega" was usually used, and sometimes, the higher-toned "Sibylla," the latter now considered antiquated, heard only in Donizetti operas. My word, he pedantically informed me, was rare. A particular seer so ancient, he assured me, that in Virgil's epic, she had prophesied to Aeneas—fleeing the destruction of Troy—that his descendants would go on to found the city of Rome.

That was all I needed to hear. The old Principessa might be a hair sensitive; I'd even allow that she was slightly psychic—she was not over three thousand years old.

Edified, if unsatisfied, I left the bookstore planning to spend the night in my pensione, reading American periodicals. Passing a kiosk just closing for the night, I made an impulsive purchase of a bar of Cadbury's with almonds. I'd already eaten it when I got to my room. I crumpled the foil wrapper as I entered, tossing it in a high arc into a distant wastebasket. This first return of high spirits cheered me, and I fell asleep an hour later, newspapers splayed over my blankets.

I awakened about four in the morning with the strangest sensations: my mouth was parched; I had a slight headache. My forehead was beaded in sweat from what seemed to be a low-grade fever. I itched in various places on my body—my forearms, around my breastbone, across my backside. No nausea: nothing remotely severe enough to be called food poisoning, never mind enough to dream of awakening the staff and trying to find a doctor at that hour of the night. But I was terrifically thirsty and I felt distinctly weird. When I got up to drink water, I noticed in the light above the antique washstand that I had red welts on my chest, rashes on both arms, and yes, when I checked, blotches on my bottom.

But I'd been lying. I wasn't allergic to chocolate. At least, I hadn't been.

I tried to recall that inane, provocative conversation: the old woman's exact words in her sharp New Hampshire accent. Could she have somehow wished the allergy upon me? Inflicted it in some way, perhaps through the enigmatic drink her grandchildren—if that's what they really were, and not instead her confederates!—had given me?

Then I had an appalling thought: what if that about the allergy to chocolate had come true, because everything we'd said—all of us—in that magnificent spot, had to be true. And did that mean ... What exactly did it mean?

I took a tranquilizer and finally managed to get a few more hours sleep. The following morning I felt better: the symptoms were gone. I had to find out if what had happened was merely a hallucination of the night, so I ordered hot chocolate with my breakfast. Its fumes were enough to make of my mouth a miniature Sahara, to cause my arms to prickle, to cause me to begin to squirm in my seat. A sip would not be needed. Damn, if I weren't suddenly allergic to chocolate!

Great, I thought. I meet an antediluvian prophetess, the very one who foretold for old Aeneas, and what do I get? A new allergy!

I began to worry. Still, there are ways around predictions, aren't there? You can't, for example, meet someone in a train corridor if you aren't in a train, can you?

I was driving a car. Yet somehow, at the customs shed in Ventimiglia, at the French border, the next morning as I was leaving Italy, I looked in the glove compartment for my international driver's license, green card for European insurance, and rental car registration, and they were gone. The customs authorities impounded the Renault, and phoned the rental agency in Calais who told them yes, I'd rented it, but for two weeks not three and they needed it back immediately. The Italians held onto the keys.

I tried hitchhiking. Dangerous on that stretch of road where cars zoom out of long waits at customs. And also, as I quickly discovered, illegal. I barely escaped arrest.

Right near the customs shed was a train stop. Okay, I decided, taking the train would be all right. Only being in a sleeping car would fulfill her prophecy. This was a regular train. Seven cars consisting of seats only. I'd buy a cheap ticket to Paris.

Outside of Lyons, however, we stopped a while for several cars from another train, including a dining car, to be added on. As I'd missed lunch and it was approaching twilight, I decided to get something to eat. A conductor pointed the way, five cars straight ahead. It was only when I had opened the door and walked a half-dozen steps inside, that I realized that the third car, which must have been added on along with the dining car, was a sleeper. Panicked, I turned and began to rush back out. I ran right into the arms of Achille l'Extringnon, the Belgian electronics billionaire, who almost fell over.

We went to Paris. We dined together, as the Principessa said we would. And Achille offered me a position as his right-hand man in Brussels at an outrageously high salary, and I said I would think about it. I mean, after all, without Sarah, there was no real reason to return to the States immediately, was there? And I'd always been intrigued by electronics.

Naturally, I've done some serious thinking about this. Who wouldn't? And I've come to the conclusion that the old woman was only partly right. True, Achille may be unmarried, unattached, but he seems an honorable enough fellow and he doesn't seem to have the least ... how can I put it ... insalubrious intentions regarding me. Or if he does, he's so far kept them to himself.

At any rate, at dinner—and what a dinner!—I made my position clear. Or at least I think I did. Yes, I must have, and Achille seemed to accept it. Of course he's insistent in some ways. The hotel suite, for example: as I had nowhere to stay in Paris, he insisted on that, and it was quite nice, as I suppose all the suites at the Crillon are. And since he owns it—he seems to own a great many things—he wouldn't dream of letting me pay for the week we stayed. You know, things like that.

Otherwise it's great. Of course two little subjects still pestered me. Try as I might, I could no longer recall the old woman's precise wording—and I was sure that remembering her exact words contained the key to how I must handle myself with Achille. Second, of course, was that damned business about the chocolate. Some of the finest in the world are made in Belgium, and from the first, Achille sent boxes of the most scrumptious-looking delicacies: white and milk and bittersweet, with hazelnut and raspberry-cream and champagne-flavored fillings. Simply irresistible. I finally told him, "Take them back, I'm allergic." But Achille had a solution to that little problem, and after the briefest of medical tests by one of his doctor friends, I received antihistamines. At least I think he said they're antihistamines. Whatever they are, the pills work wonderfully well, and now that I've moved into Achille's palais in Belgium, I can eat all the chocolate truffles I want. In fact, the pills make me feel so generally good all the time that I take four a day, as prescribed, whether I plan to eat chocolate or not.

There he is at the door, now. I should go. He's got wonderful plans for us tonight. Every night, if you must know. It's beyond my dreams. Simply magical.... Oh, by the way, did I mention that I'm absolutely certain that once I've fully settled in here, I plan to meet some nice girl and fall in love?

Felice Picano

Felice Picano's first book was a finalist for the PEN/Hemingway Award. Since then he has published twenty volumes of fiction, poetry, non-fiction, and memoirs. Considered a founder of modern gay literature along with the other members of the Violet Quill Club, Picano also founded two publishing companies: the SeaHorse Press and Gay Presses of New York. Among his many award-winning books are the novels *Like People in History* and *The Book of Lies*. His most recent novel, *Onyx*, was published to acclaim in 2001. Picano's exhibit "Early Gay Presses of New York," debuted at the ONE Institute in Los Angeles and will tour the country. San Francisco's New Conservatory Theatre premiered Picano's new comedy-thriller, *The Bombay Trunk*.

The Real, True Angel

Robin Lippincott

They called him Angel and always had, the men in his many circles of friends over the years, though his Venetian-born parents, or rather his father—for he was the only one of the two who really cared—had christened him Angelo. But the members of the various circles called him Angel always, and the name was passed on from one group—member to member—to the next; Angel not because he looked "angelic"—his hair was not golden (nor haloed), though it did fall in ringlets; Angel not because he was a benevolent innocent from above (no messenger from God he); nor could his wiry body possibly be construed as cherubic. Instead, Angel's hair was black, a black so black it shone blue in sunlight, and his almost hairless skin was fair—the sheen in his hair somehow picking up on and bringing out the delicate blue veins that coursed just beneath the surface of that marvelous translucent skin. Most of the time he simply looked electric.

And to further disprove any possible corroboration whatsoever between name and deed (or being), it must be said that, dispositionally, Angel had an attraction to danger. Nevertheless, the men in the various circles over the years persisted in calling him Angel, and perhaps the easiest answer to the riddle why (other than the wildfire theory—that it had caught on, and spread) lay in man's sheer laziness: Angel, because it was an ever-so-slightly shortened version of Angelo, and thus one syllable less to roll off the old cow tongue. So Angel it was; the name had stuck. And the one thing about it that Angel said rang true to him, though he hadn't realized it until he was in his late 30s, was the fact that he had never, not once in his life, felt grounded, of this earth—though he longed to: The unbearable lightness of being indeed!

But in the love poetry of every age, the woman (or man) longs to be weighed down by the (other) man's body. The heaviest of burdens is therefore simultaneously an image of life's most intense fulfillment. The heavier the burden, the closer our lives come to the earth, the more real and truthful become.

Angel's age? That was not a simple matter either, but a subject of some debate. Angel himself claimed, in characteristic straightforward, no-nonsense fashion, that he was now fifty-eight, though few of the men in his ever-changing circle had believed him whenever he'd divulged his age, thinking that, instead of subtracting years—as most self-respecting homosexuals and women, and even a few heterosexual men, did, subtracting ten or, if they could be so bold, fifteen, or even twenty years from their true age (this latter mathematical feat one few but Angel could actually get away with)—Angel, they said, did just the opposite (as he had so often in his life); Angel, or so they conjectured, added years to his age—so that everyone would look at him and think, and perhaps even say, "My, you don't look fifty-eight."

But there it was, the unadulterated, undoctored proof, evidence— his Birth Certificate, or "Certificate of Live Birth" as it is still known in many cities and towns throughout the South, one copy filed away in the Bureau of Vital Statistics at the State Board of Health, the other tucked away only the devil knew where, now that Angel's father Giovanni had passed on:

Angelo D'Allura, born to Giovanni and Philomena D'Allura, in The City of New Orleans, in the State of Louisiana, in the Year of Our Lord, Nineteen Hundred and Thirty-Six.

But there was Angel's body, they said—for many if not most of those who knew him also knew (or had known) his body, intimately: there was no way *that* could be a fifty-eight-year-old body, so lean and taut and, excepting certain areas of the face—those soft, dark pockets beneath the eyes and the parenthetical marks around the mouth—so smooth and wrinkle-free (nor was his hair graying).

Angel was fifty-eight, he simply didn't look it, though he had certainly and unquestionably and fully lived each and every one of those years (months, weeks, days, hours...). After his first eighteen years, growing up in New Orleans (if such a synonym for maturity could be ascribed to anyone raised in that town), in the Garden District no less, where many of the houses, Angel had always said, looked as if they were made of wooden lace, he had moved to New York—Angel had lived in and known well some of the most cosmopolitan and exciting cities in the world, always searching for home, yearning for a base, a groundedness, a world beneath his feet. From Manhattan, where he'd stayed for the better part of a decade, after which he'd moved—naturally, or so it seemed, to everyone at the time, most of whom had or eventually would do the same—to Paris, where he had felt lightness the most (another decade); from there it was Amsterdam for a couple of years (which he'd soon tired of), then Rome, his parent's native Venice, London, and, since he'd been able to avoid Australia altogether (for despite all the brouhaha about Australian men, Angel knew, intuitively, that it was not for him), back stateside in the mid-80s—to San Francisco, to lovely, funky Provincetown, and finally, once again, to a heavier place, "home"—New Orleans, still searching. Which was how—as if logic or fate had played a hand in the unfolding and development of this absurd turn in the events of Angel's life story—how and perhaps why he ended up where he was this very morning, sitting on a cot in a New Orleans prison, his head in his hands, arrested and accused of pederasty.

The police report alleged that on the afternoon of Friday, June 5th at approximately 3:30 p.m., one Angelo D'Allura lured eight-year-old Sanders Parker, on the way home from his last day of school that year, into the old St. Louis Cemetery, and therein—and for the next hour, hidden amongst the above-ground tombs—committed "heinous sex crimes" upon the boy.

The charges would have been amusing were they not so serious, as anyone who knew Angel also knew just how ludicrous such allegations were: For not only had he never favored (or pursued) children—they would never be able to bring him down, weigh him down, to earth, and their minds were not complex enough, he said, for what he liked.

What he liked; his preferences: An *almost*-violent aspect to sex. Not S/M, not theater of any sort—no *accoutrement* necessary, but an exchange between two men that was nearly vampiric, volcanic, oceanic (name your synonym for size, power, depth), in its fathomless degree of passion and intensity. Sex was successful and thus enjoyable for

Angel if and only if the lover left some sort of physical evidence of that intensity on the beloved's body each and every time (it took *that* much for him to feel it and know it was real)—a bruised knee, a scraped arm, a cut, bloodied lip, nose, or ear, a sore, tender, even slightly torn nipple, a sensitive, swollen cock, a heart murmur....

And so it had come to this—after all the years, all that space, all those cities and all that life experience (*Non, je ne regrette rien*, Angel had often said)—a 12' x 12' jail cell (6' x 6' if you considered the fact that he was sharing it). But as in every city he had ever lived, Angel had friends, friends everywhere, in high places and in low, and he quickly set them to work, searching for an explanation as to what had happened to him and, more importantly, for his key to freedom. Disallowed bail and visitors (except his lawyer), Angel passed his first few days ruminating, remembering, and wrestling with the problem, the question, of who had set him up (never mind the why just now).

That he must have a few enemies in New Orleans Angel did not doubt, because he knew, too, that the natives did not look kindly upon one who left them, as Angel had those many years ago; nor do Southerners forgive and forget easily, Angel reasoned: Witness the Civil War. But who those enemies might be Angel could not guess. A relative, he supposed, would be the most obvious choice, given natural law, but only two remained in the City of New Orleans as far as he knew: His 98-year-old maternal grandmother, Sophia Orioli, and his Uncle Luigi, his father's younger brother, who had been drunk for at least the past forty or fifty years; and Angel had seen nor heard from neither of them since he'd left the city in 1954.

June 5th: Angel remembered the day well. Rain had fallen in sheets all that afternoon, much of which he spent in the company of another man, ducking in and out of dark churches (as the air smelled of copper and the architecturally appropriate copper itself slowly refined its greenish hue, like a sunbather working on his tan). And then, late in the day, the two of them had entered the old St. Louis Cemetery. Angel closed his eyes now and tried to remember, to picture the scene that day: Had he seen anyone, or anything, suspicious looking? Or could the other man, whom Angel had met only that morning, somehow have been involved? No—Angel trusted his instincts implicitly. A friend of the family's then? Angel wracked his brain and came up empty, and it was then that he realized, after several such days of considerable cogitation and aggressive self-questioning in general and more specifically from his lawyer, that for the sake of his mental health he would have to let it go, to leave it to his lawyer and to his friends to resolve. Looking around his cell now, at everything that was cold and sterile—the iron bars over the ice cube of a window (with neither green nor blue in sight), the metallic, lidless toilet, the creaky cots, even his cell mate was cold (pale and hairy)—Angel knew that if he was going to survive this, he would need to dream.... And, he told himself (intuition?) that perhaps a trip back in time would also help him discover how he had arrived at where he was, and who had sent him there.

Because he had had so many lovers and sexual experiences in the almost-forty-five years he'd been a player (yes, Angel had long sung the body electric!), his memories of those lovers and experiences—for those were the dreams he turned to now—were fractured, cinematic, but there were a few scenes he could remember vividly. Angelo, as he was still called then, was thirteen when he lost (or *gave* would be the more appropriate, *active* verb) his virginity; it was during that still-exuberant, burgeoning time in American history between the end of WW II and the beginning of the silent, lobotomized '50s.

They had just met, Angelo and his man of choice, had run into each other amidst the wild roses growing in some rude field outside of New Orleans center, not far from the Mississippi; it was past two in the full-moon summer morning. Angelo, need it be said, was decidedly precocious (Angel sat back and let the screen roll):

Have you ever noticed, he asked the man, his voice still at the cracking stage and doing just that (much to his embarrassment), *how the texture of rose petals, not these but those of the long-stemmed variety and particularly when still buds, seems to resemble the head of a penis, especially when erect—that soft, velvety, multi-striated look? Even the shape...* (Angelo was nothing if not verbose in those years, whereas Angel was known for a much more laconic style).

The other man, somewhat older but devastatingly attractive and wearing a crimson tie (a signal to those of like mind back then), a Dirk Bogarde type, seemed caught off-guard with this rather florid display of verbal foreplay, and gave Angelo a questioning, surprised look.

Have you ever eaten one—a rose petal? Angelo went on.

The man shook his head.

They're surprisingly bitter; not at all the pleasant taste you might think.

And then I took the rose into my mouth and.... Sweet memories! The field, it turned out, was well-known for such nefarious activity, and Angelo became a frequent visitor. For at fourteen he had been inspired—*ignited* might be the more appropriate word for what he felt—by the possibility of a true brotherhood of men, *boon companions*, one which included sexuality, a utopic dream brought on by his reading of Whitman ("Twenty-eight young men..." etcetera), D.H. Lawrence, and—much to his surprise—Melville.

That was the life Angel had first envisioned and wanted for himself at age fourteen—a fantasy life really—an open, generous, magnanimous, sensual life in the natural world in which he was a part of, and surrounded by, a chorus of men. And, it was, more or less, the life he'd had.

Doesn't the warm air feel nice on your bare ass?

Another voice. Another experience. Another memory. It was something someone had said to him once, after sex, as they were standing in the weeds along the shores of Lake Pontchartrain, their pants down around their knees; (Angel could remember that the man's cock was as stiff and as long as the tongue in the bell of St. Louis Cathedral, extending a full third of the length of his leg); Angelo might have been sixteen. Such a simple statement—*Doesn't the warm air feel nice on your bare ass?*—but Angel had remembered it always, and treasured it, because of its simplicity, its sheer, simple truth and beauty, its contentment with, and in, the moment—that the moment was enough. Somehow, that one sentence seemed to capture or express the very life that he wanted.

The next day, awake before the rooster's crow, Angel lay on his cot worrying over the fact that, after a mere three days, the relationship between his cell mate, a large, bulky man named Brice (who was still asleep), and him, had begun to deteriorate—not that it had been much good from the start. But this was unusual for Angel, since he generally got along well with people, particularly men—men of all types, and he found it troubling.

All he knew of his cell mate, besides his name, was his number, 406754, and that he was in this time—his third—for raping his eleven-year-old niece, of which he'd told Angel that first day: ("Brice, Brice, red beans 'n rice," his sister had teased him when they were teenagers. Then he'd added: "Guess I got her back.") Brice had become unfriendly and downright unkind to Angel—refusing to talk much after the first day, or when he did talk, it was only to castigate or curse at Angel for something or other, something as innocent and involuntary as sneezing, for example. Brice's bullishness and *teatro di machismo* had the unfortunate effect of seeming to reduce Angel's space in the cell to something less than negligible. And then it hit Angel: Of course! Brice must have somehow found out about the charges against him—and believed them.

That same morning, after breakfast, of which Angel only drank the coffee, black, his lawyer—*the* Francis Hardin—and two of Angel's friends, men of the chorus, awaited him as he was brought into the visiting area promptly at 9am.

"Victory Number One!" the zealous young Hardin said, arms raised to the skies, his fleshy, white underarms like some white-bellied fish lost swimming in the loose folds of his short-sleeves; he was referring to the fact that he had won the right for Angel to have visitors, two at a time, other than himself.

Though Angel and his friends were separated by a wall—half of which was made of concrete and the other half of a thick, almost opaque Plexiglas, even that couldn't dampen their pleasure in seeing each other. But Hardin insisted they get right down to business, saying there was no time to lose. He told Angel that his two friends there had visited his Uncle Luigi and that Uncle Luigi could confidently be ruled out as a possible suspect: Now *that,* he said, that was progress.

"He was very sweet," one of the men said, looking Angel directly in the eyes.

"If also constantly drunk," the other said. "It's his *'lifestyle,'*" he added, winking.

"He spoke about your father," the first friend continued, "his brother Giovanni. And about how much Giovanni loved you, his only child—his son, and how he could still remember your father's happiness, the look on his face—how he glowed with pride when you were born—his Angel.

"And he told us the story about the time when your mother was out of town for a month visiting relatives in Italy. You must have been about seven or eight, he said, and the three of you—Luigi, Giovanni, and yourself—set-up house together, for the month. He said he had the both of you drunk and wearing aprons in no time!"

Angel smiled, remembering, and Hardin blushed. What was next? Hardin's body language seemed to verbalize. The grandmother—"the Orioli woman," he finally said aloud, raising his eyebrows and looking away from Angel.

Always quick, vigilant, and perceptive, Angel caught it, that *something*, an evasiveness. "What is it, Frank?"

"What?" Hardin replied, knowing he wouldn't be able to wiggle out of it. He looked down at the floor and muttered: "Advance word is not good on that."

A question mark formed in the furrows of Angel's brow, where it seemed he held an endless supply of punctuational symbols. But before Angel could say anything, Hardin stuck out the palm of his hand—like a traffic cop. "Let's just wait and see," he said. "We've got a couple of people, friends of yours, working on it." And then their time was up.

Left alone once again, virtually, spiritually alone, Angel returned to the arduous, if also ardent task of remembering. But he was tired today, and instead of actively willing his memories, this time he simply let them wash over him.

June 5th. It was the last time he'd had sex: Angel and *the man*. They'd spent much of the afternoon dancing around each other, so to speak, until finally, what they did together was so tame, yet so fulfilling—just what the doctor had ordered that particular day: *The man* stood behind Angel, his stiff cock between Angel's legs, and fucked him while jerking-off Angel with one hand, the palm of his other hand pressed tightly against Angel's heart, almost constrictingly, so that he was enwrapped; *enrapt*. Someone was practicing the organ in the church at the time, and so it was to that deep purple gothic strain that Angel—by now a connoisseur of the orgasm—came: *And in his mind's eye he saw—in quick flashes—the flying buttresses and the stained glass windows of Chartres, the open-mouthed gargoyles of Notre Dame, and in his ears he heard an aria by Callas.....*

Angel had come in endless waves that day it seemed to him now, lapping at the shore of the man who was—at least for the day, the moment—his lover; it reminded him of how—as a boy edging puberty, he had loved to kneel, naked, along the banks of the Mississippi, and masturbate into what little ebb and flow there was.

Such thoughts carried Angel past dinner—a tableaux in which he felt himself to be both the diner *and the proverbial, implattered fowl*—which he didn't touch, and into the night, further into dreams, and finally to sleep. But his sleep that night was fitful and inconstant, as he could not escape the sinking feeling that Brice, and possibly others as well, were watching him, hunting him, hovering over him even, at times—all yellow teeth and matted hair: positively werewolvian. He heard voices, too, in the night, voices saying something about "Go fish!" Voices seeming to call to him, saying, "What's she in for, Brice?" And "Sister Angel, what you in for?" "I'm gonna be in you for what!" And then a deep, sinister laughter that tingled his spine.

The next morning Angel sipped his black coffee in silence, sitting in the path of the shaft of soft light projecting in through the tiny window while Brice continued to sleep (or pretended to sleep, Angel couldn't be sure). This was Angel's sixth day in prison, *imprisoned*, and though he had awakened feeling groggy and tired from the sleepless night, he now felt energetic and was looking forward to going outside as scheduled—one hour after lunch: The exercise; the fresh air; the open space ...

That time, too, when it came—like the prospect of sleep the night before, a seeming respite which proved otherwise, was not what he'd hoped it would be. Oh, the first few minutes were delicious all right— the feeling of the air, though hot and humid, on his skin; he could feel it bristling through the hairs on his arms. The natural light on his face and on the faces of the others, shading bones and five o'clock shadow—*chiaroscuro*; and all the colors and the wide open-ness of it all ...

But before long Angel became aware of a sort-of collective bad mood among some of his fellow inmates in the yard, a foulness that apparently had something to do with him, like a conspiracy.

Fortunately, this feeling seemed to be contained to a group of less than ten men, some of whom—when they thought they were out of sight of the guards (or as out of sight as they could be)—pulled out their penises and mocked jerking-off, taunting Angel, making pronounced, exaggerated sucking noises as they did so; others pulled their pants down and mooned him. And a couple of the larger men walked past him so close that their uniforms brushed against his and whistled a secret, menacing, non-verbal message, and at the same moment they mumbled, almost under their breaths but not quite, still audible, mumbled some deep-voiced threat like "Just you wait, sister!" and "Pervert!" and "Boy-butt fucker!"

Because the group seemed relatively small and contained, Angel was hopeful; he believed in his powers to tame them, in fact he felt somewhat challenged and excited by the possibility and the danger. And yet he spent the rest of the day feeling as though he were walking in a dark tunnel—*not much space, nowhere to run*; the walls closing in around him; the entrances and exits blocked off. He was trapped; surrounded.

"I baked you a cake, honey," said another visiting member of the chorus, a petite drag queen holding out her hands as *if.* It was the next morning and Angel had somehow slept like a baby. Now he was greeting Hardin, and two *other* friends.

"But don't you go lookin' for no file," she went on, "cause there ain't one. Ain't because I didn't try, though: Mr. Hard-on here wouldn't let me."

Hardin blushed and pulled at his lapels, which Angel recognized as the opening moves of his trying to take control of a situation. "We've seen your grandmother—Madame Orioli."

Angel said he was all ears. Hardin looked at Angel's friends.

"You shoulda seen Miss Thang," Angel's petite friend went on. "I mean that girl is big, as in *huge*! And *old*! Honey, you ain't see nothin' that old since the last time you was in Europe. And that place o' hers! Splendid squalor, that's what it is. Splendid squalor! And her squattin' there in that dilapidated Peacock chair o' hers like it was a throne, and with enough chins to make a chinchilla. Why, I couldn't tell where Granny ended and the chair began. Pity that poor, sagging wicker's all

I got to say!"

Angel was smiling.

"All right, all right," Hardin interrupted, "Let's cut to the chase." He fixed Angel with a serious look. "She says she's responsible. Voodoo."

"Seems she's been practicing for years," his sober friend chimed in. "And recently, well, after Giovanni died and left everything to you, you became her chief target."

"I don't believe in that crap," Angel cried. "I mean, she couldn't have made all this happen by mixing up some, I don't know, some concoction of newts' eyes and pussywillow and a strand of my hair and a fingernail clipping and whatnot, could she?"

His three visitors, New Orleans natives all—like Angel, looked back and forth at one another without saying a word.

"She said most of what Giovanni left you was actually your mother's money, and that given how your mother felt about you, she was sure Philomena would have wanted her to have it instead of you."

"Is that all?" Angel cried. "Let her have it! I don't care about the money."

"That still doesn't solve the crime," Hardin jumped in.

"So then why is this significant?" Angel changed the subject. "Voodoo, shmoodoo. What about the boy?"

Hardin lifted a finger. "Ah, the boy! Madame Orioli says he had absolutely nothing to do with it, but that her curses are broad. She says once she casts them she can't always say exactly where they're going to land or precisely what form they'll take."

"That's not what I mean," Angel interjected. "I mean, do we know who he is, who he's related to, *why he might lie*—things like that?"

"Not yet," Hardin winced. And so the two friends and the one eager attorney left with their proverbial tails tucked between their legs. "Back to the drawing board," Angel overheard the ever-original Hardin say as they were walking out.

That night, sometime past midnight, Angel lay on his cot just barely awake, hovering between this and that other world, still mulling over the day's bad news (so many sheep to count); but he was also attuned to the unusual silence in and around his cell. Fortunately for him, though, instead of keeping him awake and alert, he was far-enough gone and exhausted to allow the quiet to push him over into sleep.

The next thing he knew something cold had clamped down on and clinched his ankles and wrists, and immediately after that some sort of cloth was stuffed in his mouth. His eyes opened and darted around, and it was then he saw Brice and four other inmates, all of whom he recognized from the yard. Angel squirmed and tried to scream, but his arms and legs were handcuffed, and his screams, muffled by the rag in his mouth, sounded more like low moans. Angel then experienced his own weightlessness and watched the ceiling seem to move past overhead as he was carried to the cell door. Once there, he was stood upright and his face was pressed up against two of those cold, iron bars. The men quickly unlocked and then re-locked the handcuffs, so that he was suspended and splayed on the bars of his own cell.

They must have stolen handcuffs from guards, Angel reasoned, *over a period of time*. The guards, where were the guards? And then Angel remembered the unusual silence he had heard earlier in the night and felt a deep, sinking feeling in the pit of his stomach. *They must be in on it, too!*

Next, Angel felt his clothes being ripped away from him, heard the sound of buttons bouncing on the cold, cement floor, the thud of his shoes, and the soft, plush fall of cloth collapsing in a heap; and then the heavy, labored breathing of his captors. Before long, amidst a deafening din of cheering and jeering, one of the men had penetrated him and begun thrusting away.

After a while Angel could no longer tell when one man had stopped and another taken over, or if, in fact, they were still fucking him. He was both all sensation and no sensation whatsoever—acutely sensitive, but also numb. His mind now took him outside the cell, where he imagined—if anyone were watching—it must have looked like some sort of medieval ritual, a feeding frenzy, as the men hovered over and around him like so many crows. What was going on in the minds of his attackers Angel could only imagine, and that he'd rather not do. Instead he would just feel what he felt, experience what he was experiencing—*get through it*. He had no other choice.

Several weeks later, having spent a full week recovering in the prison infirmary, Angel lay on his cot in a new, single cell, staring up at the ceiling. With his mind, he had projected the future onto that ceiling and, again with his mind, he could push right through it and rush head-long, out of his cell, out of his particular building, out of the entire prison compound, New Orleans, Louisiana, the United States of America—if he liked, and into blue, blue sky. Beckoned by that call of release, he projected into a future when he would be a free man, cleared of the ludicrous charges against him, a time when he would look back on and remember the horror of what had happened to him in prison. And he could also see that there, with the proper distance, he would be able to locate in that nightmarish experience a true heaviness, a solidity and closeness to the earth he had never felt before.

Robin Lippincott
Robin Lippincott is the author of three books (all still in print), the novels *Our Arcadia* and *Mr. Dalloway,* and the short story collection *The Real, True Angel*. His fiction and nonfiction have also appeared in *The New York Times Book Review*, *The Literary Review*, *The American Voice*, *Provincetown Arts*, and many other magazines. A recipient of many fellowships at Yaddo, he teaches in the MFA Writing Program at Spalding University and at Harvard Extension School. He lives in Cambridge, Massachusetts.

Rabbit Chase

Michael Carroll

One of the first things you noticed about him wasn't the way he called his school "Jew-U." Though there was something of the forbidden and wrong about him.

His name was Grant. He lived next door and was eighteen—three years older than my brother Jerry. Five years older than me.

"Jew-U" was Jacksonville University. Grant would automatically repeat his jokey moniker for the local college he'd attended for a year. It was a kind of nervous tic in which the word *Jew* popped out of his mouth whenever. But talk like that was thick in the climate, as bound up in the sticky summer heat as the humidity. Florida, after all, was only the third state to withdraw from the Union and join the Confederacy. And carpetbaggers and rednecks to this day were still in contention. "Jew-U" was so-called for the Yankees who went to JU—a college only a mile from my house—and crowded the classes, then drove out to the beach in the cars they bought with money they saved from their sunbelt tuition—to profit from the early-to-start, late-to-shut-down summers. There they were, out on the beach in March with the wind whipping their bare backs and raising goose bumps all over their covered parts. And here we were, in our jackets and sweaters.

Grant was living at home while he went to college. One of the things that bonded him to my brother Jerry was an obsession with the citizens band that had infected them both—and just about everyone else we knew in Jacksonville. We lived in a three-CB household and had a radio in our car, another in my father's pickup, and a third in Jerry's bedroom as part of a communications setup laid out on his Sears-brand office desk of wood-grain Formica and black metal.

Grant studied. He was going to be an engineer (his smarts were one of the things that attracted me to him)—but in the afternoon when he got home from class he would come over and seat himself at my brother's desk, pull the desk mike closer, and launch into five minutes of bullshit broadcasting with all the other "ratchet jaws" who, like him, "had their ears on." He didn't use the word Jew on the radio—racial slurs and obscenities being forbidden by the FCC—but he saved that for casual conversation, running it past my brother, who'd nod, and my parents, who were used to that.

When he wasn't talking to all the ratchet jaws, he was lounging with his handsome, dark head on one upturned palm as he lay on his side atop my brother's bed, bullshitting with Jerry. With his perfect posture, Jerry sat at the crowded desk touching a soldering iron to a PC board. Opening up old radios and restoring them to working order was my brother's hobby. His array of radio equipment—the CB (always tuned to channel 19), his stereo tuned to WFYV, Rock 105, and his fire and rescue channel scanner—filled the room with their crackle and hiss; the voices, guitar riffs and drum solos of Pink Floyd and Led Zeppelin; and news of all the traffic accidents that emergency crews had been dispatched to along the main arteries and streets of Jacksonville.

My brother seemed older than his true age. Already he knew he wanted to be a fireman. Once he graduated from high school, he would take the civil service exam, a test he'd already begun studying for and could probably have passed now with flying colors if it weren't for the minimum-age restriction. Jerry had had a series of girlfriends and at this moment I suspected he was seeing an older woman who worked as a checkout girl at the neighborhood grocery store where he was a bagboy. But he wouldn't tell me anything about this; maybe his buddy Grant knew something. I was sure that as soon as Jerry got his high school diploma, so he could take the fire department exam, he'd say good-bye to education forever. Already he was supplementing his academic courses by catching a bus across town to a vocational school in the afternoon. He was studying electronics repair; the guts and shells of stereo receivers and turntables he found in people's garbage during his scavenger hunts were strewn about his bedroom: under his bed, in his closet, along his bookshelves, and right in the middle of the floor (carpeted in celery-and-avocado shag). A pimply-faced surgeon with a soldering iron for a scalpel, he opened his patients up using a flathead and began to operate. With blinding speed he could spot a circuit in crisis or mend a wire that was pulled loose. He used roach clips (an implement my father would not have recognized) to hold the job in place while he twisted filaments and soldered them together.

He air-drummed (never guitared) to the famous solo of "Moby Dick." At night he went in for something mellower—*Dark Side of the Moon* or Clapton's *Backless*. He always had a soundtrack going in the background. He was working on boosters and speaker placement in his room to make the sound better and better. It was all a soundtrack to the movie of his life, but it wasn't his life. We knew nearly nothing about his real life.

Grant came along at a time when my brother wanted to be taken seriously as a grown-up. A meek younger brother, gay-acting or at least not up to the usual standard of boyish toughness, to him I was a pesky lingerer unwelcome in his room. My hobbies were reading and playing tennis against a brick privacy fence our neighbors had put up. Not that I suffered in any way from this rejection. I had my own sex life going on, and I was only thirteen. Given Grant's towering height and standard good looks, and how I always felt I had to poke my head into Jerry's doorway to tell Grant hi in the afternoon, surely Jerry knew what I was up to. Still, he never did more than mock my quick tears and excitability; he left my effeminacy (how I crossed my legs, how I'd tisk to show disapproval or interest) alone for me to deal with by myself.

My father, an engineer at a drywall plant, came home late in the afternoon and went to bed early in the evening. He worked most Saturdays. My mother didn't work. Even though she was at home most days (when she wasn't driving long distances to hunt for bargains), she preferred to check out. She would watch soaps while she unpacked the groceries and started dinner. She carried the portable TV into the dining room (a room not in use except for business dinners) and crafted dried-flower arrangements. She had grown up with a pair of younger brothers who'd gotten into trouble a lot. Maybe she thought the only way to deal with boys was to let them get fed up with themselves, get worn out. Her sister and two brothers had each married and divorced three times, and this she accepted as a casualty of malehood, not sin.

———   ———   ———

My mother was raised a dedicated, unquestioning Baptist. Getting a job and sharing an apartment with childhood girlfriends had been the first step towards breaking away from her faith. Marrying my father, himself raised in another immersion-believing denomination, was the second. Hand in hand they slowly walked away. She always *knew* she would leave it—even as a girl.

I wonder what the Baptists of the time would have thought of CBs. My mother was amused by the whole thing. So long as my brother came home at a decent hour from his part-time job, there was no conflict. She never asked us if we'd done our homework (I always had). My brother's grades rarely soared above a B average, but because my mother understood Jerry's devotion to the idea of becoming a firefighter, and because she knew his skills as a repairman would make him marketable if he didn't pass the fire department test, she assumed his future was taken care of.

Our days at home conformed to a routine. While my brother and I were at school my mother took her time getting out of bed. Once up, she had her instant coffee and headquartered herself in the dining room. The phone cord reached from the kitchen to the long celery-colored dining room table, where she sat clipping coupons, going through the week's sale flyers that freighted the daily newspaper, and calling catalog operators to place orders for new sheets and towels. The daughter of farmers who'd crawled out from the red clay fields of cotton in west Tennessee to become upwardly mobile, middle-class folks, my mother had traded in privation for luxury—if a scaled-down version of it—and a suburban sense of fullness. She told herself it was all justified so long as the lessons of the Depression were kept firmly in mind and reduced to values of thrift and saving. For her, thrift and saving had become marks of a good shopper. My mother ran a tight ship, economically.

In the afternoons, I came home and watched TV and read. Usually Mom wasn't back from her errands and shopping. If Jerry was home already from vocational school and didn't have to work, I might slip into his doorway to say hi. But it was brief; I didn't want to push his patience. Cranky and tired, he would toss me a hello that said at the same time he shouldn't be bothered. He would be in a better mood if he wasn't about to put on his tie and leave to report to his job at the grocery store. Either way, he was tending to the myriad projects laid out in his room, passing an inspecting hand over the guts and pushed-aside frames of clock radios, stereos, coffeemakers (things having heating elements were amazingly straightforward to work on, he said, and people always threw them away too fast), household appliances, blow dryers. He would worry circuits and PC boards back into shape, but some repairs were ongoing experiments, and he kept a fire extinguisher (which our safety engineer of a father had filched from work and brought home) under the Sears desk—ready for any electrical fire that might spark into life and burn the house down.

Simultaneously, his arms milled the air. His right foot tapped in time to John Bonham's steady booming bass drum and he approximated banging upon the tom-toms and their full complement of high-hat, crash cymbal, and snare. With a delicately mimed jazz-style pivot of his left drumstick to balance off the softly fulcrummed seesawing of the right, he did "Heartbreaker" and its sequel, segued in on the record like a surprise attack from the rear, "Living Loving Maid." As the music ground on, he sang, but his face, ever a studied allegory of E coolness, didn't betray the passion or the pleading in Robert Plant's bluesy vocal style. He nodded along to John Paul Jones's thrumping, haunch-throwing bass (yet never threw out his own haunches). By waggling his bottlebrush eyebrows (a family trademark) and sticking his chin out and thrusting his closed lips in time, he mimed Jimmy Page's fingering along the fretboard of his guitar as Page scoured the air clean of indifference with all his lightning licks and thunder-gathering riffs. To him, Page commanded a divine energy, appeasing the gods with the hammering arm and wrist they'd gifted him with—and such power merited respect, not mimicry. It shone for the young white men of St. John's and it mocked the charge of Page's Negro-hijacked art. It clanked and snarled like mill-town noise out the open windows of teenagers' bedrooms, their first cars. It galled the Presbyterians and the Methodists alike and it shattered the ruling Baptists' pretensions.

This my mother tolerated. Rock and roll was one of the first rebellions she'd subscribed to. She didn't seem to hear any major differences in sound or style between, say, "Be-Bop-A-Lula" and "Lola"—or to know the two songs were recorded a decade apart by bands separated by an ocean. It was free and equal rock and roll, and she'd snap her fingers and do—as best I can piece together now—the mashed potato, the monkey, the peppermint twist.

Hearing her sing on the beach as she was "Lunchin' to the

Oldies" on the AM dial, I was reminded that she'd broken with her family over precisely this music. And gyrate my mother liked to do, unlike a standard woman her age with full-dipping immersion in her background.

She was a young-looking woman, and often when we went out together strangers would ask us if we were brother and sister. There was the family resemblance—our dark, close-set eyes, our Slavic-looking cheekbones—so it only made sense. If that happened, if a storekeeper or a man at the next table in a restaurant asked if she was my big sister, my mother was transported to cloud nine. She didn't play coy games or fish for more compliments; the mere suggestion she *might* look young enough to make me her kid brother was enough to set her aloft. Then she would grab my hand and pull me through the mall. Try on clothes with girlish excitement, things she found on sale. "Be honest!"

When I asked her what perfume she liked, she paused, as if considering price as much as scent. Her birthday was coming up. An end of the summer birthday.

"L'Air du Temps."

Otherwise she was earthbound with all her responsibilities and the woes of her past. But she was free to live the present married to the "boy" she'd hung onto since eighth grade and through thick and thin (despite his other girlfriends back in high school and their open defiance of his parents and hers). Never did it occur to me she might be unhappy with my father. They got along, even if their uneventful lives and the Florida heat tired them out. They'd both gotten away from what they were escaping, and neither of their kids seemed as anguished as they'd once been, still were, but tried not to be.

So there she sat, studying her sale flyers. Non-denominational church on Sunday, an imagination lit by the comforts of her Florida house to obliterate the memory of the shabby Tennessee farmhouse she'd grown up in. My brother sat in his room working and creating a salty odor of ozone and solder. Me in front of the television, waiting for Grant to drop by.

It was as if we were all waiting. We carried on in our usual ways hoping for our reward. My mother's late-afternoon hobby of making dried-flower arrangements put an earthy, reedy pungency into the air— as of a spicy imported mud. I lay on the floor of our den watching TV. Soon my mother would start cooking a "Polynesian" dish concocted from pork chops, ketchup, canned pineapple, jars of LaChoy goops and sauces, and the onions and green peppers she took the time to slice, all simmering together beneath the glass lid of her crock pot: a miracle time-saver she'd never regretted investing in. Anything to enliven rice or spaghetti and cut corners where inflation and the fuel crisis had eaten away at our family budget.

With the air-conditioning going—and except for three or four months of the year it was always going—the vents in our ceiling moved the air around in a circular pattern all through the front of our house. The front consisted of the dining room, which doubled as my mother's work area, the den where I lay in front of the TV with a library book splayed open on the floor below for me to dip into during commercials, and the kitchen. As the central AC whooshed into action every few minutes to maintain the economy level my father had set the thermostat for, all the different activities in our house gave off their odors. Too much so. My mother had begun to get migraine headaches and she insisted that if he was home "working on his hobbies" my brother must keep the hall door leading to the back of the house closed to seal off the bizarre smells he created. The migraines upset her temper—famous for its swells as much as its calms. At her worst she lay in bed and we kept the house silent; my brother would take extra shifts at work. When she was better he would press his luck; the hall door would be shut but the crying and plaintive sex-needy howls of Robert Plant would seep through, accompanied by the salty alchemical traces of heated radio parts

Then Grant would drop by.

He would tap on a glass pane of the French doors; from my spot on the floor I could see his silhouette leaning in to catch a glimpse of what I was watching on TV; only a gauzy, celery-colored sheer curtain separated us. Immediately I'd yell him in and let my mother know we had company with one more yell. Then Grant would turn the knob and let himself in.

I would leap up to attention and say hi. There was no etiquette to tell me how to greet him. The age difference made it seem silly to shake his hand. My admiration overflowed, but I tried to conceal it; my brother kept the majority of Grant's affections for himself. So there I was standing at attention, grinning and looking as if I were waiting for something that should already be mutually understood between us. Grant might pat my shoulder.

He'd ask me about myself, what I was up to, then move on to the dining room and talk to my mother—leaving me to feel self-conscious, vaguely unfulfilled.

My mother had always been clear about teaching us to respect privacy and boundaries with people—between children, adults, or a combination of the two—and I instinctively left Grant alone with Mom whenever he went in to say hi. Already he called her by her first name, Barbara, just as he called my father by his, Doug. I could hear my mother in there with him laughing, erupting into great exaggerated girlish whoops of rapture over his charm. She did the same with me; she just loved to laugh. They would laugh and talk for fifteen or twenty minutes, sometimes longer. He was never in a hurry, since his own home next door was crowded with younger children, his father was a "certified alcoholic," and his mother sat in her room smoking and sewing and staying out of the light since some mysterious skin sensitivity forced her to avoid it (my mother was working on a Victoriana arrangement of desiccated hydrangeas, eucalyptus, sea oats, and pussy willow to soothe her). Sometimes Grant would stop and have a beer with my mother, and he'd even sometimes wait for my father to come home and join them— and already I was aware that he might be looking for a surrogate family in my parents. If so, then they were unusual ones, letting him have a drink with them. Yet he was an unusual *son*: troubled, or so it seemed to me—and I flattered myself that what he needed wasn't so much a new set of parents as a really good, dedicated friend like me.

It was on one of these days that my father happened to come home a little earlier than usual. Typically Grant would drop over, say his quick hellos to me, then his slightly chummier ones to my mother in the dining room, then I would hear his feet shump-shumping across the shag carpet, pausing on the artificial gray stone of the foyer tile as he checked his look in the mirror. He seemed to sense my paying attention to the sounds he was making; he would say again, "What's up, Tom?" before moving on back to my brother's room. There he'd man my brother's CB and break onto channel 19 to hail my father as he was crossing the bridge into St. John's from the "dark side" of town.

Today he didn't have the chance to do any of that. I heard my father's pickup moan into the driveway, the engine die and the emer-

gency brake complain as it was yanked up. It was too early for me to
be watching TV; I should have been in my room faking studying, fiddling with a set of pre-algebra math problems or leafing through a textbook. I shot up and through the hall door towards the back of the house,
but I left my bedroom door open. There were a few minutes of front-of-
the-house laughter and kitchen-chair movement. Then, soon, I heard
my father's steel-toed workshoes clunking on the foyer congoleum and
his voice calling my brother, "Jer?"

"Yep." My brother sounded almost irritated.

My father's face appeared in my doorway. He grinned at the incredible fact that he'd caught me studying and said, "Hi, son. Let me close
your door a minute," and he disappeared.

There was the hush of Jerry's bedroom door being pulled shut. I
moved over to the wall to listen.

It was about my brother's late-night forays out of the house. There
he met friends and sometimes some mysterious girlfriend. But he was-
n't ready to talk about her yet.

"Your mother and I going to bed doesn't give you automatic permission to leave the house in the middle of the night. Where do you
go?"

I imagined my father talking to his men at work this way—by strategy, alternating between a constant, hard reminder of the power struc-
ture and a gentler, more respectful inquiry.

"Just *out*," my brother was saying. He sounded cornered and angry.

At just the instant that I began having trouble hearing because
Jerry's stereo was going, and from his CB issued the blurt and verbal
strut of ratchet jaws employing the official ten-code and truckers'
lingo—at just that moment my father said, "Turn that shit down...."

This had to be serious, since my father was himself a ratchet jaw:
he'd outfitted the family with CBs—without a doubt a late-seventies
anticipation of the Internet and an act calling for togetherness and
father-son bonding.

"And what do you do?" my father said.

He tiptoes out the French doors while I'm watching TV in the middle of the night, goes drinking with friends from work, and sneaks back
in after I've gone to bed, I thought.

I couldn't hear anything.

I was standing on my bed with my ear pressed to the wall. With drywall you had to be careful because any pressure on it or brushing against it can be heard on the other side. At just the instant I was shifting my footing on the bed, Jerry turned down his stereo and CB. I heard the brushing sound of my fingertips as it carried through the hollow space in the wall, like a folkie's light strokes on the wood of his guitar near the sound hole.

I detected a hush between them, observed and protracted until the two realized that what had needed to be said was out in the open now and my brother had better watch his step. I heard my father shift his steps on the shag, rattling his keys and the change in his pockets. I could imagine him folding his arms over his chest and adjusting his stance. "I don't want you doing anything like that anymore," he said. "You do know there's a city curfew, don't you?"

"I didn't know that," said Jerry.

"You do now. I don't want you coming home with the police. 'Cause the first thing that'll go'll be your job."

"I'm not giving up my job."

"You will if I say you will."

"I'm not giving up my job—that means I'll have to give up getting a car."

"That's right."

"No way."

"Then you better stop sneaking out at night—"

"All right, all right. Don't worry about me."

"Deal?"

"Deal." He sounded demoralized, but he'd gotten himself into it with no help from me, though I knew I might still come in for some of the blame.

I wondered if this was how my father handled his men at the plant: got them to air their views and forward their requests, then ignored them since upper management would veto them, anyway. There was no union looking out for them, only the boss. As a safety engineer, my father took orders and gave orders. As a parent, he had to regard the letter of the law and the threat of a visit from the sheriff's department as the prerogative of upper management. And yet didn't know how to deal with a son who did what he wanted, who didn't have the threat of being fired from the job as leverage.

When he told Jerry that Grant was here and he was sending him back, Jerry tossed him a mournful, but still-defiant, "Whatever." Then I heard my father go back down the hall to the front of the house.

Too excited to do anything else, as if my mind had been emptied by this latest development, I paced around my room for a moment and when that got boring I started out. But when I opened my door Jerry, looking darker and more sullen, even older than ever, stood there in my way. He sucked his teeth. I knew that the smartass in him, never far from the surface, was ready to break out in fits of tripping, rising hyena laughter.

"I didn't tell him," I said. It was too late to act innocent, so I admitted I had at least eavesdropped. "I don't know how he found out."

"Uh-huh."

"Jerry, I didn't tell him!"

"Whatever." He gave me a sidelong look, disgust curling back one corner of his mouth.

Grant was coming.

"Guess you'll be more careful next time" I said, and slammed my door. I opened it back up long enough to spit out the treble phrase, "Asshole!" then slammed it again.

I heard them giggling at me—that made it worse.

I paced around the room feeling trapped. He liked to embarrass me; he was a relentless predator whose capture strategy was humiliation. Usually it worked: he had me after he'd harassed me and I'd dissolved in a pool of my own tears.

But I wasn't going to cry now.

Jerry took more shifts, determined to earn the money for his car by the end of the summer.

I took my racket out into the driveway each morning and volleyed five minutes at a time without missing the ball—for hours. My thighs and calves melted in pain each evening, then began to re-harden overnight into stronger, more sinewy limbs.

And still on some afternoons Grant dropped by to talk on Jerry's radio while I sat on my absent brother's bed and listened. He'd call for my father and welcome him back to "our" side of town, ratchet-jaw a few minutes, and sign off again. Then he'd turn to me and say, "What's up, Tommy?"

I fairly bathed in the attention and came out from a session with him glowing, but broodily.

On one of those days, though, while my mother was out, I just sat up to attention.

"You look bothered by something."

"Just tired."

"Still out there hitting the ball in this heat? That'll take it out of you."

"I guess."

"Wanna talk?"

As usual, he was sitting at my brother's desk. He slid the mike toward the edge of the desk in my direction and I got up to talk into it. He didn't get up. I was thrilled by a sense of double trespass—into my brother's room, and alone in Grant's presence. I leaned into the mike and gave it my best.

"Breaker nineteen!" I said with twangy, truck-driving glibness.

My father broke onto the channel and called for me: "That you, Denim Kid?"

"Ten-four, Crankshaft."

"You at the command post with Eagle Scout while Buckshot's out ridin' the trail?"

"Affirmative again."

The CB in Jerry's room belonged to Jerry; he'd gotten it as a Christmas present with a partial lien on his next birthday. But because my father didn't want us to run down the battery while the car was parked in the driveway, he couldn't restrict me from using Jerry's CB. I wasn't supposed to use it when Jerry wasn't in his room—but somehow it was understood that Grant could use it whenever he came around. My using it now was a risk my father was willing to watch me take—even though he might catch hell from Jerry for it later on. My father not only respected private property, but expanded the definition to include friendships.

"You better be nice to Buckshot then," my father chuckled. "Copy?"

"Ten-four."

He asked if I didn't have my summer reading list to be working my way down, and I said I was ahead on it—a fudge. Now that we we're "alone," he said, had I given my mother's birthday gift a thought?

"Four-ten." I was fooling around, talking in the bass-ackwards lingo of truckers. I felt the exhilarated rush of a boy who's just caught a baseball in the craw of his Rawlings glove—hearing the satisfying smack of the cork and hard leather sheathing at the same instant it throbs numbingly against the meat of my hand. (Just last year, little league had been an absurd episode ending in my banishment to the outfield.)

He asked about "my" tennis game. But he did not ask if I'd weeded the lawn—an ongoing project that went unspoken throughout the summer until he noticed I hadn't kept it up. He asked if I wanted him to make a reservation at the church courts this weekend and go play a real game. When we were done, we'd clean up in the church locker room and go eat, then head off to Regency Square mall for Mom's gift. I said cool.

I was a truck driver with enormous arms like two USDA-tattooed hams. I was Bjorn Bork. When I signed off ten-ten, he came back with "Ten-ten, till we do it again," even though we both knew I'd see him in another two or three minutes.

"Well all right, Denim Kid," Grant said, when I pushed back the mike and turned from the desk. I studied his smile. I'd had four teeth pulled last week so that I could be outfitted with braces—and he had the smile I hoped to end up with.

His arms were crossed and the fly and front panel of his Levis swelled out like a tent. I was sitting close enough to smell his soap and shampoo and shaving cream. We both heard the rumble of my father's Datsun pickup, and Grant's smile—big and composed of large clean white teeth not quite straight but placed here and there at odd angles you didn't notice until you were close to him—began to fade.

"You going on the rabbit chase next week?" he said, sitting up straight, looking more serious now. The swelling pushed stubbornly to one side.

We heard the French doors close at the other end of the house and my heart raced. We heard my father's voice. Grant's movements were steady. He crossed his legs in the correct "male" manner. His leg closer to the door was bent and angled so that it concealed his erection; he pressed his shin flush just above his other knee and wrapped his smallish hands around his calf. His sneakered foot oscillated up and down to some private beat.

I had just enough time to answer his question—though I don't know why I should have been so nervous or in such a rush about it. Quickly, as if in a race against time, I whispered, "Yes," which came out as a catlike hiss.

My father ducked his head into the room. "Gentlemen."

"Doug," Grant greeted him, nodding.

"Hi Dad," I said, and started out of my brother's forbidden zone.

I went to pass my father. That's when I felt my own erection pressing against the panel of my Y-fronts and poking out slightly to the left in my tennis shorts. I shoved my hands into my pockets and grunted a cheerful, if unorthodox, grunt.

My father gave me a weird look, but he always did. He was a joker and had tried to teach us to be jokers—though it hadn't taken. My brother and I were still trapped in the surly, unironic inwardness of growing-up. We didn't realize how deeply he could penetrate our concerns with his casual glances. For him it was a matter of remembering things for himself. Knowing what a kid thinks, if that kid is halfway normal. Yet the way I was hissing and grunting undoubtedly led him to wonder. Then again maybe it occurred to him Grant and I were in on a secret, protecting my brother. None of us ever saw Jerry anymore but his room, still littered with radio parts and electrical guts, was evidence of a boy becoming a man and desperate to roam. Now I realize it all must have been kind of sad for Dad, but typical of him he didn't show it.

He had low, taxi-door ears constantly red from exertion or the heat, and this color, combined with his dry stare, his fat dark eyebrows riveted matter-of-factly into place, and his wry, barely upturned mouth reminded me he was always pushing toward the outer edge of laughter and irony.

And yet I knew I was able to hide something from him—or else I wouldn't be working so hard at it now. I went to my room and, for an instant paranoid that my absence would be the occasion for some spontaneous denunciation between the two, listened over my shoulder. But all I heard was my father's laid-back, wound-down end-of-the-day drawl saying to our friend, "You ready for a cold one, son?" *Son!*

It rained all through July and August. The clouds, which hovered low over the peninsula and blocked the sun all day, smudged the pallid sky and brought the horizon low, pushing it in on us. The humidity gathered, pressing down on our skin; breezes wouldn't dry the sweat that pooled in every crook. The rain started earlier each day and trapped me in front of the TV listening to the hum and whoosh of the AC. My racket and ball were grounded. Out in the driveway the drops pattered onto the cement. The gutters sluiced with water from the roof.

It didn't let up for the weekend and so we had to cancel our father-son tennis game. I sat pouting in the pickup as we drove to the mall to find L'Air du Temps. My father hated crowds so we got there minutes after opening, parked in front of the entrance to May-Cohens, our department store of choice for price and selection, and went straight to the perfume counter. My mind was stunned by so much sudden activity given my summer-long languor. Within a few days school would start again. Lazy, I didn't even ask to smell the perfume, but at first my father made an effort to hide his surprise at this. "Not a sniff?" he said dryly. The lady behind the counter exchanged polite looks with him that I ignored. "Nope…." She gift-wrapped it for us, my father paid, and we started out of the store without a glance or turn through the rest of the mall. But as we left crowds began to flock in like wet birds, flapping their arms and umbrellas and bent on shopping for back-to-school. My father sighed. I made a show of smelling the package in its fancy bag and he looked at me and smiled.

We made a run for the car.

Two days later I found myself wading into the tepid bath of junior high. I was in eighth grade. I wore baby-blue corduroys bought as factory rejects at Goofs and a button-down madras of navy and cream. I took these off in front of a gang of boys to dress down for PE for the first time—a development more frightening than the new system of rotating class schedules, geometry, humanities, five units of homework every night and the rumors of pecking order, random fights, hazing, automatic suspensions.

Six days later I decided to pull one of my father's dry stunts the next morning and before I took off for school leave my mother's present under a pile of cattails she was using for a Florida fall arrangement.

I slid it from under my bed to memorize the odor my mother seemed to have been thinking of on those wind-fresh afternoons spent with her on the beach last spring.

When I got home from school the next day, relieved I'd accomplished at least the first week of the thing which had lurked on my own troubled horizon all summer, the house was silent for a moment—hushed by the steady tide of white noise washing down from the ceiling's AC vents. Then I heard laughter from the other room, my mother's trademark drinking cackle and something lower, more rumbling and masculine.

I called from the kitchen. "Hello … ?"

"We're in *here*!"

I moved from the kitchen through the dining room to the living room we never used—usually even forgot. Decorated in celeries and creams, it was kept pristine and cool, with the curtains drawn during the day. It was a sanctuary against the sand and headachy heat of the outside; shoes muddied from the summer rain were anathema here. The walls were covered with sedate copied oriental prints and its tables of smoked glass had twisted legs of wrought iron sprayed milky white. We entered it for company dinners and special occasions only. Or sometimes I'd cut through on my way to the kitchen—not wanting to cross my brother's line of vision as he lounged about watching TV in the den—and I'd start at the sudden knowledge my mother was sitting up alone on the beige sofa, smoking Vantages in the dark. I'd smell the fresh smoke of her cigarette (I never got far from the thought that smoke from a just-lit cigarette—in a closed-up car or a restaurant when the meal was eaten—smelled *fresh*). I'd see the orange tip of her cigarette glowing in the dark and it would be another half minute before I heard her say, "Hey Blue"—one of my father's nicknames for *her*. I'd hear the creak made by the pressure of her hand gripping a Styrofoam huggie that insulated her can of beer slipped down inside it as she lifted it to her lips and drank. And I'd know I was in for a talk, a real sit-down-in-the-dark imbibing of the past.

She drew from the Vantage, then rested it on the lip of the ashtray she'd poised on one thigh, still holding the cigarette by the filter while she paused, sipped from her Budweiser, and began sifting through the contents of a long-distance call from her mother she'd earlier managed to terminate. Or else she tried to provoke the sadness in me, as if my sitting down in one of the armchairs opposite her was an admission of my own defeat.

When she got to the part about why her mother had pissed her off this time, she laughed it off with a scratchy laugh: the roilings of a cigarette cough that did not solidify. Eroding it further with cool beer, she paused and spat out an aside, "That old bitch!" She shook her head in disbelief at any old woman who had the gall to call into question her only undivorced daughter's marriage. "The temerity! The gall!"

Now her laugh was deployed for fun. Her drawled vowels, though, were deliberate and willful, her consonants coming faster than she could deal with them. I heard the laugh. As I was coming around the corner, she anticipated my appearance and looking up said, "Hey there, Denim Kid…."

"Hi."

She was raking at the back of her black Dorothy Hamill haircut with her coral-painted nails. "Grant's back in school, too—at Jew-U. Right, Grant?"

They were each holding beers and Grant nodded. He couldn't control or hide his big-toothed, slightly crooked, and wholly entrancing smile.

She was barefoot, her body turned inward to him, with one leg pulled up onto the cushion of the sofa. She wasn't smoking.

There was a lull. I suddenly realized we were unaccustomed—the three of us—to sitting around like this. The AC vents whooshed to an intermittent standstill.

Theatrically my mother threw her arm up, turned her wrist to her face and slowly drew it toward her. Her eyebrows rose and with deep vacuum-like breaths she sniffed at herself. "My present, L'Air du Temps! Come smell." She almost sang it, holding out one wrist.

I smiled wearily and went down on one knee on the celery-and-avocado shag before her.

"Happy birthday," I said. "Did you have a nice one?"

"I'm having one *now*," she said, almost too sweetly, "with my L'Air du Temps."

Grant nodded again, grinning and speechless. I crawled back over to my chair and sat staring, studying them. I was alone with my jealousy.

"Is it hard going to college?" I said.

We were sitting in Grant's green VW Bug. The night was an uneasy mix of humid and chilly. Still dressed for summer, we kept rolling up the windows and they kept fogging over from our breath. The "pregnant roller skate"—as a VW was called in CB lingo—was parked at the end of a cul-de-sac. We were the rabbit and a bunch of ratchet-jaws in cars and pickup trucks were on the hunt for us.

"Hard?" he said. "I wouldn't say hard." It was between transmissions, and he had time to form his answer carefully.

Boundaries had been set and the other ratchet jaws were crisscrossing the streets and neighborhoods of the "lighter side of town" (a CB shorthand) in hot pursuit. They were going to find us. It was just a matter of when.

He put his seat back.

"Take it out," I said.

Grant unzipped his jeans and obeyed without comment.

"Rabbit, where are you?" came a voice over the radio.

It wasn't yet time to transmit again and he lay back in the Volkswagen seat smiling more openly.

"He ain't sayin'" said another voice.

"The hell he ain't. Rabbit, this is Crankshaft," we heard my father say. "You can run but you cain't hide!"

In the interlude of static and noise Grant and I looked at each other.

"Rabbit, it's time," somebody else said.

Grant checked his watch and sat up, hitching his fly. He pulled the mike from its hook on the side of the radio and squeezed the transmit button. He said, "It's the rabbit, poking his head out of the ground."

"Rabbit, are you looking at the river?"

"Negatory."

I eyed the signal meter on the console of the radio to see if their transmissions were getting any stronger. But the little red needle barely moved.

"*Any* bodies of water?" came my father's unmistakable deductiveness.

"Double seven," said Grant, pitching his voice low.

"Rabbit, are you looking at mostly houses, or is there some commercial property in your view?"

"Negative on the latter."

"How old are the houses?"

He let it slide. He didn't go in for anything cute. He knew the rules and they called for strictly yes-no questions and answers. He checked his watch and let the channel go blank. He turned the squelch dial up to cut down the static and crackle. He squeezed the mike button one more time and said, "Rabbit's gone ten twenty-eight for three," hung the mike back up, and yanked down his jeans. His sex sprang free and limber.

Gently he laid his hand on my shoulder. I rotated onto my left side and rested my knees on the floorboards of the VW, smelling rubber band vinyl and the tang of breath. I crouched with the small of my back just under the dash and leaned in to him. One shoulder hovered over the gearshift, the other was pinned under the steering wheel; I had to twist my torso and bob up and down at an angle.

The air in the car was close. Grant kept the windows up and the fog on the insides of them helped conceal us from the outside. As I closed my eyes I thought of the separate smells of his sex—hints of which had wafted to me when we were alone together that time and he took no pains to hide his erection.

They seemed to me distinct, separating then gradually blending like the odors that lift and come to you as you're tromping past an orange grove and the citrus is drying in the heat of the morning sun. The air in the tiny VW had gotten thick and I realized I'd broken out in a sweat; it rilled down my back under my T-shirt, dampening the waistband of my underwear. I reached down to adjust my clothes and asked him to crack a window. He reached up to open his window in a gingerly way that suggested he thought I was sleeping and he didn't want to disturb me. But when the air—which had grown suddenly cooler outside— flew in, it brought with it traces of the salt wedge in the river saying we were in for a cold front off the ocean tonight; and I was very much awake. It began clearing the windows off and making everything fresh again, wiping the slate. So much so that when Grant closed the window again (a set of headlights washed through the little window behind us and he panicked), the ecology of our little crime separated out into its component smells again. Bitter rubber and ambery-smelling gasoline. The penetrating sweetness of old vinyl. And the high viscous complexity of sex. An older guy had all the heady gradations of the boys I was used to going down on. With Grant I took my time; he doused himself with sharp, deodorizing stuff, and the process of getting intimate with him meant cutting through all his willful chemistry, with its approximated trips into the woods at autumn-time. Moss and musk broke free from my nostrils as I bent my head into his crotch again, nosing into his dark fur and inhaling deeper with crazier abandon than before—and I came up with the yellowish blossom smell (that was the color of the package, anyway) of L'Air du Temps. I attacked it with my nose, nestling my lips against the joint of flesh planted there. Easter lily and fainting gardenia. Confederate jasmine and mailbox honeysuckle, their blossoms crestfallen and burdened from a chastening rain. All at once both of us stopped; the kisses I pecked his cock up and down with died before I could lick clean the pearl from the head at the other end. A background noise like tortured steel was ripped from the airwaves and shoved calamitously through the speaker of the radio. Redneck civilization was gaining on us.

The noise modulated, attenuating back out into real voices. The rabbit chase had started again.

Grant muttered obscenities as he zipped his fly.

"Rabbit, you still in your hole?"

"Copy that."

"We go'ne *find* you!"

"Hey Eagle Scout!" my brother's voice broke onto channel 19. "Did you happen to pass an empty security booth on your way through the gate?"

Grant sat up with a grin on his face, a game look in his eyes. He looked like he was sitting in Jerry's room—on some afternoon before his best friend had started working so much.

He squeezed the mike and said, "That's a big ten-four. You're burning my ears up, Buckshot!"

He let go the mike button and listened for my brother's reply, a simple "Ten-four."

On the signal meter, the red arm had bent its way over to an incredible twenty watts in a burst of power. I looked at Grant in amazement.

"We're definitely in the neighborhood, Crankshaft and me," Jerry said.

A flurry of activity precipitated on the same channel, duller and fainter and coming in at ten to twelve watts in the background, tops.

"Buckshot, what's your ten-twenty?" came a rain of inquiries over the air.

My brother, aping the easy, studied laid-backness of the trucker's lingo that ratchet jaws had picked up over the ether, replied: "We're up on French Bluff, looking down at one pregnant roller skate parked in a cul-de-sac. Mercy sakes, looks like she's about to give birth to a whole 'nother set of wheels!"

I started in my seat. Grant closed his eyes, laying his head against the wheel.

Jerry must have been holding the mike button down. In the background we could hear my father—who was probably holding a Bud slipped into one of my mother's Styrofoam huggies—laughing beerily.

I got out of the car, leaving Grant to make a recovery and sort through things with my brother. I had my own things to figure out. I looked up at the Bluff where my brother said they were parked and transmitting, but all I saw were the frames of two-by-fours rising up from their foundations—skeletons of new houses—and beyond them the dune where once the French had looked out to see their fate as the vengeful Spanish sailed up the river to the shore, intent on slaughtering them all. I didn't see my father's little pickup, though there were cars parked up there, lovers stopping to neck and see out onto the river from atop the dune.

I started walking. I wasn't far from home. In less than ten minutes a gurgling Camaro, with an engine louder than an airplane's, passed me on the road and slowed, but I kept my head down. The engine sound died away in the distance then was reborn behind me. My heart was pounding. You never knew who was a friend and who was a redneck wanting to call you a faggot and harass you. The engine coughed as the car pulled alongside me and slowed almost to an idle. But I was on Townsend Boulevard already and it was busy enough for people to see me getting attacked.

"Hey, Tom!"

It was my father, leaning out of a sapphire-blue Camaro with orange and gold flames licking his door. I wasn't even surprised. I already knew the story. My brother had gotten his car; no wonder I hadn't seen the little puce pickup. I'd mistaken the hotrod with its metallic-flake paint for a workaday make-out vehicle.

"Go for a ride?"

My father had a bright blissful look on his face as he opened the door and pulled back the seat with himself still in it. He stuck out his tongue and made a pop-eyed face to indicate the strain against his old bones. He was thirty-five. Now I'm thirty-five.

My brother greeted me in a friendlier way than he had in months—even years. He was relieved to have his car. Proud he'd worked for it. Optimistic that it would turn out to be a means of escape. And for all I knew it was. Everything was going to change for the better now. I was going to change. Jerry said, "What's up?"

"Nothing."

We went through our usual rigmarole. I scooted forward into the space between the bucket seats in front. Jerry said, "Don't breathe on my neck."

My father turned and winked. He had a roadie sitting coolly between his legs and he said, "Denim Kid, I thought you were with Eagle Scout."

"I was."

He wasn't looking at me but was watching the road, as if he really were that responsible licensed passenger to my brother with his learner's permit. Or as if he were carefully picking through my story, dissecting it like a lie, as he'd done—respectfully, helping to preserve my dignity—when I was younger.

He said, "Well, what happened?"

I paused. I still smelled L'Air du Temps. I still tasted the tangle of hair growing in thick confusion around Grant's penis. But I'd already decided they didn't know what was going on.

"You weren't mad because we spotted you so fast?" my father said.

"That was pure luck, Denim Kid," my brother said. Calling me that was a show of confidence—of fraternity, but in the chummy not brotherly sense.

"I was bored," I said.

Except for the noise of the engine, like a prop plane's in takeoff, we rode in silence. They dropped me off at home because they had to go hide. They were the rabbit now; they'd found Eagle Scout and me.

My mother was smoking in the dark in the living room. I went to her and sat in the chair opposite and watched the orange point of her cigarette's ash move up, freeze into place, then slowly descend again. We didn't talk for a few minutes, and by the time we began it was too late for telling the truth.

The weather changed. A few oak leaves fell. One day she came home with a new perfume to try. She said it was more her style—she was really an autumn type; the lady at the counter had helped her understand all that by working on her color charts and arriving at a set of important personal conclusions.

"I'm dark-complected," she said. "So I'm early fall. Also, I'm Leo—and that makes me fiery but deep. I can mix those colors, dark and fiery, as long as I observe the polarity rule. So if I wear something lighter, I complement it with my dark eyes and complexion and put on musk." She was confiding in me even as we were growing further and further apart.

The L'Air du Temps was shelved in the vanity my father had built her in their walk-in closet.

I started taking the bus twice a week to the public library and haunting the toilets there. I was a Libra. So I came home with the stacks of books I'd check out after cruising older men and, sometimes, stepping into the last stall with one of them.

Michael Carroll
Michael Carroll's fiction has appeared in the *Ontario Review*, the *Reading Room Journal*, and such anthologies as *Men on Men 7*. "Rabbit Chase" is from a cycle of stories about growing up in northern Florida entitled *Palmettoes*. He is also at work on a novel, *The Gnostic Ghostwriter*. He lives in New York.

Disability

Vestal McIntyre

The Insurance Company sends me to a shrink because they think I've been on disability too long. They want to find out if I'm really still in pain or if I'm crazy or a liar. But he's not a very good shrink for any of these purposes. I tell him about my back pain and he just sort of nods and waits for me to go on to something else. He always acts like everything I say makes perfect sense, and I'm making all the right decisions. And if he's coming to the conclusion that I'm a liar, he must have some secret method 'cause whenever I lie to him, he acts like he believes it, no problem.

Maybe he's forgotten that I'm not one of his regular patients and that he's supposed to be finding me out rather than helping me.

He nods a lot. He crosses his legs like a girl, leans toward me, props his chin on his thumbs and nods. His thumbs fit neatly into the cleft in his chin. Maybe he wasn't born with that cleft, it's been worn in by years of leaning and nodding. At first I thought he was gay because of the way he crosses his legs, but then he says all these annoying straight-guy things. Like when I come in he shakes my hand and slaps my shoulder and says, Hey guy, how was your week? Then he nods his way through the session and doesn't say anything substantial till near the end of the hour, when he comes up with a weird summary of what he's been thinking, like Jerry Springer's Final Thought. But they never really have anything to do with my life. Like, last week he listened to me talk about this fight I had with some asshole bartender the night before that got me 86'ed, and this new ringing in my left ear, plus a few back pain references. When I ran out of things to complain about, he nodded at my quietness for a minute then gave his Final Thought, which was something like, Frank, we can't be afraid to share our needs with those closest to us, because that's the foundation of love, and the amount of patience we measure out for their response is something we learn though trial and error. Which is fine, but it wasn't for me. Maybe that was the response meant for the guy before me, and the old lady who comes in after me will get mine.

I would even understand if I talked about all that shit and his response was something about the value of honesty and hard work—then at least I'd figure Insurance was feeding him lines. But it's just senseless. Is he getting away with being weird just because I'm not paying and because I've never done therapy before, so I don't know what's appropriate and what's not?

I haven't talked to anyone about this. Maybe I should. Especially someone who's done therapy before. I'll ask around. I'll bet Rand's done therapy.

My Deal

Rand is rich—rich from his family, so he doesn't have to work. But he doesn't know his family anymore and doesn't really have anything. Except for a big loft in Soho or Tribeca—down where it's fancy and I'm completely out of place. He says he thought about buying in Brooklyn and would have if it weren't for delivery. He can't live somewhere without good delivery.

So he owns the top two floors of an old, narrow converted factory, but he only lives in the top floor. He leaves the other empty, so he doesn't have neighbors. Once I asked if I could live in the empty floor. I asked it only half-serious, hoping that he'd be into it. But he said, Then I'd have a neighbor, wouldn't I?

Rand's deal is that he has a need to be held down. His hands can't be free while he's asleep, so he had a special bed custom-made. It has a twin-sized birch frame, and about halfway down either side, posts come up from the frame with supports attached at angles. At the top of the posts are little boxes, also made of birch. They open toward the head of the bed, and they're lined top and bottom with an inch of foam rubber, then cushioned velvet. His hands fit snugly into these two boxes while he sleeps. He says he's never had trouble sleeping in the years since he had this bed made.

He also has an old-fashioned, cushioned chair that has the same kind of boxes fastened to the armrests. It stands against the wall between the two huge, naked windows. It's always struck me as odd that, with all his privacy stuff, he can live without curtains. There's no one across the street, but still.

Once I sat on the floor drinking his expensive old scotch and watching him read in his chair. He propped this little wire contraption on his lap that held the book open (it was some book on Chinese art) and he sat reading with his hands in the boxes until he had to turn the page, which he did. He even paused, holding the page to look at a picture before turning it. Then he put his hand back into its box.

I told him he was one crazy motherfucker and he said, And?

Most friends have to laugh it off when I talk to them like that, but not Rand. He was born missing a sense of humor, so he has to deal with stuff head-on.

Maybe you're thinking how can I hang out with someone who doesn't have a sense of humor? Well, he's an interesting guy. He has interesting things to say. And he's been sort of a project for me. First to figure him out. Then, when I got as far as I could with that (which wasn't far), to find him a boyfriend.

The first candidate was my friend Daniel Hamburger. Daniel's a waiter at a fancy restaurant, where all the other waiters treat him horribly. He's sort of an easy target. For one thing, his last name is Hamburger. And he's a talker. If you tell him to shut up, he won't. He'll ask you what he said that bothered you so he can avoid the subject as he continues to talk. And he's a little big around the middle, which makes him waddle. But his face is really cute and he means well.

I thought it would be perfect, since Rand never laughs and Daniel's never funny.

But before I could even begin to put my plan into action, Rand met him by accident. Rand and I were at a bar. (He does go out, but only occasionally, and he primly drinks little snifters of cognac and doesn't talk to anyone. That's how we met—I picked him up at a bar and we went to his place and talked ourselves out of the attraction before we could have sex.) Daniel came up and started blabbing to me, and then to Rand. I went to get us a round and came back to find Daniel in the middle of an involved explanation of an episode *of Star Trek: The Next Generation*. Rand was nodding, looking around the room. Daniel wouldn't try that shit with me because I made a rule that he can't go into explanations of his dreams or TV show plots. But I hadn't been there to stop him this time.

Rand hated him. All the way home he walked a halfstep behind me, the way he does when he wants to complain more confidentially into my ear. I just despise the impulse in people to drone on and on about the mundane experiences of their lives, assuming that these are shared experiences, and that that somehow makes them funny, he said. If they are shared, that's cause for despair, if you ask me. Not that they care. Most people just use their listeners as sounding boards. I have to stop myself from telling them to buy pets.

Rand never complains about people one at a time. He complains about behaviors or types of people, which is his idea of being polite, but it just makes him seem put off by entire populations rather than just, say, Daniel.

It was just as well, though. The next week Daniel was back onto girls. He's constantly going back and forth, wondering if he should go after men or women. I try to tell him to relax and go after both, but he says he has to decide. Daniel believes in that MGM sort of love. He thinks he has to narrow down the field by fifty percent if he's ever going to find the One Love who's meant for him. He thinks there's a right answer.

I just roll my eyes—not really roll them, because this is Daniel's biggest concern. Just roll them in my mind.

Candidate number two, Hector, stands a much better chance.

But before I go summarizing and analyzing all my other friends, you're probably wondering what my deal is, right? Other than being in everybody's business. Well, here in a nutshell is My Deal:

Remember Chaka from *The Land of the Lost*? The squirmy little ape-boy with bucked teeth, friend of the humans, always running around his family's dusty cave? That was me at eight. My dad was usually out selling things or cheating on my mother. We lived in East Brunswick, New Jersey, and our living room with all its browns and wickers was like a dusty cave.

Then my dad left. My mother shut the curtains and started sleeping in the living room. That was 1976, the year Judy Collins came out with the album *Judith*. My mother sat for a year listening to "Send in the Clowns" again and again. Do you know the cover of that album? It's a head shot of Judy. Her hair is blowing and her hands gently frame her tilted head. Her lips are parted, just a little. She has these incredible gray eyes that are sort of vacant and knowing at the same time. If you added makeup and a tear it could actually be a face from a sad clown painting. My mother wore that same expression as she listened to "Send in the Clowns."

I started missing school to take care of her. We went on welfare. She started sharing her pills.

That was before the invention of CD players, with their repeat function. My mother had to creep back and forth between the sofa and the record player all day. It was also before the government started cracking down on fathers who skipped out on child support and doctors who made a business of over-prescribing sedatives to nervous women.

A few years later, my mother got into self-help. She read books and went to a group every Wednesday night in the rec room at the Presbyterian church. This helped her get off pills. She took a course to become a real estate agent, and she became beautiful again. She was too busy for me now, but I had my own business—I had appointments with the Doctor and sold the surplus pills to kids at school. Remember Wesley from *Mr. Belvedere*? The half-cute kid who's always conniving to either make a buck or get himself out of trouble, able to fool everyone but, of course, Mr. Belvedere? That was me in high school.

With my mother and me both making money, I didn't have to go to the grocery store with those embarrassing food stamps anymore. She gave me real money to eat out.

By the time the Doctor went to jail, it was no big deal because I had other suppliers to fall back on. Then, just a couple weeks after high school graduation, I went to jail myself. My mother was shocked, which didn't make sense. She hired me a lawyer, and when I was released after two weeks, she introduced me to all these creepy people who wanted to help get me off drugs. I said no thank you and quit by myself. My main connection had been arrested too, and I was afraid of breaking my parole and going back to jail. I was satisfied to carry a thermos of vodka and ginger ale in my backpack. I still do, as a matter of fact. I don't know why people use flasks or worse, paper bag it. A nice old-fashioned plaid thermos holds more, keeps it cold, and is far less obvious.

My mother married an older guy who makes less money than her and they moved deeper into New Jersey. I moved to New York City. At different points over the years, she would refuse to support me and I'd get some job. Then, three years ago she said she'd had it, I was nearly thirty and it was time to quit hitting her up for money. She swore she'd

never give me another cent as long as I didn't have a Career. I reminded her that she owed me for the years I took care of her. Her husband
pounded his fist on the kitchen table and said how dare I speak to her
like that, I was a deadbeat, and so on. I stomped out and didn't speak to
my mother for over a year. I wasn't really mad at her, just waiting for
her to give in and call me to offer money. But she didn't.

So I got a job as a courier of confidential documents for a gigantic
law firm in Queens. It was the best job I ever had. I got a decent wage
plus benefits just for driving around New York and Long Island picking up file boxes full of papers so completely uninteresting I wondered
why they bothered making them confidential, and taking them to this
courthouse or that insurance company, where I'm sure they would
never get read. Luckily, I left my thermos at home the day when, on my
way out to a firm on Long Island, a truck slammed me from the side
and rolled me off the LIE. When I woke up, I had this heavenly feeling
that I recognized as heavy-duty painkillers. There was my mother's
concerned Judy Collins face and, hallelujah, a muffled pain in my right
lower back.

That was a year and a half ago. I'm still on disability. I go for physical therapy and get massages. I have doctor's appointments twice a
month, and now this shrink. I tell them all I'm still in incredible pain.

I am in a little pain actually, but not like I say. You're getting the
extra-confidential version here, 'cause I don't tell anybody I lie about
the pain. *Nobody*, not even my friends. It's the one thing I lie about, and
that's not so bad considering how most people wrap themselves in lie
after lie after lie.

Remember, in *Hello Dolly*, how Ephram Levi, Dolly's dead husband used to say that Money, pardon the expression, is like manure. It's
not worth a thing until it's spread around encouraging young things to
grow. That's me now. I live on disability, but only because it allows me
to give everything to others—friends and strangers. I don't hoard anything—my time, my things, nothing—for two reasons: 'cause I'm driv-
en to out of Love, and 'cause it's actually easier for me if I don't have
anything. It sounds like I'm joking but I'm not. I've thought about this.

Nori

On Tuesday evenings I have to baby-sit the girls. Marcie and Bill
go to their marriage counselor and then out to eat or to a movie by

themselves—it's their weekly Marital Improvement Time. I stay home and watch TV with Missy and Tina. See, I live in their house for free in return for baby-sitting twice a week—Tuesday nights 'til ten or eleven and then Sunday afternoons when Bill goes for golf and Marcie sees her girlfriends. They've had this rigid schedule thing since they decided to try to work it out and he came back. That was a year before I moved in.

Marcie was a paralegal at the firm, and sometimes we'd have a drink after work. Just after the accident, my lease came up for renewal and, not knowing I'd get disability, I gave it up. Marcie offered to let me live in the basement of her house out in Queens. It's sort of its own apartment—there's a little refrigerator and a hot plate. Separate phone line. The street winds back and forth, trying to make it seem like a roomier neighborhood than it is. All the houses were built at the same time and are variations on the same theme. The neighbors eerily remind me of my neighbors growing up in Jersey.

Marcie said, You'd be doing us a favor as well, the girls adore you, Bill likes the idea and so on—but Bill doesn't really like the idea. It was just something he was giving in on to save the marriage. A concession.

I put the girls to bed at ten and go back to the living room. I pour myself a drink. Now I can watch what I want.

Bill and Marcie get home. I think they've been fighting. Marcie goes up to check on the girls and Bill stands in the dark living room with his fists on his hips watching the TV. He's thinking about something else though.

Have a seat, Bill.

No, I think I'm going to bed.

He stands there a minute, then sits down anyway. You want a drink, Bill? He looks at my glass of Stoli on Ice. He hadn't realized I was drinking. I shouldn't have said anything, but I try to be friendly to the guy.

Um, no thanks, Frank. Then he says, Just out of curiosity, you weren't drinking when the girls were still up, were you?

Of course not, Bill.

No, I'm just saying, it's fine to have a drink sometimes. I mean, Marcie and I have a drink in front of them once in a while—they definitely know what it means—but we try to keep that at a minimum.

Understood, Bill. I've never even had a drink in the same room with the girls.

Oh sure, he says, no problem. Just curious.

Well, I say, I'm actually feeling tired. I'm gonna go on down. I leave Bill watching TV and take my drink downstairs to watch my own TV even though it doesn't have cable. But I'm restless. I slept in today and didn't really do much.

I call Rand to see if he wants to meet for a drink. The answering machine picks up and I leave a message knowing that he's probably listening. Rand's like that. He'll tell you later, I heard you leaving that message but I didn't pick up. I didn't feel like going out.

He's been acting sort of odd lately. He gave me a set of his keys and told me that if he ever goes a few days without returning my calls to come check on him. I guess it's because he does things like gag himself and shut himself in the closet for hours at a time. Sometimes he works with this older prostitute named Belinda, and I told him it would be safer for him to just stick with that. They don't have sex, she just comes over and ties him up or holds him down, I don't know. I actually met her once. I was coming in as she was leaving. She was in her forties, very sturdy looking, polite, professional.

He doesn't really know I'm trying to find him a boyfriend. He would just dismiss the whole thing. When I started my search, I sort of nonchalantly asked him if the guys he dates have to be into bondage. He said, oh, definitely not. That's something I take care of on my own.

I would call Hector tonight to see if he wants to go out, but he never wants to go into Manhattan. He goes to the local straight bars or to the nasty gay bar on Northern Boulevard.

So I go in by myself. I park on Tenth Street and try to decide which bar to go to, then realize I'd really rather just go to the porn theater on Third Avenue.

It's a slow night—I count eight guys as I sit down in a dark corner seat and pour some Stoli and ginger into the thermos-lid coffee cup. On screen, a bunch of skinny blond boys from the seventies are having group sex on a houseboat. That's what I like about this place—they don't just play the new-release video stuff. They show older porn too, stuff shot on film. The sex goes on and on and I wish it would end and the plot would progress. I'm completely immune to porno sex scenes. If I'm going to get turned on at all, it's by the in-between scenes, especially if there's a cute boy who stays dressed for a while, keeping me in suspense.

The secret about this place that everyone who comes here knows is that if you go downstairs, past the bathrooms and through a door marked Employees Only, that's where you'll find most of the guys. There's long dimly lit corridors lined with little dark rooms. They play tinny gay dance music and there're guys cruising the corridors or waiting in the doorways for someone to join them. Most of the guys tonight are old or unattractive. (I take them twenty-five and younger unless I'm too drunk or bored to care.) Then I see him. Tall, square-jawed, Asian, probably Japanese, bored-looking, dressed in black. He walks down the corridor and I follow him.

I go for the direct approach, which is unusual for this place. I tap him on the shoulder. He sort of jumps and turns to me. I indicate an open doorway. He follows me in and I lock the door.

What's your name?

Nori. name?

What?

Nori, N-O-R-I.

Okay, I'm Frank.

Thick accent.

I kiss him. He's handsome, handsome, handsome and I'm a little drunk. He smiles and puts his arms around me and I kiss him again for a long time. Then I offer him a drink. When I pull out the thermos, he says, Coffee? I pour him a little. He tastes it and likes it and drinks it down. I put my hand inside his shirt and feel his tight warm body. For a second I think he's calling me Papa, which is weird, but he's actually just offering me poppers. I pass. They'd just make me weak-kneed and headachy. He puts the bottle to his nose and sniffs.

We fool around for a while, light stuff, until the air in the little room is stifling with body heat and the smell of his poppers.

It is very hot in here, he says.

Yeah, do you want to go somewhere else? Your place?

He shakes his head. I have roommates, he says.

I can't take him all the way out to Queens. Do you want to go to a different room? I ask.

Uh … yes.

We pull on our clothes and step out into to the hall. Everybody turns to look at us. I find us a new room, but Nori hesitates.

Maybe I'll go home, he whispers, it's late.

I don't want to let him go, and I don't really care if I show it.

Oh come on. Don't you like me?

Yes I like you. He smiles.

Then come in here with me.

I don't like these little rooms.

Then I have an idea. It's a bad idea, but I do it anyways.

I know a place we can go. It's an empty apartment. We'd have to be quiet if we go there 'cause the neighbors are asleep.

Okay.

I think to myself, we should take the long walk down to Rand's just to be more certain we get there past his bedtime.

It's late April and the streetlamps in Washington Square Park filter through the tree branches and their tender, light-green leaves. I wish we could walk through the park but it closes at midnight. It used to not matter, I tell Nori, but now the place is crawling with police.

We have a halting conversation. He's an engineering grad student at NYU. He's from Japan but wants to stay in New York. We duck into doorways and kiss. My feet are like bricks and I'm walking unevenly. Watch out, he says and pulls me, but I've already stepped on whatever he was warning me about. It's stuck to my foot and I try to kick it off. Then I look. It's a glue trap with a mouse stuck to it. The mouse is still wriggling, trying to get free. Someone must have thrown it out the window.

Ugh! Pull it off! I yell, but Nori is laughing and won't come near me. I can't bring myself to touch it. I limp over to a metal trash can, lift it up, and slide the glue trap underneath it. I push the trash can down. It crushes the mouse, and I can pull my foot away. Good. Put it out of its misery.

Nori is still laughing, but he realizes that I'm really disgusted so he hugs me and says, I'm sorry but it is so funny.

When we get to Rand's I can see that the lights on his floor are out. Remember, quiet. We climb the stairs and I turn the key very, very slowly but it still scrapes and knocks as it unlocks and I cringe. The empty apartment is lit by a streetlight. Rand stores some boxes and furniture down here and they cast long shadows across the floor toward us.

Wow, says Nori, this is a nice place. It's yours?

Sorta, I say.

I pull the dust cloth off a sofa, and we fool around for a while, mostly me doing stuff to him 'cause I can't really get hard. He's affectionate, which I like. He looks me in the eye and touches my face.

At one point I think I hear something upstairs. I hold Nori tight and say shhh. Rand is definitely walking across his apartment. I'm terrified, because if he finds me out, he'll never forgive me. This is a shitty thing to do, and I don't know why I thought of it. The footsteps go back to the end of his apartment where the bed is. He was probably just taking a piss. Maybe we should leave, I think.

Nori asks, What's wrong?

Nothing, I say, and go back to his smooth, narrow body.

It starts to get light outside and I tell Nori we have to go. We can't fall asleep here. We dress, carefully put things back as they were, and lock up.

We share a cab back up to the East Village.

I'm so tired, says Nori. I have to get up soon and go to class.

I'm sorry.

Do you have to go to work?

No.

That is good.

Nori writes his number on a little pad he has in his pocket, and tears it off. He says, You can call me if you like, and I tell him I will.

The cab pulls up at his building. We kiss good-bye. We kiss and kiss until the cabbie says, C'mon!

Bonus

I'm not a morning person. Especially when I was up all night. The phone wakes me and it's Missy and Tina asking if they can come down. They're home from school so it must be 3:00. I tell them no, I'm still sleeping, I'll let them know when I'm up.

They used to just come down and pound on my door. Then Marcie told them that Frank's room is his own separate home and you have to call him before you go visit, just like your other friends.

The phone rings again and I let the machine pick it up. Frank, it's Rand. Pick up.

Hi Rand, I'm sleeping.

Frank, I'm freaking out here. Could you come over?

What's wrong?

I think someone broke into the apartment downstairs.

What? Why do you think that?

I thought I heard something in the middle of the night. I went down there this morning and I could tell someone had been there.

Did they take anything?

I don't think so. They could have, though. I don't remember everything I had in there.

How did they get in?

I don't know.

Did you check the windows?

They were all locked.

And nothing was broken?

No.

Are you sure you're not just imagining this?

I think so.

You think you're sure, or you think you're imagining it?

I think I'm sure.

Okay, well you're not in any danger now, are you? I'll come over tonight. I've got to go back to sleep.

All right.

I pull the covers over my head and feel ashamed. I never lie to my friends. You can never ever do that again, I tell myself.

The guilt won't let me sleep so I call Missy and Tina. They come down and jump on the bed with me still in it. You sleep all day, they say.

I stay up late, that's why.

Doing what?

Stuff.

What kind of stuff?

Grown-up, none-of-your-business kind of stuff.

I go shower, leaving them to root around in my stuff and play my CDs. All the porno and booze is out of their reach, locked up.

Then Hector calls and talks me into meeting him for happy hour at the Broadway, this corny straight bar in Forest Hills decorated with posters from Broadway musicals. When I get there, he's slouched in front of a beer, but his face is beaming. Let me buy you a drink, Frank, he says. I got a raise today.

He does computer stuff. He's my most sensible friend. His face is shiny and his hairline is receding. He's short and has a strong little body. He lives in Jamaica, Queens, down the hall from his parents who immigrated from Guatemala before he was born. I adore his mother, but she has no patience for me. His dad works as a maintenance man, comes home, drinks a lot.

Hector goes to Mass with his mother on Sundays. She goes to Mass daily, and tells him he should too, it's a ticket straight to Heaven bypassing Purgatory, but he tells her he doesn't have time, and once a week is plenty.

Once he told me that a psychic he trusts told him he would die before the age of thirty-five. I told him that's bullshit, and he just shrugged sadly. He's twenty-nine. Maybe that's why he goes to Mass.

I think he and Rand would balance each other out nicely.

I've been hoping for this raise for a long time, Hector is saying. And they gave it to me as a reward for my one-hundredth contract. They also gave me these other bonuses. It was great.

Hector stutters just a little. It's not really a stutter, his jaw just gets stuck on a few words and he has to push them out. You wouldn't even notice it the first time you met him. I think it's sort of endearing.

Like what? I ask.

A better parking space. And a gift certificate for a nice dinner. Do you want to go with me?

Where?

This restaurant in Tribeca. Nobu. Robert DeNiro owns it.

Actually, Hec, I know someone who could really use a nice dinner. My friend Rand.

What do you mean? he says suspiciously.

What do you mean, what do I mean?

Isn't he rich? Why would he need a nice dinner?

It would be good for him to get out, you know. Meet a new friend.

Wait a minute, he says. Isn't this that guy who's into bondage and stuff?

I think to myself, I should really keep my mouth shut, and I say, No, just forget about all that. Rand's really attractive—tall, thin, shaved head, very striking-looking. You'd like him.

Maybe, says Hector. I'll think about it.

Hector has a couple of beers and I have a couple of Stolis, then he suggests we go hang out at his place. I've noticed he always stops himself at two drinks.

I sit on the couch in the living room of his dingy apartment and he plays these new records that he's excited about. Hector's sort of a record freak. He has hundreds and hundreds of them—lots of Latin stuff, all the old '80s New Wave he used to listen to, female jazz vocalists, and this weird stuff he's been collecting lately. He doesn't like CDs.

Now this is genius. There's nothing else in the world like this. It's a Disney movie from the '50s called *Grand Prize*. No one's ever heard of it, right? But they released this record of the songs from the movie and Cubby—remember, the littlest Mouseketeer, the one who plays the drums?—narrating the story.

He puts on the record and this cheery little boy's voice starts telling about the County Fair and how a little orphan goat named Sissy hopes to win grand prize. Then Sissy in her little goat-voice sings a song. Hector sort of mouths the words along with it and laughs.

Hector, what in the fuck am I listening to?

Isn't it just bizarre? laughs Hec.

You have too much time on your hands if you find this stuff entertaining, I yell.

Oh, come on, he says. It's wonderful. Listen.

You are in bad shape, my friend. You work these long hours and come home and listen to children's records all night. You've completely lost touch.

Frank, please don't start, he whines, taking off the record. He's used to this treatment. Sometimes I feel like I have to abuse my friends a little, especially Hector, who isolates himself so much. He needs to be toughened up and sent out into the world.

You've got to get out more before you disintegrate into this totally reclusive Catholic hermit fuckup. And quit going to Mass. Psychics are bullshit and you're not going to die at thirty-five.

Dios mio, he says, looking to heaven. Why did I tell you about that?

And don't start speaking Spanish like you're some native. You grew up in Queens, New York and have never been anywhere. That's why you should go to dinner with Rand.

What sense does that make?

He might tell you something new, I say.

I'm not really serious about any of this. It's just for my fun and his betterment.

There's a knock on the door. Hector? It's his Mom.

Oh, allow me, I say and I open the door. Hello, Mrs. Cordova, how are you? I hold out my hand.

Oh. Hello, Frank. She shakes my hand faintly. She turns to Hector and starts speaking in Spanish, because she doesn't trust me. He answers in English out of politeness to me: Mama, call them on the phone. They're nice people. You don't need me. She speaks even more quickly and he answers her in Spanish. Back and forth.

Then she shuffles back down the hall to her own apartment.

What was that all about? I ask.

Oh, she wants me to ask the Puerto Ricans next door to her to turn down their music. She doesn't want to do it herself 'cause she's afraid of them. She says island people cast spells. I told her to call them.

She hates me, doesn't she?

She doesn't hate anybody, says Hector.

Did she say anything about me?

He hesitates. She said you smell like alcohol.

Shit! I put my hand over my mouth and try to smell my own breath. Do I?

Hector shrugs sadly.

I remember that I'm supposed to go over to Rand's, and this is a good time to exit.

I drive in, and Rand's wringing his long hands, though he says he feels better. He takes me down to the empty apartment and asks me what I think.

Well, what makes you think there was someone here?

He shows me faint streaks in the dust on the floor. Doesn't it look like someone walked across the floor?

That could be anything, I say.

And this is the other thing. I have a method for covering things. I fold the cloth here and here. He shows me a chair covered by a dust cloth. But this is just thrown over, he says, indicating the sofa.

Now that is sort of weird. But how do you think they got in?

I don't know. Maybe they picked the lock. It might have been a homeless person who just spent the night then left, he said.

Maybe you should have another lock put on.

I already did. The man came today. Here, he says, handing me a key, keep this with those other keys I gave you.

We go back up to his apartment. He puts on opera, sits in the chair and puts his hands in the boxes. I tell him we should go out to eat, but he just wants to order in. I call for Vietnamese, he pays, and we sit down to eat at his long, bare pine table.

My shrink says the weirdest shit, I say.

Like what?

Just stuff that has nothing to do with me and doesn't make much sense. Have you ever done therapy? What kind of things are they supposed to tell you?

My parents sent me to a psychologist when I was young, but I wouldn't speak to him. Then I tried some different types of therapists a few years ago, but they didn't help me much.

Why?

I don't think it was their fault. They were just trained to deal with one facet of the whole, I felt, and I needed something more … inclusive … or nothing at all.

Mine, he acts like he's listening, but I don't think he really is. Or at least he doesn't take it into account when he sums things up. He just invents something. For a while I wondered if he had some big, different idea of what my problem was and how to fix it. Like he was using some technique on me. But now I just think he's making shit up.

Then you should quit, says Rand with his mouth full.

Well, I can't really quit yet. The Insurance Company is having me go. It has to do with my injury.

How is your back, by the way?

Ugh. It's awful. The pain is just horrible. But it's like second nature to me now, you know, I just live with it.

He nods and wipes his mouth.

We finish our food and when I'm about to leave, I say, You know Rand, I have a friend who lives out near me, Hector, maybe I've talked about him. No? Well, he got this bonus from work—a gift certificate to that restaurant Nobu.

Robert DeNiro's place.

Exactly. He asked me if I wanted to go and I'm not really interested, too fancy for me, but I thought maybe, since you live so close …

Are you trying to set me up, Frank?

No. I was just thinking, you know. Just a friendly thing. He couldn't think of anyone else to invite, so I suggested you.

Does he think you're setting us up?

Definitely not.

Well …, says Rand and he fades away for a minute, face frozen, … I've been meaning to try that place … and they don't deliver.

Good. I'll give him your number.

But it's a couple of days later, Friday, when I call Hector to give him Rand's number and he tells me he already used the gift certificate, for lunch with his mother the day before.

Damn it, Hector, you said you would go with Rand!

No, Frank, I told you I would think about it, he says. Well, I thought about it and decided I'd rather take my mom. Can't I just meet this guy for coffee or something informal? Or, better yet, why don't the three of us go do something together? That would take the pressure off.

No, no, no, that won't work.

Why?

I have to call you back.

I go to my PO Box where my trusty disability check is waiting for me. I cash it, then I drive into the city, down to Hudson Street where Nobu is. It's pretty impressive, with ceilings so high it's sort of echoey, huge, abstract paintings, and all these yuppies lunching. I ask to look at the dinner menu, and the host says they're serving lunch right now, and I say I know, I'm going to buy a gift certificate. He opens a dinner menu for me and, Jesus, this place is expensive! Better make it for one-fifty. But I want them to have wine, too. Two hundred.

I buy the gift certificate and order a spring roll appetizer to go, because it's the only thing on the menu I'm willing to pay for myself.

It's sunny and breezy, so I go sit on a bench in the park and open the little box they gave me. These are the littlest spring rolls I've ever seen. There are two—the size of my pinkies. They're pretty good though.

I have to see my shrink uptown at four, so I have a few hours to waste. I haven't talked to Daniel Hamburger for a while, and I know he works the lunch shift on Fridays, so I walk up Hudson to the West Village to visit him. It's this fancy French place—the Something Bistro.

It's so good to see you, Frank. I've been meaning to call you. I have big news. Big, big news. Here, sit at the bar, do you want anything to eat? How about a drink? He has a breathy voice and he doesn't pause between sentences.

It's sort of early, I say. Maybe a Bloody Mary?

Good. He steps around the bar and starts mixing. It's good that you visited. I'm bored out of my mind, it's been so slow. But anyways I've got big news.

Someone calls from the kitchen, which is just beyond the bar, Hamburger? Hamburger? Why am I the only one running food? Oh, I'm sorry. I didn't know you had a friend.

It's an ugly little waiter with red hair. He gives me a little smile, then says, Never mind, Daniel. Take your time.

I wonder if he would have been so nice if he didn't think I was cute.

What's your news, Daniel?

Well, I met someone.

That's great, I say. Male or female?

Female. Her name is Ana and she just moved here from Idaho. She's really pretty. Her attitude is sort of dark. She's quiet and you'd think she's brooding, but she's just shy. When you get talking she's so smart and nice! She's really getting me into shape. Wise beyond her years, you know?

How old is she?

Daniel pauses. Seventeen.

Oh my God, Daniel, what are you doing? That's not even legal. What, is she some NYU freshman?

No. She doesn't go to college. But she wants to. She dropped out of high school. She's gonna get her GED.

I can't help but laugh. Seventeen-year-old drop-out fresh from Idaho? Was she hustling on the street when you met her?

Don't talk like that, Frank, I'm serious.

Let me guess, I say. She's staying with you.

Well, yeah. She's been great. You know how disorganized I am, how I never get anything done. She's been helping me. I really like her a lot.

I think for a minute. Who am I to criticize, if he's happy? Especially when it's so easy for him to find people he likes, but so hard to find people who like him. So I say, Well then, Daniel, God love ya. Whatever makes you happy.

He grins and goes on about her. And on and on. Everything spells disaster, but I bite my lip, and nod like my shrink. He asks me if I want some food, and I say, Sure, just bring me whatever's good. He brings me a big bowl of mussels in the shell and a basket of bread, and goes on and on about Ana.

When I leave he hasn't asked me one thing about how I am, but that's typical. It's not that he doesn't care.

I tell my shrink about Nori and Rand and the guilt. I tell him the pain is so bad I can't even get out of bed some mornings.

He tells me about the beauty of released aggression and suggests I pile up the pillows on my bed, and punch them.

That night I give Hector the gift certificate. I put it in his hand and say, Here. This is another gift certificate to Nobu. Don't you dare say no and don't you dare thank me. And here, I put another paper in his hand. This is Rand's phone number. You will call him tonight.

My friends are such babies, I think.

Jeez, Frank, says Hec. Thanks.

Fuckup

Marcie comes down to visit me one afternoon. The first time in a while. We have to talk, she says, and puts her hand on my knee. Is this working out for you? I mean, are you happy living here?

Are you happy with me living here? I ask, 'cause I can see what's coming.

Well, yes. You're great with the girls and it's been a real help … her voice trails off.

But … I say to help her along. Out with it, Marcie.

But Bill and I worry that we're allowing you to stagnate. It's been a long time and you haven't progressed as far as we can see. Your back's not getting better, you're not working.…

Marcie, does Bill want me to leave?

Don't get defensive, Frank. It's not that we want you to leave, we just want you to step back and evaluate things. Think of why you're here.

Marcie, you've been very good to me, so let me make this easy for you. I've been here too long. I'll start looking for another place.

Well, she hesitates, do you feel okay about that?

I nod.

No rush, you know, she says. You're welcome here as long as it takes.

Thanks, Marcie.

She gives me a confused half-hug and gets up. We'll still be friends, right, Frank?

I don't know. Will we?

She smiles and says, Sure.

But we won't.

That night, I go out with Nori. We eat at a diner on West Fourth and in his bad English he tries to explain what he studies. It's engineering but it also has to do with architecture and for some reason he has to take sociology. It's about how people use space. He's obviously excited about it and he knits his eyebrows as he tries to explain.

Then he sits there and eats while I smile at him. He's so handsome. And fresh and clean and smart. I'm so afraid that he'll ask me what I do and I'll have to say, Nothing.

I'm a fuckup, and I'm okay with that, always have been. There are very few moments when I'm not okay with it and this is one of them. I'm ashamed of myself in front of Nori, and, although it makes me sad, that probably means that this isn't going to work.

We walk quietly toward his building. On the way there, I'm surprised to see Rand on a corner hailing a taxi. Rand! What are you doing out?

Oh, hello, Frank, he says nervously. Nothing, just heading home.

Rand, this is Nori. They both nod. Oh! I say. Did you go out with Hector?

Yeah. A cab pulls up. I'll call you and tell you about it. Nice to meet you, he says to Nori.

Nori nods, then says to me when Rand's gone, Strange man.

Yeah, I say.

When we get to his building he asks if I want to come up. His roommates are away. No, I have to get home. Sure? he asks playfully and nudges his face against mine. Yeah, I'm sure. I'll call you.

It would be easiest just not to call, of course. He still doesn't have my number. But that would be cruel, and I'm not cruel.

The next easiest would be to make up an excuse—I have a boyfriend or whatever—but that would be a lie, and I don't lie.

So I get home, put my keys on the dresser, and call before I even take my shoes off. Nori, I say, this isn't going to work. I can't go out with you again.

Why? he says. Don't you like me?

Yeah, I like you a lot. But I'm not right for you.

I don't understand.

That's okay, I say. You don't need to understand, all right? I'm sorry.

He doesn't respond.

Bye-bye, Nori.

He doesn't respond again, so I hang up.

I drink. I fall asleep with the TV on.

The next morning:

Dinner was delicious, says Hector, and don't worry. I didn't mention that I had just been there with my mom.

The place was a little overrated, says Rand. Places owned by celebrities get a lot of undue attention.

I liked him. He was interesting, says Hector

He was very nice, but I don't know if there's really a spark, says Rand.

I mean, he's definitely a bizarre guy. I would have to think about it if he asked me out again. But I enjoyed myself. Very, sort of, friendly, you know? says Hector.

He's not really my physical type, but he was handsome, says Rand.

So you guys didn't sleep together? I say.

Yeah, we did.

Yes, he slept over.

The sex was okay, says Hector. But he's very, you know, distanced. He kept me at arms length the whole time. And I had the feeling that he was thinking about every little thing. Not letting go.

It was nice, at least, to have sex, says Rand. It's been a while.

His bed was sort of small, and it had these boxes....

I know, I say.

I couldn't fall asleep with him there, says Rand. But it was all right. I napped the next day.

I don't know, Frank, says Hector. Maybe we could all get together as friends. I don't know if there's a lot of excitement.

He says I can borrow some records, says Rand.

Maybe you should give it another try, I say.

Maybe, says Hector. I gotta go. My boss is coming.

You know who was attractive? says Rand, that Asian man I saw you with on the street. Are you dating him?

No.

Mother's Day

Not to be a Daniel Hamburger, but I'm going to tell you about a dream I had. It's a sad dream:

My mother, her husband, and I are all sitting by a swimming pool. They look like they normally do—my mother has big sunglasses and a wide-brim hat with her orangish dyed hair curling up from underneath. Her husband's sleeping with a towel over his head. This is all from when they took me to Florida a few years ago. My mother tells me I should take a dip in the pool. So I get up and start to go down the stairs into the water when I realize, this is a special pool. It looks like a normal pool, but there's only an inch or two of water, then there's air underneath. I put my head down there, and sure enough it's dry and I can breathe. The sun shines though the ripply border of water above my head.

There's a woman lying on the pool floor, down at the deep end. I walk down and kneel beside her. It's my mother, but from when I was little. Her hair is long, straight, and brown, she's wearing a '70s granny dress with crocheted sleeves. I touch her hand and it's cold. Her face is still and her gray eyes are open, but she's dead.

I wake up missing my mother. It's been weeks since I talked to her. I'm such a bad son, taking care of everybody but her. Not once in my life have I even bought her a Mother's Day present.

But Mother's Day is in May, right? I look at the calendar and see that it's just over a week away. I'll do something special for her this year. Then the idea comes to me: Why don't me and my friends all take our mothers to a nice brunch together on Mother's Day. That way I'll have my friends with me, and our mothers will be meeting each other, which will distract them from what fuckups their sons are.

I start making phone calls. Hector likes the idea. Daniel will call his mom in Philly and see if she wants to come up for the day. He also gives me some suggestions of restaurants with outdoor seating. I call them, but they're all booked so I put myself on waiting lists. Should I invite Rand? He's not in touch with his mother, but I don't want him to be left out, and it would be a chance for him to see Hector again. I call and leave him a message, thinking he'll probably say no.

I call Marcie upstairs and ask her if I could take the day off from baby-sitting. She'll get her niece to do it, she says.

Then I call my mother, who I should have called first, and she says,

That's such a nice thought, Frank, but we're leaving for Atlanta that afternoon.

Ah, really? What time is your flight?

Five.

That's plenty of time! We'll meet at noon. Just bring your luggage and leave it in the car. You can go straight to the airport.

You know I like to get there early, says my mother.

I know, but still.

Okay. Sounds wonderful. How's your back, honey?

It's so bad, I tell her, sometimes I can hardly get out of bed.

A few days later, one of the restaurants calls—Emily's, in the West Village. There's been a cancellation and they can take us. I go by the next day just to check it out. It's perfect—little courtyard in back with ivy growing up the walls and birds chirping.

Rand decides that he'd like to come after I assure him he won't be the odd man out.

My one worry is that people will sit in the wrong places and no one will mingle. I want Rand as close to Hector and as far from Daniel as possible. Would it be weird for me to make a seating arrangement with little cards telling people where to sit? Weird or not, I do it, seating Hector by Rand, me by Mrs. Hamburger, whom I've never met, Hector's mother by mine, and so on.

But on Mother's Day, everybody ignores the cards I printed so neatly. Hector sits next to me and his mother, next to him. Then my mother arrives with her husband. Why'd you bring him? I ask her under my breath. I told you—we have to go to the airport soon, she says. Don't worry, he'll just sit at the bar inside and read the paper.

I seat her next to Mrs. Cordova and introduce them. Before I can re-arrange the name cards, Rand arrives, solemnly introduces himself, and sits next to me.

I glance inside and see my mother's husband sitting at the bar in his off-white suit, looking sort of like Blake Carrington from *Dynasty*. Then, at the opposite end of the bar … Hector, isn't that your dad?

Yeah. He had to drive us in. My car's in the shop and he doesn't let anyone else drive his car.

His dad was already having a beer. I tell Hector, At least go introduce him to my stepfather. Hector says that *he's* never even met my stepfather, but he goes anyways.

Daniel Hamburger arrives with someone much, much too young to be his mother. Hi, everyone, he says brightly, I'm Daniel and this is my girlfriend Ana. Ana's scowl breaks into a momentary tight smile, then sours again. They sit in the two remaining seats, Daniel next to Rand, Ana next to my mother.

Why is everybody bringing all these extra people? I ask Rand. He smiles. Never before a sense of humor, but he thinks this is funny.

They all introduce themselves to Daniel and Ana, visibly disturbed that this man in his late twenties is dating a teenager. Mrs. Cordova in particular finds it difficult to meet their eyes. When Rand introduces himself, Daniel puts his hand on his shoulder and says, Oh yeah. We've met. Rand, who doesn't like to be touched, cringes.

Daniel explains to me that his mother canceled at the last minute, so, knowing we had a reservation for seven, he invited Ana.

Well, you're very welcome, I tell Ana, who ignores me 'cause the waitress is here to take our drink orders. Brunch comes with a Mimosa or Bloody Mary. Everyone orders Mimosas except for me and Mrs. Cordova. I order a Bloody Mary, Mrs. Cordova asks for plain orange juice. The waitress doesn't card Ana, thank God.

At least the two mothers are sitting together, I think. I strain to hear what they're saying. My mother compliments Mrs. Cordova on her lovely black hair. Do you dye it? she asks, then chuckles, I hope you don't mind my asking.

Oh, I don't mind, Mrs. Cordova answers. And no, I don't dye it. She twists and strokes her cloth napkin.

My mother gasps. You don't have a single gray hair. If I didn't dye mine it would be as white as this tablecloth.

You want to know my secret? says Mrs. Cordova. Daily Mass.

In at the bar, the men seem to be getting along as well. Mr. Cordova has bought my mother's husband a beer. They stand, elbows resting on the bar, chatting.

My Bloody Mary arrives and we all order. I propose a toast to mothers, Rand says, Hear hear! and my mother and Mrs. Cordova raise their glasses, smiling bashfully like Homecoming queens.

Everything's going well, so I relax and try to draw Hector and Rand into conversation. Eventually they're talking over me, so I tell Rand to switch me places, so I can talk to Daniel who, so far, has been occupied with Ana.

Our food comes—lots of sausages, hollandaise sauce, runny eggs—everything's delicious. Ana is a dark little thing, and even though I'm perfectly friendly, she divides her attention between Daniel and her food, nothing else.

She doesn't like Mother's Day, Daniel says when she goes to the bathroom. You'll have to meet her again when it's just the three of us.

Rand taps my arm and whispers, There seems to be a dispute at the bar. Sure enough, Mr. Cordova is talking forcefully and throwing his arms about. My mother's husband is flushed red, answering him. All the nice people inside, all the mothers, are looking. Why did Hector have to bring him? He's got a horrible temper. Hector knows that better than anyone.

Hector, I say, go calm your dad down. But too late. He's stomping across the courtyard to our table. He starts speaking to his wife in Spanish. Hector tries to answer him soothingly.

Hector, what's going on? I ask.

He says we have to go now. I guess your father said something about immigrants.

Mr. Cordova, please, I say, standing up. I apologize for my stepfather. But we're in the middle of our meal.

I don't care, he says. I'm leaving.

Mrs. Cordova starts to get up. No, I say, Mr. Cordova, you go ahead. I'll give them a ride home, all right?

He says something to Hector, Hector answers, and he leaves.

Oh my, says my mother, and goes to check on her husband who's still sitting red-faced at the bar.

I excuse myself too. I find our waitress. Excuse me, I say, could you bring me a second Bloody Mary, only this time, give me twice the vodka, okay? They're a little spicy for me.

All right.

You can charge me for a double.

All right.

And use Stoli, if you don't mind. I don't like the cheap stuff.

Certainly.

I go back to the table, and people are getting over the excitement, but Mrs. Cordova looks upset. I hope you don't mind riding home with me, I say to her, trying to be kind.

No, Frank. That'll be fine.

Do you want another drink?

I guess, some more orange juice, she says. I call over the waitress.

My mother returns to the table, and she and Mrs. Cordova sit picking at their food and apologizing for their husbands.

As soon as the waitress clears our plates, my mother lays her napkin on the table and says, Well, this has been just lovely, but we've got a plane to catch.

Mother, you've got hours. Sit back down and have some coffee.

I wish I could, honey, but they have these new rules at JFK since that plane blew up. You've got to get there very early.

Come on, Mother. Just stay for a little, then we'll all go. We've barely finished eating.

It was so nice meeting you, she says sweetly to Mrs. Cordova. She says good-bye to the others and I follow her from the table. I can't believe you're leaving so soon, Mother, we haven't even gotten a chance to talk.

Now listen, Frank. I told you I was going to leave early. She takes my hand and changes her tone. Thank you very much for this, honey.

I take my hand away.

Don't spoil it, Frank.

I go back to the table. We all sip coffee and chat politely, but it's spoiled.

When we get the bill, the boys all put in their cash, and I count it up. It's not enough to cover even the food, not to mention the tip. But rather than make a big deal, I make up the difference, using most of my remaining disability money. Check comes in a few days anyways.

On the way out of the restaurant Rand takes me aside and says, Frank, I want to ask you about something. Remember that guy Nori you introduced me to? I met him again.

Where'd you meet him? I ask.

At that porn theater on Third Avenue.

I didn't know you went to porn theaters.

He shrugs and goes on, We sort of fooled around there at the theater, and he gave me his number. I want to call him, but I thought I should ask you first. Do you mind? You said you weren't seeing him, right?

We're standing on the street corner now and Daniel and Ana are saying good-bye. I'm numb. What if Rand invites Nori home and, climbing the stairs, Nori says, Oh, I've been here before—that empty apartment.

So how about it? says Rand.

Um, sure Rand. Do whatever you want.

You seem unsure.

No, it's fine. Do what you want.

What am I supposed to say? No?

On the drive home, Hector's mom is spitting out grumpy Spanish words, and Hector's answering in Spanish. It's driving me crazy. Could you guys at least speak in English when you're in my car? What is she upset about, Hector?

I'm upset because you were mean to your poor mother on Mother's Day, she says.

Mean to her? I planned this whole damn thing for her!

She had to go catch a plane and you made her feel bad.

Look, Mrs. Cordova, you don't know about my mother and me, all right?

You should have respect for her, like Hector has for me, she says. Instead you yell at her and make her feel bad.

Hush, Mama, says Hector.

You don't know what it's been like for me, I say. I've had a hard time and this brunch was a big deal.

You don't have a hard time, she says. You don't even work for a living.

I'm injured! I yell. I'm on disability. I can't work.

Injured, she laughs. I'm in pain my whole life and still I work. You're lazy.

Hush, Mama.

I drop them off and drive straight to the nasty gay bar out on Northern Boulevard, where I drink myself silly.

Silly

Late that night, I park my car in front of the house. I get out and have to stifle a laugh 'cause the car's half on the sidewalk. I get back in and park it right.

Concentrating so hard on driving right distracted me from the nausea, but now, walking across the lawn, it hits me in wave after wave and I don't want to puke in the middle of Bill and Marcie's lawn, so I jog over to the trees and let go. I cough and sputter and look up and, uh-oh, here comes the neighbor guy yelling, Get off my lawn, you drunk! He shoves me and I turn around to see Marcie coming across the grass, arms crossed to keep her bathrobe closed. Then Bill passes her, grabs me by the arm, and drags me, tripping and stumbling, across the lawn.

What the hell do you think you're doing, Frank? You can't live like this. Not here in front of the girls.

Let go of me, Bill. I yank my arm.

I want you out of here tomorrow, Frank! Hear me? Out!

Out, out, out! I say and Marcie's crying as she takes me down to my bedroom. Fucking straight prick, I say. I feel sorry for you, Marcie.

Oh shut up, Frank, she cries. You're drunk.

I feel sorry for all you straight women who have to marry straight men like Bill. I go on about it, but the light's out and Marcie's gone.

In the morning, Missy and Tina sit in the living room bawling as I take stuff out to the car. Bill's nowhere to be seen. I find Marcie paying bills at the breakfast table, and I ask if I can store some things in the basement closet until I'm settled. Sure, Frank, she says, with a complicated look on her face.

I hug the girls good-bye. Their narrow, warm little backs heave and sob. I tell them not to worry, that they'll see me all the time. They nod breathlessly.

I get in the car and head toward Manhattan. I'm crying a little too now. Oh well, I think. Maybe this will get them on the road to hating their father. And the earlier the better, you know?

Where should I go? If I still had a set of keys, I'd go out to Jersey until my mother returns from Atlanta. If I hadn't spent my disability, I'd treat myself to a night at the Mariott, just to cheer myself up. If I felt like seeing any of them, I'd call my friends.

I park in a garage and spend the day walking around to little shops and having meals at cheap restaurants. The weather is beautiful and I love all the freaks in the street. I have conversations with the waitresses. I start to feel better, 'cause who needs entertainment when you live in New York? And who needs a place to go at night when you can sit in the porn theater on Third Avenue and watch the movies until you doze off? Till they turn the lights on at six A.M. and say, All right guys, time to go home.

Then you can go sit in the park by the Hudson and watch the sun glint on the windows over in Jersey. At eight, the city gym on Carmine Street opens and you can show your membership card that you use next to never, and they let you in to shower.

Everything's okay, I think, 'cause if you know what you're doing, New York is like your own big hotel.

But by that evening, I've had enough, so I call Hector, who has a roomy apartment and a fold-out couch. We sit in his kitchen and I tell him what happened. He just sort of shakes his head. He wants to tell me things, to drink less and so on, but he bites his tongue, and I'm grateful for that.

Instead he entertains me with records. He says he can make me cry by playing sad songs, and I say he's wrong.

He starts with Tammy Wynette and I roll my eyes. He tries Sarah Vaughn, then Frank Sinatra, and I say, you don't know me very well, do you? As usual, he's putting on songs and taking them off before they're even half-through.

I know what'll get you, he says. Back-to-back he plays "Vincent" by Don MacLean, "You Needed Me" by Anne Murray, and "Superstar" by the Carpenters, each one all the way through. Nice technique, I say, but no.

He puts on "Careless Whisper" by Wham, and takes it off almost immediately.

Then it's Judy Collins, and my life comes rushing at me. Turn it off, I say. You win.

He walks over and there's a grunt as he takes the needle off the record. He slides it back into the sleeve. He can see that I'm genuinely sad, but can't help saying, quietly, Softie.

He turns on the TV, and I'm glad for the noise, but I'm not watching. I'm going over my life and thinking of how worthless everything is. I feel desperate, and I want to feel close to Hector, so I lie across the couch and rest my head on his lap. He lays his hand on my shoulder and we watch TV like that for a while. It makes me feel a little better—his hand is heavy and warm. In my mind, I try to spread that warmth through my whole body. Friendship is the one thing I need, and the one thing I've got. That's something I tell myself all the time. So I try to make Hector's warmth enough.

His hand leaves my shoulder and begins to stroke my hair. I close my eyes and he rubs my neck. Now my thoughts are melting into sensations, as if I were drunk. I roll onto my back and look up at Hector, and his hand rests on my chest. His eyes are glassy, still fixed on the TV, and his jaw shifts back and forth. He swallows. He's nervous. That's good, it means I don't need to be.

I touch his face and pull him down to kiss me. I should be wondering if this is a good idea, considering how it'll change our friendship and so on, but I don't care. Good idea or bad, it's what I want. His hand moves across my chest, under my arm to my back. He lifts me and we really kiss.

We leave my stuff in the living room and spend the night in his bed.

Our Deal

And the next night, and the next.

The sex is surprisingly good. I guess I always imagined it'd be boring, but it's fun. It's like playtime, we laugh a lot.

We sleep in each other's arms, which scares me just a little. If we were just friends fooling around for the fun of it, wouldn't we sleep on our own sides of the bed? But our bodies fit together so nicely and I sleep so well when I'm right up against him. Mrs. Cordova hasn't been coming by since I've been here, and I feel a little weird about that too, but Hector says, She's got to realize I have my own life.

I leave Rand the third message since Mother's Day. He isn't returning my calls. I have this horrible feeling that Nori gave away my secret, and that Rand's furious. But then, didn't I promise to come check on him if we went for a few days without speaking? If he doesn't call by tomorrow, scared or not, I'll go over.

Hector gets home from work and before we can even order food, we're kissing in the kitchen, and I'm taking his clothes off, and we're fucking on the couch. Afterward, we lie there naked and he flips on the TV. And I sip on the drink I already had going.

So Hec, I say, is this one of those situations where the guy's in love with his friend for ages and finally, just when he gives up hope, the friend sort of turns around and they start screwing?

I don't know, Hector says. Have you been in love with me for ages?

No, I'm saying *you're* the one in love, I say.

You sure talk about love a lot, he says.

Listen, I say, don't tease me. Just because we're having sex doesn't give you all sorts of rights and privileges, all right? I'm still the aggressor in this friendship.

He rolls over on top of me to prove he's the aggressor.

My shrink's response to all this is a Final Suggestion rather than just a Thought: I want you to close your eyes and return to that day when you were ten years old and your father left. I want you to pretend I'm your father and tell me what happens to me. Predict my life, Frank. Tell me where I went, and what I did. Tell me if I succeeded or failed, if I'm alive or dead.

No, I say.

What?

Look. I was eight, not ten, and besides that makes no sense to me. The things you say never make any sense. This isn't working, so I think that I should quit coming.

Well, he says carefully, I'm sorry you feel that way. His chin lifts from his thumbs and there's a red impression in the cleft. Maybe we should work on communicating more clearly with each other. You are free to discontinue sessions … but I should warn you, your disability payments are contingent on your attendance here.

Oh, I say, contingent.

On the way home, I consider going by Rand's, but there's tons of traffic so I decide to give him one more day.

I pick up the *Village Voice*, go to Hector's and sit in the kitchen looking at the apartment listings. Everything's so expensive, even in the outer boroughs. Hector's going from room to room, picking things up, piddling around.

What are you reading? he asks.

I tell him.

He goes into the living room for a minute then comes back. You know, he says, then his jaw locks and he pauses.… I was thinking that maybe I'd offer you to stay here.… sort of, for a while. Like indefinitely.

You were *thinking* of offering that, or you are offering that?

I *am* offering that, he says, but with a condition.

What's that? I ask.

That you limit yourself to two drinks a day.

Hmmm, I say. I think for a minute. How 'bout this: I'll stay here, and I'll drink only two drinks a day if you quit going to Mass.

He looks down at his shoe, which is tapping on the brownish marbleized linoleum.

Okay, he says.

The following week, Hector's mother talks him into going to Mass on Saturday night. The next night I go out drinking. I only let myself get moderately drunk, but the headache I didn't realize I had is washed away and I recognize myself.

The day after that, we reinstate our agreement and say we'll try to stick with it this time.

It's a start, at least. Right?

Vestal McIntyre
Vestal McIntyre was born and raised in Nampa, Idaho, and attended Tufts University. He now lives in New York City.

Japanese For Blurred Image

Robert Williams

keshiki: the landscape

I am there, in the dusty bus station, a boy of fourteen with blond feathered hair, still wearing my soccer uniform from the morning's game. A game I'm sure we lost because I spent too much time staring at Bruno Carifi's legs, which were the most muscular and hairy of anyone on our team. I'm in my bright orange jersey, blue polyester shorts, black cleats, socks pulled up to my knees over massive shin guards, dried sweat salting my forehead. Today, as we did last summer and the summer before, my family will pick up our Japanese exchange student for his four week visit to Southern California, or more specifically to our suburban neighborhood with its addresses black-stenciled into cement curbs. Streets named La Jolla, cul-de-sacs called Venice Beach. Communities known as Birdrock and Kensington, where palm trees sway in the smaze of exhaust fumes and where bougainvillea creep up and over fences and the sides of Spanish-style houses. I am anxiously waving a small American flag. Under my arm is my Japanese-American dictionary. At a moment's notice I can look up words like older brother: *oniisan*, or family: *kazoku*.

My mother and grandmother, in pastel sundresses, their hair recently done (they go to the salon twice monthly—together—a day of magazines and gossip), pink lipstick freshly applied, are wiping the sweat off the back of their perfumed necks, fanning each other with brightly colored Magic Marker signs they themselves have made. Other families around us also hold homemade signs boldly emblazoned with "Welcome Keiji," or "Hello Shinji," or "Konichiwa! We're the Johnson Family!"

My father, in Hawaiian shirt, corduroy shorts, and sandals with tube socks, looks at his watch every two minutes. He's probably wondering why we can't for once get a nice Japanese girl exchange student. A nice, kimono-wearing Japanese girl. He is thinking, "What'll it be tonight, pizza or fried chicken?" He is itching for a cigarette.

tsudoi: gathering for a purpose

There are a dozen or so families like us here. Many from my neighborhood, waiting for their *natsu musuko*, their summer son and brother. We are California families, two to four kids, one or both parents, stepfathers, stepmothers, grandmothers grandfathers, girlfriends, boyfriends. The Wilsons, Mr. and Mrs., and their three kids live across the street from us. Their kitchen table and floors are always sticky. But they have a pool with a slide and Jacuzzi and a wide-screen television. The Petersons from further down the street also have a pool and used to live in Santa Monica. Their son Phillip is my age and already a world traveler.

Phillip has greasy hair and a small head and wears tiny glasses that look like they came from a doll or ventriloquist's dummy. Still, I wonder if Phillip ever swims in a Speedo or swims in his pool naked, for that matter. I find myself wondering these things quite often.

If I climb on the roof of my house I can see their backyard. Sometimes, if I stand by the chimney, I can almost see into the window of Phillip's room—but not quite. The roof is slanted and steep and so I hold onto the chimney for dear life, scraping my palms on the rough edges of brick. Last summer the Peterson family didn't have an exchange student because they went to Europe.

"Eight countries in nine days!" Phillip bragged in school.

"Next year," his parents tell mine while we wait at the bus station for the Japanese boys to arrive, "Phillip gets to be an exchange student in Japan for the summer."

shonen: boy

The Greyhound bus arrives, with large, mysterious black-shaded windows, like movie star sunglasses that we cannot see behind. Japanese boys file out slowly, cautiously, as if they are soldiers coming back from a battle, clutching suitcases and duffel bags. They remind me of the black-and-white pictures of my grandfather, handsome with his hair combed slick, back from the war, a wide, dashing smile spread across his face because he is finally seeing my grandmother after months, maybe years.

The program director, Mr. Ishyama, is last to step out from the bus. He is a jolly, chubby Japanese man wearing a pink polo shirt and white pants with a blue and red nylon belt who comes to America every summer with thirteen boys from Yokohama, ages fifteen to seventeen. Mr. Ishyama and two other American instructors will teach the boys conversational English here for the summer. Though Mr. Ishyama claims to have a beautiful wife in Japan (a Geisha girl, the Japanese boys once told me), he always comes out of the bus alone, then he smiles at the families, many of whom he recognizes from previous summers. He waves to my father, who makes a beeline for him. He shakes my father's hand, says "Hello, hello once again!" and gives him a carton of Japanese cigarettes—he does this every year. Mr. Ishyama then walks over to us and tells my mother and grandmother that they are "always most beautiful," and they fan themselves even faster with the homemade signs. He pats the top of my head.

It is time for Mr. Ishyama to read the names of the boys and their respective families.

"Masahiro, you belong to the Peterson family."

He belongs to the Petersons, I think to myself. This boy intrigues me. He is tall, lean, with a pompadour hairstyle and black high-top sneakers. He smirks and saunters over to the Petersons, all Japanese cool; a Japanese commercial for jeans. He even has a pack of cigarettes rolled into his short-sleeve T-shirt. He pushes his sunglasses up to his forehead, not on top of his head, and surveys the scene, looks at the other families, at the bus station ticket booth, the vending machines. He is still smirking when Mr. Peterson extends his hand to him, stiff and businesslike, and Mrs. Peterson pushes Phillip forward.

"Masashi, goes to the Wilson family." And Masashi does, most diligently. He is smart-looking and serious, and clean, with thick dark hair, and a mouth tightly closed. He is wearing all white, except for his shiny black shoes, and his pants are pulled up high, almost to his chest. I am quick to note that his penis is parted on the left. I look down to my own blue soccer shorts, but my penis is nowhere to be found. I am wearing a jockstrap, which makes simply a tiny, dome-like hill in my shorts, as indistinct as a wrinkle in the fabric. Masashi, I decide, is not going to like the sticky floors and tables at the Wilsons.

"Fumiyuki, you belong to the Comford family."

Mr. Ishyama directs Fumiyuki to us. Fumiyuki is small, smaller than I am, with fine, closely cut black hair, a thin smile and glasses. He is wearing a letterman-style jacket with a picture of Woody Woodpecker stitched on the back, and pants that, though wrinkled from the long flight, still have the sharp crease down the front of the leg.

My father tries some of the textbook Japanese that I have taught him and explains that we are "happy to be your *shujin kazoko*, your host family." At this Fumiyuki's smiles again, and he removes his glasses to rub his eyes.

"*Kazoko*," he tells my father, "means volcano." My father's face turns a bright red.

"Well, hell," he says, "I never could master a foreign language. And especially not Japanese, with all those crazy symbols and pronunciations!" He laughs a big, overblown laugh in Fumiyuki's face. "So, do you like fried chicken or pizza?" Fumiyuki's smile gets smaller and thinner and curves down in a confused frown.

My mother introduces me and then puts her hand to her chest and pats her breast bone a few times, "... and my name is Claire, but you can call me host mother if you like."

Fumiyuki has a hard time saying my mother's name, he calls her *queer*.

"He thinks your name is Queer," my father says with a laugh. "That's funny Claire, he thinks you're queer."

My mother smiles and shrugs it off, though my dad keeps saying, "Queer, that's a good one. Queer."

"This is our *obasan*, our grandmother."

Grandmother bows, holding the sign to her chest.

"Hello, I am Fumiyuki," he says, also bowing slightly.

My grandmother calls him Fuck-ee-yoo-me. I've never even heard my mother, let alone my grandmother say the word *fuck*, or anything close to that. My mother gasps and cups her hands over my ears, my father laughs harder, and then he tears the clear, shiny wrapper off the Japanese cigarettes and smells them.

"Ah," he says, "these are great cigarettes, you can tell by the smell."

dotabata-kigeki: slapstick

The Wilsons and the Petersons join us at the pizza parlor/video-game arcade. We spread out, our three families, three Japanese students, over two long picnic-style tables with paper liners over them and broken crayons for coloring. Above our tables and against the carpeted wall is a pull-down movie screen playing old silent comedies. Piano roll music blares from two wood-paneled speakers anchored in the corners of the ceiling; this, and the buzzing, exploding sounds of video games make conversation almost impossible. Laurel and Hardy, Charlie Chaplin, Buster Keaton are all hamming it up above us while we eat platters of pepperoni, ham and pineapple pizza and drink pitcherfulls of root beer. Laurel (or is it Hardy?)—the fat one—gets hit with a plank of wood and we all laugh. Root beer sprays out of the youngest Wilson kid's nose and onto the table.

Over the noise I catch bits and pieces of my father telling the other grown-ups how my grandmother had mispronounced Fumiyuki's name. The adults lose it. Mr. Wilson beats the table with his fist and laughs so hard he turns almost purple. The kids laugh too, but nervously, as if we aren't supposed to know a word like *fuck*. My grandmother doesn't quite get that she is why they are all laughing, but she laughs with them anyway. Then I see my father mouth the word *queer* and point to my mother. He is holding a piece of pizza in his hand, pointing with his pizza and calling her queer. They all laugh again, and I laugh too, just a little.

The Japanese boys sit at the end of the table, eating their pizza and speaking Japanese, occasionally nodding their heads at us.

Masahiro, who is leaning against the wall, has taken a crayon and drawn someone's portrait on the white paper of the table. Someone with a beautiful face and big, dewy, deer-like eyes and almost shoulder-length hair like mine. Masahiro catches me looking at him and for a moment I think it is me that he is drawing. He studies my face a little, and then he blows his cigarette smoke in my direction and shades in the hair with the black crayon. I decide that he is very handsome, in a James Dean sort of way. Tough, slick, smooth.

On the movie screen someone gets a cream pie in the face. I look away from Masahiro, and down at my chest. A greasy hunk of cheese from my pizza has fallen onto my soccer jersey.

hakobu okurimono: bearing gifts

At home we gather around Fumiyuki in what has become a Japanese exchange student family tradition. Fumiyuki slowly reads a letter from his mother in Japan to my mother. He translates in quiet, halting English. In this letter are suggestions of how my mother can best take care of her son. This includes keeping him away from *seriously spicy food, alcohol*, and *cigarettes*, and making sure that he bathes every day.

Fumiyuki then passes out gifts to my family and me: another kimono for my mother and father, which my father, in his tube socks, wears for the rest of the evening; delicate wood and china sake cups and a tiny carafe-like bottle of sake; a small comb and mirror set for me, its case decorated on the front with a picture of a fierce warrior swinging a huge sword over his head, who, with his pony tail and white makeup, looks almost feminine; Hello Kitty products—including an intricate set of stationery and envelopes, mini-pencils and sweet-smelling erasers; packets of miso soup and dried wasabe peas; an elaborate wood-and-red-ribbon wind chime; a jewel box for Grandmother made from thin, fragrant, pink-and-yellow origami paper.

"For my clip-on earrings," she says as she removes one and rubs her dented earlobe.

My father, as if it were Christmas, says, "Hell, we made out like bandits this year, didn't we? I bet we're the only folks on the block with his and her kimonos," he sits back in his easy chair and lights up a Japanese cigarette. My mother swats at the smoke.

"Not now, honey," she says to him as she gathers up the torn tissue paper that Fumiyuki's gifts came wrapped in, "not in the house with Fumiyuki here, you told me you wouldn't smoke."

My dad dismisses her with a wave of his hand and my grandmother gets up from the couch and bows again at Fumiyuki.

"Goodnight, Fuji ... Fuki ... goodnight." She goes to her bedroom.

In the morning, all throughout our neighborhood, kimono-clad mothers cook eggs and toast waffles, while kimono-clad fathers proudly gather the newspapers off their driveways.

ichinichiju nigeru: day escape

The Japanese boys go to Tijuana and a few of the host families and their children, including myself, go with them. My parents are both working and my grandmother doesn't like the heat, so she stays at home. Unlike the previous year, I have decided to attend all of this summer's field trips. Many of the boys listen to Walkman radios on the hour ride to Mexico, nodding their heads in almost unison to the cooing of a female Japanese singer called Hiroko. I move from my seat on the bus to the empty one next to Fumiyuki. I ask him if I can listen to Hiroko, and he hands me his Walkman, brushing my arm with his own hairless arm. Fumiyuki smells like the tiny, Hello Kitty erasers—sweet and soft and clean. I am not sure how to use his Walkman so he helps me clip it to my belt and then touches my head and face to point out which earphone goes in which ear.

"I like the hair that is blond," he says, "blond hair is much better than black hair."

I nervously fidget with the volume on the Walkman.

"Blond hair," he continues, "is hair of the gods. In Japan, you would be *top idol*, with hair like this." He touches my hair again with his small hand and I shudder somewhat, not quite sure how to react. I quickly take off his Walkman and hand it back to him.

"Hiroko," I say, "sounds like a hungry baby bird."

I return to my seat and watch the quiet, brooding Masahiro, who is not listening to a Walkman. Instead, he scribbles into a tiny notebook and stares out of the bus window. He catches me looking at him and I blush and feign interest in a Japanese book that Fumiyuki has lent me, though I have a sneaking suspicion I am reading it upside down.

In Tijuana, the Japanese boys buy blankets and panchos, clay pots, and cheap silver that will turn their wrists and fingers green before we even reenter the States. Fumiyuki and Masashi, the Wilson's student, buy large ceramic cartoon character piggy banks: Woody Woodpecker and Mickey Mouse. Several students, including mine, stop at a roadside cart selling small tacos and hot dogs wrapped in bacon.

"I'm not allowed to eat those," I tell Fumiyuki and his friends as they hand over their pesos to the vendor, "those are made of rat hair and sewage."

"My stomach," says Fumiyuki, "is one of intense steel." He lifts his shirt and slaps his smooth, tight abdomen several times.

Masahiro walks past us down the street where Mexican men, like carnival barkers, stand out in front of bars and strip clubs, luring customers inside with the promise of beautiful women and cheap beer. I want to follow him down the street, to see where he goes. I want him to run his fingers through my hair and touch my face. But Fumiyuki and Masashi pull me by the arm.

"We are still very hungry," he says, and we head for a Mexican restaurant.

We find a small cafe painted in bright orange and green with an open back patio and extremely hot salsa. A young Mexican girl, probably seven or eight years old, wearing a white dress and a red bandanna on her head sells roses from table to table. She has a sad, unsmiling face and large eyes and I am reminded of Masahiro's crayon drawing from the pizza parlor a few nights earlier. I wonder if Masahiro is smoking a cigarette and sitting in one of those strip clubs on the avenue.

Three of the Japanese boys buy roses but then realize they have no one to give them to except for the Wilson's oldest daughter, who is fourteen with a mouth full of braces and a nose too big for her face. She smiles, embarrassed, and one of the boys tells her that they are married now.

The next morning only Masahiro comes to the door to pick up Fumiyuki for the five-block walk to the school for their English lessons. I am fumbling out of my pajamas in order to catch a glimpse of Masahiro when I hear my grandmother ask Fumiyuki where Masashi, the missing student, is.

"Masashi," Fumiyuki tells her, "cannot come to school ... for he has ... brown water from the spicy food in Mexico."

I slip on a sweatshirt and shorts but only catch the back of Fumiyuki and Masahiro as they turn the corner.

kaisu-pantsu: swimming trunks

The Wilsons from across the street throw a pool party for all of the Japanese boys and their host families. They have a 25-foot, peanut-shaped pool in their backyard with a smooth, slick, light blue slide that hurls you into crystal-clear water. On the bottom of the pool are a dozen water whips that swirl and twist like snakes, blowing dirt and leaves and other debris into the drain. The Wilsons have set up a volleyball net across the pool and the Japanese boys frolic and splash, dunk each other and spit water. Inside their one-story house with the flat roof, Mrs. Wilson, in kimono, is showing off her collection of sake cups to my mother, to Mrs. Peterson, and to the other host mothers, which she has displayed behind glass next to their sticky dining-room table. The host fathers gather around a wide-screen television watching football, drinking beer, smoking, and yelling, *Hakai Suru! Hakai Suru!* Which is Japanese for destroy.

From my lawn chair in the shade, I try to read my Japanese-American dictionary but instead I find myself watching the boys play in the water. Their hair is shiny, wet, pasted to foreheads, their lithe, smooth bodies bob up and down, waiting for the serve.

Beneath the cool water their thin legs look distorted and massive, like tree trunks which then sprout into lean, taut stomachs and curved, defined chests. Masahiro sits on the wooden deck next to the Wilson's barbecue. A group of boys, including Fumiyuki and Masashi, have ascended from the pool, surrounding another young boy with a shaved head named Koko. They are repeating the word *fukurami* and pointing to his bathing suit—a small, tight-fitting Speedo. I quickly look up the word *fukurami* in my dictionary. It means bulge. One of the boys moves out of the way, and I see that Koko has an enormous erection, pointing straight up the front seam of and barely contained in his red swim suit. They continue pointing and laughing, and one of the boys flicks Koko's penis through his bathing suit as if it were a game of marbles. Soon the other boys are flicking at Koko's erection, and touching their own penises through their wet Speedos, saying *masatsu masatsu* and *fukurami.* I notice a stirring in my own suit and quickly turn over onto my stomach, pressing into the vinyl of the lawn chair. The Wilson kids are busy at the other end of the pool, spraying each other with the water whips. No one else seems to notice the Japanese boys and their game. I look up the word *masatsu*, it means to rub or to cause friction. I look up more words: *inkei* means penis; *nekkyo suru* means excite; *kin ' niku*: muscle; *sekkusu*: sexual intercourse; *jii-ni-fukeru*: masturbate; *doseiaisha*: homosexual.

maho okoku: Magic Kingdom

Two weeks into our Japanese summer I join the boys on a field trip to Disneyland. On the bus, with the air-conditioning blowing up the sides of the windows and cooling my cheeks, I am reminded of the family trips we would take to Anaheim, to Disneyland and Hollywood, my father, my mother and me. I remember holding my father's hand tightly as the creaky elevator descended deeper into the Haunted Mansion, and burying my face into his neck to hide from the animatronic Pirates of the Caribbean. At Grauman's Chinese Theater in Hollywood, my father once set my feet into John Wayne's footprints, as if hopeful that this action might re-enhance my already fading masculinity. While the family trips to Disneyland continued, the hand holding, the embraces between father and son soon ended; somewhere around age ten or eleven these are replaced by gestures, by affectless slaps on the back and punches on the shoulder.

The Magic Kingdom seems less magical to me on this particular trip. I no longer feel the need to explore Sleeping Beauty's Castle or sit in the slow-moving It's a Small World boatride, no longer charmed by the cheery voices singing the dreary song in fifteen different languages. I'm wanting to be someone different than who I am, someone far removed from the California streets that I have always known. As we wait in line at yet another ride, I begin to imagine that I am one of them, one of the Japanese boys, and I nod and laugh with them as they talk to each other in Japanese. My foolishness makes them laugh back and stare in wonder at me.

"You understand what we are saying?" asks Fumiyuki, whose forehead is already peeling from too many afternoons spent swimming in various neighbors' pools.

"I understand some," I lie. "I learn very quickly."

As the line slowly moves forward, I begin to take my act even further. I perform, pretending that I am fluent in Japanese, spouting out the words and phrases I learned from my dictionary.

"*Arigato, Arigato.*"

"*Ohayo gozaimasu.*"

"*Genki desu ka.*"

These are simple words of *thank you*, *good morning*, and *how are you*, but I make a spectacle of them. I speak loudly, with elaborate gestures and enunciation. Fumiyuki and the group of boys we are with respond with even more laughter. Not so secretly, I revel in the idea that I am giving off the impression to the tourists around us that somehow, by some twist of fate or miracle, I too am Japanese, or that perhaps I was adopted as an infant by a Japanese family. Or that maybe my family is like Phillip Peterson's—well traveled and cultured. That my father is a dignitary, my mother an ambassadress. Something. Anything but the reality. Anything but the truth.

hijoguchi: emergency exit

It is late at night and I hear something outside my bedroom door. I think I am dreaming but the noise gets louder. At first I am sure that it is the sound of the dishwasher in the kitchen, a deep and guttural steady hum that used to lull me to sleep. But soon the sound becomes more human, throaty. It is my father, wheezing and gurgling in the hallway. His voice is raspy, his words almost inarticulate, though I begin to piece the fragments together.

"I …"

"… can't."

"… breathe.

He gets them out, somehow, though I have never heard him like this.

" … call … hospital…."

I look out of my bedroom door and watch my father as he sinks in slow motion down on to one knee, his face is pinched, red, his right hand squeezing his left shoulder.

"He's having a heart attack!" My mother screams, looking like a ghost in her white nightgown and slippers. My grandmother opens her door and scurries down the hallway to her son, my father. She kneels next to him, without a word and puts his head in her lap. There is a chaotic fusion of sights and sounds, lights turning on, wheezing and screaming.

"The ambulance is on its way," my mother yells, or is it my grandmother?

Fumiyuki's door stays closed.

A siren wails outside for what seems like an eternity and then two paramedics tear a stretcher through our house, banging and scraping the walls of the hallway, knocking down pictures of us: family portraits taken in a studio against a cheap maroon backdrop, a trip to the Grand Canyon, grandma on her seventieth birthday.

Where is Fumiyuki?

I'm crouching in my doorway, leaning against the door frame, unable to speak. But not knowing what to say anyway, not knowing if I should be screaming too.

They take my father away in the ambulance with my mother. I am to stay home with my grandmother and Fumiyuki. Maybe I should wake him, I think. Maybe he will let me sit with him on his bed or let me lie next to him and sleep. I go to his door and press my ear against it to listen, but I don't hear anything. Not a sound. Not stirring, not snoring, not breathing. I decide not to knock.

My grandmother sits on a bar stool in the kitchen. She has called various aunts and uncles and other nearby relatives. And now she waits by the quiet phone in her housecoat with a cup of tea. A whisp of gray hair has loosened itself from her bun and hangs in her face.

I return to my room and sit on my bed. I don't know how to feel, how to act. I decide to pray to God so that my father will survive. So that we won't be left alone. I'll stop thinking bad things, sexual things, I pray. I'll think only good clean thoughts from now on. I'll try every day to be the son my father wants me to be.

In the morning Fumiyuki tells us that he heard the commotion, the banging and the voices, but that he thought it was a dream from eating too much spicy food.

kanja: patient

My father will be all right. A mild heart attack, my mother tells me, he will be in the hospital for about a week.

The Wilsons, the Petersons, and other neighbors come by our house bringing casseroles and pies. Mrs. Wilson invites Fumiyuki and me over to their house for swimming but I politely tell her, "No, thank you."

I look up heart attack in my Japanese/American dictionary—*shinjo hossa*—and explain it to Fumiyuki.

"Too many cigarettes, and too much stress," I tell him.

Fumiyuki goes with us to the hospital and in the car he tells us that in Japan, his grandfather had a *nosotchu*, a stroke, which left him partially paralyzed. In the backseat next to me he stiffens his body, then he tightens and distorts his mouth to demonstrate how his grandfather looked.

"This was … very difficult time for my family," he says.

He continues, telling us that he and his family nursed his grandfather back to health so that he could eventually almost feed himself. My grandmother likes this story; she wipes at her eyes with her handkerchief and smiles.

"What a nice family you have," she tells him.

At the hospital my grandmother cries when she sees my father, which makes my mother cry as well. My father is sitting up in his bed watching television, the sound is coming from a tiny speaker on his pillow. He has an oxygen tube under his nose that hisses and whistles, helping him breathe. I feel lost, confused, unaware of what I should say or do.

"I'm fine. I'm fine," my father says, his voice soft and scratchy, almost a whisper.

"I know, honey," says my mother, "It's just the room and the tubes and everything." She sits down next to him on the bed. Her eyelids are red and her face blotchy, devoid of makeup.

"Fumiyuki!" My father whispers, "How are you doing?" He beckons Fumiyuki closer to his bed. Fumiyuki walks slowly over to him with a shy, courteous smile.

"Fumiyuki," he rasps, "have you seen my nurse? She's a dirty old hag who steals glimpses of my backside when I get up to use the bathroom."

"Oh, heavens," says my grandmother, who sits in a hospital-issued chair near the window.

Fumiyuki wrinkles his brow but continues to smile. My father places his hand on Fumiyuki's elbow and pulls him even closer.

"I'm serious," he says. "What I want to know is, what happened to all of the pretty young nurses you see in the movies? The ones with the big bazookas?" He puts his hands up in front of his chest as if he were holding two cantaloupes.

"Now, now," my mother says, putting her hand to her cheek and looking at my grandmother.

I try to explain bazookas to Fumiyuki. The word is not in my dictionary so I find the word *breasts*. He seems to understand this and nods and smiles at my father.

"Well, Fumiyuki," Dad says while glancing toward me, "looks like you two are the men of the house now. Think you … can … handle it?" He begins to cough. A quiet, breathy cough that he tries to stifle with a grimace. My mother places her hand on his shoulder and my grandmother sits on the edge of the chair. Fumiyuki moves away from my father's bed.

"I'm fine.… I'm fine." My father says again, patting my mother on her knee. His breathing becomes easier, less labored.

"Time to be a man," my dad whispers to me, "No time for wimping out."

"Yes, sir," I mutter.

Except for the sound coming from the oxygen tube, there is a sad, protracted silence in the hospital room.

"Isn't that right, Queer?" says my father, laughing and coughing, to my mom.

oyogi benkyo: swimming lessons

I am in my backyard, sitting on the steps of our black-bottom pool, surrounded by dry bark and bird of paradise. Under the water my bathing suit has inflated like a blowfish, my feet look stark white and huge. I'm feeling something strange inside of me. Inside, I'm somewhat empty, and unlike my bathing suit, somewhat deflated. The feeling began in the hospital, or maybe even before that, but I don't recognize it as loneliness, not just yet. Above me, a skywriting airplane buzzes, leaving its message in the air. Because of the bright sun and the reflection off the pool I can't read the writing; it looks to me like white-dashed lane lines in the street, slowly fading away. It is probably an ad for suntan lotion, but I imagine instead that it is a message to me from an unknown admirer. Someone who has been watching me from afar, on the soccer field perhaps, just as I watch Bruno Carifi and his fuzzy legs, or Masahiro and his moody gesticulations. I'm wanting to be wanted, missed, needed. With the Japanese boys, I'm a master at getting attention, but only at provoking laughter and merriment. Why wasn't I the recipient of the roses in Tijuana two weeks ago, or my face that Masashi had drawn in crayon at the pizza parlor?

The sliding screen door that leads from our family room to the backyard scrapes open and I look behind me. It is Fumiyuki, who walks over to the pool in his Speedo and baseball cap with the L.A. Dodgers insignia stitched onto the front. He sits down on the step next to me.

"*Ototo*," he says to me, which means little brother, "what do you dream of?"

"I don't understand," I tell him.

"I see you looking at the sky ... for long time. Isn't this what you call today's dream?" He takes the baseball cap off of his head and tosses it onto our stained, wooden patio, then he eases himself off the step and into the shallow end of the pool, swirling his arms around him like mermaids' tails. "Oh. *Hai*," I say, meaning yes, "daydreaming. I was … I guess."

"Daydreaming." Fumiyuki repeats, then he dives under the water and does a handstand for several seconds. When he comes up, the bangs of his straight, fine hair form a perfect line across his forehead. "Don't be sad … about your father," he says to me, "everything will be okay." He makes the sign for okay with his small hand. The shadow of which looks like the head of a rooster.

"I know. I'm not worried about that."

"Don't worry, be happy," Fumiyuki sings and then he dives under once again.

"Your father," he continues when he comes up for air, "is always very funny, always with a joke … but always … a man of few words and even fewer … emotion?"

"What do you mean?" I pull my legs up and rest my chin on my knees. A cloud passes in front of the sun, shading the pool, the back-yard.

"Tell it's the truth," Fumiyuki says to me, and then he dog-paddles up to my feet on the first step. "It is same, in Japan … with my father. Only my father is … always silent to me, to my mother, to my sister, to my brother."

"It's not easy." I tell him, and I cup my hands in the water and then pour it over my knees. I'm not sure of what else to say, and Fumiyuki is still looking at me, unblinking. There are tiny drops of water hanging from his eyelashes.

"Sometimes I am … to daydream too," he says, "I have learned to … imagine the words … the words I wish my father would say." He sinks lower into the water, grabbing onto my knees with his hands. This time I don't push his hands away. I cup my hands again and pour water over his head.

"*Yume*," he says, "is the word for dream. *O Yumemiru* … to dream of. Maybe … this can work for you, too."

"Maybe. Maybe it can."

Fumiyuki takes in a mouthful of pool water and spits a stream of it into my face, then he kicks away from the stairs and into the deep end of the pool.

fureru koto: touching

It is after dinner, and the Japanese boys have taken to playing baseball in the street. They wear their baseball hats backwards and roll up their jeans at the ankles. The smell of charcoal and freshly cut grass lingers in the humid air. The neighborhood host families sit on porches in lawn chairs, drinking beer and wine coolers and sharing funny stories about their respective exchange students, zany incidents inevitably involving miscommunication or misunderstanding.

"I thought he was telling me he was horny," I overhear Mr. Wilson say to one of the other host fathers, "turns out, *horny* means 'the truth' or something in Japanese!"

The two men laugh and then I hear Mrs. Wilson ask my mother about my father.

"He'll be home in a few days," my mother says, "just in time for the students' farewell party."

"He's off the oxygen for now," my grandmother offers.

I am sitting on the curb in front of my house. Someone up the street is watering their lawn. A steady stream flows through the gutter, below my legs. I remove my flip-flop sandals and place my feet in the gutter, letting the cool water run over them. The boys take a break from their game and Fumiyuki, Masashi, and Masahiro sit next to me on the curb. Masahiro lights a cigarette and inhales deeply. I watch his chest heave as he takes in air and smoke.

"O ... P ..." Fumiyuki says. He is reading the initials on my shorts and my tank top, which also sports a picture of a seagull and beach.

"It means Ocean Pacific," I say, "Pacific Ocean."

Masashi pokes his finger at the dime-size pockmark that stands out like a tiny moon on my freckled shoulder. "Your skin is very brown." He says, then he pokes his finger into Fumiyuki's wet, sunburned forehead. "And your skin is very red, Fumiyuki!"

Fumiyuki pokes Masashi in his belly, then Masahiro does the same. They all laugh, even Masahiro.

"Japanese boys are always touching each other," I blurt out to them, remembering the pool party and Koko's erection.

"Oh?" Fumiyuki says, "you think this is the truth?"

"Isn't it?" I say, and Masashi laughs and covers his mouth with his hand. Masahiro smiles and flicks his ash into the gutter. I quickly pull my legs out of the flowing water.

"Yes … maybe it is so," Fumiyuki pokes at my ribs, "we like to do this."

"Why?" I ask, pushing the point.

Masahiro drops his cigarette into the gutter. He gets up from the curb then he crouches in front of me. I can smell the smoke on his breath. He puts his forearms on my knees, to hold himself up. This is the closest Masahiro has been to me. I notice that his teeth are brilliantly white, despite the smoking. My heart jumps and I feel a slight stirring in my shorts.

"You know what?" Masahiro's voice is gravelly and deep.

"No. What?" I repeat.

"We touch each others so many … times …," he continues, slowly, "because in Japan, we cannot touch the young woman … as we would like…."

Fumiyuki and Masashi snicker at this.

"What … what do you mean?" I say to Masahiro.

"We cannot," he says again, lowering his voice this time, "touch the woman … like … *this*." Masahiro then takes his arm off my knee and touches my penis through my shorts. It is a move so quick and unexpected that I push myself backwards like a crab, onto the sidewalk, shocked.

The three boys laugh at this, then Masahiro says something in Japanese to the other two and they laugh even more, throwing their heads back. Fumiyuki's baseball hat falls off. They are grabbing at their own crotches and saying over and over, *kataku suru*. I sit stunned on the edge of my grass. Fumiyuki breaks away from the other two and sits next to me. He puts his arm on my shoulder and speaks into my ear.

"Masahiro … he say that your penis … was hard. *Kataku suru*, it was made hard," he says this and laughs into my ear. The other boys resume their laughter, or maybe they had never stopped.

"Is this the true?" Masashi says from the curb, his face is red and sweaty from laughter.

I push Fumiyuki away from me and he rolls on the grass like a stuntman rolls from a speeding car. The other boys join him on the grass and they begin to poke at each other again, still laughing.

"Get away!" I shout at them. "Get away from me. I hate you. You are all stupid. Stupid Japanese."

I get up from the grass, which sticks to my feet as if I've been tarred and feathered. I run past my grandmother and mother, who both call my name, and into the house, dropping clumps of grass on the carpet. I hide in the bathroom, where the electric fan in the ceiling, the *courtesy fan*, as my mother calls it, drowns out the sounds of my anguish. There is a knock at the door.

"Go away!" I shout.

"*Ototo*," Fumiyuki says, "*Ototo*, it is okay." He jiggles with the doorknob. "We are only making joke."

saigo odori: last dance

It is the night before the boys return to Japan. There is a barbecue and potluck in the grassy quad of the school where the Japanese boys have been practicing their English. Everyone who has a kimono wears one; there are host fathers in bright, multicolored kimonos, drinking beer and flipping burgers on the grill, host mothers in kimonos with red and purple and green sashes around their waists, setting out paper plates, napkins, potato salads and Jell-O.

The Petersons, the Wilsons, all of the host families are here. My father is seated in a lawn chair on the grass in his kimono. He looks frail and white, and the kimono hangs on him like a small boy wearing his father's sport coat. He is itching for a cigarette, one of the Japanese cigarettes, but my mother gave them back to Mr. Ishyama. The Wilson's oldest daughter, in bare feet, does cartwheels across the grass in front of him and to the delight and applause of the Japanese boys.

After everyone has eaten, the host mothers begin cleaning up the tables and putting left-overs into Tupperware containers. A group of host fathers surround my own father, who hasn't moved from his chair.

"You're looking just great," says Mr. Wilson, who has taken his wife's purple sash and tied it around his head. "One beer's not going to kill you, is it?"

"No, no. I promised the wife. No beer and no cigarettes. For a little while anyway."

"No beer and no cigarettes! Damn!"

"Don't you worry," my father takes a belabored breath, "I'm no sissy. I'll be smoking and drinking before you know it."

They both laugh.

When everything has been cleaned up the host families move chairs and spread blankets onto the grass. The boys and Mr. Ishyama line up on a makeshift stage in front of us and sing nervously and out of tune to a cassette tape of "Yesterday," by the Beatles. Fumiyuki, Masashi, Masahiro, Koko, all of the boys are on the stage, in suits, shiny shoes, and thin, colorful ties.

They sing, sweet, stumbling when they get to the word *believe*.

My grandmother tells the Peterson's how brave and helpful Fumiyuki has been while my father has been recovering. How he made sushi and egg rolls for us one night, and how his mother in Japan called us to wish my father "good health and prosperity."

After the performance the host families join their students near the stage, hugging and laughing and congratulating the boys for making it through a difficult song.

"*Ototo*," Fumiyuki says to me, messing up my hair with his hand. "You are not so angry at us today, is this true?" Masashi and Masahiro are next to him. They look to me like Bible salesmen, in their suits and ties, and I can't help but give in and smile. Masashi tries to hide his smile with his hand, but Masahiro's is wide and it consumes me.

Tomorrow the Japanese boys will move on, and in a few weeks I will return to school for the fall. For a few months we will exchange letters and trade photos from their trip to America, and then one day they will stop coming, the letters, the photos, the feelings. But tonight it's the Beatles and barbecue, and the moment is as clear and vivid as the colors on the boys' thin ties.

Someone puts in a tape of fifties rock and roll and turns up the tape player and the boys begin to dance on the stage. Fumiyuki pulls my mother and grandmother up on to the stage with him as do the other boys with their host families. We are all bouncing and shimmying and swaying and spinning. Fumiyuki takes my mother's hands and pulls her to him and then pushes her back. He spins her around like a ballerina, which is not so easy to do in a kimono. My grandmother claps her hands and rotates her shoulders. My father taps his feet to the music from his lawn chair. I am rocking my hips from side to side when I feel someone's back pressed against my own. It is Masahiro, with his cigarette dangling from his lips, and for a solid minute he is next to me again. He has taken off his coat. I feel his warm back, his sweaty skin through his T-shirt, his belt against my spine, smell a faint whiff of cologne and cigarettes. I look over my shoulder and see his profile, the sweat glistening on his forehead. I press back against Masahiro and he doesn't give, he lets me press, he lets me rest my head, sweaty, spinning, in the hollow of his shoulder blades.

Robert Williams
Robert Williams was born and raised in San Diego, California. He holds a degree in English from Arizona State University and recently completed the graduate Creative Writing Program at Columbia University. He lives in New York City, where he is wrapping up a collection of short stories and working on a novel, both of which are set in California.

The Incontinents

Andrew Holleran

I t had taken him years to be able to wear a Speedo—although the same thing could be said of the entire country, he thought as he entered the shower room of the gym on his way to the pool. In the fifties, when he was growing up, Americans considered red wine and skimpy bathing suits not only European but decadent—now, at the dawn of the millennium, wine was sold in supermarkets and Americans wore thongs. He wasn't sure how this had happened. Once, in the mid-seventies, a friend of his, temporary-typing in Manhattan, spent a summer at an advertising agency compiling a report on strategies to get Americans to drink wine. Well—as with almost everything the advertising agencies had turned their attention to—that had been accomplished, and with that, somehow, came all sorts of other things—including that product of Australia heretofore confined to Olympic swim meets and beaches abroad: the Speedo.

He thought men almost looked better in a Speedo than they did naked—some men, that is. It wasn't just that the Speedo revealed the heft and content of the genitals, though surely that was one of the reasons men had started wearing it on Fire Island; it was something else. The previous year a friend had sent him from Sydney, where he'd retired, a stack of postcards with photographs of lifeguards in Speedos on the beach; he kept them on the table by his bed, and occasionally leafed through them before he fell asleep. That's how wonderful Speedos were—though he had always been too modest to wear one himself.

The summer he was sixteen his family spent a month in Maine at a resort with a community pool. Their neighbor, a deeply suntanned man with a fleshy, dissolute face, would come over at five for cocktails in a black bikini with two Doberman pinschers, and he could tell it was not the dogs that bothered his mother, it was the bathing suit—even if she never said so. That same summer, however, a boy his age came to the pool in the same black suit accompanied by a voluptuous blond in a bikini who would sunbathe with him. One afternoon, while showering in the little men's room beneath the pool, he noticed the boy's black swimsuit hanging on the handle of the shower, and one day when there was no one about, he put it on. It was the first time he had ever felt the erotic charge an article of clothing can provide. It was as if he could—by slipping this swimsuit on—become the muscular young man; or touch him by wearing a garment that had rested on his skin too. That black swimsuit—so striking on the muscular youth his age with the thick brown crew cut; so embarrassing on the fat middle-aged bachelor who came over with his two Dobermans for vodka every day—had been the emblem of everything he wanted to possess but was too shy to even consider owning, the unapologetic masculinity of that sullen young man.

Since then he had possessed such people, but now, forty years later, his possession had proved frustratingly impermanent, and he was come full circle—sharing the pool, the shower room, with young men he dared not look at directly, much less approach, and men his own age who wore bathing suits that only made their bellies look bigger.

In fact, in the middle of the day, when he went to the gym, there were only two kinds of people there: students from the University of Florida and the elderly. Nobody else could go at two in the afternoon. When he entered the poolroom after his workout, he always found the elderly doing exercises in a roped-off portion of the pool on one side, the students swimming laps in the lanes on the other. Who else did not have to be at work? The elderly had retired and did not have to show up at an office—the college students, like lambs before slaughter, were still being fattened to take their place on the assembly line—not quite adults, though at nineteen and twenty they already had the bodies of adults. And their beauty.

This seemed to bring them little pleasure, however. "Adolescents are often prudish about their bodies," a friend had told him when he commented on the downcast eyes, the grim expressions, of the students when they came into the poolroom. Whatever the reason, these college men hardly ever wore Speedos, unless they had been on a swim team—a link that was confirmed when they sliced through the water at twice the speed and half the effort of the boys in baggy shorts. He liked to think it was the latters' just-dawning awareness of how powerful their bodies were that accounted for their voluminous bathing suits; but he suspected it was probably the opposite—some painful self-consciousness, some prudery, some disapproval of their own appearance. At nineteen, he remembered, one is supremely conscious of one's shortcomings and, by no means, always ready to plunge into erotic life. Only the old could realize the beauty of youth; youth couldn't see it, even if they knew, intellectually, that old people kept telling them these were the best years of their lives. These Greek gods in baggy shorts came to the pool with morose expressions, papers overdue, loans unpaid, exams looming, while the shapeless older men sprouting hair from every orifice, with most of their life struggle behind them, wore the Speedos. (And not just Speedos—black Speedos, it had been wordlessly established, were the appropriate swimsuits for the mature men who swam laps.)

He wore a Speedo himself because he didn't want to expend any more effort swimming laps than he had to, and believed the baggy shorts were literally a drag; but in part it was because his own life, he felt, was drawing to a close, and he might as well use this excuse to do something he had been too shy to do till now. Yet clearly the system was backwards—it was the young who should have been wearing the tank suits, which they refused either because they were indeed prudish, or because—he preferred to think—they knew exactly how beautiful they were, and were not about to waste it on this audience.

This audience could not possibly count in their eyes: this audience consisted of a row of gray heads lined up along the west wall of the pool in an aqua-aerobics class, doing what the instructor standing above them told them to. To him the silvery figures looked like rows of the newly dead—waist-deep in the river Styx, receiving an orientation lecture to Hell. Though it was not Charon welcoming them to Hades, it was a young big-breasted woman in yellow Lycra tossing her curly head of black hair in rhythm as she told them to roll their heads to the left, then back, then to the right. Only one woman was perfectly still, her attention caught by the golden light falling through the trees outside the big plate-glass windows—unless she was demented, he thought, or had been distracted by a memory, or her head was stuck in that position. Whatever the reason, there was something wistful about her vacant stare; the only head in the whole row not turned to the instructor, while the students swam their oblivious laps in the adjacent lanes.

They were three this afternoon. The smallest swam his laps and then paused at the far end, where the sunlight coming through the tall windows illumined a corner of the pool and threw reflected light up his half-immersed, still form. He was the most beautiful, though the other two swimmers were bigger and more chiseled. His small head, his shoulders, the glowing collarbone, the smooth white chest, were illumined from below, like a statue lighted in a niche. Outside a bright white light fell on the terrace where people were sunbathing. But the light inside the pool room was indirect, save for the corner in which the student stood as still and beautiful as a stone kouros, bathed in light.

Swimming with the gods was thrilling, or rather between the gods and the recently dead; a place one could only be in the mid-afternoon at this gym, suspended between these two poles of existence, these two manifestations of Time: those just about to begin their lives, and those about to end them.

His father had died in a hospital in this town—university towns are always hospital towns, too—and during that awful time, when he took breaks from the bedside, he would go swimming, not in this pool but another he belonged to at the time, on the east side of town; a pool owned by the Knights of Columbus, an outdoor pool, deep and clean and crystal blue. The swimming had been a bright spot in what seemed to be a tale with no possible happy ending, the laps an orderly activity in a world of horrible change. His sister had gone shopping on her breaks; he swam up and down the pool in comforting straight lines. He went around three, when usually the only other swimmer was a crew-cut young blond who wore a blue Speedo, and on this blue Speedo he would see, after making his flip turn underwater, thousands of tiny silver bubbles, clinging to the young blond's butt. The blue bathing suit, the silver bubbles, the muscular butt seen underwater in the lane next to his in that split second were a vision of strength and happiness—contrasted with the sight of his own father trying to pull the catheter out, tossing his head, delirious, as he decomposed and struggled with death. It was awful—dying—there was no way around it, only through, he thought, and when you came out the other side you'd vanished.

That pool had been crystal blue; this one was murky green. A man from Chicago had been flown down to improve the clarity of the water but so far there was no improvement. Some days, when few people were there, the pool was lucent. Most days it was not. A friend of his attributed this to the Incontinents—his nickname for the people who used the pool for aqua-aerobics. "I'm writing a musical," he'd said. "I'm going to call it *The Incontinents*. Big aqua-aerobics numbers. Lots of pee. We'll bring Esther Williams out of retirement!" In truth the murk annoyed him as he swam up and down the pool, trying to make sure his head was underwater when the big, well-built student in the baggy red trunks passed him in the adjacent lane; even in baggy shorts, even in cloudy water, the sight of those flashing legs, the arched back, was exciting.

So much of desire was looking—even when young. Now he really was a voyeur. Toward closing, according to his friend, men displayed themselves while toweling off in the little corridor between the shower stalls; but mostly the erotic life of the place lay beneath the surface.

His friend—an erstwhile Presbyterian minister who had given up preaching to study German, and now spent hours in the gym, and loved to tell him at dinner about the sexual display he witnessed in the showers and locker room—was often courted, though he never encouraged these exhibitions. The minister was lucky, he thought. No one had ever approached him—though he still found the place exciting. No matter how depressed he might be on entering the lobby, his exercise, his swim, always made him feel glad to be alive by the time he emerged into the crowded parking lot. The pool really was rejuvenating—or at least the people he saw in and around it.

Today was different, however, because an old family friend—a woman he'd known since childhood—was probably dying at this very moment in a hospital five minutes' drive from the gymnasium, and he had not gone to visit her. He could not go. The thought of it brought back too many memories of his own parents in the same place; though he knew that was no excuse. There was never any excuse, really. Yet he could not make himself go to the hospital and enter her room to see her pale, emaciated form lying there connected to tubes. It was as if the experience of suffering—the loss of his own parents—had made him not a better person but a worse one. When he'd mentioned this to the minister, his friend had just laughed, and refused to absolve him. "Everyone has trouble visiting the dying," he'd said, "even—you might be surprised to know—their doctors. Because there's nothing you can say. I was good at it, actually—that's why the parish in Providence liked me. And it was fairly simple. All you have to do is sit there—and listen," he said with a laugh.

The laugh only chilled him when he heard it—a laugh filled with a fortitude he did not have, he thought as he swam his laps this afternoon, while she lay dying, or improving; he did not have the courage to learn which.

"Do you think vanity is connected to the fear of death?" he asked his friend another night as they were discussing the psychology of people who go to a gym. "No doubt about it," his friend replied.

Perhaps that was it—everyone here, the students, even the elderly, were, to some degree, sufficiently vain or narcissistic or afraid of illness to make the effort to keep their bodies supple. They were to some extent aesthetes; they valued their own beauty. So did he; it was all that assuaged his depression some days.

He was depressed—he knew that: A sweet, still sadness pervaded his life, or a still sad sweetness, he didn't know which. It wasn't unpleasant, though it was depression. It was mostly still and sad— above all, still. He felt quiet inside. He stayed home a lot by himself now since retiring and went to bed sometimes in the middle of the afternoon and simply lay there, watching the light flicker on the leaves of the garden outside the bedroom window—till he roused himself and went to the gym, if for no other reason than to look at people.

The people he was looking at now were beginning to come to the end of their exercise class. There were remarks made by the people in the pool to the instructor. Then the elderly women all moved at once, like a flock of blackbirds, to the hot tub; where they settled into the Jacuzzi beneath the presiding outspread legs of an elderly man perched on the side in his black Speedo, a gold coin on a chain buried in his silver chest hair, like an erotic talisman, advertising his own belief that he was still virile. Surely erotic currents were passing between these septuagenarians, he thought. On the other hand, he assumed the young men with chiseled torsos swimming beside him were total snobs. Youth was hard and firm. Old age was wrinkled and soft. Never the twain would meet. He swam back and forth between the two, wondering in the middle of the sunny afternoon where he would die, and with whom, and how. Strange, he thought as he made his flip turn, how, in your fifties, one actually began to think about death as a logistical problem, a question of where, and how and when.

With the women all in the hot tub, stilled by the heat or demands of modesty, the pool room was so quiet it reminded him of kindergarten. There was something infantile, pre-school, about the diffused sunlight, the watery glow on the walls. He was back in the womb. But this womb was equipped with three young men. The huskiest student continued to swim with a slow, deliberate stroke, moving faster than the others with what looked like less effort, though the mechanics of a stroke were mostly invisible above the water. The more chiseled student on his opposite side was doing a choppy backstroke.

He thought of tourists allowed to swim with the porpoises at a resort. Their beauty was what got him through an otherwise dull routine, a routine he followed, theoretically, to prolong his own time on earth. All of a sudden the elderly women rose at once from the Jacuzzi and went into their locker room, while the student who had been standing at the far end lost in thought got out and walked the length of the pool toward the men's locker room. His lower body was more pear-shaped than one would have assumed. The pool emptied further of its patrons. He continued to swim, and swim, and then, after the last two students left, he stopped and stood up at the end of the pool to clear his goggles.

It was the first time he'd paused in twenty minutes. A middle-aged woman with dark hair was standing against the north wall of the pool, beside an elderly man whose face wore a docile, childlike blankness— a man who looked as lost and submissive as a small boy.

The woman holding the strange man's arm by the elbow looked at him and said, "Are you his son?"

He stared at her a moment, not understanding, and then said, "No! No!" and, rather than get involved, put his goggles back on and resumed swimming his lap. When he returned to that end of the pool a few moments later, however, he paused an instant while changing direction to hear what the woman was saying to the people gathered on the edge of the pool above her. She was talking about an ambulance; the old man had just had a stroke.

He pushed off from the wall and swam to the opposite end, reconstructing the events. The man had had a stroke, in the pool, the woman had come to his aid, had asked him whom he belonged to, the man had said his son was somewhere in the pool, and now, whether the son was or not, whether he even existed, they could not find him. Are you his son? he thought as he swam through the cloudy water. It sounded like a religious question. Of course I am, he thought, in some sense, in the sense we are all brothers and sisters, children and parents, related if you go back far enough through Time, all of us descended from the same couple. Are you his son? he thought as he switched to the breaststroke. But he had already done that duty—with his own father; he could not repeat it with this perfect stranger in the pool. Yet to have said "No," so energetically, so firmly, to have rejected the man at such a terrible moment in his life—when suddenly all was lost, at a single, yes, stroke, when he went from being the captain of his destiny to a helpless child in a public pool in a crowd of strangers, one of whom had just said "No!" (I am not your son) and gone on doing his daily laps—was not good. Are you his son, are you his son? he thought as he reached the opposite wall. Of course I am, and he is my father, I who have none of my own, neither son nor father.

When he got out of the pool, the old man was still standing waist-deep in the water, the woman still holding his arm, the gym staff in their red polo shirts and web belts huddling above. Twenty minutes later, when he emerged from the men's locker room showered and dressed, the old man was going through the doors in front of him on a stretcher. Outside, he was put into the back of an ambulance by two paramedics. Are you his son, are you his son? he thought as he got in his car and drove away. How could I say "No"? I who will die alone?

He drove faster than usual past the hospital where his neighbor lay dying, went home, got in bed, and saw the postcards on the table. The one on top was his favorite: a lean, golden man in a baby blue Speedo jumping into the air, the outline of his cock visible on the surface of the blue nylon. There was not an ounce of fat on his torso; he had no love handles; his pectoral muscles, flattened by his uplifted arms, were flat to begin with, his stomach corrugated, his upper thighs swelling out-ward from the blue bathing suit's borders, his whole body perfectly proportioned and lean—and all of it dusted, it seemed, with a golden pollen. There was no face. The photographer had cropped the photo so that his head and lower legs were both cut off—as if the man in the blue Speedo was already entering heaven, his body left behind.

He turned the card over and looked at the credit on the back. The photo had been taken in 1986—so the man in the blue Speedo could still be alive, he thought, somewhere in Australia.

This is my father, he thought, as he stared at the blue nylon pouch, this is my son, this is the man I belong to and love. Then he put the card down and fell into a vacant trance, staring at the light on the hedge beyond the window.

Andrew Holleran
Andrew Holleran is the author of *Dancer from the Dance* and *In September, the Light Changes*. He lives in Florida.

The Wrong Kind Of Queen

W.C. Harris

Todd, as usual, is in a spot. Trying to balance Erica on his right hip with one hand, trying to unwrap and eat his burger with the other. As soon as he has her small frame secured in the wedge between his arm and waist, he returns to the burger, using his teeth to tug back another corner of the foil-lined, grease-soaked paper. Just when he manages to take another diet-breaking bite, however (Kris will never find out: Erica isn't old enough to grasp the idea of dietary restrictions and Sam is lost in the depths of the Keep), Erica wriggles loose and begins to slip away. He may never finish his meal. Scoffing at the idea of purchasing one of those Juggling for Klutzes books in the mid-eighties takes on, not for the first time, the stature of a life mistake.

Two bites left, and Erica must sense it because her wriggling has progressed to writhing. "Keep! Keep! I wanna see the Keep!"

"I know, honey, I know. We have to wait till your brother gets out." Sam is seven and deemed old enough, at least by Todd on these solo trips to Ye Olde Burger Queen, to watch over a four-year-old while she worms her way through the Keep. Or makes it as far as the second portcullis, by which point being pulled back out and finishing her saliva-soggy fries usually wins out over her desire to match her brother's triumph. Until it does, Sam stands guard, patient, a little bored, while Todd pretends to stray, far enough to make him feel a little important as well.

"Sam, are you almost done? Sam?" He shouts in the Keep's general direction, since there is no way to tell what part his son is in. "Sammy? Your little sister wants to go, too." No answer. Maybe the combined weight of all those plastic balls, infinitesimal by themselves, oversized Ping-Pongs really, has borne down and trapped the boy, critical mass obtaining even here. How will he explain it to Kris? Will a child's suffocation in a crenelated playpen be as hard a sell as that fountain he'd proudly brought home from the garden center but which she'd made him return? No returns on a smothered son, at least not a dead one. Will the manager try to settle out of court, plying the bereaved father with free coffee with any breakfast order, throwing in Hash Pops, finally, desperate to obtain a signature on the appropriate release form?

"In a minute!" Though muffled, Sam's catchphrase echoes inside the Keep, seemingly from loopholes in two opposite walls. Is it possible that, somewhere within the bowels of this ersatz medieval jungle gym, plastic siding molded in some hope of resembling battlements, the boy has been transformed, Merlin-fast, into an unwitting ventriloquist? Perhaps he has mastered throwing more than his voice, adept at evasions beyond the merely verbal. Todd means to ask him, if he ever emerges. With little to do but wait, Todd moves to the glossy, molded bench and sits down, letting the girl free, the battle of restraint ended predictably but gratefully. There's no need to tell her to wait her turn; she's sensed, somehow, it's almost here. She runs over to the cubicles where entrants are instructed—assuming they are able and/or patient enough to read the eleven-item list of rules (*Who's inside enforcing them?* Todd wonders)—to remove their shoes and place them in one of the child-sized cubicles. Bright gold hooks—for coats, scarves—span the molding nearby. This corner of the Keep enclosure resembles nothing so much as an open locker room, like those the children already know from daycare and pre-school: demanding for now only shoes, coats and lunch boxes, but preparing them for the more intimate dispossessions that less open spaces will someday demand. Todd half-smiles as he watches his daughter struggle with her small aquamarine Jellies, stopping only for a dull thud in the far left corner of the Keep, parallel to the Jousting Grounds, which confirms that her brother is nearly out. The turn she's been promised is upon her.

A nap is what I need. Thank Christ there's not some yokel in here making a production with her screaming, sticky-fingered brats. No wonder. Who'd want to eat in, with this choice view? Refinery to the right, car graveyard to the left. This far out, you don't have much choice if you're hungry, but you sure don't have to eat it here. Who knows why they bother with indoor seating, when a kitchen with a couple of windows would do.

"Daddy, please."

He opens eyes that were no more than half-closed. She's primed at the entry tunnel, one bare foot poised nervously on the tunnel's lower lip while she looks back eagerly. She waits for permission but seems ready to do without. Todd leans over to look for his son—as far as he can without actually getting up—when he suddenly has to squint, blinded by a knife of sunlight glancing off the windshield of a van headed for the drive-thru. One wary eye reopens and spots Sam at the Keep's exit, stepping onto the drawbridge.

"You go ahead, sweetie, it's okay." But Erica's gone, well on her journey to the inner charms of the Keep, the sort of privacy she hasn't grown too large for. Kris would say it isn't safe, she's not old enough, didn't you read the rules for god sake? Todd knows the truth about rules from work: clauses in a contract, fine print below the dotted line—they're precautions, denials of liability in advance; rules pretend to care. Kris isn't here, so he decides to rely on something else he knows: hell hath no fury like younger siblings who don't get what they want. Anyway, Sam will be serious and dutiful, once commissioned, giving Todd time to rest his eyes or take a quick leak before the twenty-seven-minute drive home. Of course, it helps that Sam has already gotten his own way. But he grows up in these moments, too, because his father asks it of him, deputizes him; because it's a chance to play secret agent, despite the sting of demotion to baby-sister detail.

Suddenly, a loud smack, accompanied by a duller thud, makes Todd's glance swivel from one side of the elaborate playhouse to the other. He sees Sam laid out flat, legs and feet on the drawbridge, his half-turned upper body on the institutional terra-cotta tile. It's happened so fast it doesn't seem real, but then Todd's up and halfway across the room when the boy's surprise at tripping (from where his right foot lies, sock halfway off, it's clear this is what happened) has yielded to the shock of pain.

"Sammy? What happened?" An idiotic question, it occurs to him, one he wouldn't ask so often if he didn't constantly feel like he'd just missed something, an important detail. Just as he rounds the last corner of the swag rail that separates him from the grounds of the Keep, the door to the outside just behind Sam opens—one of the several doors granting adult visitors escape from this overcrowded room—and a Ye Olde Burger Queen worker is crouched beside the footbridge, gently lifting the boy's torso into his arms. *Beaten to the chase once again*, Todd thinks to himself, intoning privately what Kris will glibly editori-

alize when he tells her about this over dinner. The cap obscures the face
of the employee who bends over Sam, but the arms are smooth and
nearly hairless. *Another munchkin*, Todd thinks, lumping him in with
the army of twelve- to fourteen-year-olds who seem to run this place,
making Todd feel more and more as if he's stumbled on the Pied Piper's
sweatshop. But Sam's cry is diminishing, which must say something
for the nurse's skill; maybe this one doesn't have a dozen facial pierc-
ings.

"Lemme see. Where'd you hurt yourself?" The voice is young but
steady, not exactly a munchkin's. Perhaps it's that steadiness, as well as
being held, that the patient responds to, whimpering unintelligibly: a
sign of life, which Todd takes, in what some women have called his typically masculine way, as a sign of nothing seriously wrong. To be fair,
there's no blood or torn skin. He thinks of what his older brother used
to say—"nothing that'll leave a scar"—but in most cases his brother
had also inflicted the injury, so the phrase seems inappropriate.

"You all right, there?" Todd adds, close on the heels of the worker's question. To emphasize his presence, Todd lays a hand on Sam's
nearest leg, just below the back of the knee. "That was a nasty fall." It
is in the next instant that a whole series of necessary actions occur:
together, Todd and the worker get the boy turned over, they lift him off
the footbridge, finally steady him against his kneeling father, but for
Todd, all this takes place without direct awareness of his own partici-
pation. Righting Sam takes less than a minute, but that minute is elon-
gated, obliterated for Todd when the employee finally lifts his head,
bringing the face that had been hidden thus far into view. *He's no
munchkin*. Todd forgets why he's holding his son, distracted by the heat
spreading across his forehead and earlobes with a speed he's not known
since puberty. *Look at those forearms, and that neck*. Seeing the dark
blond hair on its nape, darker where sweat has dampened it, Todd has a
single, clear, and paralyzing thought: *I can almost smell his tight, pink
balls*.

"Stupid bridge," Sam pouts, tenderly rubbing the arm that seems to
have broken his fall.

"Can you move it there?"

"Yeah. Hurts."

He inspects the arm: "I know, stings a little. No cuts or bruises,
though. Hate to disappoint you, sport, but you're gonna live." Sam,

propped against his father's knee, grunts, reserving judgment.

"Thanks, uh"—Todd turns back to the worker long enough to spy the name embossed in red tape on one of BQ's bejeweled name tags—"thanks for the assist … Jay." *Don't stare him in the face like that, you idiot. What the hell's wrong with you?* The catch in his voice will be attributed, one can hope, to parental concern, to the time spent deciphering the white, unevenly raised letters on the name tag.

"No problem, sir. Just lucky the little guy didn't break anything. Ever since that lawsuit about the Hash Pops, the manager really goes ape shit over stuff like this. Oh, geez—" Jay breaks off, freezing in the act of getting to his feet. Professionalism is the furthest thing from Todd's mind right now, as thoughts pass from Sam's distress, which has almost completely subsided, to a slight but familiar pressure below his navel.

"Don't sweat it. I'm not litigious." Jay frowns, but Todd doesn't look up. "I won't sue anybody. Sammy's shipshape, aren't you, tiger?" Todd's distracted by his son's arm: moping over the lack of even a scrape, Sam cups it and lets it go slack against Todd's thigh. He does it again. Each time, the elbow inches higher on Todd's leg, perilously closer to the swelling he can feel but can't yet see.

"Cool. So everything okay here, sir?"

Todd holds his breath.

Sam's elbow inches closer: ignorant of certain barriers, innocent of a heat he will not know for some time.

Todd knows he needs to answer the question. The weight of the pause only makes it worse. If he just holds still, relaxes his groin, it will go down before anyone notices. Looking up, he's mortified to realize he must have been staring right at it, because Jay and Sam both seem to have followed his gaze. Above where Jay stands, Todd's distracted by a neon-red and -yellow sign: IF YOU NEED ANYTHING AS OUR ROYAL GUEST, JUST ASK YOUR LOYAL LIEGE. Catching Sam's wandering arm, he makes a final assessment of the damage.

"Yeah. We're okay, aren't we? Listen, Jay—I hate to ask, you're probably on break, but would you mind staying with Sam here for a sec? I really have to … use the john." Jay stares, blank. "Or whatever you call it these days."

"I get you," Jay says. Todd's eyes meet his, but this time remain, seeking permission. Jay swallows a laugh, and shoots a hand under his back collar to scratch between his shoulder blades. Innocent enough, but Todd finds himself mesmerized by what Jay's hiked-up shirt reveals: a pristine inch of pale obliques. "Regal-size Coke, huh?"

"What? Oh, right." Another catch in his voice. "That must be it." By this time, Sam has left them and headed over to the cubicles to retrieve his shoes and nurse his wound. He's quiet, as if piecing together details, hatching the appropriately pained grimace that will ensure an extra Whippey Cone for the ride home.

"Go ahead," Jay says. As if emboldened by Todd's nonchalance and the child's distance, he adds, "Anytime I drink one of those things, I have to piss like a racehorse."

An "Appreciate it, guy" to Jay and a word to Erica through the walls of the Keep is all Todd has time for. If he doesn't get to the bathroom, he's going to burst like an overheated can of aerosol. His dick continues to swell in his briefs as he makes for the rest rooms. Tucked down and to the right a minute ago, when it was only slightly tumescent, it bobs up now with a surge of blood and lodges against the leg elastic—which only increases the friction it receives as Todd strides to the men's room door, pacing himself but feeling as if he's going faster than an incontinent who's been set on fire. Row after garish row of tables with under-mounted swivel seats, a gauntlet of Santa Claus red and forest green. Panicked that he won't make it but not caring (*I'll just blow my load right here in the restaurant, who'll notice?*), Todd shuts his eyes tightly, thrusts out an arm (on the off chance he actually reaches the door labeled MERRY MEN), leans into the last few feet, and readies himself for impact. It's not until he is safely inside a stall, seated on a toilet, Dockers down around his ankles and hard-on in hand, that he allows himself to open his eyes. To breathe. To see his anger standing swollen between his legs, a tear of precum just welling up at the tip. To know again, as before, that the pain of one-eyed vision comes from a lack of perspective.

Todd slows his stroke.

He knows he has to hurry, but thinking of why he needs to reminds him of why he's in here in the first place, about to explode. What started as a little stress-reliever in the men's room at work is starting to feel less commendable than a pastime, less defensible than a kink. It's almost as if each workaday orgasm has been not relieving a pressure, discharging some hormonal obligation, but instead bringing compulsion to its boiling point. Every time Todd comes, and returns to his desk and cubicle, what was boiling over cools, and what he thought he'd left in the men's room precipitates right back into sight: crystalline, solid, telltale.

He speeds up a little now. The sooner he gets out of here, the better; two or three minutes to get Sam and Erica in the car, buckled up, two more minutes on the access road, twenty-one on the interstate, and four last minutes to his front door. Todd prides himself on immaculate timing. Another set of strokes, a measured dozen; another marginally faster set; three tugs with thumb and forefinger on his snug, resistant balls, squeezing down and holding before releasing his hold; another five strokes, a penultimate pass over the glans with his palm. A final pinch of his left nipple will clinch it. He wants to finish. He wants to finish with this.

There, he's pinched his nipple, and head back, squinting up into the stark fluorescent lights overhead, he braces himself, anticipating not just the orgasm itself but its announcement: the palpable instant when your balls relax, right before clinching, that much tighter, to shoot. Todd bites his lower lip, his balls tighten, *shoot it, shoot it, yes, fuck, fuck*. He pulls down and holds fast—when the door to the rest room leaps opens.

He freezes, head still back, but eyes open wide. Calf muscles flexed, heels arched, he listens. Todd is not totally unprepared. He's been interrupted once or twice before by coworkers with colitis or simply bad timing. Now he hears a few footsteps, shoes squeaking on the wet floor in front of the sinks. *Maybe they only need to piss*. A few more steps, and this other guy is in the stall next to Todd—the handicapped one—and, from the sound of it, letting his pants down. *Great. This bozo's gotta take a dump*.

The feeling of the toilet pipes, suddenly cold against his back, shocks Todd into relaxing his legs and loosening his grip. Crouching forward on the toilet seat, he waits for his erection to soften. All he can do now is breathe evenly, and wait. He tries to help the process along by distracting himself—thinking first of his basset hound being put to sleep when he was nine, then Kris' early, bungling attempts at fellatio—when he hears a sound, though not the one he was expecting. A familiar sound, like eight ounces of cold cuts being slapped down on a deli scale. The hefty cut of meat in this case, however, is between his new neighbor's legs. Whoever it is has similar ideas about the uses of public bathrooms. Next to the toilet-paper dispenser, just below eye level, Todd notices two small, corroded holes in the partition—where a previous dispenser was mounted, he guesses. One is a dark pinhole; the other apparently goes through to the other side. Todd leans over and peers through; the hole is large enough to admit light, but little else. The slapping sound, meanwhile, is replaced by an equally familiar whispering, rubbing sound. Nearly imperceptible unless you know what you're listening for, but unmistakable. Spotting another hole, about the size of a dime, Todd hits the jackpot: a hand passing back and forth over a pale shaft—twice as thick as his own, and it doesn't seem to be totally hard. Sensing the tenacity of his own erection, Todd sits back on the toilet seat. He hesitates, thinking that this kind of thing doesn't happen when he's masturbating at work. Part of him is stunned by the intrusion on a previously solitary experience, a whole spectrum of images and imagined acts, of which Kris is entirely ignorant. He wants to keep it that way. And certainly no man knows what Todd thinks about when he's like this: the locker rooms where (as early as eighth grade, when he first saw pubic hair on Johnny Lizscinski) he first heard guys joke about circle jerks and brandish "Blow me!" as the lowest insult. In the following years, he felt more and more the shame of that insult, when it became clear that his fantasy spaces were spaces populated by men. Saunas, locker rooms, shower rooms: anywhere men showed each other freely what they usually kept guardedly out of sight; where it was okay to lather yourself into a boner because no one was supposed to be looking, because desire was a jockstrap, crusty with use and genital sweat. You leave that in your locker; no one but a retard would wear it in the shower. But listening to this guy in the next stall jacking off right next to him—imagining that he's matching the other guy stroke for stroke—Todd realizes he's been masturbating for months in yet another masculine space: the men's room. Aching to ejaculate, he speculates whether what's he doing now is pushing his luck. He tells himself he was *already* hard, wonders why he can't look away. Because looking makes him harder, makes him *want* to come, and to come *because* he's looking. Is he finally confirming what he knows every male fears, especially during adolescence—being labeled a faggot—but what he feels like, now, he alone deserves? He feels his heart beating. He swears he can hear it.

A tingle like static electricity jolts him out of what seems like indecision. He lowers his head, drools a generous string of saliva onto his cock (if he had some Lubriderm, his wedding band wouldn't rub the vein on the underside so hard) and begins to work up a passable lather. He thinks, *I'll finish myself off real quick, just come real fast and quiet, and go.* He thinks, *This guy's not gonna notice.* Whatever gets you through it. Todd tells himself it's a competition, without sensing how true that is.

When he looks again, he's surprised by a lateral view of his neighbor: leaning on the assistance railing mounted in the wall behind him. Facing Todd and whaling away. With the other hand, rubbing a flat, pale stomach, disappearing above, then returning to groin and thighs. When a thumb brushes the lightly haired balls growing redder with the beating, all Todd can think about is putting them in his mouth. Now the hand leaves the dick, beached on a hairless thigh, and beckons slowly. Knowing this guy's aware that he's watching makes the head of Todd's dick even wetter. As the precum dribbles onto his left hand, he hears a click. Before Todd can accept the invitation—the handicapped stall door creaks, halts ajar—he brings the wet hand to his mouth and slurps up the clear, viscid juice. Standing, he pulls his underwear and pants halfway up, unlocks the door of his own stall. With a middle finger he probes under his foreskin, he needs one more taste. He plunges the sticky fingertip into his mouth, and before he removes it, he's opened the wide door to his right.

"Hey guy," Jay whispers.

Todd's thinking, *Shit, I should have known. Fucking little perv*, but he isn't pursuing the thought. He considers running, but he locks the door behind him. Todd doesn't come any nearer for the moment. Jay cocks his head, adding, "Don't worry. Someone's watching 'em." Todd wants to ask who exactly this "someone" is, but with naked desire standing so prominently before him, he finds it hard to focus. To take in anything except this young man, this urge as demanding as his own.

He stares at Jay's sturdy hard-on. He tells himself, *You really are a pansy-ass faggot, after all*, yet he still gets on his knees. Seen straight on, it appears even thicker, bouncing slightly in anticipation, fully distended, a bare few inches from his face, close enough to feel its heat graze his lips. *Go ahead. You know you're all wet for it.* Pausing long enough to find Jay's face—the glint in the green eyes, the tip of his tongue piercing an impossibly inviting smirk—Todd opens his mouth and gorges himself. He doesn't gag (*Five inches, tops*, he tells himself with surprising confidence) but his jaw is fully extended to take its hot girth. "Yeah," Jay whispers, "suck it. Suck my dick." No argument from Todd, who laps greedily at the swollen underside, then the corona. He grasps the smooth white ass with one hand, kneads the warm balls, all while he works his own dick with the other. "Man, that feels so good," Jay whispers, "yeah, take it." His voice sounds muffled, as if by the weight of summer heat. Todd pulls off to look up, punch-drunk, his lips sloppy with spit; Jay's face is turned to the right, screwed up with pleasure, and all Todd can think of to say is, "You have the most beautiful cock." It's enough; it seems like a good start. Jay looks down and leers. Todd mutters "shit" and knows he's about to come. "Get up, man, get up," Jay says quickly, pulling Todd to his feet. Their legs touching, Jay works Todd's nipple with his free hand, takes his own dick back in the other. Within ten seconds, Todd sprays a gluey stream across the plastic seat; the next spurt hits the wall with a grunt; the third lands on the chrome fixtures; the last one, weakening, dribbles back over the porcelain and into the bowl itself. Jay takes a little longer. Up on the balls of his feet, he leans on Todd and works with both hands, furiously, as if for takeoff. Just when his blunt, short fingers begin to blur, he lets out a long sigh, squeezing out two milky beads, then a single, heavy dollop, which sloshes aside Todd's already diffusing semen as it strikes the water below.

And Todd's outside, headed back to the Keep. Where, he tells himself, he left his children, with a stranger bearing as credentials no more than a BQ uniform, who *himself* left them with God-knows-who. The part-time employee from the special school, whose sole duty is refilling the straw dispenser? Some stoner dropout pal, fresh out of juvie for maiming several neighborhood pets? Todd deliberates over which two photos he and Kris will provide for the police (*Will Erica's chipped tooth show on a milk carton?*) and tries to remember if it was pictures from last year's trip to his parents' that didn't come out, or the year before.

Rushed, he recalls only a few sensations after orgasm: the cheap, thin toilet paper tearing twice as he swabs off his penis and mouth; the difficulty of getting his belt buckled at the right notch; and Jay's hand, clammy and hot, pressing his own against the boy's slight, distinct chest. Cracking an impenitent smile, Jay kissed him, sealing their complicity with a hot, earnest tongue.

Todd looks at his watch. Barely eight minutes. Hardly anything at all. Blink, and you'd miss it—which is hard to do with the vile mural that assaults him right past the door marked LIEGES ONLY. It's one of a series of efforts afflicting almost every wall in the building; this one, which depicts a market square, reminds him less of the PBS costume dramas Sam watches (and claims to follow) and more of the Renaissance Fair that invades the county fairgrounds. *I suppose thirty-year-old virgins can't play D&D all the time; they're not in high school anymore.*

The mural finally comes to end when the wall mercifully does, and there they are. Erica and Sam. Intact. Unabducted.

Sam, fall forgotten, sits cross-legged next to the Keep, straightening and re-straightening his own shoes in two adjacent cubbyholes, with the studied care of a lepidopterist mounting his latest catch. He tidies up like that at home, as if the havoc of playtime requires its own contrition. Erica is doing her Miss America, but as usual, it comes out more like Princess Anne. Tricked out in the tiara and scepter from her Little Milady Meal, standing up in the booth and waving stoically: a cherubic but constipated monarch. Today, though, she's giving audience to someone new at court. Todd blinks. Jay's surrogate is no juvenile, but a nondescript retiree—lured out of his Craft-Matic, no doubt, by the prospect of getting a Senior discount on an eighty-nine-cent cup of coffee.

"Hi, honey. Hey, tough guy."

Erica levels her eyes at Todd. "Off with his head!"

"That's not right," Sam insists, admiring his work but sighing as if over an old dispute. "That's Alice in Wonderland, dummy. Hey, dad."

"You okay there?" Todd goes and kneels by his son. "No visible scars, eh?"

"We don't have to tell Mom, do we? She won't let me anymore."

"Well."

"But you just said. No scars."

"I guess so."

"What you don't know can't hurt you," the old man chimes in. "Your boy is very shrewd for his age. Wouldn't you say?"

Todd opens his mouth. A thank-you seems awkward.

"I apologize for not introducing myself," the retiree continues, "but I was so absorbed by your little girl's charming performance. Drew Perry: harmless old coot. I do hope everything's all right."

"Daddy," Erica says, "fix my tiara. It's crooked."

"Oh, right," Todd says, obliging. "Daddy had too much soda, did-n't he?"

"Ah yes," nods Drew sagely, "the Regal size. Gets me every time."

"Yeah," says Todd. He manages a smile.

Drew takes a careful sip from his coffee.

"We'd better head back, guys." Todd looks over at Sam. "What do you say, sport? Shoes on." He helps Erica down from the seat. "Your majesty."

"Dad?" asks Sam, edging up to his father. "Can I maybe have another"—and the pained grimace hits its mark—"another Whippey Cone?"

"All right. You were pretty brave. Take your sister's hand, here. Now I want change: all I have is a five. Go on, I'll be right there."

Todd watches them go. "Don't run inside."

"A careful father," the older man says. "Always encouraging. I wish my own children were so attentive with theirs."

"Thanks for watching them."

"Nonsense. Children's games can be tedious; fathers gets bored, especially. That's why Jay and I provide this little service for each other, as the need arises."

"What do you mean?"

"Well, we don't want anyone getting nosy and self-righteous, call-ing the police, making silly, fallacious charges like endangerment. Or indecency."

"Look, I don't know what you're talking about."

"Calm yourself, my boy. The single, true danger is refusing what life puts forth." He lifts the Styrofoam cup, pausing before he takes another cautious sip. "I hope you enjoyed your visit."

Todd flushes. "Can you keep it down?" he says through his teeth. "I don't believe this. Kids." Sam is at the counter on tiptoes, collecting his prize. "Come on, let's go." He starts off.

"Don't blame yourself, my boy," he hears, over his shoulder—an understanding, measured purr. "Youth and beauty are redundantly irre-sistible." Todd turns back. "I've shocked you," Drew continues, "confused you with the wrinkles and talk of grandchildren. How can I possibly disapprove of what I understand too well." He pauses, facing Todd's glare with a veiled, steady eye. "Hard as it may be to believe, I myself was once a teenage Burger Queen."

Suddenly, Sam is back, cone in hand. Erica, sulking over being refused a bite, renews their argument. Todd shepherds them toward the door.

"You're the dummy," she lectures. "I'm Miss America, not Alice."

"The story, not her. The *Red* Queen says 'Off with his head!' You can't be Miss America and say that, you're the wrong *kinda* queen."

The drive home is more of the same.

Every day this past week, Todd has found an excuse on his way home from the office to return to the BQ. He picks up a Little Milady Meal for Erica; they have a new prize, some bug-eyed version of the animal host from her favorite show. So of course he has to get a Little Milord Meal for Sam. Two nights of fast food, and Kris finally balks. Now he drives by. He doesn't order. Jay smokes out in front, by the Keep. Two days in a row, Drew stands beside him, lighting his cigarette, watching him exhale. From where Todd parks in back of the Winn Dixie, he can make out the curve of Jay's ass, impudently pressing against the brown polyester tights. The rest of the time, he sits in his car, studying the litter of signs and decals, amazed at the overkill, wearied by such tireless promotion: OVER HALF A MILLION SERVED. *You have to start somewhere*, Todd tells himself. He stares at the Giant Combo cutouts that dot the landscaping—their logic relentless, almost intuitive—and wonders whether anything still comes by itself. *I just want one. Just that one, please, nothing else.*

It's Monday, lunch hour; he's learned Jay's schedule. He uses the entrance back by the rest rooms. He wouldn't mind company, but it's easier to do it alone. Today, on his way back to his car, he sees the old fruit, sipping his goddamn coffee. And Jay sits across from him, giggles over some unheard comment. He laughs and the bill of his cap obscures his face, but Todd guesses that the pug nose is wrinkling, as it did when he came. *Likes the old ones, I guess. It was a fluke, then, a one-time thing.*

Jay's companion nods, looks like he is about to wave. Todd does not feel like civilities.

Saturdays are the hardest. With Sam in Cub Scouts at the Youth Center, and Erica at Gymboree across the street, he has nothing but time. Say he gives in: even if he catches every light, he has a good hour. Erica has spent the entire car ride pining for the broach-and-pendant set that comes with this week's Little Milady Meal. And he doesn't want either of them near the old man; deviants like that don't draw lines, do they? The food can be warmed up again; the Center's rec room will have a microwave; all they really want is the prize.

When Todd pulls in the lot—in back, avoiding the Keep—he parks and goes inside. Those drive-thru half-wits will put in last week's prizes, because that's what's closest, and then he'll have to go inside, after all. Plus, the old man is nowhere in sight.

Jay stands at the counter. Behind the grill, the manager teaches an overweight trainee the finer points of sandwich assembly.

"Welcome to the Kingdom, can I help you today, sir?" No hint of a smirk.

"Yeah." Todd knows what he wants but consults the overhead menu. "Two kids' meals, please."

"So that's one Little Milady, one Little Milord?"

The overdone inflection gets Todd's attention. He looks down. Jay is grinning at him, but the eyes are somewhere else, fixed on someone behind him. Todd feels disappointed and relieved: *This kid doesn't miss a beat—onto the next one already.* At the same time it occurs to Todd: It might be a woman. *The way this kid looks, he probably bats for both teams. Shit—with my luck it's one of Kris' well-scrubbed friends, picking up meals for her own brood. If it is and I don't say hello to her, I will never hear the end of it.*

But looking around, he doesn't see anybody in line. At a booth over by the window, he spots the Burger Queen, who raises his coffee, as if in a toast.

Todd turns back with a sneer. "What is he, another satisfied customer?"

"Huh?"

"Grandpa told me about your little sideline, the service you give each other. Same kind I got, I guess."

Jay blinks. "We sort of baby-sit for each other, is that a crime or something?" A shrug. "He's the guy who listens to me."

Todd feels his face start to tingle. "Just the Little Meals, please." He shuts his eyes. When he opens them, Jay is back, bags in hand.

"I made sure they got the new toys," Jay says, evenly. Then he reaches in his jerkin, pulls out an envelope. "And this," he catches Todd's eye, "this is for you." Jay's hand hovers over the two bags, as if unsure which to put it in. He settles on Sam's.

It is not until Todd starts his car that he lets himself open the bag, another minute, with the car idling, before he takes out the envelope.

The outside is blank. What could he have written, when Todd never told him his name? Inside the envelope he finds not a letter but what looks like a page torn from a magazine. "Certainly not *U.S. News & Report*," he mumbles to himself: two columns of print, listings for BARS and BOOKSTORES. Some kind of nightlife guide, he assumes, a bit confused, *like you find in hotel rooms, in cities that* have *a nightlife*. The ads on the lower half of the page suggest that the Marriott doesn't furnish this particular guide. If the names aren't suspicious already (THE PIPELINE and THE BOSSA NOVA), the illustrations seal it: a hairy bruiser wearing chaps and not much else; a woman holding a cigarette holder and a martini, propped against a piano.

Todd's seen *Philadelphia*. He remembers that embarrassing Village People movie. He's not stupid. And that's no woman.

Then he sees it, printed at the bottom of the page, in neat, square capitals: "WHERE THE BOYS ARE...." That's the worst of all. He wads the page up and throws it out the window somewhere between the BQ and his house; he can't recall exactly where.

This should take only a minute. Five minutes and no more, unless he gets distracted by a sale on something he doesn't honestly need. It's happened before. He can be in and out of here as long as he stays focused, intent on what he came to get.

The bare concrete floors ripple a sickly yellowish gray as Todd passes under the fluorescent lighting, regularly spaced but perched so high in the cavernous ceiling that it's a wonder the customers can see well enough to distinguish high-grade sandpaper from medium. Or whatever. Todd is here for one reason. Really Kris' reason, she's the one who wants the tile in the guest bathroom finished before her parents arrive. Never mind that Thanksgiving is four months away, never mind they'll stay at a hotel again because they're that kind of in-laws, spitefully selfless, unobtrusively disapproving. He wonders how many times Ann-Marie will ask about the promotion which hasn't materialized quite when predicted. *Just never mind. Where the hell is the grout? I don't know how you're supposed to find anything in this goddamned maze.* He moves to the next aisle, another mile of yellow steel shelving lined with twenty more brands of what he isn't looking for. After combing the store a second time, he's about to give up and ask for help, though that would mean finding someone to ask—a waste of time better spent finding it on his own. He tries another aisle, thinking, *Probably in the last place I look, or right in front of my nose, which is where it'll turn out to be if I* do *ask someone.* Which he is about to do—not for directions but to ask how long you have to work at Hardware House before you can locate anything.

"I see we share another interest." He's standing by a display of roller-and-pan kits, the old perv from Ye Olde Burger Queen, whom Todd had almost forgotten, or hoped he'd seen the last of, like a ghost confined to a particular house. *And of all places, here, where you think you'd be safe from that type. Just keep walking, he's not talking to you. Probably senile at that, he thinks you're one of his pals from the home.*

"It must be true what they say."

Todd has passed him, but stops. Against his better judgment, but then he's always been a sucker for generalizations; collecting platitudes is not exactly a hobby, but they tend to come in handy at cocktail parties, when you're trapped into a conversation. "What was that?"

"I say, it must be true what they say."

"Which is?"

"That D-I-Y is the new Esperanto."

"Oh," Todd responds, halting for a second, "the international language, right."

"A tongue that knows no barriers, yes. A nice idea, perhaps this one will pan out." The man turns back to the shelf in front of him, but Todd senses this isn't over.

"Drew, isn't it?" Otherwise they'll be standing here all day.

"I see I made an impression. That is reassuring. I'm glad you prefer first names also, though I'm afraid … " Drew hesitates, expectant-ly.

Todd draws a blank. For some reason, all he can think of are names that aren't his. He even remembered the old timer's. He thinks perhaps he *should* give a fake name, in case this fruit tries to track him down, in case he's graduated from baby-sitting to blackmail. Just as Todd pictures himself going to the ATM, trying to remember his daily withdrawal limit, he blurts out his first name.

"Yes, Jay's discovery—and yours, I hope."

Todd bites his tongue. He could end it right now; he should. "Look, what the hell are you doing here?"

"Just looking. The same as yourself, I expect."

"Oh, sure," says Todd, ashamed by his attack of paranoia. "Yeah, me too."

"There, as you said. The international language."

A thought occurs to Todd. "What else would I be doing here?"

"The only question is, looking for what? No, let me guess. Caulk, perhaps?"

"What did you say?"

Drew blinks, meeting his eyes again with a faint smile. "Caulking, I suppose, is the more correct term, one that avoids confusion. Myself, I prefer the ambiguous reference. It helps one reach a wider audience."

Todd picks up a can of spray enamel, avoiding the other man's eyes, but oddly not so panicked. He spots what seems to be grout just down the aisle, after all, and he hates making scenes. *Maybe Jay* …

"I trust you understood my little note."

"So that was from you."

"Naturally. I don't deface books as a rule, even though guidebooks don't really count as books, do they? It was an old edition, Jay's in fact. The message was mine, the choice of stationery was his idea."

"Yeah, what the hell was that?"

"Todd, my dear—do you mind my calling you Todd?—I thought it would have been clear. A road map, or the beginnings of one. The one page won't do, of course, but I thought you would find out the rest on your own."

"I told you once," Todd begins, before realizing he doesn't recall exactly what he said, or what he can say now. "I'm not—"

"Some of the bars *are* quite a drive, but if one lives this far out—"

"I mean I'm not. Not like that."

"I wasn't implying you were. We're not all barflies, no matter what Bill Bennett says."

"No, I mean I'm not a fag." He breathes in sharply, through his nose, hoping he wasn't too loud; even if not, he senses he's gone too far, used one of those words they don't like. He recalls a sensitivity-training class a few months ago, where an hour spent making lists on giant legal pads was supposed to open everyone's mind, or scare them into pretending it had. "Look, I'm sorry, I shouldn't't've."

"No, I apologize. Now that I think about it, I know quite a few straight men who use that book. I've met them. In *those* sorts of places."

Feeling flushed, Todd puts down the can he's been holding, making to leave, when a yellow-aproned employee passes by at the end of their aisle. He picks up another brand of enamel.

"I'm not following you, if that's your concern. There are, however, only so many places one can go to find a ball cock."

Todd's grip tightens. He feels his pulse thud against the can's cool surface.

"The humor," Drew adds, "is juvenile, I admit, childishly derivative. We'll blame the surroundings and move on to the point."

"Please do." He can feel his pulse in the pit of his stomach now, hollow and irregular. He wonders if he's too young for a stroke, unable to recall the symptoms.

"What you're looking for … well, it can be found almost anywhere."

"I'm afraid I don't know what you're talking about."

"You said that before," says Drew, lingering for a moment, as if a new idea has occurred to him, then continuing as if he's decided to ignore it. "One merely has to be alert, alive to the possibilities. You see that humpy number, for instance, down by the drop cloths?"

Todd looks to his right, expecting to see someone in a wheelchair or a brace. *"Humpy" like Quasimodo?* What he sees instead is some guy in a dirty baseball cap, scratching his cheek, debating between flat and semi-gloss. *And out of hearing distance*, Todd hopes, when the man strolls off.

"He may have a mullet," Drew says, apparently unflustered, "along with a farmer's tan, but I assure you, he's not looking for pussy."

"Christ." Todd considers an escape route, but passes. He might run into the guy in the cap, or Drew would follow him.

"Now they're not all looking for head, either. All the same," Drew catches Todd's eye and directs it to a man in neat khaki shorts just passing their aisle at the other end. After he's gone, Drew continues, in that sickening purr Todd remembers from before. "It doesn't take an hour to decide on an outdoor sealant. That's how long that one has been here. At least that's what he was looking for when I saw him an hour ago."

Todd feels a line of sweat trickle down his back, grateful for its coolness. He notices the old man has stopped speaking, and he's grateful for the silence. *Not me, no way, you've got it all wrong.* He can't think of what to say, he's run out of ways to say no. *Not here. Not here, too.*

But Drew isn't done. He steps closer, his voice softer, almost confidential. "And Todd, while you're thinking about men, and finding them, be careful not to box it off. It's easy to think of it as a sideline, what you do because you're not thinking, or because it's been a rough week. Because of where it happened or when it happened, it's irrelevant, not real. No. Wherever you do it, it's still your life."

Todd looks down at his hand, still gripping the can, tendons rigid, finger joints knotted with pain. He lets go, with a wince, surprised at how tightly he was holding on. His voice, when he finds it, sounds equally constricted. "I don't think … I don't think I need this." As he puts down the can, turns to leave, he looks Drew in the face. He's remembered another way to say no. "I'm married," he says, weakly.

"Coffee, then. You must tell me all about yourself."

"I'm married."

"So many men are," Drew replies. "So many of us are."

Todd starts off. What do you say to that?

Although it contradicts his memory of events, although he's at his car inside of a minute, it seems to Todd, later, that Drew was somehow the first to leave.

What do you say to something like that?

Todd needs some space. Driving back, he thinks about what awaits him at home. He didn't find the grout; what's Kris going to say when he comes home empty-handed? He didn't even check out, left what he was carrying in the nearest empty cart, walked as fast as he could without breaking into a run. But Todd doesn't worry about the unfinished grout work, or the argument with Kris; he pictures the stack of work he brought home Friday because he'd let himself get behind. He concentrates on finishing quarterly reports, juggling dividends and pie charts. He looks forward even more to the end of the weekend, getting back to the office. Typing up interdepartmental memos, whose boilerplate language is boring but plain. Reliably unembellished, and comfortably abstract. Passive clauses meant to pass the buck, indirect phrases to keep competitors in the dark. He recalls what a professor once said, during the first week of business school: "Corporate Rule of Thumb Number One: Cloak all indiscretions and let the auditors sort them out."

Sterling advice, thinks Todd, already behind his desk, back in his cubicle where fresh air and sunlight are unimaginable. Anything beyond these upholstered walls, potential, fantastic. Safely partitioned from view.

W.C. Harris
W.C. Harris was raised in Memphis, Tennessee, and has received degrees from Amherst College and The Johns Hopkins University. He currently teaches at a state university in Pennsylvania, where he resides with his partner. Although he has published several essays in academic journals, this is his first published piece of fiction.

Same Situation

Paul Lisicky

The crowd throbs, raucous and agitated, heat wafting off bare muscles. Bicycles with bells, pedestrians, roller bladers, gym boys, baby carriages—the street's a pachinko game; we roll in and out of each other, miraculously avoiding collision. Though it's an Indian summer weekend on Commercial Street, it might as well be July—at least my idea of July. "You think this is insane," says my friend, Hollis, "wait till you see the real summer." Someone crushes the back of my shoe. "Hey," I say, annoyed, but the stranger's already out of earshot. On the wharf-side of the street there's a red rectangle in the window: SUMMER BLOWOUT. People stream from the store with dazed faces and plump shopping bags, and like the good gay boys we are, we lurch toward the door.

"What about this?" I hold an aqua-striped, olive-gray sweater to my face.

"Nnnn," Hollis says, shaking his head. "J. Crew doesn't work here."

I must look wounded, though I try to hold my smile. It's not that I feel any particular allegiance to my old style; still, it's disconcerting that there's so much I don't know about Provincetown culture and customs. Only last week I slept with a certain Townie who biked up to me on the street and introduced himself by saying, "Hi, do you want to get high and have sex?" When I proudly (yet discreetly) pointed him out the next day, my friend Billy winced as if he'd caught me snacking on a loose Oscar Mayer wiener I'd found on the sidewalk.

Listen," Hollis says, more softly now. "You're a spring. Not a summer. *I'm* a summer." He squeezes my shoulder, then picks through the overstuffed rack. He hands me something meager. "Try this on."

I put on an absurdly tight Tom of Finland tank top over my button down and try to imagine standing on my parents' front porch in Florida. (*Uhh*, says my mother, covering her face, crumbling to the floor.) I put it back. I've been in town but two weeks, since October 1st, and already it seems that half the populace has participated in my makeover. Billy has accompanied me to the optician in Orleans, where he's tried to persuade me to buy lipstick-red frames, which I almost assent to (does he want them for himself?), until I choose a more sensible tortoiseshell pair. My friend Jimmy has already shorn off the hair on the sides of my head and left the dark, foppish waves on top—a look that really seems to understand who I am, as an aging boy who has one foot planted in his past, the other in who he wants to be. I can't help but wonder whether this kind of tutelage is part of any boy's welcome to town. Who, for instance, facilitated Hollis', Billy's, and Jimmy's welcomes, their respective entries into the frat? And who before them?

I couldn't be more grateful for my new friends. Certainly, they want to see me flourish and thrive. They must get that I'm hungry to slough off my old skins, that I've had enough of being a good boy, so desperate to please. They must know that I need to be a little bad before it's too late.

"What did you get?" I say to Hollis outside the store.

He holds up a cluster of socks—mustard-green, graphite, cadmium yellow—like some mad bouquet while I show off my new polo shirt.

"Paul," he says, eyes rolling.

"What?"

Instantly he takes the shirt from me and rips off each sleeve in two expert tears. I don't know whether to thank him or to weep.

"Now that's a Provincetown shirt."

It comes in like a white speck on the water. Then something with more dimension: a wedding cake; an igloo; a string of white boxes, in descending order, hooked together on a floating raft. It's the last arriving ferry of the season. I stand on the town beach and herald its arrival. I wave stupidly, then dip my hand in the harbor. On this fine, fair Columbus day morning, the water's freezing, cold enough to scald.

I step through the kelp on the shoreline. The smell of the water, the tolling of church bell and foghorn: How intricately lovely the world seems, how precise and expansive. Who knew what I'd been holding back? I see things more deeply; clouds tower; even the pale pink roses outside Billy's apartment window seem to vibrate. I've already written thirty pages of a new novel; I've already made more friends in two weeks at the Fine Arts Work Center than I'd made in the past ten years. My shoulders ease backward; I hold my head higher as I walk into yet another party. I speak more fluently, expressively, not afraid to display my silly side, the cast of selves I've kept expertly hidden for too long. One minute I'm the "Sissy Priest," the next I'm a comic strip character, "Fancy Boy," the next I'm devising theme nights for a fictitious night-club: *Lola Falana! Jack Wrangler and his Corn Cob! Star Boy in Flames!*

And yet?

Why is love still missing from my life? I haven't been in town all that long, but I don't understand why I haven't been asked out. And why is it that every time *I* ask someone out, he only seems to be interested in fooling around? Not that I have anything against sex, but I'm frustrated that the boys I've slept with don't seem to be much interested in anything more. While we certainly say hello to each other on the street the next day, it's all a bit casual. I think, if it was good that time, well, wouldn't it be even better the next? My hints at further explorations seem to be appreciated but it stops at that. Is something wrong with me? I tick off all possible permutations—body type, body chemistry, smell—and kick myself for even entertaining such common thoughts. Or does it have something to do with New England culture, where the direct, forthright expression of desire seems unseemly, if not low-class, even among those who are convinced they're above all that? Obviously it would be mistaken to expect an extravaganza of everlasting devotion from the aforementioned guy who biked up to you on the street with a lit joint between his fingertips, but *still*. I wake up in the morning, groggy, a bar of sunlight blinding my eyes. I feel hope—what will happen today?—before the melancholy settles: dust beaten from a mop. If only someone's face were on the pillow next to mine. If only to watch another man sleeping, his mouth twitching as he dreams.

I am 31 years old. Do I already sense my future creeping up on me: the narrow bed and the crock pot, the smell of cooked cabbage wafting up from the one-room apartment below?

I certainly can't live in Provincetown forever.

I try not to fret. Maybe it's just that what I want is too specific and my desire is caving in on itself, the roof of my soul buckling under that weight. Or maybe it's this *place*: maybe there's no point in being coupled if there's so much fresh "talent," as Hollis says, waiting to be discovered at the town version of Schrafft's every weekend. Still, I'm not ready to let go. One night, I walk into Gallerani's with my friend, Polly, and see two handsome men, obviously a couple, sitting along the opposite wall of the restaurant. Their faces are underlit by the candle between them. One reaches across the table for the other's hand, and in that easy, intimate gesture, I know everything I need to know about them. We're not talking about Idea here, but something earthier and sexier than that. I just know: you can see it in their eyes.

"Who are they?"

"That's Mark and Wally," says Polly. "Let's go over and talk to them."

"No, no, don't bother," I stay seated in my booth, stopping her. "They're so sweet together."

Food is brought to the table. I lift my wineglass to my lips. And Polly reaches over to touch my hand, as if she realizes that I can see suddenly, in the deepest sense, what I've been missing.

I decide to be practical. Billy has already indicated an interest in joining the gym with me. He's been spending far too much time inside, he says, and his doctor thinks working out would be good for his health. So one day, after squeezing my paltry biceps before the medicine-cabinet mirror, I give him a call: "Let's do it." If I cannot find a boyfriend, then I can control other aspects of my life.

Yet joining the gym is a bigger commitment than I think it is. It entails entering into a complex relationship with the body in which nothing is ever good enough, in which one's always examining one's failings. I'm not sure I'm ready for this intensified scrutiny. Doesn't my body already take up far too much of my attention? And aren't bodies succumbing to illness all around me? At certain moments I can't help wishing I were born something other than human, mammal. I look down at the gray-beige pebbles around the shrubs outside my window and think how much more reliable to be stone—not to worry about temporality, perfection, and the mucky place where love and lust meet. At least not to be goaded by these hormones, which prickle the skin, and lead me to all sorts of charged, complex situations in which I'm not even sure I want to participate.

We sign up at Betty's. Though Billy has promised to suggest a program for me (he's worked out at other times in his life), he immediately wanders off toward the free-weight area and leaves me on the floor like a seventh-grade girl with braces and thick, thick glasses who's just been publicly dumped at the junior-high canteen.

"What should I do?" I call out.

"Try the leg machine."

Well, thank *you*, Mr. Forlenza. I plop onto some Frankensteinian contraption then lift my legs feebly. Dumbbells thump and chime; everyone's focused; everyone seems to know exactly what he's doing. Unlike me, who's too ashamed to let anyone see how inept I am. It's one thing to look like a big old sissy among straight boys, quite another to accomplish that among men you want to look sexy for.

"What in Christ's name are you doing?"

Is that man with the shaved head talking to *me*? I swallow hard.

He steps toward me. "You're cheating. Make sure you squeeze your legs at the top. Go for the full range of motion. There, there, that's right." And he stands beside me as I execute a perfect rep.

There's something lulling about the authority of his voice. I can't help but be drawn to its parental quality: that conflation of concern and control. I'm partly flattered, partly offended: who asked for his help? I let him watch me. Without my realizing it, his face (half hard: mouth, brow; half soft: eyes, nostrils) imprints itself in my consciousness like a deer paw in clay.

"I have to go, honey," says Billy, huffing, his hand to his chest. "I'm exhausted."

"Are you okay?"

But he's already hurrying down Commercial Street to his apartment.

The doorman's a big black fellow in a floor-length duster and a red, rubbery hat with points like a jester's crown. He makes me think of an oversized, overage Little Rascal. If only he were so charming, though. Does he grimace at everyone else the way he seems to grimace at me? He seems to take particular offense at my desire to be admitted into the

A-House for free. Five dollars, he barks. But aren't all Work Center fellows allowed in for free? I squeak. Five dollars, he says, more softly now, and jabs my chest with his finger. I fork over my cash, hurrying past him, a little pissed, but still hoping that one day soon I'll be recognized by him as the Townie I truly am.

I've worked hard all week on a book that makes me deeply uncomfortable, if only because I'm writing about things I'd rather avoid feeling. I've been waiting for this night the whole week. I order a Rolling Rock from Ken, the bartender, and practically shotgun it. The voices around me are booming, baritone. The boys stand around the postage stamp of dance floor, heads nodding to the beat, clutching their bottles to their chests or belts. The fireplace roasts the room. Everyone's waiting for something to happen. I'm all loose and woozy, as if the beer has dripped down into the emptied cave of my stomach. I stroll onto the floor. Perhaps I'm lucky that my eyesight's so poor, that I still have on the same pair of gummy, protein-coated contacts I've worn for the past three and a half years; otherwise, I'd feel self-conscious if I could see those faces looking back at me. But my body feels right tonight, that pleasant combination of tensile and supple. I'm ready for trouble. I chug my arms and I shimmy, focus on the bass line rumbling the floorboards.

I raise my head. I'm unnerved to see that the man from the gym is dancing not two feet from me, his palms facing outward at his collar bone, eyes closed. His grin is sly, the left corner of his mouth turning upward. For the first time I see how muscular his body is, how thick across the chest, and for the first time I see that he's attracted to me, which quickens my heart, in part because I hadn't known it before. He grasps my hand, drags me off the floor, and buys me another beer. It's too loud to talk. He puts his lips to my ear, says something wickedly cutting about the boy to our left, and I laugh, pretending to understand every word, though all I can think of right now is the warmth and weight of his shoulder through his sweat-drenched T-shirt, its dense, meaty quality.

"Let's get out of here," he says finally with a controlled triumph. As we walk past the boys at the bar, I try to maintain a look of cool composure. My pulse beats inside my back teeth. I tell myself: Of course, *of course*.

To this day, I can't even recall the route to this house: did we walk, ride bicycles? Was it cloudy, or did the moon silver the surface of the harbor? All I know is that we're inside his living room. He latches his fingers together, stretches his arms overhead, and to his shock, I tear his shirt up out of his waistband and fix my mouth to his left nipple. "Oh, Jesus," he says, as his knees weaken.

Soon enough I'm leading him to *his* bed (how sexy, how profound this feels), just the way he led me off the dance floor. We lie down for a minute, still, a little shy, then all at once we're on each other, thrashing, voracious. He lifts his face from mine after a while. "That's one fierce mouth on you, boy," he laughs.

I lick my way down to his tight, tight stomach. I am hungry for forgetfulness, greedy to be an animal.

I'm still awake at four-thirty in the morning. The bedroom is too cold, the floodlights outside shine through the blinds, throwing slatted patterns on the ceiling. V. sleeps beside me, absolutely calm and contained. He snores delicately. What is it about me when I have sex with someone I'm excited about? Why can't I sleep afterward? Why do I feel this lump in my throat like I'm about to have a heart attack—but a satisfying heart attack?

"I have to kick you out," says V. affectionately.

Sunlight pools on the floor. As I focus, V's face is just inches above my own, the tiniest thread of spit jeweling the space between his open lips. "What time is it?"

"It's ten," he says, glancing at his watch. "You have to leave before my boyfriend gets home."

I sniff. I almost say it: *Boyfriend?*

His voice is calm and rational as he explains the situation to me, how he and his boyfriend of three years spend one night apart each week to sleep with other people, even though they're deeply devoted to each other. The sincere expression in his eyes suggests that he doesn't think he's hurting me and that there's no reason in the world why I should be offended. And while I know in my heart that it's his absolute right to be in an open relationship, I wish I'd had access to this news a little earlier. I'm peeved. And yet it would seem indelicate to express such feelings, akin to wearing sneakers at a Park Avenue dinner party hosted by the princess of a long-gone republic.

I step into my jeans as expertly as I can.

"Well, bye," I say, extending my hand at the door.

A tinge of sorrow flickers in his eyes (the color of tea leaves in this light), as he pulls me close to him. His hug is tight, unguarded. His shirt collar smells of fabric softener, a hint of shaving cream. "I had a wonderful time," he says.

A branch cracks outside. "Me too."

I walk home. Sunlight shines on the shards of a broken Coke bottle by the street.

Danella thinks it's time to lie low. We're in her Work Center apartment with its knotty-pine paneling, its sweltering fireplace. She stirs the contents of an enormous pot, preparing one of her low-fat soul food recipes she's trying out on me. (A dud of a cook, I couldn't be more grateful.) She's on vacation from men after having ended a long, exhausting relationship with someone with whom she shared a Kings Croft condo in my hometown of Cherry Hill, of all places. This hard-won detachment gives her a special assurance, a self-effacing, Zen-like wisdom. We adore each other like brother and sister. (She calls us Laurel and Hard-on.) I walk over to the stereo and put on our favorite music of the day: first De La Soul, then Queen Latifah. Before long we're moving our arms, dancing casually around her apartment. It's never been at such ease with my body, and it pleasures me no end that she doesn't make fun of my white-boy moves. Later, slouching on her bed, we'll watch John Waters' *Desperate Living* until we laugh so hard that the tears run hot down our cheeks.

For now, we sit down to eat. The greens are fabulous: zesty, spiked with lemon and garlic: church bells on the tongue. Once again, I'm talking about my lovelorn-ness, a topic which must tire the patience of even the best of my friends.

"You're kicking and fighting," she says.

I lift my head. Do I detect the slightest hint of scorn in her voice?

She salts her corn, takes a spoonful, then cocks her head. She salts it again. "You're going to get what you want, honey. But you can't force it. It will come to you." She has a way of investing these tired, New Agey expressions with such freshness. But why am I so unwilling to have faith?

"There's not very much time."

"You're *young*," she insists.

But then a tender recognition settles inside her gaze. We've just been talking about how many people are sick in town, how so many of them are not going to make it through the winter. Even her beloved younger brother has been in and out of hospitals for years. As far as I know, I'm healthy, but, like most of my friends, I'm scared to death to go to the doctor to find out. Could this be one of the reasons why she loves me so much?

"Eat." And she spoons another helping of greens onto my plate.

The tide advances on the town beach outside the gym's sliding-glass windows, foam swirling around the boats' rusted red hulls. It's twilight. A nor'easter gangs up on the coast; ions rush and tumble through the atmosphere. Yet everything's safe inside this little corner of the gym: no water seeping under the sill. There's Polly, leaning on the Roman chair. There's Hollis, by the window, doing his shoulder shrugs. There's Tim Callis, who's just passed a homemade cassette of dance music—"Butt Party"—to S., the woman behind the counter. There's Jasper, up from New York; there's Jack Pierson; there's Scott Frankel; there's Ryan Landry—all the people I'm fond of, the inimitable combination of souls who give this town its peculiar vitality and panache. Unfortunately, Billy's stopped coming: I can't tell whether he isn't feeling well or whether he's lost interest.

I'm much more committed to working out than I'd ever expected. On my better days, I'm convinced that I've actually remade my entire body (look: a blue ropy vein's popped out on my biceps!), and when I tell my friend Elizabeth, whom I haven't seen since our time together at Iowa, that she might not recognize me when she comes to town, she'll kid me about it mercilessly for years to come. Of course, it probably helps that I've shaved off my hair and grown a goatee, which gives me a certain Luciferian quality.

We're all engaged in our reps and our sets when S., the woman behind the counter, switches off "Butt Party." She claps her hands like a drill sergeant. "All *right*," she bellows, "who in this gym *smells*?"

We're silent. The room positively vibrates with collective shame. She has tapped into our deepest dreads. *It's me*, each one of us thinks.

Then a few of us start snickering, nervously, quietly, expelling air through our nostrils. Immediately, S. herself seems to realize how extravagant and over-the-top her outburst was, how it expresses some lurid deep phobia. What rage has she kept bottled up inside? It probably makes it worse for her that no one's willing to back her up; all at once, all the shame in the room boomerangs on her. She crumples down in her seat. We might have stepped onto the set of *A Woman Under the Influence*.

The combination of the approaching storm and the complex energy in the room has my hair practically standing on end. *Is it you? Is it you?* Now everyone wanders about the gym, sniffing, laughing. Arms are raised. We smell; we're smelled back. And all at once we're creating one of those quintessential Provincetown moments, weirdly intimate, something we'll remember for the rest of our lives, when people who've never spoken before laugh together. All the while S. sits up front, moistening her lips, as if she's on the verge of tears.

On my way out I feel a tapping on my arm. V. smiles, slinging his gym bag over his shoulder.

"Were you here the whole time?" My voice sounds harsher, more authoritative than I'd intended.

"Can you believe her? Maybe she'd like to spray us all down like little piggies in a trough."

We stand outside in the howling wind, leaves rasping the pavement around our feet. Like me, he, too, is caught up in the spirit of camaraderie and happy feelings. He lifts his head. A door swings open inside me. In the porch light his eyes smile and gleam with just the right hint of wickedness. "Your place?" he says.

I grab for his hand. Where is death tonight? We walk down Pearl Street. The world couldn't be more achingly beautiful; the sky glows beyond the stark, thrashing trees.

And so it starts, the events that conspire to make love, or whatever this is, the center of your life. At first, you don't even realize how much of your attention it consumes. You still have a life, don't you? You still get up to brush your teeth and pour your milk on your honey puffed wheat. You still send off your student-loan payment on the first of the month. And yet you jump when you hear the phone or a knock at the door—is it him? You keep yourself sexually focused and groomed at all times because you never know when the opportunity will arise. Worse, you don't leave town when your brother offers you a free plane ticket to Miami for fear that when you come back he'll have revised his feelings. You don't even insist on your right to see him because he tells you—quite cheerfully, in fact—the story of Renaldo and Bobby. The single Bobby, who's having an affair with the coupled Renaldo, has started to make demands, and the way V. sees it, "That's going to kill things." The whole thing becomes more precious to you because it's provisional, forever on the verge of vanishing. You lacquer it the way an oyster lacquers a grain of sand: layer upon layer until it shines.

You're walking down Commercial Street. You think you see the back of his shaved head in a group of people standing outside Cafe Express and your steps quicken. He's happy to see you, and you him, but when you talk you can feel a tension, the possibility of sex beating beneath everything: should we do it? Are all the conditions right? In public, you carry on something resembling a friendship, but you wonder whether the others know what's going on between you. You *hope* they can see it in both your eyes, for at the very least it will prove to you that there's something real between you, that it's more than just sex, which is what V. thinks it is. Or so he says.

You look at his unchanging gaze sometimes. Is he hiding something? How could he not be as torn-up as you are?

But in spite of the fact that the terms aren't equal here (he's unavailable a certain portion of the time; you're *always* available), you must admit that it's incredibly intoxicating. Life has never seemed as dense and as rich: a fancy Italian cake. You love the way he makes fun of you. You love his warmth and his wit, his sweeping assessments of the pretentious and the absurd. He takes a particular pleasure in exposing the true essences of people who present themselves one way and are actually something else. One man, who's known as sensitive and sweet by many of the available straight women in town, is branded a "cunthound." Truth be told, he's hard on everyone. The fact that he approves of your character makes you feel like a million bucks.

Now if only you could sit at your desk for more than five minutes at a stretch. Your new novel has come to naught. You stare out the window, then get up to pee. You stare again. You wonder whether you have adult attention deficit disorder.

You're standing outside the First Old Store one night when his boyfriend bikes toward you. A valve in your heart flutters. Too late to run. You know you should probably be feeling guilty and contrite about what you've been doing (once is one thing; again and again is another), but you know he's probably doing the same thing himself with somebody else. And besides, you must confess that you feel some warmth toward the fellow. You talk about Alicia Henry's show of new paintings at the Work Center, which both of you happen to like very much. You both complain about the music at the A-House. You look in his Nordic-blue eyes. You can see the edge of asperity in them. He knows; of course he does. You are breaking up the relationship. Still, this doesn't stop you from wanting to tear the flashing red light from his handlebars to throw it against a building.

Danella offers me a cup of Earl Grey as I sink into her sofa. Over in the barn, there's a party still going on for a visiting writer. Things have been getting a little wild around the compound. Is it just the cold, the fact that there's nothing much else to do out here on the edge of the world besides our work, and we need to blow off some steam, in a manner of speaking? Or is it simply that we trust each other?

Within the last couple of weeks we've heard rumors of all sorts of couplings: lesbians with straight boys, black girls with white boys, straight boys with gay boys—every possible combination you can imagine. Only last week, as part of a collaborative art project, Itty poured an assortment of canned foods from her cupboard over my naked body and photographed the results—something which we both found amusing, compelling, and a little kinky.

Sometimes, though, one needs to take refuge. Through the window I can hear the strains of Public Enemy drifting out across the parking lot.

"We haven't gotten together since last month," I say to Danella. "Do you think something's the matter?"

She tosses carrots into her juicer, a thoughtful, sleepy expression on her face.

"I mean, if things were really great between them, this wouldn't be happening. I can tell what he thinks when he sees me. It's just too much for him to take in right now."

The sleek machine makes a grinding noise before she switches it off. She will not proffer the easy answer, though she knows that's what

I want from her. "Then why are you so worried?" she says finally.

"What?"

She pushes the dreadlocks off her forehead and presses her hand against the small of her back. She sips from the carrot juice, which leaves a pale, creamsicle-colored mustache on her upper lip before she wipes it off. "If he's the one, he'll come to you."

"You mean I shouldn't try to bring this up?"

"Sit tight for now." She walks over to the sink and rinses out her stained glass. "Just trust me."

"But what if this is it?"

"It's not over, sweetheart."

I lift the cup. My tea burns the tip of my tongue

A burst. I've been writing since dinnertime, and now it's half past three in the morning. I've accumulated two chapters, fifteen more pages of my novel. I think they're good, but who can tell such things when you're in the storm and fire of it? Whatever's transpired, though, I've had a conceptual breakthrough: my protagonist till now hasn't been active enough. He simply hasn't taken charge of his daily affairs; everything's been done to the poor guy: a baffled, inert observer. I want to shake him; I want to whack him upside the jaw. As soon as I make him choose, the stalled narrative takes off. He comes alive. The story sings for the moment, one unexpected event leading to the next.

Is my book trying to tell me something about myself?

I decide to sit tight. Outside my bedroom window the entire compound's dark, with the exception of Jim and Jane's window, in which a little lamp burns. I lie down on my spongy, narrow mattress. I think about what Danella told me, but her words don't stick. What's the worst that can happen? Am I only going to make an ass of myself? Or am I going to find out that he really doesn't care about me, that I simply don't have that much meaning for him? Well, if that's the case, then screw it.

I down cup after cup of coffee. I must have courage. I must keep hold of my convictions. I throw on my leather jacket, my scuffed Doc Martens, and a pair of torn 501s. I am walking down the stairs, walking out the door. The town couldn't be more beautiful this mild December night. A loose clapboard bangs softly against a building. A white star fires, fizzling out over Long Point. The breadth and depth of the landscape. I shudder inside. And I couldn't be more pleased with myself, for I'm thinking: This is what it means to be an adult. This is what it means to throw off the yoke of childhood uncertainty: to be able to ask for what you want.

The lights are on in V.'s bedroom window. I creep up the driveway, careful not to make too much noise on the gravel. Music plays inside. Is it Joni? "Same Situation." I take a step further, sidle up against the car, and stop at the foot of the stairs. Voices. I clench. Not two inches from my shoes a skunk ambles by, white tail flaring. My mouth opens. My arms move frantically about as he wobbles away down the hedgerow, as scared of me as I am of him. Luckily, he keeps his scent to himself. I prop myself against the sideview mirror, practically falling to my knees. Then another step. Voices again. And this time I see them—V. sits in the hot tub, his arms wrapped around his boyfriend from behind. Steam hovers over the deck; the water bubbles. I think I should be angry, but it only feels like I've been hit by a bicycle and I can't feel anything. Their backs are pale and broad in the moonlight. V. nuzzles the bluish hollows behind his lover's shoulder blade; the leaves shiver, and that's enough. I see it all: the heft of their time together, their successes and missed opportunities, and suddenly I know why they're up this late: they've been talking about me, them, how they're going to move onward from here. Their eyes are closed. They're too caught up in the moment to notice the intruder standing on the deck.

I turn back down the steps. I wait till I'm far enough away from the house. I glance back over my shoulder, and this time I really do fall down on my knees. I stay there until it hurts, the gravel digging into my skin.

I shouldn't be surprised when V. tells me that he and his boyfriend have broken up. He tells me in the calmest, most workaday fashion, two years after I happened upon them in the hot tub. I've been involved with someone else, Eric, fresh from India by way of Montreal, and my attentions are too much turned toward him to feel anything like surprise. I suppose I'm still a little in love with V., but I've tossed that love aside, turned it inside out, and lost it like a sock beneath a bureau. All over town, seemingly in-it-for-the-long-haul relationships are falling apart.

And much, much worse, people are dying. How many friends have we all lost over the last couple of years? It's 1993, the height of the Epidemic. Billy, Lon, Richard, David, Chico: even if they haven't died, they're getting sick. The medicine is lousy, the doctors have thrown up their hands, and we all know it's only a matter of time. And now Wally—I've been looking in on him while Mark's away teaching at Sarah Lawrence—isn't doing so well. One night I walk by their house to see a clear-glass votive burning in the living-room window.

A couple of days later, Eric and I attend Wally's memorial service inside the white clapboard UU church. I'm reasonably composed throughout. I reach for Eric's warm, broad hand, and think of that scene back in Gallerani's, which seems like so many lives ago, when I first saw Mark reach for Wally across the candlelit table. Shyly, I walk up to Mark after the final hymn. He says, "Thank you for being in Wally's life." And he says it so plainly, with such simple austere truth, that I burrow my eyes into the soft part of his shoulder. The world falls silent. The church empties out. Too much at once: Wally's death (I should have stopped by more often in those last, difficult weeks!); Mark's efforts to hold himself together; Eric's protracted indecision—whether to go back to Canada, or move on, or … *what?* Death after death after death in town. And V.—what about him? The fractured globe turns, the cold clear light of its core burning through the rift in its surface, but there isn't any globe in the sanctuary, just time going round and round inside our heads, and Mark holds me tighter before letting go, and lets me know that I shouldn't be sorry for losing my composure

Some days I can't believe that Provincetown's still standing.

But there it is along the beach: a little battered, some days a little unsteady on its feet, but walking forward, a trace of wryness in its expression.

And who could have imagined that the story would turn out this way? Polly certainly saw it; so did Jenny, Dan, and others. Lynda, who caught me on the street a few days after Wally's death (she herself would die in a car accident outside Plymouth in two months), hugged me, saying, "Watch out for Mark."

How would things have been different had we not started out in anguish, had someone else not died first?

Love in the new world.

Mark and I stand in our living room, stepping back from the windows, and wait to see who takes what from our giveaway pile at the foot of the driveway. Sometimes it feels okay to let a few things go—not all, but a few. I'm ready to go back to work when I see a young man sifting through a milk crate full of my old shirts. He's new to town. He has that hungry look; it barely masks his vulnerability, the squint, the touch of trouble in his eyes. He picks up a shirt, chews on his lip. It might very well be the shirt from which Hollis tore off the sleeves all those years ago. The trees shake for a moment. The clouds part, sun bronzing the tips of the leaves. I want to tell him, watch out, dangerous currents in the forecast. Instead, Mark and I stand side by side at the window and wait to see what he'll do.

Paul Lisicky
Paul Lisicky is the author of the novel *Lawnboy* and the memoir *Famous Builder*. His work has appeared in *Ploughshares*, *Boulevard*, *Mississippi Review*, and in the anthologies *Open House*, *The Man I Might Become*, *Best American Gay Fiction 2,* and elsewhere. A graduate of the Iowa Writers Workshop, his awards include fellowships from the National Endowment for the Arts, the Michener/Copenicus Society, and the Fine Arts Work Center in Provincetown. He teaches creative writing at Sarah Lawrence College and lives in New York City and Provincetown. He is currently at work on a new novel.

To My Former Mother, Mrs. Callahan

after Eudora Welty's "Why I Live at the P.O."

Tom House

I cannot explain how annoyed and mortified I was to have you waking me up yesterday with that loud rapping, only to open my door and find you standing there with a vase full of carnations—green, no less, and how appropriate in a way I can't think of, with all those fairy fern leaves and baby-whatevers to boot. There's nothing I hate more than a holiday.

"Who the fuck are they for?" I said, and I apologize for the use of the word *fuck* to your face, but you have to understand my predicament, and also take into account I didn't get to sleep till after five in the morning and was standing there in my underwear feeling like I'd just been ripped from the womb.

Well, that smile fell right off your face, and I could tell by your overcoat and makeup you were home for lunch, which just made me marvel at my rotten luck—once in a blue moon you eat at home, and that's just the moon these things arrive.

"They're for you," you said, handing them to me, as if I might've wanted any part of them.

"How could they be for me?"

"The woman said—"

"What woman?"

"Your name's on the—"

And yes, I was rude: I grabbed the vase from your hand, ripped the card off the tissue paper and planted that mutant hellspray on my dresser. Again, I apologize for my lack of whatever, but to be perfectly honest at the moment I was wishing either you or the flowers would disappear, and you were both staying stubbornly present.

"Aren't you going to open the card?" you said, with your hand on your hip that way that makes me cringe.

"No, I'm not going to *open the card,"* I said, shoving it in a drawer.

"Don't you want to know who they're from?"

"I know who they're from."

"Oh?"

"Oh." And believe you me if that ... *jerk* had been standing in this drafty, one-windowed, converted-garage of a room, I would've strung him up by the toes and torn out both of his eyes for your viewing satisfaction—sending me flowers at my parents' house.

"Well, who?" you said.

And I was shocked. "What do you mean, who?"

"Who are they from?"

Now you had no right. Don't think I've forgotten the day you sat me down at the kitchen table and told me the whole drawn-out story about how Cousin Marybeth was living with some guy and she went and told Aunt Kathy right out, and how upset your poor sister was, and how the least Marybeth could've done was lie—no, you didn't say *lie;* the least she could've done was misrepresent the situation, was the gist of it, like whichever one of your friends' darling son who forbade his girlfriend to answer the phone and all other kinds of elaborate schemes, and you looked me wide in the eyes the whole time like there was something enormous behind your words you wanted to get across. And don't think, either, it was any mystery to me that from that moment on you stopped hounding me about when I was going to get a girlfriend, and I'm sure you noticed I stopped dropping all those glaring little hints, like the time I held up *People Magazine* and said, "I can think of sexier men than Mel Gibson." Well, those conditions were fine with me, and I was under the impression it was the beginning of a nice long détente, but then all of the sudden you came breaking your own rules, asking me who the flowers were from.

"Mom, I am twenty-six years old," I said.

And there your blue-green eyes were, staring me down like oh so many years ago, and I was staring back just as hard wondering which of us was going to break first—neither (and isn't that always the way?); you just turned with the swish of your polyester pants and big-belted overcoat, mumbling, *"Well, excuse me for living,"* and slammed my own door, leaving me face-to-face with my timeworn *Partridge Family* poster, sick souvenir of my youth: Shirley & David et al., smiling brightly before the multicolored bus, *Com'on get happ-y!* And it was while staring at those big-collared crooners that I realized how much neither of us understood what I'd just said, because I felt I'd answered your question to the best of my ability, though I couldn't have said how.

Meanwhile I was willing to forget the whole scene and go back to bed, which is exactly what I tried to do the second you left the room. And maybe I would've been successful if the faces of those damned dogs hadn't come plaguing my brain again, which they seem to be doing more and more frequently these days, and usually at just this kind of inconvenient moment. Mind you, I've never seen these dogs, but I'm convinced they were Dalmatians—remember, like Pongo, the Shaws' dog, that died of whatever it was that made him piss all that blood and stain the trees? But of course you know nothing about the learned helplessness of dogs and I am wasting time and paper. I wouldn't have known about them myself if you and Dad hadn't been so kind as to pay for me to go to college against my will, and so I am indebted to you both for this bit of mind-expanding knowledge, even though I failed psychology like I failed every other course I took. I'm sure Jimmy knows all about the dogs, ask him. Or ask that bitch of his, Jennifer (and don't tell me you don't share that opinion). And then maybe I'd be interested in hearing what they might have to say about them—that is, if any of us are on speaking terms by then, which I entirely doubt.

Well, I'll have you know it wasn't long after your car screeched out of the driveway that I got up and did all my showering, breakfasting, laundrying, and everything else I needed to be in another room of the house to do. Of course I did not respond, as you're aware, when you came rapping on my door at dinnertime asking if I was going to eat corned beef and cabbage with the family. Now, did you really expect me to come popping out to the kitchen table like nothing had happened? For your information, I walked up to the corner and had a couple slices of pizza and a normal-colored beer. What's more, when I came back I sat at my desk for the longest single period of time I can recall, just flipping through my old psych textbook. If I hadn't had to pass through the den to brush my teeth before leaving for work, I wouldn't have done that, either, but as it never seemed to occur to anyone when you were having this "extra room" built that its occupant would have to travel cross-country to get to the can, it's not like I had a lot of options.

Lord knows I wasn't prepared for Phase Two: Dad, stirring from his vegetable state in the easy chair to announce, "Here's the one who's too old to give his mother a straight answer." So what the hell was that? You went and told him about the whole thing—you told him about the *flowers*? And how do you think I felt with Jimmy and Jennifer in that plaid love seat, gaping up at me in unison like I was the main attraction in a freak show? My private business, out for everyone to consider.

And you can tell Dad that so far as his *straight answer* is concerned, I have also not forgotten the day we were watching *Deathtrap* on cable, and the second Christopher Reeve's and Michael Caine's lips touched he let out the most profound and guttural *yech* I've ever heard. And that kiss wasn't even real! Not even in the movie was it real—it was just part of this ploy the Reeve character was using to steal the old man's play (and then, incidentally, they edited that scene when it was shown on television, not that I ever expect you to understand what that has to do with anything).

Well, I'm sure you noted I said nothing in response to Dad's unusual remark, but just kept right on walking through your dining room and kitchen and down your rubber-runnered hallway to the bathroom—there was nothing more on my mind than getting out of firing range just as fast as I possibly could. But then, as if I hadn't gone through enough for one day, I had yet another door rapped on.

"What is it now?" I had to scream through the foam in my mouth. Little did I suspect I was in for Phase Three.

"It's Jimmy. Can I speak with you a minute?" Which I knew meant Jennifer as well, seeing how they can never be pried apart; I'm expecting their hands to permanently fuse any day now.

I had the door open one second and Jimmy blurted out with, "Mom and Dad want you to tell them about yourself."

I knew right then it was a full-fledged family conspiracy—all of you sounding off so loud and brave about something you wouldn't have whispered the day before. And you think I didn't know what spurred it all on? The four of you last Sunday, huddled in the den watching that made-for-TV bullshit about the minister's son dying, and when I passed through, same as I passed through yesterday, you all looked up at once with these dog-tragic eyes—no, it wasn't at all obvious. Well, I hate to disappoint everyone, but to the best of my knowledge I am as healthy as the day I was born, and you are stuck with the reality of a living son and brother for an indeterminate period of time to come. What do you think I am, careless? Did it ever occur to you what might happen to me if I ever did die and found out God really was a Catholic? You think I'm eager for an eternity in hell? So don't come weeping at me, because I plan to outlive you all.

Meanwhile I spat in the sink. "Tell them about what?"

"Yourself," Jimmy said, nodding like he was alluding to the most apparent thing in the world.

And then Jennifer, "Don't you think it's about time?" Where does she get the nerve?

"What the hell do you mean?"

"You know very well what we mean," Jimmy said, and—oh my god—letting go of her hand, he crossed his arms and squinted those small brown eyes of his behind the wire glasses. I'm sorry, but I have my limits, and at that moment just about the last thing I had patience for was my baby brother magna-cum-whatever engineer and his lion-haired magna-cum-whatever computer scientist fiancée telling me how I should conduct my life—two friggin' eggheads whose children will probably drop out of the womb babbling new theories of relativity no one will ever understand.

I slammed the door in their face, as I'm sure they told you. What you may not have known was I happened to have my house keys in my pocket, which explains how I managed to walk around the front yard to the side door of the garage—that is, my room—and grab my coat without passing through the den again. Probably the only thing you heard was my car starting on the street, or maybe you didn't even hear that but just some time later lifted your head and said, "Oh yeah, did Kenny leave?"

Then, of course, all the way to work the dogs came back to plague my brain, and I suppose I had my family to thank for that again. Do you have any idea what it's like to be able to see nothing but big amber eyes in a white-and-black fur face, the rims of the eyelids a pure sagging pink? Imagine that staring at you a long time, and not having a clue as to why.

And as I seem to be harping on the subject of these dogs, maybe it's best I explain a thing or two about them. Personally, I think it would do you a world of good to read the story of their predicament; it'd probably give you something to think about for the rest of your life:

It so happened that twenty-some-odd years ago a team of sadistic psychologists got it into their heads that, for the sake of science and the betterment of people everywhere, they'd go strapping a pack of Pongos in hammocks so that all four of their spotted legs hung out into the air— then they applied shock to the hind ones. Some of the dogs were able to stop the shock by pressing their faces against a kind of panel, the others just had to live with it. These first shocks were applied *sixty-four times,* then the psychologists moved the dogs to a shuttle box—two small rooms separated by a shoulder-high wall. The floor in the first room was rigged with a grid that provided shock to the dogs' paws, while the floor in the second had no grid at all. Each dog was led into the rigged room, and there was a code: ten seconds after the lights were turned down, the shock came through the floor; the dogs quickly learned the code.

As it turned out, the dogs from the escapable shock group figured out by the third or fourth trial to jump over the barrier into the safe room; eventually they became quite smart about it, and waited by the barrier for the lights to go down and gracefully leapt right over, avoiding shock altogether. But the dogs that had been given shock they couldn't control didn't have it so good—at first they ran frantically about, trying to lift their paws from the floor, then they finally stopped, lay down and just quietly whined for the duration of the shock, about *sixty seconds.* Again and again they failed to escape, and those were the dogs said to have learned helplessness.

Well, after thinking about this whole bit, I decided completely against your straight answer, for reasons then obvious to me, though if I'm to judge by your reaction when I came in this morning—that way you breathed out loudly over the bathroom sink and penciled your eyebrows faster—they hadn't even begun to occur to you. All right, I said to myself, I can handle a loud breath; but of course you had no intention of stopping there. I wasn't within five feet of my room in outer Siberia before I heard your shoes booming after me.

"*I* want an explanation!" you called, at which point I thought it best to slam and lock the door before you could reach it. And so there I was again, face-to-face with Shirley & David, *Com'on get happ-y!,* when those trademark thunder-raps rained down—*wump! wump! wump!*— even louder and faster than yesterday's, if that's possible.

"Explanation for what?" I said through the poster and pressed wood.

"Why you're coming home at seven thirty in the morning."

"I'm coming home at seven thirty in the morning because I was foolish enough not to wait till eight when you'd be out of the house altogether."

"And I want an explanation for that, as well, smarty-pants."
"And what's 'that, as well'?"

"Why you have insisted on avoiding me and every other member of this family."

"*I'm* avoiding *you*?"

"That's right."

"Well, maybe you can give me an explanation why all the sudden you're so hot for explanations. Seems to me there haven't been any explanations going down in this house for years on end. Seems to me those were very peaceful years."

And if I'm not mistaken you had nothing to say to that, unless you said it so softly it got lost somehow in the hollow of the door.

"And I am twenty-six years old," I added.

"Ooow, ooow, *ooow!*" you said, booming back up the hall. "Don't think this is finished!" And I could tell by the tone of your voice this was a very determined conspiracy set on achieving its final aim, which was the disruption of peace and the law of rooms.

So fine, I'll give you a straight answer, but don't think it's going to be the one you had in mind. Don't think I'm just going to *name* the person who sent me the flowers, or give you some phrase like *learned helplessness* you can walk away with—I don't see it that simple. If you really want to know about me, then I insist you live in the room. And I can think of no better way of accomplishing that than by describing everything that transpired from the time I snuck out the side door till the time you breathed out and ooow-ed. Those are the conditions I'm setting, and I warn you in advance that this is not going to be tailored to your squeamish hearts.

Nine o'clock as usual, I arrived at Raptures (which is the real name of the bar I've worked at for the last five years, the one in the heart of the industrial park in Edgewood that high-school jocks throw bottles at from car windows; and now I'm sure you're just picking yourself up off the floor with the astonishment of discovering there was never any

"Club O" out in Nassau County—and then by the way, if you ever want to see the expression of terror that would flood your face every time someone asked what kind of clientele we get there, I do a good impression). Right away I started setting up—stocking beer and juice, icing down the wells, cutting lemons and limes; everyone was saying how the phone had been ringing off the hook.

Then around eleven, in the middle of getting a couple Guinness from the tap, I heard, "Pardon me, laddie, but did ya by any chance get any flowers delivered to ya today?" (in a voice I'm sure you'd recognize, having beaten me to the phone several hundred times this past year—imagine that voice trying to cop a brogue).

I looked up, and bad enough he had to be dressed in green from head-to-toe, but he'd even gone and put glitter in his *eyelashes*. Now picture that—a rich sparkling emerald batting across the bar at you; well, to say the very least, it wasn't exactly charity I was feeling for The Leprechaun Princess.

"Did *I* get your goddam flowers," I sneered, and almost doused him with one of those dark, frothy pints. "What the hell do have on your eyes?"

He drew his chin back. "My eyes?"

"What is that stuff?"

"Nothing. It's just a joke, Kenny."

"Well, you look like a little faggot."

I gave the guys their beers, and as I was putting their money in the register, he scuttled across the bar and whispered, *"What did you say?"*

Then when I turned with their change in my hand, I noticed the *Fuck me, I'm Irish* pin on his windbreaker, and that was just the outer limit of my limit. "And what's *that*?"

He looked down at it and blushed.

"What do you want people thinking, you're some kind of slut?"

"A *slut*?"

"Well, who's it for, Robby? Who do you want to fuck you?"

"Who do you think it's for?"

"When you figure that out, why don't you let me know."

"What's gotten into you?"

His eyes are a light bluish gray, but right then in the bar they just looked ashy, like anyone else's. I knew I was doing something terrible, but the only way I could've stopped myself was if he would've disappeared, and he just continued to stand there, waiting. "You've gotten into me, asshole. Get the fuck away from my bar unless you plan on washing your face."

"*Asshole?*" His eyes stretched wider, searching over the black Formica counter before he turned and walked away; never before had I seen him so hurt. Whether or not you realize—well, of course you can't realize—but Robby's a sensitive guy, and still I went and lit into him like that for no reason; still I ignored every impulse to leave the bar a minute and apologize, four hours of impulses.

When he came stumbling back, it was right before closing, and by that time I was in deep conversation with a horny little bodybuilder named Ralph who was drinking margaritas and tipping me well. For years he's been trying to get into my pants, but I never paid him any mind till last night, particularly once I saw the nice-looking Italian guy in a cut off sweatshirt Robby had in tow.

"This is the fella who thinks I'm a faggot and a slut and wha' was the otha one? *Ass*hole, let's not forget *ass*hole. I'm an asshole, Mike." He hiccupped and glared at Ralph, who took a step backwards.

"Huh?" the new guy said; he was having a hard time peeling his eyes off Robby's ass.

"Who's he?" I asked.

"Oh yeah," Robby said, rolling his eyes and swaying backwards into the shithead like it was all some hilarious joke, "Mike's an ol' frien' a mine." Which is when the guy finally looked up—all red-faced and grinning, and then he slipped a finger through a loophole of Robby's jeans, just right before my eyes.

"What are you doing?" I said to Mike.

"Huh?" Extensive vocabulary, the shithead had.

"Get your hand off his pants."

"Escuse me?" His own bar-gray eyes were bloodshot, like a mutt's.

"I said get your hands off his fucken pants."

"Who?"

"Hey, Kenny," Robby said, "whada you care?"

"What do you mean?"

"Lissen." He removed the hand himself. "I'm goin'."

"Now?"

"Yeah, now."

"You can't wait twenty minutes?"

"No," he said, "Wha' for? Wha' shou' I wait for?" and wobbled off a couple steps. "Com'on, Mike."

Then the shithead held up his hand and said, "Happy St. Patrick's Day, everybody!" before he was at Robby's heels again, practically stepping on them.

"Cunt," I called after them. I don't know which one I meant it for—both, probably. But that was the icing on the cake; Robby whirled right around, or tried to, but ended up spinning too far and having to back-track a little.

When he regained his balance, he said, "I was wonderin' if you were gonna get aroun' ta *that* one." Then he pulled Mike closer and slipped a hand into a back pocket of his jeans, and they wove their way toward the door.

Ralph just leaned there on the counter, watching me bang ashtrays, rinse glasses, wipe down the bar; I didn't have much to say to him at that point, so I set him up counting ones from the register. Then as he was handing me rubber-banded stacks, he came out with something to the effect that his parents were away and they had a hot tub in their house, like fooling around in a hot tub wasn't one of the last things on my mind.

Just as soon as I had the bar packed up, I went for my jacket in the coatroom, with Ralph following me like a homeless puppy. At the door he said, "Will you come?"

I considered it for a moment—it'd be a certain way of putting this Robby business to rest once and for all, if I hadn't managed to already. But a policy I've always tried to adhere to is, if you're not sure about something, hold off till you are. "I don't think so," I said.

"What if they went home together?" A shrewd little hard-on, Ralph. "Then I don't know what I'm doing."

"Here," he said, handing me a little map he'd drawn on the inside of a Raptures matchbook. "Any time you want to drop by—I'll be there all night."

I slipped the thing in my pocket out of courtesy; I had no intention of meeting him. But then as I was pulling out of the parking lot, I saw Robby's Honda across the street, just plopped right in front of the club. I got out of my car and ran over to it; there were all kinds of grunting and ummphfing going on inside, though I couldn't make out a thing for the steam. I opened the driver's door.

And so you wanted me to tell you about myself, and I asked you to live in the room. Then picture the interior light flashing on. See the guy you've supposedly been hanging out with for the last year with some loser's dick jammed down his throat; see his lips kissing up at a puff of black pubic hair, his emerald eyelashes batting over a snow-white groin. Probably you can't picture that. And probably you have even less of an idea what it's like to actually witness such a scene knowing it's being put on for your benefit.

"Kenny?" was all he had to say for himself, his slicked-up mouth in a wondrous O—like seeing me just then was one of the last things he expected. And those eyes of his, once that clear blue gray, now just a dumb reflection of the yellow streetlight.

"Don't be sending me any more flowers, Robby," I said, "don't be sending me a goddam thing." Then I just slammed that sweaty door shut and walked back to my car; he didn't even peep his head up to the window to watch me go, at least so far as I could tell; probably he just heard the sound of my engine fading down the road and then whispered to himself something that meant regret; maybe he even cried; or maybe he was too preoccupied to do any of that, maybe he was even grateful I left, and I'm the only one feeling bad in this town.

Which explains me arriving home at seven thirty this morning smelling like chlorine.

And so there you have it, all laid out for you—everything that happened from the moment you came rapping on my door. Now I'll leave it for you to decide who pushed who into something so foolish as telling about himself.

But while you're thinking, you might want to question the wisdom of calling those dogs helpless. I, for one, am not about to believe they didn't know there was a room on the other side of the barrier—they knew, and would've leapt over in a flash if they felt it would've made one bit of difference. What were they supposed to do, *help* themselves by diving headfirst into a room they knew they didn't belong in? All that voltage and the psychologists thought none of it managed to creep up and become part of their brains? They thought their paws hadn't become part of the grid? I've got news for you—those dogs couldn't have left the room any sooner than the room could've left the room.

Your ex-son,

Kenny

P.S. As you can see, I've left. The few personal belongings I couldn't fit in my car I'll be back for while you're all off at work, so don't worry about us running into each other. Meanwhile if anything of earth-shattering importance needs to be conveyed to me, I can be reached at Raptures. Henry, my boss for the last five years, has been kind enough to let me make a room for myself in the attic, and he says I can stay there for as long as it takes me to decide what I'm doing next with my life, seeing how you have so hastily put it up for the planning.

Tom House

Since 1995, Tom House's fiction has been published in a wide range of literary magazines and anthologies, including *Harper's*, *New England Review*, *The Antioch Review*, *Chicago Review*, *Men on Men 2000,* and the *Best American Gay Fiction* series. His first novel, a dark comedy called *The Beginning of Calamities*, appears this spring from Bridge Works. An excerpt of the new book, along with other short fiction by the author, is posted at www.housestories.net.

Afterword:

by Karl Woelz, Editor

In thinking about the state of contemporary gay writing and publishing, I'm reminded of the widely reported sociological study from the late 1980s that suggested an American woman over the age of thirty-five had a better chance of dying in a terrorist hijacking than she did of finding a man with whom she could settle down. The assertions of this study, of course, were eventually proven to be grossly mis-represented, though the attention given to their retraction was negligible at best. But the idea propounded by this study, the idea it embedded in our cultural consciousness, reminds me of the plight of a great many gay writers at the dawn of the new millennium; writers of literary fiction who, especially in this new era of heightened Homeland Security, have a better chance of being killed in a terrorist attack than getting their gay-themed fiction into print and into a bookstore somewhere near you.

That probably sounds either harsh or hyperbolic—especially at a time in gay American history when so many people are telling us that we've Arrived. That most of our fighting is done. That all we really have to do—now that we've more or less assimilated and proven ourselves to be "just like" our straight counterparts—is sit back, fingertips clicking like mad, and shop our way into happiness and fulfillment like everybody else in the country. Since our Arrival in the American mainstream is both predicated and dependent upon our identities as consumers—via the highly touted success of "niche marketing"—we must, above all else, prove our economic clout (our worth, both individual and collective) by showing those Big Money corporate types just how well we've been trained to trade our political (and personal) souls for our fifteen minutes of Superstar Consumer status. I shop, therefore I am ... validated, wanted, respected. (Besides, political activism is exhausting, rarely appreciated work; shopping on the Internet in your underpants, preferably with a tumbler of Skyy vodka in hand, is fun!)

But hitching our rainbow wagon (complete with dancing go-go boys) to the vagaries of the Market is problematic, at best. I'm reminded of Sally Field's infamous Oscar acceptance speech. I mean, we've been waiting so very long for corporate America to acknowledge our existence that we're more than a bit intoxicated by the sudden rush of attention: "You like me! You really *like* me!" The most obvious danger in attaching our political worth to our much-touted economic clout—though I rarely hear it articulated—is that the Market cares about one thing and one thing only: profit. The Market doesn't care about our safety or our civil liberties or our unmolested pursuit of happiness. It doesn't care about the substance of our lives in any real sense. In embracing our exploitation as a "market niche"—and then confusing it with social equality—we reduce ourselves to nothing more than a demographic market segment, ripe for the proverbial pickin's, and valued only in as much as we prove ourselves worthy (via our wallets) of whatever attention the corporate Big Boys have decided, suddenly, to pay us. And that spasm of overdue attention has nothing to do with altruism or progressive politics. The corporate Big Boys are interested in profits, in bottom lines, and we would be wise to remember that unprofitable products don't stay on the shelf. The minute a "gay" product, of whatever kind, ceases to generate profits, it will be gone, and all of Dusty's "wishin' and hopin'" won't bring it back. More significantly: if gays themselves, as an exploitable market segment, cease to be profitable, they too will be gone.

This, I sadly believe, is where the writers and readers of gay literary fiction now find themselves. We have been deemed an unprofitable market segment consigned to the remainder table of contemporary American literature. As I said in the Introduction to this book, there are now *fewer* choices for those of us who want to read "books for grownups" than there were just four years ago. All three critically acclaimed gay short fiction anthologies of the 1980s and 1990s no longer exist, almost all periodical venues for gay short fiction have dried up, and many (if not all) of the mainstream publishing houses have either abandoned gay-themed titles altogether or so drastically reduced support for them that it amounts to the same thing.

Building upon the post-Stonewall literary boom of the late 1970s, the mid-1980s produced, as former St. Martin's Press editor Michael

Denneny has pointed out, "a burst of writing such as ha[d] never been seen before," a veritable explosion of gay literary culture remarkable for the strength of its authors' "talent, diversity, and sheer numbers." It was a truly extraordinary moment in our cultural and literary history: a handful of years when it seemed there would be no end to the wealth of authors and titles from which we could choose. But within a decade this literary revolution was more or less over, and it could be argued that, today, what little remains of it is either on life support or in its death throes. This is not to say that there are fewer talented gay writers at work today than there were in either 1987 or 1997—nothing could be further from the truth—but rather, that the market for their work has been scaled back so radically as to be almost nonexistent.

This doesn't sound right, I'm sure. Gay bookstores (or at least those few still in existence) are filled with plenty of titles. Super-chains like Barnes & Noble not only feature gay books on the display shelves at the front of the store (space, I might add, for which the publishers have paid dearly), but they also include gay and lesbian sections (albeit small and arranged, it would seem, by autistic ferrets). Online bookstores and book clubs include gay titles. And while Oprah more or less glossed over the gay experience in her celebrated Book Club days, the corporate-sponsored copycats bobbing in her wake have been quick to include gay writers among their selections.

But if you take a closer look at the *kinds* of gay titles being published, you'll find a demoralizing sameness to them: lots and lots and lots of collections of erotica, almost as many self-help books (both decidedly earnest and thoroughly tongue-in-cheek), celebrity biographies, picture books of partially clothed or fully naked men, travel books, "lifestyle" books, "gift" books, and most recently, romantic comedies of the boy-meets-boy, boy-temporarily-loses-boy, boy-finds-boy-again variety. And almost every one of these books, regardless of content, will feature a "humpy number" (preferably shirtless, pantless, or both) on its cover. (That *any* gay-themed book, regardless of content, *must* include such a "beefcake" photo if it hopes to sell is an unfortunate reality, a sad commentary on the hyper-sexualization of our culture, and the "skin sells" mantra that keeps it in perpetual motion.) Like the increasingly slick and content-less "lifestyle" magazines for gay men, a disproportionate number of gay books are heavy on "style" and light on "life" (real, adult life, that is). Is it just coincidence, I wonder—

in light of the much-heralded disposable incomes and vacationing habits of middle-class gay men—that a significant number of our most talented and well-respected writers either have been asked to write, or have recently published, what amounts to little more than upscale travel guides for cities that might top the list of any reasonably well-off gay man's choices for a high-end summer getaways?

The publication of a spate of such books sounds like the kind of editorial decision made by people who know an exploitable market when they see one; people who like the idea of what they perceive as a no-brainer/easy-money/win-win proposition; people who know a lot about marketing and very little about literature. As American publishing houses have been taken over by either media conglomerates or multinational companies with little knowledge of, and interest in, books, they have been ever-increasingly driven by the bottom line. With their attention focused only on profit margins, the executives in control of such companies are interested only in what sells—there is very little room, or no room at all, for anything that doesn't perform like a blockbuster smash. And it's this "Hollywoodization" of publishing that bothers many industry insiders.

Under the management of these mega-corporations, books are treated like motion picture "spectacles," wherein creating the proper "buzz" about a project is frequently more important that its content, and costly promotional campaigns are waged in order that a book "opens" well, selling fast and furiously in its first few weeks. Books that don't "open big" (and that would be most books) are abandoned, either drastically discounted or returned to the publisher.

There are significant problems with this approach to publishing, and one of them is the very different way in which books and movies are consumed. Eighteen million people don't go out and buy a new book on Friday night, read it, and then tell all their friends to do the same thing the next day. Books are not movies, and they can't be expected to generate the same kinds of profits, in the same amount of time, as cinematic entertainments. But that's what's increasingly being asked of them. You can probably think of the very small handful of writers who could generate immense profits for their publishers (though nowhere near the money a big-budget Hollywood movie would pull in over the course of seventy-two hours). Their names start with Stephen and Tom and Danielle, and end in King, Clancy, and Steele.

They do not start with Christopher, David or Jim, and end in Bram, Leavitt, or Grimsley.

In the not-so-recent past, when the publishing industry was run by people who knew books, read books, and understood how books *don't* operate like movies, there was much more space given to all manner of books—with the understanding that the big blockbuster best-sellers would allow publishers to take chances with—in terms of mass appeal—infinitely less popular or marketable work. But now that those in control of the publishing business think of books as just another product (one among many) to be hyped and hawked, they are interested in selling only those books upon which they think they can make a sizable return on their investment. This thinking has proved deadly for what are called "mid-list" writers—authors of literary fiction—who do not generate levels of income like mass-market or genre writers. Several years ago, publishing giant HarperCollins shocked the industry by simply *canceling* the contracts of more than one hundred of its mid-list writers.

This rapid abandoning of literary fiction should be of particular concern to gay writers and readers because gay writers are *inevitably* mid-list writers. Because the publishing industry has already "ghettoized" gay writers (that is, gay-themed books are only ever "about" being gay, and thus are directed only towards readers who publishers think would be interested in the subject—namely, gays) gay-themed books can *never* perform like those of their straight counterparts. Gay books are *rarely* reviewed by critics outside the gay press, gay writers are usually *not* sent out on book tours to promote their work, and gay books are *never* marketed to straight audiences. Thus, gay writers and their books are completely contained, by the publishing industry itself, within prescribed boundaries that guarantee they will never break out of the mid-list ghetto. There is, of course, a very small handful of gay writers for whom this does not apply—and you can count them off on the fingers of one hand—but for 99.8% of gay writers at work today, the chances that their work will be picked up by a mainstream publishing house and distributed to a wide, not exclusively gay, audience are almost nonexistent.

Of course, mainstream publishing is not the only game in town. There are other options. There are smaller presses, both straight and gay & lesbian, and there are really small presses. The really small presses, of course, are at a marked disadvantage (to put it mildly). For one, they're being rapidly killed off by the big-money houses. Those who've managed to survive (and their survival is always tenuous), can't compete with the behemoths, nor can they pay to get their books in the prime display areas inside the huge super-store chains. They are, quite literally, a dying breed.

While the smaller presses have a little more economic weight to throw around, they face more or less the same problems. Some smaller presses are very much involved and invested in publishing gay books, but their fundamental ignorance of all things gay means that, all too often, they don't really know what to *do* with their gay product—and so their books languish, never really getting the attention, or generating the sales, they deserve. Other smaller presses seem to care less about their gay product and gay consumers, but are savvy enough to know that they've tapped into a niche market that's been abandoned by the Big Boys, a veritable sitting duck, both historically starved for attention and loyal to those who throw it a bone.

When gay writers cannot get their books into print because they're told there's "no market" for their work … when gay anthology series like *His* and *Best American Gay Fiction* and *Men on Men* are unceremoniously dumped … when mainstream publishers like St. Martin's decide to abandon their gay imprints altogether … and when gay publishers offer readers little else but "husband-hunting" guides and jack-off books, we are left with a disturbing and demoralizing conclusion: the writers and readers of gay literary fiction are worse off *now* than we were little more than a decade ago.

Several years ago, I was reading a short piece in the back of *The Advocate* by Gabriel Rotello, both detailing the demise of yet another gay and lesbian bookstore and outlining the sad state of affairs in queer publishing. In the letters to the editor section of the next issue, a reader responded to Rotello's piece, hailing the demise of the bookstore as a sign of *progress*. Such places, the letter writer argued, were relics— useless antiquities from the days of early Gay Lib, reminders of a ghetto mentality, which we were wise to jettison in this New Age of mainstream acceptance. Good riddance, the writer declared, for we no longer need something so irrelevant to our ever-ascending position within the dominant culture—something that reeks so pungently of our old, subcultural second-class status. And what's more—who reads anyway?

Naturally, I was horrified by the man's letter, but it's too easy to dismiss him as a mere philistine, an exception to the rule of well-heeled gay sophistication. That he understood a bookstore to be irrelevant doesn't surprise me, since so many gay men would never dream of picking up a book (unless, perhaps, it were filled with lots and lots of glossy pictures of shirtless men). The days of the well-read homosexual are over, it would seem. Who has time to read, after all, when there are episodes of *Will & Grace* and *Queer As Folk* to watch (not to mention all those naughty amateur webcams)? But the letter writer's sense of gay literature being somehow a part of a history that no longer had any currency, that no longer *mattered*, was truly appalling because in that perception, of course, is a complete dismissal of our literary, cultural, and political past. A past which has very much shaped our present, and more likely than not, will continue to inform our future.

Of course, many gay men think that gay bookstores are insignificant or irrelevant. Well, let me rephrase that: gay bookstores are good places to pick up free copies of the local gay paper, buy porn, buy saucy greeting cards, buy nudie refrigerator magnets, buy anything-&-everything with a rainbow on it, buy lube, and of course—cruise for sex. That books written by, for, and about gay men can be found in gay bookstores doesn't seem to matter to a great many gay men. And in light of this disinterest, many gay bookstores are becoming less and less about books and more and more about videos, DVDs, CDs, and "gifts." If, as is so often the case, gay bookstores make the bulk of their money from everything that *isn't* a book—pornography (there's a skin mag, or two or three, for just about every conceivable taste and predilection out there) and "gifts" (rainbow *everything*) comprising an increasingly large portion of those profits—then books themselves are like the hoary old nag struggling in vain to catch up with the long-limbed thoroughbreds forcing her to eat their dust.

Having worked in a gay bookstore for several years—where I was more frequently asked to describe the differing viscosities of I.D. Glide vs. Wet lube than which new gay novel was worth reading—I've seen what gay men buy, and do, in gay bookstores. And for the most part, it's not about books. And on those infrequent occasions when it is about books, those titles all too often come from either the erotica section (*Jizz Bucket 12*) or the self-help section (*I'm Not Kidding This Time— Your Dream Boyfriend Really IS Right Around the Corner!*), the pseudo-biography section (this month's effort from last year's prostitute-turned-memoirist), or most recently, from the growing hunk-meets-hunk "fluff romance" genre.

In and of themselves, there's nothing wrong with "fluffy" romantic comedies or plot-driven mysteries or hard-pounding jack-off stories— and there are, of course, many talented writers at work in all of those genres. But there *is* something wrong when these kinds of narratives become the bulk of our available choices; when they are offered to us (or forced upon us) to the increasing exclusion of just about everything else. But in that age-old game of "chicken and egg," publishers will tell us that these are the books we *want* to read—that they are only responding to the demands of the market. I have to wonder, of course, to what extent such publishers are *creating* markets, regardless of what consumers actually want, rather than *responding* to them. You know: the ol' lowest common denominator, the easiest buck, the path of least resistance … that is what marketing types *do*, isn't it?

We have been reminded, again and again, by both gay and mainstream media outlets, that gays are now more visible in the popular culture than they have ever been before. And while this is true, it's true only if we're talking about network and cable television—and even then, reports of our Arrival in the promised land of the hetero-mainstream are greatly exaggerated. There's *Will & Grace* and *Queer As Folk*, to be sure, along with a significantly well-integrated plotline on *Six Feet Under*, and the urban campiness and super-gay-friendliness of *Sex in the City*. There are also gay characters scattered throughout much of MTV's programming, whether in reality-based shows like *Road Rules* and *Dismissed* or series like *Undressed*, and gays have been included, too, among the telegenic combatants of prime-time reality TV programs like *Survivor* and *Big Brother*.

So, yes, we are undeniably more visible on television than we were a decade ago. But those who would herald our ascendance should keep in mind that we are talking about a very small handful of programs, most of which are not broadcast on the major networks, and which—no matter how well-written or engagingly acted—offer viewers a very narrow vision of white, middle-class, urban gay life. (Ellen is long-forgotten and there is, presumably, no such thing as an African-American or Latino gay man as far as TV executives are concerned). Further, we should keep in mind that there is, for all intents and purposes, only one network television show that is really "ours"—NBC's *Will & Grace*. One show out of the hundreds of television programs that air each week. Others—CBS's reasonably engaging *Some of My Best Friends* and ABC's poorly conceived *Normal, Ohio*—have come and gone, to borrow from an old Whoopi Goldberg routine, "like a fart in a dust storm." This suggests that, as far as TV executives are concerned, one show "for the gays" really is enough. Further, it suggests that we might want to temper our enthusiasm with a long, hard look at just how far we've come in this widely touted era of Visibility and Acceptance. I mean, what happens when *Will & Grace* or *Queer As Folk* go belly-up? If the Powers That Be think that one show "for the gays" is enough, do you really think they're going to go out of their way to offer us *more* choices?

Our recent limited success on television, however, has *not* been replicated in the publishing world. Again: there are fewer and fewer books of gay literary fiction being published with each passing year. Part of this maddening and dispiriting trend is directly connected to the corporate powers who rule the publishing business from on high—men and women who don't see enough of a profit margin in gay literary fiction to bother with it at all. But indifferent corporate types don't shoulder the blame alone. Gay men, too—whether as publishers or consumers—have done their literary fiction a grave disservice by either ignoring it or abandoning it. We're enjoying the unprecedented spectacle of big ol' fags on prime-time network and cable TV, the even more salacious spectacle of countless gay men jacking off on amateur webcam sites, and the equally slick stroking of corporate America telling us how valued (and valuable) we are—but we are not reading.

Five years ago, at the first *Behind Our Masks* writers' conference in Washington, D.C., former Firebrand Books publisher Nancy Bereano noted that gays and lesbians, "rather than reading serious fiction, [are] reading lightweight, chatting on the Net, and watching *Ellen*." Today, of course, we're reading even *lighter* (if at all), chatting (and so much more ...) on the web, and watching *Will & Grace*. Who knows what we'll be doing in another five years (the mind boggles), but there's a real chance that reading literary fiction may no longer be an option.

One of the most frustrating things about my years at the gay bookstore was taking note of the alarmingly large number of people who came through the store without buying anything. *Ever*. Of course, these were the men who usually complained the loudest when the free gay paper was delivered late, or who threw a hissy fit if we'd sold out of the latest issue of *Black Inches* before they could slobber all over it, or who wanted to know *why* we weren't open on Christmas Day, too. They never gave a dime of their money to the store (well, *maybe* once a year they'd buy a skin mag), but they came in often enough to be considered die-hard regulars. Of course, one of the great things about gay bookstores is that they really *are* much more than a business; they transcend their role as mere purveyors of goods. They're safe spaces in which gays can meet. They're one of the only places in the entire culture where everything is *for* gays. They allow us to feel connected to some larger community of like-minded others. And when we're totally exhausted, physically and emotionally, from the relentless onslaught of shiny, corporate-sponsored heterosexuality that's shoved down our throats twenty-four hours a day, seven days a week, a gay bookstore can seem like the most beautiful and refreshing place on earth.

But gay bookstores *are* businesses. And without our support they die. It used to frustrate me that so many people came through the store without ever feeling the need, or desire, to do anything to keep it alive—and worse still, that they assumed it would always *be* there. Far too many people took the existence of that store for granted, assuming that it would always be around, whether they supported it or not, to provide them with a meeting place, a source for free information about what was going on in the community, and/or a place to cruise.

I think far too many gay men take the existence of gay literature for granted as well. But gay lit is *not* a given. It is constantly under threat. And it *cannot* survive unless we support it. As readers of gay "fiction for grown-ups," we need both to consume as much of it as possible ourselves, and to encourage *others* to read it, too. If you're holding this book in your hands, chances are you're already a regular reader of gay literary fiction—and that's fantastic—but we need *more* people like you. Instead of buying your best friend a copy of *Jizz Bucket 12* for his next birthday—even if that's what he really wants—get him a copy of David Leavitt's *The Marble Quilt* instead. Or Mark Merlis' *An Arrow's Flight*. Or Stephen McCauley's *True Enough*. When you're out shopping, take the book about pubic topiary out of your buddy's hand and put Scott Heim's *Mysterious Skin* in it. Or Andrew Holleran's *Dancer from the Dance*. Or James Baldwin's *Giovanni's Room*. *Share* your enthusiasm for literary fiction with your friends. *Encourage* them to read something that isn't "disposable." And above all else, continue your *own* reading. Read as much as you can, whenever you can. Be promiscuous—there is *no* shame in being a literary whore!

Remember, too, that our literature has *always* sustained us. Think about the books you love; about what good friends they've been through the years. Always fresh. Always engaging. Always offering you something new each time you return to them. I still vividly remember the weeks I spent circling the block of the bookstore across the street from my college dorm, palms sweaty and heart aflutter, before finally mustering the courage to go in and buy my first "gay book," Edmund White's *A Boy's Own Story*. Until that moment, I couldn't envision what a "gay book"—never mind a gay *life*—might look like. And what a magnificent time I've had in the years since then! The characters I've met ... the places I've gone ... the ideas I've entertained. Nervous nineteen-year-old gay boys today might be searching for a copy of Paul Russell's *The Salt Point* or James Earl Hardy's *B-Boy Blues* or Brian Malloy's *The Year of Ice*, rather than White's now "classic" text, but I know they're still looking for books to help them understand both the world around them and their new place in it. And the nervous nineteen-year-old gay boys of tomorrow? I'd like to think that their options will be no less varied than my own were all those years ago.

I'd like to think that gay literary fiction will continue to show *all* of us the limitless possibilities of our gay lives. It can—and it will—but only if we demand more from the publishers who, rather than treating us like adults, insist upon infantilizing us. Only if we prove to those corporate number crunchers that there *is* a healthy and hungry market for gay literary fiction. And only if we take it upon ourselves to support, today and tomorrow, wholeheartedly and without fail, both the books and the writers who continue to compel, to complete, and to sustain us. That means we must *buy* the books, *read* the books and *talk about* the books that deal with our real lives—both inner and outer. Along with music, theater and the rest of the Fine Arts, *literature creates culture*. It is our culture and if we don't create and support it, the corporate world will. In whose hands do you want your culture—theirs or yours?

Karl Woelz
Karl Woelz is a recipient of both the Lambda Literary Award and the
National Gay & Lesbian Press Association's Vice Versa Award. His
short fiction, articles, and reviews have appeared in *Best American Gay
Fiction 2*, *Men on Men 6*, *Diversity & Social Work*, *The James White
Review*, *Link*, *asspants*, *Cottonwood*, *The Gay & Lesbian Review
Worldwide*, *Lambda Book Report*, *The Baltimore City Paper*, and *The
Baltimore Alternative*. He is the co-editor of Dutton/Plume's *Men On
Men 2000: Best New Gay Fiction for the Millennium*.